Anonymous

Every Man his own Lawyer

And general legal Form Book

Anonymous

Every Man his own Lawyer
And general legal Form Book

ISBN/EAN: 9783337189501

Printed in Europe, USA, Canada, Australia, Japan

Cover: Foto ©Andreas Hilbeck / pixelio.de

More available books at **www.hansebooks.com**

EVERY MAN
HIS OWN LAWYER,

AND

GENERAL LEGAL FORM BOOK,

A COMPLETE GUIDE ON MATTERS OF LAW AND BUSINESS FOR CONVEYANCERS, JUSTICES OF THE PEACE, CORONERS, CONSTABLES, MERCHANTS, FARMERS, MECHANICS, AND BUSINESS MEN GENERALLY THROUGHOUT THE DOMINION OF CANADA.

BY SEVERAL

BARRISTERS-AT-LAW.

The Law as regards all matters treated of in this work, has been carefully revised in accordance with the recent Statutes, down to date.

BROCKVILLE, ONT.
Published by McMULLEN & Co.,
WHOLESALE BOOKSELLERS,
1882.

Price, - - $2.00.

Entered according to Act of the Parliament of Canada, in the year one thousand eight hundred and eighty-one, by McMullen & Co., in the office of the Minister of Agriculture.

INTRODUCTION.

For several years back a reliable and simple book of legal and business reference, adapted for the use and information of the general public, has been much needed in this country. Works of this character, published hitherto in Canada, have been very limited in their scope, and not infrequently, also, inaccurate and misleading, the object of the compilers, in the latter case, evidently being to make money by their books, and not to add to their own reputation or to be of real benefit to the community. The work which we now submit to the public is of an entirely different character; and while it reaches almost every ordinary phase of the legal and business transactions of every-day life, it will be found, on careful examination, to be as accurate as it is comprehensive. The Publishers feel confident that no equally useful work of the same character has ever before been issued from the press of this country, nor one so well adapted to educate the public mind on the rights and duties which appertain to every good citizen of the Dominion, and with which every one within its borders should be more or less acquainted. The time has come when a work of this popular character, freed from legal technicalities and couched in plain language, which the most unlettered could understand, is a real necessity. Since the creation of the New Dominion the scope of legislation has became greatly extended. As regards various phases of even ordinary business transactions, the people of Canada have now to make themselves acquainted, to a greater or less extent, as necessity may arise, not only with the Common Law of the Empire, but also with the laws of the Dominion Parliament, and of the particular Province in which they may happen to reside. Some simple classification, therefore, of such of these laws as bear more directly on the rights and interest of the people generally, cannot fail to be of great value to them ; and to supply that classification is one of the objects of this work. It will also be found valuable from another point of view. While the members of the legal profession of Canada are being constantly supplied with ably written and copious works for their better information, and to direct their practice, the public at large has been almost entirely left without any reliable popular guide in ordinary law and business matters, and such as would enable any intelligent person to draft simple legal instruments, or to know precisely what he should consult his lawyer about. EVERY MAN HIS OWN LAWYER will fully meet that want.

While this work is not designed for the use of the legal profession it will be found, nevertheless, exceedingly useful to its younger members in many ways ; and will give them a ready clue, owing to its simplicity of arrangement, to a variety of subjects which would take a great deal of time and labor to look up in technical law books. They will find some information, too, in its pages which will be quite new to them, while notes of decided cases are added very frequently for their benefit, and to enable them the more readily to refer to the law reports. The grouping of the applying laws down to date, as in the case of Landlord and Tenant, and under other headings as well, cannot fail to be also very useful to them.

INTRODUCTION.   5

To the Justice, or *ex-officio* Justice, of the Peace the information supplied in this work will be almost invaluable. Never before have the duties of his important office been so clearly and plainly traced out for his benefit as they are in this book; and never before has so much valuable information been rendered so simple and so easily accessible to him. It is, indeed, true that many excellent books have been written, from time to time, for the use of Justices of the Peace; but the authors of these books being always lawyers, their own well-trained legal minds could hardly realize the opposite condition of the minds of many persons outside the profession, and as a necessary consequence their works were, without any exception, much better adapted for the use of their brethren of the bar than for the Justice of the Peace. The author of most of the original matter in this work has been a Justice of the Peace for nearly a quarter of a century, and having had great experience in that position, now gives his brother Justices, all over the Dominion, the full benefit of that experience. He has traced the history of the office from its first statutory creation, and placed its nature and duties so plainly before the reader that they cannot be misunderstood; while, at the same time, the index which he supplies to the Dominion and Local Statutes, under which Justices of the Peace are empowered to do some official act, will save them much weary wading through their law books, and enable them to make up their minds more easily, and more promptly as well, in cases submitted for their decision.

In the same way the Constable, also, will find the various important duties of his office very plainly defined, under the different headings of Constable, Coroner, and Landlord and Tenant; while the Coroner is supplied with full instructions, and all the necessary forms, for his guidance.

Whenever it became necessary to do so during the preparation of this work for the press, (a labor that has extended over the better part of a year) the publishers obtained the best legal advice. The public may rely, therefore, on this work being a safe and certain guide in all ordinary matters of law and business. In every case where it was possible or necessary to do so, we give the text of the applying statute, and all alterations of the law have been carefully noted and brought down to the present year. We may state, however, that since the paper under the head of "Naturalization" went to press a new Naturalization Act has been passed by the Dominion Parliament, being 44 Vic., Chap. 13, which embodies some of the provisions of the Imperial Statute, 33 Vic., Chap. 14, and makes some slight changes in the law, but the substance of which still remains the same.

THE PUBLISHERS.

INDEX.

Affidavit.
	PAGE.
Nature of an Affidavit, &c.	17
General Form of Affidavit	19
General Form of Affirmation	20
Form of Oath	20
Form of Affirmation	20
Statutory Declaration	21
Form of Affidavit of Execution of Agreement	21

Agreement.
Law and nature of Agreements	24
General Form of Agreement	24
Agreement for the Purchase of a House and Lot	25
Agreement for the Sale of Real Estate	26
Agreement for Building a House	27
Agreement respecting a Party Wall	29
Agreement for a Sale of Grain	31
Agreement for the Sale of Standing Timber	31
Agreement to Sell Goods on Commission	32
Chattel Security Agreement	33
Agreement to Rent a Furnished House	33

Arbitration.
General Law of Arbitration	34
Fees of Arbitrators. (Ontario)	37
Acts of Ontario as to Arbitration	37
Form of Arbitration Deed	38
Form of Arbitration Bond	40
Appointment of an Umpire	41
Enlargement of Time for Making Award	41
Enlargement of Time by the Parties	41
Appointment of Third Arbitrator	42
Oath to be Administered by Arbitrator to a Witness	42
Appointment by Arbitrator for Attendance before him	42
Peremptory Appointment for the same purpose	43
General Form of Award	43
Award where the Submission was by Mutual Bonds	44
Award where the Submission was by Agreements	44
Clauses which may be inserted in an Award where they suit the circumstances	45
Affidavit of execution of Arbitration Bond	46
Affidavit of execution of Award	47

Assignments.
Legal View of Assignments	47
Law of Assignments in Ontario	47
General Form of Assignment	49
Assignment. (Crown Lands)	49
Affidavit of Execution	50

Assignment of Partnership Property and Debts.......... 50
Assignment of Partnership Property and Debts by one
   Partner to another for a Certain Sum............... 52
Assignment of Bond by Endorsement.................. 54
Assignment of Lease 54
Assignment of Lease by Administrator............... 56
Assignment of Judgment............................ 57
Assignment of Mortgage............................ 58
Assignment of Mortgage (by Indorsement)........... 60
Assignment of Debts............................... 60
Assignment of a Policy of Fire Insurance by Indorsement 61

Auctions and Auctioneers.
General Law as to Auctions, &c..................... 62
Law of Ontario as to the same...................... 62
Memorandum to be Signed by an Auctioneer after a Sale
   of Land 63
Memorandum to be Signed by Purchaser.............. 63
Conditions of Sale of Goods......................... 64
Conditions of Sale of Land.......................... 64
Conditions of the Sale of the Court of Chancery........ 66

Bills of Exchange and Promissory Notes.
Nature of Bills of Exchange......................... 67
How Accepted...................................... 69
How Presented for payment......................... 72
Form of Protest for a Bill of Exchange or Promissory Note 74
Form of Notice of Protest........................... 75
Inland Bill of Exchange or Draft..................... 75
Another Form of Bill of Exchange or Draft........... 75
A Set of Bills of Foreign Exchange................... 76
Ordinary Promissory Notes......................... 76
Note Payable to Bearer............................. 76
Interest Note Payable on Demand.................... 77
Note with Collateral Security....................... 77
Note Payable by Instalments........................ 77
A Joint and Several Note........................... 77
A Joint Note...................................... 77
Demand Due Bills.................................. 78

Bill of Sale.
General Features of Bill of Sale..................... 78
Law of Ontario as to Bills of Sale................... 79
Bill of Sale of Goods............................... 79
Another Form of Bill of Sale........................ 81
Bill of Sale of Vessel............................... 82
Affidavit of the Bargainee.......................... 83
Affidavit of Execution of Bill of Sale................. 83

Bonds.
What a Bond is.................................... 84
General Law as to Bonds............................ 85
Single Bond, without condition...................... 86
Bond with Condition............................... 86

INDEX.

Bond to Convey Land 87
Bond for Payment of Purchase Money 88
Bond of Indemnity 89
Bond for a Leasee and his Surety to pay rent according to
   Lease 89
Bond, with Interest Condition 90
Bond of Indemnity on paying Lost Note 91
Bottomry Bond 92

Chattel Mortgages.

Explanatory Remarks as to nature of Chattel Mortgages. 93
Extracts from Revised Statutes of Ontario as to Chattel
   Mortgages 94
Discharge of Mortgage (Ontario) 96
Amending Statute (Ontario) 97
General Law as to Chattel Mortgages 98
Ordinary Chattel Mortgage 100
Affidavit of Mortgagee 102
Affidavit of Witness to Mortgage 103
Chattel Mortgage by way of Security against Indorsement 103
Affidavit of Mortgagee 107
Affidavit of Witness 107
Chattel Mortgage to secure further advances 107
Affidavit of Mortgagee for the same 111
Form of Chattel Mortgage, under the Revised Statutes of
   Ontario, Chap. 119, Sec. 1 111
Affidavit of Mortgagee for the same 116
Affidavit of Witness 116
Form of an Assignment of Chattel Mortgage 117
Affidavit of Assignee 119
Affidavit of Execution of an Assignment of Chattel Mortgage 119
Warrant of Seizure under Chattel Mortgage 119
Amending Act of 1881. (Ontario) 120

Constables :—Their Powers and Duties.

History of the Office 121
Powers of a Constable 121
Duties of a Constable 123
Law to protect Constables 125
Who may be appointed to the Office 125
Law of Ontario as to Constables 126
Law of Ontario as to Special Constables 127
Constables must not purchase goods at sales by them (Ontario 130
Constables' Fees (Ontario) 130
(*For other duties see under the heads of Landlord and
Tenant and Coroner.*)

Coroners :—Their Powers and Duties.

General Law as to Coroners 131
Dominion Statutes as to Coroners 133
Ontario Law as to Coroners 134

Fees of Coroners. (Ontario).... 138
Jurors' Fees.. 139
Proceedings by the Coroner............ 139
Form of a Warrant.. 139
Form of the Summons........................... 140
Foreman's Oath.. 141
Form of Recognizance to appear and prosecute.......... 146
Form of a Recognizance to appear and give evidence.... 147
Form of Recognizance by Husband and Wife 148
Form of Recognizance by a Master, (parent or guardian,)
   for the appearance of an apprentice or minor.......... 149
Form of an Inquisition on a Lunatic...................... 150
Felo de se, by Drowning................................... 151
Upon an Accidental Death occasioned by a Cart........ 151
Se Defendendo.... 155
Form of the Warrant to Summon a Jury....... 158
Form of the Constable's Summons..................... 158
Warrant to Bury after a View...................... 159
Warrant to Bury a *felo de se*, after inquisition found.... 159
The Return thereto....................................... 160
Warrant to Bury without a View, where no effectual In-
   quest can be taken.................................. 160
Another Form of Warrant to Bury without a View...... 160
Warrant to Bury without a View when the Body was
   found Drowned.. 161
A Warrant to take up a Body Interred................... 161
Warrant to Apprehend a Person for Murder............ 162
Commitment for Murder................................. 162
Summons to a Witness. 163
Warrant for Contempt against a Witness for not appear-
   ing to give evidence 164
Warrant to Commit a Witness refusing to give evidence... 164
Commitment of a Witness for refusing to sign his In-
   formation... 165
Commitment of a Witness for refusing to enter into
   Recognizance to appear to give evidence.............. 166
Recognizance by Husband for Wife's appearance, and by
   Master, &c., for the appearance of an Apprentice &c... 168

Deeds.

Nature of a Deed... 169
How a Deed should be Drawn........................... 170
How Registered.. 172
Deed of Bargain and Sale. (Absolute Covenants.)....... 174
Deed with Qualified Covenants.......................... 177
Deed of Land belonging to Married Woman (Ontario)... 179
Short Form Deed with Dower. (Ontario)................ 180
Statutory Deed. (Ontario).............................. 181
Deed of Right of Way..................................... 182
Deed of Gift of Personal Property 183
Deed of Gift of Lands.................................... 184
Affidavit of Execution of Deed in Ontario... 185

Division Courts. (Ontario).
General Summary of Division Court Law 185

Guarantees.
Law and Nature of Guarantees 200
Guarantee for a fixed sum 201
Continuing Guarantee 202
Guarantee for a Servant 202
Guarantee for a Clerk 202

Exemption from Seizure under Writs of Execution.
Exemption in Ontario 203
Exemption in Quebec 204
Exemption in New Brunswick 204
Exemption in Nova Scotia 204

Justices of the Peace.
History of the Office of Justice of the Peace 204
General observations as to the great importance of the Office 206
Improper appointments 207
Justice can be compelled to Act 208
How he may be dealt with for corrupt acts 209
How he should fit himself to act 209
How he should hold Court 211
Nature and Powers of the Office of Justice of the Peace .. 212
Property Qualification 214
His Court one of Record 215
Acts to Protect Justices 217
Oath of Qualification 217
Oath of Office 218
Form of the Commission of the Peace 219
Explanatory Notes to Commission 221
Articles of the Peace 224
General Law as to Articles of the Peace 224
Complaint of party threatened for Sureties of the Peace.. 227
Form of Peace Warrant 228
Form of Recognizance for the Sessions 229
Condition of the Recognizance to keep the Peace, &c., without appearing at the Sessions 230
Form of Commitment in Default of Sureties 230
The form of Supersedeas to be used where the defendant finds surety before the warrant is executed upon him ... 231
Release of the Surety of the Peace, &c 232
Discharge of one Committed for want of Sureties 233
Form of Articles of the Peace in the Courts of Chancery or Queen's Bench 233
Commitment for Contempt 234
Public Statutes of the Dominion of Canada under which Justices of the Peace are empowered to perform some official act 235
Public Statutes of the Province of Ontario, under which Justices of the Peace are empowered to perform some

Ministerial or Judicial Act.................. 245
Dictionary of the Criminal Law of the Dominion of Canada not treated of otherwise........................ 250
Fees of Justices of the Peace........................... 257

Landlord and Tenant.

General observations............................... 259
Law of Landlord and Tenant....................... 260
Distress for Rent................................... 261
What goods may be Distrained..................... 266
Concerning Replevin................................ 269
As to Fradulent Removals.......................... 269
Case of Tenant holding over........................ 271
Deserting the Premises 271
Rents Recoverable by Execution................... 272
Warrant upon the preceding Complaint and Oath........ 273
Information and Complaint under the 11 George II, ch. 19 of Tenant having deserted the Premises 274
Notice to be affixed on the Premises so deserted. (Burns) 274
Record of Putting the Landlord into Possession........ 275
Form of Notice to Quit............................ 276
Distraining for Rent ; what the Constable must do....... 277
Laws of Ontario as to Landlord and Tenant............ 282
As to Costs of Distress 282
Respecting over-holding Tenants.................... 289
Ejectment by Landlords............................ 288
Landlord's Claim as to Goods Taken in Execution........ 290
Misconduct of Bailiffs.............................. 292
To protect Lodgers and Boaders against distress by Superior Landlords................................ 293
Lease of House..................................... 294
Lease of Land...................................... 297
Lease of a House and Farm......................... 299
Short Form of Lease, (Ontario) 303
Simple Agreement for the yearly Tenancy of a House..... 304
Agreement for a Lease............................. 304
Landlord's Agreement of Lease..................... 306
Tenant's Agreement................................ 306
Agreement for a Part of a House................... 306

Line Fences and Water Courses. (Ontario.)

Summary of the Law............................... 307
The Line Fences Act............................... 308
Schedule of Forms under Act...................... 313
The Ditches and Water Courses Act............... 314
Schedule of Forms under Act...................... 319
Amending Act...................................... 320

Marriage and Rights of Married Women.

General Remarks as to the Law of Marriage in English Speaking Countries............................. 321
As to Breach of Promise........................... 322
The Marriage Act (Ontario)........................ 323

Schedule of Forms under Act.................................. 328
Separate Rights of Property of Married Women............ 330
The Law of Dower.. 334
A Husband must maintain his Wife............................ 335

Master and Servant.
Recent alterations in the Law................................... 337
Nature of Contract of Hiring and Service.................... 339
Extracts from Master and Servant's Act. (Ontario)....... 340
Relating to Apprentices... 342
Apprenticeship Indenture... 344
Indenture of Apprenticeship for a girl to learn Housework 345
Assignment of an Indenture of Apprenticeship............ 346

Mortgages.
Nature and Law of Mortgages................................... 347
How they should be Executed................................... 348
Mortgage of Lease.. 349
Statutory Mortgage. (Ontario).................................. 353
Affidavit of Execution... 354
Mortgage with Dower. (Ontario)................................ 355
Mortgage to Secure Future Advances. (Ontario).......... 356
Discharge of Mortgage. (Ontario).............................. 358
Discharge of part of Mortgaged Premises.................... 359

Naturalization.
General Remarks... 359
Extracts from Dominion Statutes............................... 360
Extracts from Imperial Statutes................................. 365

Partnership.
General Law of Partnership....................................... 367
What a Partner may do.. 368
How Dissolved... 370
Limited Partnerships. (Ontario)................................. 371
Declaration of (ordinary) Co-partnership..................... 374
Declaration of Dissolution of Partnership.................... 375
Partnership Deed.. 375
Dissolution of Partnership.. 377
Notice thereof.. 377
Notice when business is to be continued..................... 378

Patents of Invention.
General Remarks as to Patent Law............................. 378
Extracts from Patent Act of 1872.............................. 380
Tariff of Fees... 381
Extracts from Rules of Patent Office.......................... 382

Power of Attorney.
Nature of Power of Attorney..................................... 384
General Power of Attorney....................................... 385
General Custom House Power................................... 386
Power to Sell and Convey Real Estate........................ 386
Power of Attorney to Transfer Stock.......................... 387
Proxy, or Power to Vote at Election of Directors.......... 387

Substitution to be Indorsed on the Power of Attorney.... 387
Revocation of Power of Attorney.................. 388

Protection of Game, and Fishing Laws of Canada.
Explanatory Remarks.. 388
Act for the Protection of Game and Fur-Bearing Animals.
(Ontario)... 389
Extracts from Dominion Fisheries Act........ 392
Orders in Council under Act..... 394

Province of Ontario Laws of General Interest.
Free Grants and Homesteads' Act...... 395
The Mechanics' Lien Act............ 395
Mills and Mill-Dams.......................... 395
Planting Trees along Highways.............................. 396
An Act respecting Pounds............................·.......... 396
Protecting Cheese and Butter Manufacturers................. 397
For the Protection of Birds beneficial to Agriculture. 397
To Prevent the Profanation of the Lord's Day (Sunday).. 397
Registration of Births, Marriages and Deaths............. 397
Right of Property in Swarms of Bees.... 398
Returns of Convictions and Fines by Justices of the Peace 398
Support of Illegitimate Children... 398
Form of Affidavit of Affiliation under this Act........... 399
To Prevent the Spreading of Canada Thistles............. 399
To Prevent Accidents by Threshing Machines........... 400
Travelling on Public Highways and Bridges 400
Tolls on Turnpike Roads............... 400

Province of Nova Scotia, Laws of General Interest.
Landlord and Tenant.... 401
Rights of Married Women.................................... 401
Law of Inheritance........... 402
Wills of Real and Personal Property....................... 403
Mechanics' Lien.............. 404
Deeds, Bills of Sale, &c.......................... .. 404
Crown Land Grants.. 405
Master's, Servant's and Apprentice's Act........ 406
Nature and Jurisdiction of Small Debts Courts.......... 407
County Court.................. 408
Limitations of Actions............... 408
Magistrates' Court.—Justices' Fees................... .. 408
Constables' Fees.................. 409

Wills and Intestacy.
Explanatory Remarks.. 409
The General Law of Wills..................... 410
Law of Ontario............................. 412
Descent of Property of Intestate. (Ontario).............. 412
Law of Ontario respecting Wills.......................... 413
A Short Form of Will 417
General Form of a Will to dispose of Real and Personal
  Estate in Legacies...... 418
Codicil to a Will......,............................. 419

EVERY MAN
HIS OWN LAWYER,

—— AND ——

GENERAL LEGAL FORM BOOK.

A COMPLETE GUIDE IN MATTERS OF LAW AND BUSINESS FOR THE DOMINION.

AFFIDAVIT.

The word affidavit is an old law term of the English language, literally meaning he made an oath. In accordance with practice and precedent, it is a written statement of facts sworn to before a magistrate, a commissioner for taking affidavits, a notary public, or any person specially appointed by some statute for a particular purpose, such as returning officers, municipal clerks and others. In cases where persons object to taking an oath, from conscientious scruples, they can make an affirmation. In point of law the oath and affirmation have precisely the same binding effect on the conscience, and making either falsely is alike regarded as perjury, and subject to the same penalties. Oaths and affirmations being solemn engagements before Almighty God to state the truth, should always be administered with due form and decorum in a standing position, so as to impress their great responsibility on the minds of the persons taking them. All magistrates and others administering oaths should be careful that they administer none without due legal authority, as otherwise they render themselves liable to prosecutions of one kind or another. The practice of taking improper or voluntary and extra-judicial oaths and affidavits in matters not the subject of any judicial enquiry, nor required or authorised by any law, has heretofore been so prevalent in the Dominion of Canada, that it became necessary in 1874 to pass an Act expressly prohibiting it. This Act provides that any Justice of the Peace or other person administering any oath, affidavit, or solemn affirmation, contrary to its provisions, shall be deemed guilty of a misdemeanor, and be liable to be imprisoned for three months, or to be fined fifty dollars.* It also gives a special form of Declaration for the statement of matters of fact, the false taking of which Declaration it constitutes a misdemeanor. Magistrates especially should always consult this Act before taking any affidavit outside the regular routine of their ministerial and judicial functions.

In drawing up an affidavit, care should be taken that dates in the body of the instrument are written at full length, and that figures should not be used in any case therein. It should also be framed in simple and explicit language, and interlineations and erasures avoided as much as possible. When these become absolutely necessary, the initials of the person before whom the affidavit is made should be put in the margin opposite them, or close to them between the lines of the document thus (A. B.). If it becomes necessary to erase any word, strike the pen through it, and do not use a knife. When an affidavit embraces several subjects the numbered paragraph form should be used, each paragraph covering one distinct subject.

It is absolutely necessary that a person presenting himself

---

*Vide Dominion Statutes, 37 Vic. Chap. 37.

or herself to make an affidavit should be fully acquainted with its contents, and should not ignorantly swear or affirm thereto. This knowledge should be acquired either by personal perusal of the affidavit by the person swearing or affirming thereto, or by its being read over in his (*or her*) presence, and so as to prevent subsequent denial of a full acquaintance with its contents and character. In cases where the person swearing or affirming cannot write, he appends his mark in the form of a cross, above which should be written "*The mark of,*" and below the name of the marksman in full. Whenever an affidavit is made by a person who cannot write, the magistrate, or whoever takes the same, should append his certificate of execution in the following form, viz.: Sworn (*or affirmed*) before me, &c., and I certify that the foregoing affidavit (*or affirmation*) was read over by me (*or in my presence*) to the said A. B., who appeared to fully understand the same, and made his (*or her*) mark in my presence.

General Form of Affidavit.

Province
County of   (or
United Counties)
To wit :

I, George Allen, of   in the County of   yeoman (*or other proper designation*) make oath and say :

1. That, &c., (*Here state the facts to be sworn to, confining each paragraph to a distinct subject matter, and commencing each with a new line as in this form.*)

2. That, &c.

3. That, &c.

Sworn before me at
in the County of   this
    day of   A. D. 18

GEORGE ALLEN.

J. P., or a Commissioner, &c., for the County of or United Counties of   as the case may be.

General Form of Affirmation.

Province
County of

To wit :

{ I, George Allen, of   in the County of   yeoman (*or other proper designation*) do solemnly and sincerely affirm and declare as follows :

1. That, &c.
2. That, &c.
3. That, &c.

(Follow the same instructions as given for Affidavit.)

Affirmed before me
at
in the County of   GEORGE ALLEN.
this   day of
A. D. 18

J. P., *or a Commissioner, &c.*

(If the affidavit or affirmation is joined in by more than one person, then their names should be stated in the certificate of execution, thus :)

Severally sworn (*or affirmed*) by the Deponents, A. B, C. D., &c., before me, at, &c.,

---

Form of Oath.

You swear that this affidavit by you subscribed is just and true to the best of your knowledge and belief. So help you God.

Form of Affirmation.

You do solemnly and sincerely declare and affirm, as you shall answer to Almighty God at the great day of judgment, that this affirmation by you subscribed is just and true, to the best of your knowledge and belief.

Statutory Declaration.

Province⎫ I, George Allen of the
County of ⎬ in the County of   Yeoman.
   To wit:⎭

Do solemnly declare, that, (*Here state the matter declared to, in simple and direct language, using the paragraph form as in an affidavit when there is more than one subject to be declared to.*)

And I make this solemn declaration, conscientiously believing the same to be true, and by virtue of the Act passed in the Thirty-seventh year of Her Majesty's Reign, intituled " An Act for the Suppression of Voluntary and extra Judicial Oaths."

Declared before me ⎫
at   in the ⎬
County of   this   ⎬   GEORGE ALLEN.
day of   A. D. 18 ⎭

J. P., or Commissioner, &c.

Form of Affidavit of Execution of Agreement.

Ontario,   ⎫ I,   , of
County of   ⎬ the   of   , in the
   To Wit. ⎭ County of   , make oath
and say :

1. That I was personally present and did see the annexed (*or within*)   (and duplicate, *if any, according to the fact*) duly signed, sealed and executed by
and   the parties thereto.

2. That the said   (and duplicate *if any, according to the fact*) were executed at the
of

3. That I know the said parties (*or one or more of them, according to the fact*).

4. That I am a subscribing witness to the said (and duplicate, *according to the fact*).

Sworn before me ⎫
at   ⎬
this   day of ⎬   GEORGE ALLEN.
   A D. 18   ⎭

J. P., or a Commissioner, &c.

AGREEMENTS.

An agreement, or contract, is a bargain or engagement entered into between two or more persons for the due performance of some special act, or acts, or for the sale of some kind of real or personal property. An Agreement may be of two kinds, viz., verbal or written. In order to make it binding, it is absolutely necessary that a fair and reasonable consideration, of a good or valuable character, should be made by one party thereto, and be accepted by the other; and where such consideration cannot be shown an agreement is void in law. A good consideration is that of close relationship, or the love and affection which a man has for his wife and children, or other near relatives. A valuable consideration represents money, real or personal property, marriage, or the like. Unless in the single instance of a verbal lease of property (which may be valid for a term not exceeding three years), a verbal, or word of mouth, agreement is only good for one year; and if an agreement is designed to be for a longer period it should be in writing.— Every agreement should distinctly specify the time in which, or at the end of which, its conditions should be complied with, in order to prevent any future misunderstanding. But if no time is mentioned, the contract must be construed as permitting a reasonable time for its fulfilment, and the courts will enforce this construction. If it is designed to hold the party charged with the fulfilment of an agreement to the date specified therein, a clause should be added to contract stating that time is considered of the essence thereof. If an agreement is special in its character it should always be made under seal. As every instrument is better in law with a seal than without one, and as many persons may not be able to understand clearly when a seal is, or is not necessary, all agreements of any importance had better be made under seal whenever it can be conveniently done. Although the signature of the party charged with the fulfilment of an agreement is sufficient to make it binding, yet it is always better to have it signed by all the parties thereto, and duplicate copies made for the use of both sides.

In drawing up an agreement the simplest and most easily understood language should always be used. No figures should be made in the body of the instrument, and whether for dates, or for sums of money, or for other purposes, they should always be expressed in words. Erasures, or other alterations, should be made with the pen only, and be initialed by a witness to the instrument.

While what is known in law as a simple agreement, or contract, or, in other words, a contract inferior in degree to a deed, may be either made by word of mouth or in writing, a special contract must always be a written one. Under the provisions of an act passed in England in 1676, in the reign of Charles II, which is still in force in this Dominion, for "The Prevention of Frauds and Perjuries," an agreement for the sale of goods under the value of $40 is not binding, unless there is a part payment of the money, or part delivery of the goods, or an understaanding that the contract is to be completed at some future time. Hence, if John Doe should agree to pay so much for the goods, and their owner, Richard Roe, should agree to take the specified sum, and they should then separate without saying anything more about the transaction, there would be no definite agreement for delivery, and no sale. But if Richard Roe should offer to pay the money, or even pay a single cent of it to John Doe, or should a delivery take place of the smallest portion of the goods, or if the payment or delivery, or both together, should be put off by mutual consent to a future day, the sale will be held good, and the property in the goods will pass from the seller to the buyer. But, at the same time, the agreement will involve the necessity on the part of the seller of doing all acts required for the due performance of the sale, such as the weighing or measuring of the article or articles sold, or their due separation from other goods, or of the manufacture and setting apart for the benefit of the buyer of goods to be subseqnently made ; and of the due performance also on the part of the buyer of his part of the contract.

By Chap. 117 of the Revised Statutes of Ontario, respecting "Written Promises and Acknowledgements of Liability," the provisions of the Statute of Frauds are declared to extend to all contracts for the sale of goods of $40 and upwards.

In cases where agreements are of importance, they should be drawn up in duplicate, and, if made in the Province of Ontario, registered in pursuance of Chap. 111, Secs. 2 and 38, of its Revised Statutes. The proper form of Affidavit of Execution in this case, will be found under the head of affidavit.

General Form of Agreement.

THIS AGREEMENT, made this first day of May, one thousand eight hundred and eighty, between JOHN GILES, of the Town of Brockville, in the County of Leeds, and Province of Ontario, merchant, of the first part, and JAMES ALLEN of the Village of Maitland, in said County and Province, yeoman, of the second part :

WITNESSETH, That the said JOHN GILES, in consideration of the covenants on the part of the party of the second part, hereinafter contained, doth covenant and agree to and with the said JAMES ALLEN, that *(here insert the agreement on the part of John Giles.]*

And the said JAMES ALLEN, in consideration of the covenants on the part of the party of the first part, doth covenant and agree to and with the said JOHN GILES, that [*here insert the agreement on the part of James Allen.*]

In witness whereof, we have hereunto set our hands and seals, the day and year first above written.

Sealed and delivered,
  in presence of
JAMES STRONG,
JOHN TAYLOR.
}
JOHN GILES. [L.S.]
JAMES ALLEN. [L.S.]

(*When required this clause may be inserted :*)

And it is further agreed, between the parties hereto, that the party that shall fail to perform this agreement on his part, will pay the other the full sum of *fifty* dollars, as fixed and settled damages for such failure.

Agreement for the Purchase of a House and Lot.

THIS AGREEMENT made this tenth day of July, in the year one thousand eight hundred and eighty, between JOHN ROWLEY, Printer, of the city of Toronto, and CARLTON BRYANT, Merchant, of the same city, *witnesseth*—That the said JOHN ROWLEY agrees to sell, and the said CARLTON BRYANT agrees to purchase, for the price or consideration of six thousand dollars, the house and lot known and distinguished as number ninety-nine, on Yonge Street, in the said city of Toronto. The possession of the property is to be delivered on the first day of May next, when twenty-five per cent of the purchase money is to be paid in cash, and a mortgage on the premises, payable in five years, bearing seven per cent interest, (such interest payable quarterly (*or half yearly*), is to be executed for the balance of the purchase money, at which time also a deed of conveyance in fee simple, containing the usual statutory covenants and warranty is to be delivered, executed by the said JOHN ROWLEY and his wife CATHERINE ROWLEY, and the title made satisfactory to the said CARLTON BRYANT : it being understood that this agreement shall be binding upon the heirs, executors, administrators or assigns of the respective parties ; and also that the said premises are now insured for three thousand dollars, and, in case the said house should be burnt before the said first day of May next, that the said JOHN ROWLEY shall hold the said insurance in trust for, and will then transfer the same to, the said CARLTON BRYANT, with the said deed.

In witness, &c., (*as in General Form*)

Agreement for the Sale of Real Estate.

ARTICLES OF AGREEMENT made and entered into this   day of   between A. B. of   , of the one part, and C. D., of   of the other part, as follows: The said A. B. doth hereby agree with the said C. D. to sell him the lot of ground, (here describe it,) for the sum of   ; and that he, the said A. B., shall and will, on the   day of   next, on receiving from the said C. D. the said sum, at his own cost and expense, execute a proper conveyance for the conveying and assuring the fee simple of the said premises to the said C. D., free from all encumbrances, which conveyance shall contain a general warranty and the usual full statutory covenants, and release of dower. And the said C. D. agrees with the said A. B. that he, the said C. D., shall and will, on the said   day of   next, and on execution of such conveyance, pay unto the said A. B. the sum of   aforesaid. And it is further agreed between the parties aforesaid, as follows: The said A. B. shall have and retain the possession of the property, and receive and be entitled to the rents and profits thereof, until the said   day of   next; when, and upon delivery of the conveyance, the possession is to be delivered to the said C. D. And it is understood that the stipulations aforesaid are to apply to and to bind the heirs, executors, administrators and assigns of the respective parties. And in case of failure, the parties hereto bind themselves each unto the other in the sum of   which they hereby consent to fix and determine as the amount of damages to be paid by the failing party for his non-performance of this agreement.

In witness, &c., (*as in General Form.*)

Another Form.

ARTICLES OF AGREEMENT made and entered into this tenth day of June, A. D., one thousand eight hundred and eighty, between JOHN SMITH, of the Township of Yonge, in the County of Leeds, and Province of Ontario, Yeoman, of the first part; and RICHARD JONES, of the village of Newboro, in the said county, Merchant, of the second part:

1. WITNESSETH that the said JOHN SMITH and the said RICHARD JONES, do hereby respectively for themselves, their

heirs, executors, administrators and assigns, agree with each other as following, that is to say, that the said JOHN SMITH shall sell to the said RICHARD JONES, and that the said RICHARD JONES will purchase from the said JOHN SMITH, all that parcel or tract of land and premises, situate, lying and being, &c., (*here fully describe the property to be sold,*) and the freehold and inheritance thereof in fee simple, free from all incumbrances of dower or otherwise, for the sum or price of three thousand dollars, of good and lawful money of the Dominion of Canada, fifteen hundred dollars, or one-half of which said sum, are to be paid by the said RICHARD JONES to the said JOHN SMITH immediately after the signature of these presents, and the other half on the first day of August next ensuing, when the purchase is to be completed, and the said RICHARD JONES put in full and peaceable possession of the land and premises aforesaid.

2. That the said RICHARD JONES, at his own expense, shall procure inspection, and make copies if needed, of all deeds, wills, or other documents relating to the land and premises aforesaid, not now in possession of the said JOHN SMITH, and which may be required for the due completion of the purchase.

3. That on payment of the second half of the aforesaid purchase money, being the sum of fifteen hundred dollars, on the first day of August next ensuing, as already set forth herein, the said JOHN SMITH shall execute and deliver to the said RICHARD JONES a proper Deed, with full Covenants, Warranty and release of Dower (or under the Statute of Ontario respecting Short form of Conveyances), of the lands and premises as aforesaid.

4. Should the purchase not be fully completed on the said first day of August next ensuing, the said RICHARD JONES shall pay interest on any balance of the purchase money remaining due from that date until the full completion of the purchase.

In witness whereof, &c., (*as in General Form*).

Agreement for Building a House, the proprietor to find the material.

ARTICLES OF AGREEMENT made and entered into this third

day of June, A. D. one thousand eight hundred and eighty-one, between JOHN SMITH, of the Town of Brockville, in the County of Leeds, and Province of Ontario, Builder, of the first part, and RICHARD JONES, of the same place, Merchant, of the second part:

Witnesseth that it is hereby agreed between the said JOHN SMITH and the said RICHARD JONES, in manner following, that is to say, the said JOHN SMITH, for the consideration hereinafter mentioned, doth for himself, his heirs, executors, administrators and assigns, covenant with the said RICHARD JONES, his heirs, executors, administrators, and assigns, that he shall and will, within the space of six months next after the date hereof, in a good and workmanlike manner, and at his own proper charge and expense, at the town of Brockville, well and substantially erect, build, and finish, one house, or messuage, according to the plan and specification hereunto annexed, with such stone, brick, timber, and other materials, as the said RICHARD JONES or his assigns shall find or provide for the same: In consideration whereof, the said RICHARD JONES doth for himself, his executors, administrators, and assigns, covenant to and with the said JOHN SMITH, his heirs, executors, admistrators and assigns, that he will well and truly pay unto the said JOHN SMITH, his executors, administrators, and assigns, the sum of   of lawful money of the Dominion of Canada, in manner following, viz.:   part thereof at the beginning of the said work   another part thereof when the said work shall be half done, and the remaining   in full for the said work, when the same shall be completely finished to the satisfaction of the said RICHARD JONES, or the architect or other person appointed by him to inspect and superintend the same: And also that he, the said RICHARD JONES, his executors, administrators, or assigns, shall and will from time to time, as the same shall be required, at his and their own proper expense, find and provide stone, brick, timber, and other materials necessary for making, building, and finishing the said house. And for the performance of all and every the articles and agreements above mentioned, the said JOHN SMITH and RICHARD JONES do hereby bind themselves, their executors and administrators, each to the other, in the penal sum of   firmly by these presents.

In witness, &c., (*as in General Form.*)

(*The foregoing form will also answer where the builder provides the materials by making the necessary alterations. Special covenants can be added in every case as may be required.*)

Agreement respecting a Party Wall.

THIS AGREEMENT, made this   day of   , in the year A. D.   between D. L. of the City of Winnipeg, Merchant, of the first part, and P. S. of said city, Merchant, of the second part, *witnesseth* :—

Whereas, the said D. L. is the owner in fee of the lot and store known as number 90 in   street, in the third ward of the City of Winnipeg, and the said P. S. the owner in fee of the lot known as number 92 in   street, aforesaid, immediately adjoining to and on the southerly side of said lot and store number 90, on which lot of the said P. S. he is about to erect a brick store. And whereas, it has been agreed, by and between the said parties, that the said P. S., in erecting his said store, shall make use of the gable end wall of the said store of the said D. L., immediately contiguous to and adjoining the said lot of the said P. S, as a party wall, upon the terms, conditions, and considerations hereinafter mentioned, the said gable end wall of the said D. L., so to be used as a party wall, standing and being entirely on the said lot of the said D. L. Now, therefore, this agreement witnesseth, that the said D. L., for and in consideration of the sum of   dollars to him in hand paid by the said P. S., at or before the ensealing and delivery of these presents, the receipt whereof is hereby acknowledged, doth for himself, his heirs, executors, administrators, and assigns, covenant, grant, promise, and agree to and with the said P. S., his heirs, executors, administrators, and assigns, forever, that he, the said P. S., his heirs and assigns, shall and may, in erecting and building the said store upon the said lot of the said P. S., freely and lawfully, but in a workmanlike manner, and without any interruption, molestation, or hinderance of or from the said D. L, his heirs or assigns, make use of the said gable end wall of the said store of the said D. L., immediately adjoining or contiguous to the said lot of the said P. S., or such parts and so much thereof as he the said P. S., his heirs or assigns, may choose as a party wall. And further, that should the said wall, hereby made a party wall, be at any future time or times injured or destroyed, either by decay, lapse of time, fire, accident, or other cause whatever, so as to require to be either repaired or rebuilt, in whole or in part, then and in every such case, the said D. L. and the said P. S. by these presents, for themselves respectively, and their respective heirs and assigns forever, mutually covenant and agree, to and with each other and their respective heirs and assigns forever, that such reparation or re-building, as the case may be, shall be at the mutual joint and equal expense of them the said D. L. and P. S,, their respective heirs and assigns forever; as to so much and such parts of the said wall as shall be used by the said P. S., his heirs and assigns, in erecting and building the said store which he is now about erecting on his said lot, and as to all coping of the said gable end, whether such coping be used by the said P. S., his heirs and assigns, in erecting and building the said store or not, and as to the residue of the said wall not used by the said P. S., his heirs or assigns, in erecting and building the said store, such reparation or rebuilding of such residue of the said wall shall be at the sole and separate expense of the said D. L., his heirs or assigns forever; and that in every case of such reparation or rebuilding, should the same be necessary and proper, and either party, his heirs or assigns, request the other to unite in the same, and to contribue to the expense thereof, according to the true intent and meaning of this agreement, then the other party, his heirs or assigns forever, may cause such reparation or re-building to be made and done, and charge the other party, his heirs and assigns, forever, with the proportion of the expenses, costs, and charges thereof, according to the true intent and meaning of this agreement; and that in every case of such reparation or rebuilding, as the case may be, such repairs shall restore the said wall to the state and condition in which it now is in all respects, as nearly as may be; and that in every case of rebuilding, such wall shall be rebuilt upon the same spot on which it now stands, and be of the same size and the same materials, as far as they may go, and as to the deficiency with others of the same quality and goodness, and in all respects shall be made of the same quality and goodness as the present wall.

It being further in like manner mutually understood and agreed, by and between the said parties, that this agreement shall be perpetual, and run with the land, and be obligatory upon the heirs and assigns of the said parties, respectively, forever, and in all cases and on all occasions, shall be construed as a covenant running with the land; but that this agreement shall not have the effect or operation of conveying to the said P. S., his heirs or assigns, the fee simple of the one moiety or any other part of the ground or land on which the said wall now stands, but only the right to the use and benefit of the said wall as, a party wall, forever.

In witness, &c., (*as in General Form.*)

Agreement for a Sale of Grain.

MEMORANDUM.—It is agreed, by and between E. F. of &c., That he, the said G. H. in consideration of three hundred bushels of wheat, sold to him this day by the said E. F., and by him agreed to be delivered to the said G. H., free of all charges and expenses whatsoever, at, on, or before, &c., next, shall and will pay, or cause to be paid to the said E. F., or his assigns, within three months after such delivery, the sum of, &c. And the said E. F., in consideration of the agreement aforesaid of the said G. H., doth promise and agree, on or before, &c., aforesaid, at his proper expenses to send in and deliver to the said G. H., or his assigns, the said three hundred bushels of wheat, so sold him as aforesaid, and that he the said E. F. shall and will warrant the same to be good, clean, and merchantable grain.

In witness, &c.,(*as in General Form.*)

Agreement for the Sale of Standing Timber.

ARTICLES OF AGREEMENT made and entered into in duplicate, this second day of June, A. D., one thousand eight hundred and eighty, between GEORGE BROWN, of the Township of Bathurst, County of Lanark, and Province of Onario, Farmer, of the first part; and HENRY ROBERTSON, of the Town of Perth, in the said county, Lumberman, of the second part:

Witnesseth, that the said party of the first part, in consideration of the sum of one thousand dollars, of lawful money of Canada, now paid to him by the said party of the second part (the receipt whereof is hereby acknowledged), hereby grants, bargains, sells, and assigns, to the said party of the second part, his heirs, executors, administrators or assigns, all the trees and timber over ten inches in diameter at the point where they are cut, (said point being at least two feet from the ground), now standing or growing in and upon that certain parcel or tract of land and premises, situate, lying and being, in the Township of Drummond, in the County of Lanark, aforesaid, containing by admeasurement four hundred acres, be the same more or less, and being composed of lots ten and eleven in the said Township.

And it is hereby further agreed between the parties to these presents, that the said party of the second part, his agents, servants or workmen, with such horses and vehicles as they may need or require, shall for the space and term of two years, to be fully completed and ended from this date, have full right and liberty, at all times, to enter into and upon the said land and premises, to cut down and remove the said trees and timber as he or they may think fit.

And the said party of the first part, covenants with the said party of the second part, that he is the owner in fee simple of the said lands ; that he has the right to sell the trees and timber thereon ; and that they are free from incumbrances of any kind or description whatever.

In witness, &c., *(as in General Form)*.

(If for Registration append the proper Affidavit of Execution).

Agreement to Sell Goods on Commission.

THIS AGREEMENT made the tenth day of May, one thousand eight hundred and eighty, between JOHN JONES of the City of Hamilton, in the Province of Ontario, Merchant Tailor, of the first part ; and THOMAS ROBINSON, of the same place, Commercial Traveller, of the second part :

Witnesseth, that the said party of the first part hereby agrees to furnish the said party of the second part, with such articles of clothing of his manufacture, as he the said party of the second part may personally select, or order in writing, from time to time, at a discount of one-third from his regular retail prices.

And the said party of the second part, agrees to pay, at

the end of each month, the said party of the first part, for all such articles of clothing sold by him; and then to account for, and surrender if required, to the said party of the first part, any articles of clothing supplied by him, and still remaining unsold.

This agreement to terminate at the pleasure of either party thereto.

In witness, &c., (*as in General Form*).

Chattel Security Agreement.

THIS AGREEMENT made the first day of June, one thousand eight hundred and eighty, between JOHN DOE, of Brockville, in the County of Leeds, and Province of Ontario, Tailor, of the first part; and RICHARD ROE, of the same place, Merchant, of the second part:

Whereas the said JOHN DOE hath this day deposited (at his own risk of loss or damage by fire or otherwise) with the said RICHARD ROE, a quantity of wearing apparel, according to the Schedule marked A, and hereto annexed, as a security for the payment of the principal sum of one thousand dollars now in hand paid to him (the receipt of which is hereby acknowledged), and interest thereon at the rate of eight per cent per annum, to be computed from this date, it is hereby agreed between the parties to these presents in manner following, that is to say:

That should the said JOHN DOE, on the first day of August next ensuing, pay to the said RICHARD ROE the said principal sum of one thousand dollars now loaned to him, and interest thereon at the rate specified, the said wearing apparel shall then be delivered up to him. But if he should fail in such payment, or any part thereof, then the said RICHARD ROE, after giving three clear days' notice in writing to the said JOHN DOE, may sell the whole of said wearing apparel, or such part thereof as may be required, to fully indemnify himself for the amount due him, and for all costs and charges incurred by such sale.

In witness, &c., (*as in General Form*).

Agreement for a Furnished House.

THIS AGREEMENT made this first day of June, one thousand eight hundred and eighty, between JOHN JONES, of the

Town of Cobourg, and RICHARD ALLEN, of the same place :

1st. The said JOHN JONES lets his house on Ormond Street, with the furniture and effects therein (as per Schedule hereto attached marked D) by the month to the said RICHARD ALLEN, who agrees to take the same at the rental of twenty dollars per month, payable each month in advance.

2nd. One month's notice from either side to terminate tenancy.

3rd. The said RICHARD ALLEN agrees for himself, his family and servants, to do no damage to said house, furniture or effects, and to leave them at the expiration of his tenancy in as good a condition as he now receives them, the wear and tear of ordinary occupation and use excepted, and to make good on notice all damages and deficiencies.

4th. The said JOHN JONES is to have the right to enter upon, and make a monthly inspection of, the said house and furniture.

In witness, &c., *(as in General Form)*.

ARBITRATION.

Arbitration is the settlement of differences or disputes, either as regards suits at law or otherwise, by a person or persons chosen by the parties themselves who differ or dispute, or under the order of some competent court. The principle of arbitration has been interwoven for centuries with the practice of the British Courts of Law. In cases of questions of account, and in others, also, where the matter in dispute could better be settled out of court, a verdict was taken for the plaintiff by consent, subject to the award of an arbitrator, or arbitrators, mutually agreed upon by the parties to the suit, and the reference was then made a rule of court. In this way the arbitrators (as well as the parties to the suit) were subjected to the jurisdiction of the court, which could reduce the award should it regard it as excessive, or compel the disputants to abide thereby. This plan is still continually adopted in courts of law throughout the British Empire, and has always been found to work most satisfactorily. Under these circumstances it was only natural that the progress of time should see the principle of arbitration more widely diffused, and more fully recognized in the British Constitution. Hence we find that in the reign of William III. an Act of Parliament was passed to extend the benefits of arbitration to all cases of dispute between merchants and traders or others, as to matters of account, or other matters ; and directing how awards should be enforced by the courts of law, or set aside if procured by corruption or other undue means.* This Act still remains in force, not only in Great Britain, but in all the Colonies of the Empire where it has not been superseded by local legislation. In Ontario its principles have been extended by the Legislature ; and under the Common Law Procedure Act ‡ submission to arbitration if once made a rule of court, cannot be revoked without permission of court ; and the arbitrator, or arbitrators, will be bound to proceed with the reference, whether the parties to the suit are willing or otherwise. But the court may at its pleasure enlarge the time for making the award. Arbitrators whether appointed by any court of record, or by consent of the parties to any dispute, having authority to hear, receive, and examine evidence, may administer an oath or affirmation to all such witnesses as are legally called before them, and any witness wilfully and corruptly giving false evidence is guilty of perjury, and liable to be prosecuted therefor, just the same as if he had given his evidence in a court of law.

The authority of arbitrators may be terminated by an order of court, or by the death of either of the parties to the suit or dispute. In order to meet, however, the unsat-

---

*Vide 9 and 10 William III., Chap 15.
‡Vide Revised Statutes of Ontario, Chap. 50, sec. 204.

isfactory condition of things which may arise in the latter case it is now usual to insert in the Arbitration Order, or Rule of Court, that the authority of the arbitrators shall not be abrogated by the death of either of the parties thereto, and that the award shall be delivered to, and be binding on, their executors or administrators. And this stipulation may also be made where the arbitration is consented to by private agreement, and not entered upon under the rule of any court of law. If no specified time is stipulated in the Deed of Arbitration the award must still be made within a reasonable time; and if a certain day is specified, the award must be ready for delivery by that day unless the time has been enlarged. When the arbitrators are ready to proceed to business, they must notify the parties to the dispute to be in attendance, and so take charge of their respective interests. But if, after due notice, either party fail to attend in person or by counsel, the arbitrators are at liberty to proceed with the case without them. Evidence should be properly taken in accordance with the rules of law, and the final award should be signed by the arbitrators in each other's presence. Should the arbitrators disagree, and they select an umpire, the latter ought to hear the whole evidence over again to enable him to give an intelligent and proper decision. His doing this, however, is not required by law, if the parties to the dispute are satisfied with the case or statement conjointly submitted to him by the arbitrators. As many difficulties may enter into complicated matters of arbitration, the advice of counsel is always desirable in order to prevent any misconceptions of matters of law, as well as of fact, and to make the award legally binding. If the award is not in accordance with the rule of court, or violates any general principle of law, it may be set aside by the courts on application; and in any event is not competent to be enforced. When arbitrators are appointed by the parties to the dispute, their award will create a debt from one party to the other, which can be sued for in a competent court. Should, however, an award be made a rule of court, it can at once be enforced by execution without any suit. In Provinces where a Court of Chancery exists, an award made under its order, which cannot be enforced by an action at law, will be enforced under a specific equity decree. Under the provisions of Chap. 64 of the Revised Statutes of Ontario, it is enacted that the fees to witnesses before arbitrators shall be the same as those of any court having jurisdiction over the subject matter of reference. The same Act provides for the payment of an Arbitrator who is a Barrister, Attorney, Engineer, Architect, or Provincial Land Surveyor, according to the following schedule :—

For every meeting where the cause is not proceeded with, but an enlargement or postponement is made at the request of either party, not less than..................	$ 4 00
Nor more than.......	8 00
For every day's sitting, to consist of not less than six hours, not less than...	10 00
Nor more than	20 00
For every sitting not extending to six hours (fractional parts of hours being excluded) where the arbitration is actually proceeded with, for each hour occupied in such proceedings, at the rate of not less than	2 00
Nor more than	3 00

Arbitrators who do not come under any of the foregoing heads, are to be paid according to the annexed Schedule :—

For every meeting where the cause is not proceeded with, but an enlargement or postponement is made at the request of either party, not less than	$ 2 00
Not more than........	4 00
For every day's sitting, to consist of not less than six hours, not less than..	5 00
Nor more than	10 00
For every sitting not extending to six hours (fractional parts of hours being excluded) where the arbitration is actually proceeded with, for each hour occupied in such proceedings, at the rate of not less than	1 00
Nor more than	1 50

Various Acts of the Province of Ontario prescribe how arbitration shall be exercised in particular cases, and under special circumstances. Chap. 158 of the Revised Statutes

Sec. 17, provides that the dispute between members and officers of co-operative associations, shall be decided by arbitration without the right of appeal; the Drainage Act, Chap. 33, Sec. 25, provides for an arbitration court to settle disputes arising under it between municipalities; and the Act, Chap. 134, also of the Revised Statutes, makes provisions to adjust disputes between masters and workmen by a board of arbitration. The same wise principle enters into the construction of several other statutes of this Province, so that a great variety of disputes and differences may now legally be arranged by arbitration, and the expense and uncertainties of suits at law thus avoided.

Form of Arbitration Agreement or Deed.

THIS INDENTURE made, in duplicate, the first day of June, A. D., one thousand, eight hundred and eighty-one, between JOHN DOE, of the City of Belleville, County of Hastings, and Province of Ontario, Yeoman, of the first part, and RICHARD ROE, of the same place, Merchant, of the second part.

Witnesseth that whereas disputes and differences have arisen, and are now depending, between the said parties of the first and second parts in reference to (*state matters in dispute*), and in order to put an end thereto, and to obtain an amicable adjustment thereof, the said parties of the first and second parts have respectively agreed to refer the same to the award, order, arbitrament, final end and determination of John Smith and George Jones, both of the City of Kingston, in the Province aforesaid, arbitrators, indifferently chosen, by and on behalf of the said parties respectively: And in the event of the said two arbitrators hereby appointed not being able to agree within one month from the date of these presents upon their said award, then it shall and may be lawful for them to appoint some fit person as third arbitrator, by a memorandum, in writing, under their hands, to be endorsed on these presents; and the award of any two of them shall be final and conclusive, both at law and in equity, upon both of the said parties hereto: such award to be made in writing on or before the first day of August next.

Now this Indenture witnesseth, that the said parties hereto do, and each of them doth, each for himself severally and respectively, and for his and their respective heirs, executors and administrators, covenant, promise and agree, to and with each other, his and their heirs, executors and administrators, well and truly to stand to, obey, abide by, observe, perform, fulfil, and keep the award, order, arbitrament and final determination of the said arbitrators hereby appointed ; or, in the event of it becoming necessary, to appoint such third arbitrator as aforesaid, to stand to, obey, abide by, observe, perform, fulfil and keep the award, order, arbitrament, and final determination of any two of them of and concerning the premises ;[aforesaid, or anything in any manner relating thereto, provided such award be made in writing, under their hands, or under the hands of any two of them (in the event of any such appointment as aforesaid), on or before the first day of August next.

And it is hereby agreed, that the said arbitrators shall be at liberty, by writing, under their hands, or the hands of any two of them, respectively endorsed on these presents, to enlarge the time for making the said award when and as often, and to such times, as they shall think fit. And also, that all the costs and charges attending the said arbitration shall be in the discretion of the said arbitrators hereby appointed, or in the event of such appointment of a third arbitrator as aforesaid, of any two of them so making their award as aforesaid, and shall be paid and satisfied pursuant to their award. And also, that these presents may be made a rule of Her Majesty's Court of Queen's Bench or Common Pleas, at Toronto.

And for the full performance of the said award so to be made as aforesaid, the said parties hereto bind themselves, severally and respectively, their several and respective heirs, executors and administrators, each to the other of them respectively, in the penal sum of one thousand dollars of lawful money of Canada, firmly by these presents.

In witness whereof the said parties to these presents have hereunto set their hands and affixed their seals, the day and year first above written.

Signed, sealed and delivered
in the presence of   JOHN DOE, [L. S.]
    E. F.   RICHARD ROE, [L. S.]

Arbitration Bond.

Know all men by these presents, That I JOHN DOE, of &c., am held and firmly bound to RICHARD ROE, of, &c., in the penal sum of one thousand dollars of lawful money of Canada, to be paid to the said Richard Roe, or to his certain attorney, executors, administrators, or assigns, for which payment to be well and truly made, I bind myself, my heirs, executors, firmly by these presents.

Sealed with my seal. Dated this first day of June, 1881.

Whereas disputes and differences have arisen, and are now pending, between the above-bounden JOHN DOE and the said RICHARD ROE, touching and concerning (*state suject-matter in dispute as in deed.*)

And whereas the above-bounden JOHN DOE, and the said RICHARD ROE, have agreed to refer such disputes and differences, as well as all actions, suits, controversies, accounts, reckonings, matters, and things in any wise relating thereto, to the award, arbitrament and determination of John Smith and George Jones, arbitrators nominated, appointed and chosen, as well as by and on the part and behalf of the above-bounden JOHN DOE as of the said RICHARD ROE, and who have consented and agreed to accept the burthen of the said arbitration :

Now, the condition of the above-written bond or obligation is such, that if the above-bounden JOHN DOE do and shall well and truly submit to, abide by, and perform, the award, arbitrament and determination of the said arbitrators so nominated, appointed and chosen as aforesaid, touching and concerning the matters in dispute between the above-bounden JOHN DOE and the said RICHARD ROE, and so referred to them, the said arbitrators as aforesaid (provided such award be made in writing under the hands and seals of the said arbitrators, ready to be delivered to the said parties, or such of them as shall apply for the same, on or before the first day of August, one thousand eight hundred and eighty-one): Then this obligation shall be void, otherwise to be and remain in full force and virtue. And the said obligor hereby consents and agrees that this Bond of Submission, and the Award to be made thereunder, shall and may be made a

Rule of Court of any of the Superior Courts of this Province.
Signed, sealed and delivered
in the presence of JOHN DOE. [L. S.]
E. F.

(NOTE.—*A similar bond must be executed by Richard Roe, substituting Richard Roe for John Doe wherever it occurs.*

Appointment of an Umpire.

We, the within-named JOHN SMITH and GEORGE JONES, do hereby nominate and appoint William Robinson, of the city of Toronto, to be umpire between us, in and concerning the matters in difference within referred, (on condition that he do, within   days from the date hereof, by some writing under his hand, accept the umpirage).

Witness our hands this   day of   , 18
Witness,   JOHN SMITH,
W. W.   GEORGE JONES.

(NOTE.—*The foregoing appointment should be endorsed on the arbitration deed or bond.*)

Enlargement of Time for Making Award.

We, the undersigned arbitrators, by virtue of the power to us given for this purpose, do hereby appoint, extend, and (*if a second enlargement,* "further") enlarge the time for making our award until the   day of   next, on or before which said day our award in writing of and concerning the matters in difference within mentioned and referred to us shall be made and published.

In witness whereof, we have hereto set our hands the day of   , 18   .
Witness,   JOHN SMITH,
W. W.   GEORGE JONES.

NOTE.—*The observation appended to the last form applies to this form and the two next forms also.*

Enlargement of Time by the Parties

We, the within-named JOHN DOE and RICHARD ROE, for ourselves severally and respectively, and for our several and respective heirs, executors and administrators, do hereby give, grant and allow unto the within-named arbitrators, further time for making their award of and concerning the several matters within referred to them, until the day of   next.

In witness whereof, we have hereunto set our hands (*or, if the submission was by bond or deed, say*, " our hands and seals") the   day of   18   .

Signed, (*or* Signed, sealed and delivered)
in the presence of   JOHN DOE,   [L. S.]
    W. W.   RICHARD ROE. [L. S.]

Appointment of Third Person as Additional Arbitrator.

We, the within-named John Smith and George Jones, do by this memorandum under our hands (made before we enter or proceed on the arbitration within mentioned) nominate and appoint William Robinson, of the City of Toronto, the third person or arbitrator, to whom, together with ourselves, all matters in difference between the said parties within mentioned shall be referred, according to the tenor and effect of the within submission.

Witness our hands this   day of   , 18
Signed in the presence of   JOHN SMITH.
    Y. Z.   GEORGE JONES.

Oath to be administered by Arbitrator to a Witness.

You shall true answer make to all such questions as shall be asked of you by or before me touching or relating to the matters in difference between JOHN DOE and RICHARD ROE, referred to my award (*or* "to the award of myself and G. H."), without favor or affection to either party; and therein you shall speak the truth, the whole truth, and nothing but the truth. So help you God.

Appointment by Arbitrator for attendance before him.

DOE ⎫ I appoint   , the   day of   next,
  v.   ⎬ at   o'clock in the evening, at   , for
ROE. ⎭ proceeding in this reference. Dated the
day of   , 18   .   A. A.

To Messrs. JOHN DOE and RICHARD ROE, and their respective attorneys or agents, and all others whom it may concern. } *(The Arbitrators' signature, or the signature of one or more of them if more than one.)*

Peremptory Appointment for the Same Purpose.

I appoint   , the   day of   instant (or "next"), at   o'clock in the   noon precisely, at   , peremptorily to proceed upon and conclude the reference now pending before me between JOHN DOE and RICHARD ROE: And I hereby give notice, that in case of non-attendance of either party, I shall nevertheless proceed, and immediately make my award.   Dated the   day of 18 .

E. F., Arbitrator.

To Messrs. JOHN DOE and RICHARD ROE, and their respective attorneys or agents, and all others whom it may concern-

General Form of Award.

To all to whom these presents shall come, I, A. A. of, &c., send greeting: *(proceed to recite the instrument by which the matters was referred to arbitration, and so much of its terms as may be essential to show the authority of the arbitrator or umpire with respect to the subject-matter of reference, and the time, power of enlargement, and manner of making the award. Thus if it be by indenture, the recital may be as follows:* Whereas by an Indenture bearing date, &c., and made between, &c., reciting that various differences had arisen, &c., *so stating all that may be material to warrant the following award, and then proceed thus:* Now know ye that I, the said A. A., having taken upon myself the burthen of the said arbitration, and having heard and duly considered all the allegations and evidence of the said respective parties of and concerning the said matters in difference, so referred as aforesaid, do make this my award in writing of and concerning the said matters in difference so referred, and do hereby award, order, determine and direct that *(conclude with a distinct statement of the arbitrator's decision on all the points referred to him.)*

In witness whereof I have hereunto set my hand this day of   18   .
Signed in the presence of   A. A.
W. W:

Award where the Submission was by mutual Bonds.

To all to whom these presents shall come, I, A. B., of, &c., send greeting ; Whereas on   , by a bond made and sealed with the seal of RICHARD ROE, &c., he became held and firmly bound unto JOHN DOE, of, &c., in the penal sum of   dollars : And whereas on the day and year aforesaid, the said John Doe, by another bond sealed with his seal, became held and firmly bound unto the said RICHARD ROE, in the like penal sum, with conditions written under the said several bonds that the said JOHN DOE, his heirs, executors and administrators, and the said RICHARD ROE, his heirs, executors and administrators, should well, and truly stand to, abide by, perform, fulfil, and keep the award, order, and final end and determination of me, A. B. an arbitrator indifferently named and elected, as well on the part and behalf of the above-bounden JOHN DOE, as the above-bounden RICHARD ROE, to arbitrate, award, order, judge and determine of and concerning (*&c. here set out such parts of the bond as bear upon the award, and state the enlargement, if any*). Now, I, the said A. B., having taken upon myself the burthen of the said arbitration, and having heard, and duly and maturely weighed and considered, the several allegations, vouchers and proofs made and produced on both sides, do in pursuance of the said submission make and publish this my award of and concerning the said premises in manner following ; that is to say, I do award, &c.

In witness, &c. (*as in last form.*)
Signed in presence of   A. B.
W. W.

Award where the Submission was by agreement, and stating an assent to an enlargement.

To all to whom these presents shall come, we A. B., of &c., and T. A., of, &c., send greeting : Whereas, by a certain agreement in writing under the hands of JOHN DOE, of, and RICHARD ROE, of, &c., bearing date on or about the   day of   reciting that (&c. *here set out such parts of the agreement as bear upon the award:*) And whereas by an endorsement on the said agreement, bearing date on or about the   day of   last under the hands of all the said parties to the said agreement, they the said parties mutually and reciprocally consented and agreed that the time for the said arbitrators making the said award should be enlarged to the   day of   then next, and that they would in all other respects abide by the terms of the said agreement. Now know ye that we the said arbitrators having taken upon us the burthen of the said reference, and having examined all such witnesses as were produced before us by the said parties respectively, and having fully weighed and considered all the allegations, proofs and vouchers made and produced before us, do award &c.

In witness, &c., (*as in preceding forms*).
Signed in the presence of   A. B.
   W. W.   T. A.

Clauses which may be inserted in an Award where they suit the circumstances.

1. I award that RICHARD ROE do pay to JOHN DOE the sum of $ within   days after demand.

2. I award that JOHN DOE do pay to RICHARD ROE the sum of $ within   days after demand.

3. I award and direct that RICHARD ROE do, within one month after demand, pay to the said JOHN DOE the sum of $, and that the said JOHN DOE do, upon such payment, deliver to the said RICHARD ROE a good and sufficient conveyance in fee simple, free from incumbrances of all and singular, &c., (*describe lands*).

4. I award and direct that the said JOHN DOE do pay to the said RICHARD ROE the sum of $, and that thereupon the said JOHN DOE and RICHARD DOE do execute and deliver the one to the other good and sufficient releases of all claims and demands which they may have one against the other.

5. I award that the costs of the reference and award be paid by RICHARD ROE to JOHN DOE.

6. I award that each party bear his own costs of the re-

ference, and that the costs of the award be paid by the said JOHN DOE (*or Richard Roe, or in equal portions by the said John Doe and Richard Roe.*)

7. I award and direct that the said RICHARD ROE do pay to the said JOHN DOE, the costs incurred by the said JOHN DOE, of, and incidental to, the reference and award, (*when the arbitrator is to ascertain the amount add the following words*) and I assess the amount of the said costs of the said JOHN DOE, at $, and the costs of my award at $

8. And I further award and direct that the said JOHN DOE and RICHARD ROE do each bear his own costs of the reference, and pay one-half the costs of the award, and if either party shall, in the first instance, pay the whole or more than half of the costs of the award, the other party shall repay him so much of the amount as shall exceed the half of the said costs.

9. I award and direct that one moiety of the costs of the reference and award be borne and paid by JOHN DOE, and the other moiety by RICHARD ROE.

Affidavit of execution of Arbitration Bond.

Province of } I, W. W., of, &c., make oath and
County of   } say,
  To Wit :   }

1. That I was present and did see the annexed Arbitration Bond duly signed, sealed and delivered by the therein named JOHN DOE, and that I am the subscribing witness to the execution of the said bond.

Y. Z.

Sworn before me at
    , in the county of
    , this   day of   ,
18   .

E. F.,
a Commissioner, &c., in B. R.
  for the County of   .

If the affidavit is intended for use in a Court of law, it must be entitled in the Court.

A affidavit of the execution of a submission by deed or otherwise, may be easily framed from the above.

Affidavit of execution of Award.

Province of ⎫ I, W. W., of, &c., make oath and
County of   ⎬ say,
To Wit :   ⎭

1. That I was present and did see the within (or annexed) award duly signed by the therein named A. B. and T. A., and that I am the subscribing witness thereto.

W. W.

Sworn, &c.

ASSIGNMENTS.

The word assignment, in ordinary acceptation, means the writing or instrument by which an interest in some real or personal property is transferred from one person to another. From a legal point of view, it means the special transfer to a second party of a mortgage, lease, bond, note, bill of exchange, contract, or any kind of property, whether real or personal. In countries where a bankrupt law exists, the phrase "made an assignment" conveys the single idea of the transfer of a debtor's estate to an assignee for the benefit of his creditors. As an assignment is a special contract it must be executed with the same formalities as other deeds, and be duly made under seal, and properly witnessed. It must also be placed on public record, in accordance with the laws of the province in which the instrument is made. In the Province of Ontario an assignment of land, or of any interest in land, must be registered in the County Registry Office, in pursuance of the Act, Chap. III, of the Revised Statutes. When the assignment only covers goods and chattels where the sale is absolute, as by bill of sale, or conditional, as by chattel mortgage, and is not accompanied by an actual change of possession, the instrument must be filed with the Clerk of the County Court in the County, or in the United Counties, as the case may be, where the transaction takes place.* An assignment is only valid when made in good faith, and on equitable grounds; and any creditor of the Assignor, either by himself or his agent, may at his pleasure bring an action to test its validity. If any assignment is found to be fraudulent, the courts will grant the necessary relief to the suing creditor, and it will be set aside. If an assignment is made by a debtor for the benefit of his creditors, the unconditional surrender of all his effects, (excepting those articles which may be exempt by local statute) must be made; and he will not be permitted to fraudulently hold back any property. In Ontario Chap. 118 of the Revised Statutes provides that no person in insolvent circumstances, or who cannot pay his debts, or knowing himself to be on the eve of insolvency, shall have the right to give a confession of judgment to any favored creditor to the prejudice of other creditors, or to make any assignment of a preferential nature. The same act provides that the destruction, mutilation, or alteration of any books of account or other documents by a debtor, to defraud or mislead a creditor, shall be deemed a misdemeanor, and be liable to be punished by six months' imprisonment. A debtor who gives or makes away with any real or personal property of any kind with intent to defraud a creditor; and any person who receives such property with such intent, is also guilty of misdemeanor, and may be imprisoned for twelve months, and fined eight hundred dollars. But a debtor has the right to make an assignment in good faith to any person he pleases for the benefit of all his creditors, and this right remains even after an action has been brought against him by any one of his creditors. In the absence of a general Bankrupt Law for the Dominion, the same state of things, with certain modifications, prevail in its other

---

*Vide Revised Statutes of Ont., Chap. 119, Sec. 7.

provinces, if we except Quebec, where the French Civil Law, in force there, provides a better method for dealing with insolvent debtors' estates. ‡

General Form of Assignment.
TO BE WRITTEN OR ENDORSED ON THE BACK OF THE INSTRUMENT.

Know all men by these presents, that I, the within-named JOHN DOE, in consideration of one hundred dollars to me paid by RICHARD ROE, have assigned to the said RICHARD ROE, and his assigns, all my interest in the within written instrument, and every clause, article, or thing therein contained; and I do hereby constitute the said RICHARD ROE, my attorney, in my name, but to his own use, and at his risk and cost, to take all legal measures which may be proper for the complete recovery and enjoyment of the assigned premises, with power of substitution.

In Witness whereof, I have hereunto set my hand and seal, this tenth day of May, one thousand eight hundred and eighty-one.

Signed, sealed and delivered   JOHN DOE. [L. S.]
in presence of
    GEORGE BURNS.

Assignment (Crown Lands.)

Know all men by these presents, that I, JOHN DOE, of the   of   , in the County of   and Province of   for and in consideration of the sum of $, of lawful money of the Dominion of Canada, to me in hand paid by RICHARD ROE, of the   of   in the County of   and Province aforesaid, at or before the date hereof, (the receipt whereof I do hereby acknowledge,) have bargained, sold, assigned, transferred and set over, and by these presents do bargain, sell, assign, transfer and set over to the said Richard Roe, his heirs and assigns, all my estate, right, title, interest, claim and demand whatsoever, both at law and in equity, of, in and to, that certain parcel or tract of land and premises, situate, lying

---

‡ The Creditors Relief Act of 1880 of Ont. had this object in view. But this Act has not been proclaimed according to Sec. 29, and is therefore not in force. It exceeded the legislative functions of the Province.

and being in the Township of   , in the County
of   and Province aforesaid, containing by admeasurement   acres, be the same more or less, being composed of   Lot number   in the
Concession of the Township of   aforesaid (*insert if necessary*, " subject to the conditions. as to settlement and otherwise, of the Crown Lands Department, which are to be performed.")

To have and to hold the same with all and every the benefit that may or can be derived from the said
acres of land, unto the said Richard Roe, his heirs and assigns forever.

In witness whereof, I have hereunto set my hand and seal, this   day of   , 188 .

In witness, &c., (*As in General Form of Assignment*).

Affidavit of Execution.

Province :   I,   of the
County of   of the County
        To Wit : of   make oath and say,
that I was personally present and did see the within-named   duly signed and sealed, and as   act and deed, deliver the within Assignment on the day of the date thereof. and that I, this deponent, am a subscribing witness thereto, together with   of   in the County of
and that the said Indenture was executed at
Sworn before me at
  in the County of
  this   day of   in
  the year of our Lord 188   .

A Commissioner in B. R., &c.

Assignment of Partnership Property and Debts,
BY ONE PARTNER TO ANOTHER, IN TRUST, TO CLOSE THE CONCERN.

Whereas, a co-partnership has heretofore existed between JOHN DOE and RICHARD ROE, both of the city of Hamilton, which co-partnership has been known under the name of Doe & Roe, and which it is the intention of the said co-partners forthwith to dissolve and determine :

Now, this indenture of two parts, made this tenth day of

June, one thousand eight hundred and eighty-one, by and between the said John Doe, of the one part, and the said Richard Roe, of the other part, witnesseth:

First. That the co-partnership aforesaid is hereby, by the mutual consent of the said parties, dissolved and determined.

Second. The said John Doe doth hereby sell, transfer, assign and set over unto the said Richard Roe, his moiety of all the stock in trade, goods, merchandise, effects, and property of every description belonging to or owned by the said co-partnership, wherever the same may be, together with all debts, cases in action, and sums of money due and owing to the said firm, from any and all persons whomsoever, to hold the same to the said Richard Roe and his assigns forever, in trust, for the following purposes, namely: that the said Richard Roe shall sell and dispose of all the goods, property, and effects belonging to the said firm, at such time and in such manner as he may think prudent; and shall, with reasonable diligence, collect all the debts and sums of money due and owing to the said firm; and shall, out of the proceeds of the said sales, and with the money thus collected, pay and discharge all the debts and sums of money now due and owing from the said firm, as far as the proceeds of said sales and sums of money collected will go; and, after fully satisfying all demands against the said firm, if there be any surplus, shall pay over one moiety thereof to the said John Doe or his assigns.

Third. The said John Doe doth hereby constitute and appoint the said Richard Roe, his attorney irrevocable, in his, the said Richard Roe's own name, or in the name of the said firm, to demand, collect, sue for and receive any and all debts and sums of money due and owing to the said firm; to institute and prosecute any suits for the recovery of the said debts, or to compound the same, as he may judge most expedient; to defend any and all suits against the said firm, to execute all such paper writings and acquittances as may be necessary; and generally to do all such acts and things as may be necessary or proper for the full and complete settlement of all business and concerns of the said co-partnership.

Fourth. The said Richard Roe, for himself and his heirs, executors, and administrators, hereby covenants to and with the said John Doe and his assigns, that he will sell and dispose of all the partnership property and effects to the best advantage; that he will use his best diligence and endeavors to collect all debts and sums of money due and owing to the said firm; and that he will truly and faithfully apply the proceeds of said sale, and the moneys collected, to the payment, discharge, and satisfaction of all debts and demands against the said firm, as far as the same will go: and, after discharging all such debts, will pay over to the said John Doe, or his assigns, one moiety of any surplus that may remain; and further, that he will keep full and accurate accounts of all moneys received by him for goods sold, or debts collected; as well as of moneys paid out, and will render a just, true, and full account therefor to the said John Doe.

Fifth. The said John Doe, for himself, &c., covenants to and with the said Richard Roe, &c., that, upon settlement of accounts, if it shall be found that the debts due and owing from the said firm exceed the amount of moneys received from the sale of the said goods, and the debts collected, he will pay unto the said Richard Roe, or his assigns, one moiety of any balance that may then be due and owing from the said firm.

In Witness, &c. (*as in General Form of Assignment.*)

Assignment of Partnership Property and Debts by one Partner to another for a Certain Sum.

This Indenture of two parts, made and concluded the first day of June, one thousand eight hundred and eighty-one, by and between JOHN DOE, of the city of London, printer, of the first part, and RICHARD ROE, of the same place, printer, of the second part, witnesseth:

That, whereas, the said parties were lately co-partners in the business of printing, which partnership was dissolved and determined on the first day of May last; and whereas many debts, due and owing to the said parties on account of their said co-partnership, are still out-standing, and debts due by the said firm are yet unpaid; and whereas it is agreed that the said party of the second part shall assign and release to the said party of the first part all his interest in the stock in trade, goods and effects, belonging to the said firm, and in the debts now owing to the said firm, and that the said party of the first part shall assume all the debts and liabilities of the said firm, and shall discharge and indemnify the said party of the second part from all liabilities and losses arising from the said partnership :

Now, therefore, in pursuance of the said agreement, and in consideration of the sum of   dollars, paid and secured to the said Richard Roe, he, the said Richard Roe, doth hereby fully and absolutely sell, assign, release, and make over to the said John Doe, all his right, title, interest, and share, in and to all the stock in trade, goods, merchandise, machinery, tools, books, leasehold premises, and effects, belonging to the said partnership, of whatever kind or nature, and wheresoever situated ; also, all his right, title, and interest in and to all the debts and sums of money now due and owing to the said firm, whether the same be by bond, bill, note, or account, or otherwise, and the said Richard Roe doth hereby make and appoint the said John Doe, his executors, administrators, and assigns, to be his attorney and attorneys, to receive all and several the debts and sums of money above mentioned, to his and their own use and benefit; and doth hereby authorize the said John Doe, his executors, &c., to demand, collect, and sue for the said debts and sums of money, and to use his, the said Richard Roe's name in any way or manner that the collection, recovery, and realization of the said debts and demands may render necessary, as well in court as out of court, but at their own proper costs and charges, and without cost or damage to the said Richard Roe. And the said Richard Roe doth hereby further authorize the said John Doe to convey and transfer to his own name, and for his own use and benefit, any and all sums of money and effects, real and personal estate, which may be taken or received in the name of the said firm, and to hold the same free from all claims by the said Richard Roe, his executors, administrators, or assigns.

And these presents further witness, that, in pursuance of the said agreement, the said John Doe, for himself, his executors and administrators, doth hereby covenant to and with the said Richord Roe, his executors and administrators, that he, the said John Doe, and his, &c., shall pay and discharge, and at all times hereafter save harmless and indemnify, the said Richard Roe, his, &c., from and against all and every the debts, duties, and liabilities, which, at the dissolution and termination of the said partnership, were due and owing by the said firm to any person or persons, for any matter or thing touching the said partnership, and of and from all actions, suits, costs, expenses, and damages, for, or concerning the said debts, duties and liabilities, unless the said Richard Roe shall have contracted any debts or incurred any liabilities, in the name, and on account of the said firm, which are unknown to the said John Doe, and do not appear in the books of the said firm; for which, if any such exist, the said John Doe does not hereby intend to make himself responsible.

In Witness, &c. (*as in general form of Assignment.*)

Assignment of Bond by Endorsement.

KNOW all men by these presents, that I, the within named JOHN DOE, for, and in consideration of, the sum of   dollars, to me paid by RICHARD ROE of   , at or before the sealing of these presents, (the receipt whereof is hereby acknowledged,) have granted, bargained, sold, assigned, transferred, and set over, and by these presents do grant, bargain, sell, assign transfer and set over unto the said Richard Roe, his executors, administrators and assigns, the within bond or obligation, and the sum of   dollars, mentioned in the condition thereof, together with all interest due and to grow due for the same, and all my right, title, interest, claim, and demand, whatsoever, of, in, and to the same. And I authorize the said Richard Roe, in my name to demand, sue for, receive, have, hold and enjoy the said sum of   dollars, and interest, to his own use absolutely forever.

In Witness, &c. (*as in general form of Assignment.*)

Assignment of Lease.

This Indenture, made the   day of   , one thousand eight hundred and eighty   , Between JOHN DOE, of, &c., of the first part, and RICHARD ROE, of, &c., of the second part, Witnesseth, that in consideration of the sum of   dollars now paid by the said party of the second part, to the said party of the first part, the receipt whereof is hereby acknowledged, he the said party of the first part, Doth hereby assign unto the said party of the second part, his executors, administrators and assigns, All

and singular, the premises comprised in and demised by a certain Indenture of Lease, bearing date the   day of   , one thousand eight hundred and eighty
and made between &c., which said premises are more particularly known and described as follows, that is to say : All and singular that certain parcel or tract of land and premises situate, lying and being, &c., together with the appurtenances, To hold the same unto the said party of the second part, his executors, administrators and assigns, henceforth for and during the residue of the term of   years from the   day of   188 , thereby granted, and for all other the estate, term, and interest (if any) of the said party of the first part therein. Subject to the payment of the rent and the performance of the lessee's covenants and agreements in the said Indenture of Lease reserved and contained.

And the said party of the first part, for himself, his heirs, executors, and administrators, doth hereby covenant with the said party of the second part, his executors, administrators and assigns, that notwithstanding any act of the said party of the first part, he hath now power to assign the said premises in manner aforesaid. And that subject to the payment of the said rent, and the performance of the said lessee's covenants, it shall be lawful for the said party of the second part, his executors, administrators and assigns, peaceably and quietly to hold and enjoy the said premises hereby assigned during the residue of the term granted by the said Indenture of Lease, without any interruption by the said party of the first part, or any other person claiming under him, free from all charges and incumbrances whatsoever, of him the said party of the first part. And that he the said party of the first part, and all persons lawfully claiming under him will, at all times hereafter, at the request and costs of the said party of the second part, his executors, administrators and assigns, assign and confirm to him and them the said premises for the residue of the said term as the said party of the second part, his executors, administrators, or assigns, shall direct.

And the said party of the second part, for himself, his heirs, executors and administrators, Doth hereby covenant with the said party of the first part, his executors and administrators, that he, the said party of the second part, his executors, administrators or assigns, will, from time to time pay the rent, and perform the lessee's covenants in the said Indenture of Lease contained, and indemnify and save harmless the said party of the first part, his heirs, executors and administrators, from all losses and expenses in respect thereof.

Signed, sealed and delivered
In witness, &c., *(as in General Form of Assignment.)*
The usual Affidavit of Execution.

Assignment of Lease by Administrator.

Know all men by these presents, that I, A. B., of &c.; administrator of all and singular the goods and chattels, rights and credits, of the within-named C. D. deceased, for and in consideration of the sum of $. lawful money of Canada, to me in hand well and truly paid by E. F., of, &c., at or before the sealing and delivery of these presents, the receipt whereof is hereby acknowledged, have bargained, sold, assigned, transferred and set over, and by these presents do bargain, sell, assign, transfer, and set over, unto the said E. F., his executors, administrators and assigns, all and singular the parcel or tract of land and premises comprised in the within-written Indenture of Lease, and all the estate, right, title and interest, which I, the said A. B., as administrator of the said C. D. as aforesaid, or otherwise, now have, or at any time hereafter shall or may have, claim, challenge or demand, of, in, or to, all or any of the said premises, by virtue of the said indenture of lease or otherwise, as administrator of the said C. D. To have and to hold the said parcel or tract of land, and all and singular other the premises, with their and every of their appurtenances, unto the said E. F., his executors, administrators, and assigns, for and during all the rest, residue, and remainder yet to come and unexpired, of the within-mentioned term of   years, subject, nevertheless, to the yearly rent of $ in and by the said indenture of lease reserved and contained, and to become due and payable, and to all and every the convenants, clauses, provisoes and agreements therein contained.

In witness, &c., *(as in General Form of Assignment.)*

Assignment of Judgment.

This Indenture, made the   day of   18 , between A. B., of, &c., of the first part, and C. D., of, &c., of the second part.

Whereas, the said party of the first part, on or about the   day of   , one thousand eight hundred and   , recovered a judgment in the Court of   for the Province of Ontario, at Toronto, for the sum of $ against   .

And whereas, the said party of the first part hath agreed to assign the said judgment, and all benefit to arise therefrom, either at law or in equity, unto the said party of the second part, in manner hereinafter expressed.

Now this Indenture witnesseth, that in pursuance of the said agreement, and in consideration of the sum of $, of lawful money of Canada, to the said party of the first part in hand paid by the said party of the second part, at or before the execution hereof, the receipt whereof is hereby acknowledged, he the said party of the first part, Hath bargained, sold and assigned, and by these presents Doth bargain, sell and assign, unto the said party of the second part, his executors, administrators and assigns, All that the said hereinbefore mentioned judgment, and all benefit to be derived therefrom, either at law or in equity, or otherwise howsoever.

To hold, receive and take the same, and all benefit and advantage thereof, to and for his and their own proper use, and as and for his and their own proper moneys and effects, absolutely.

And the said party of the first part hereby constitutes and appoints the said party of the second part, his executors and administrators, to be his true and lawful attorney and attorneys, at the proper costs and charges of the said party of the second part, his executors and administrators, to take and prosecute all and every remedy or proceeding at law or in equity, which the said party of the second part, his executors or administrators, shall hereafter consider advisable in reference to the said judgment, the said party of the second part, for himself, his heirs, executors, and administrators, hereby agreeing to indemnify and save harmless the said party of the first part, his heirs, executors and administrators, of and from all damages, costs, charges and expenses in respect thereof.

In witness, &c., (*as in General Form of Assignment.*

Assignment of Mortgage.

This Indenture, made in duplicate the   day of   one thousand eight hundred and   , Between A. B., of the   , in the County of   and Province of   of the first part, and C. D., of the   , in the County of   and Province aforesaid,   of the second part.

Whereas, by an Indenture of Mortgage bearing date the   day of   , one thousand eight hundred and   , and made between E. F. of, &c., of the first part, and the said A. B. of the second part, it is witnessed, that in consideration of the sum of $, of lawful money of Canada, to him the said E. F. paid by the said A. B., He, the said E. F., did grant, bargain, sell, alien, release, enfeoff, convey, and confirm unto the said A. B., his heirs and assigns, all and singular that certain parcel or tract of land and premises situate, lying and being in the, &c.; To have and to hold the same unto the said A. B., his heirs and assigns, forever. Subject, nevertheless, to a proviso therein contained for redemption upon payment by the said E. F. to the said A. B. of the sum of $ of lawful money aforesaid and interest, on the day and time and in manner therein mentioned.

And whereas, the sum of $ is now owing to the said A. B. on the said in part recited security, and the said A. B. hath agreed to sell and assign the said lands and premises, and all the moneys thereby secured, as well as the said Indenture of Mortgage, and all his interest therein, unto the said C. D. for the consideration hereinafter mentioned.

Now this Indenture witnesseth, that the said party of the first part to this Indenture, in consideration of the sum of $ of lawful money of Canada aforesaid, to him by the said party of the second part to this Indenture in hand paid, the receipt whereof he, the said party of the first part, doth hereby acknowledge, and of and from the same, and every part thereof, acquit, release and discharge the said party of the second part, his heirs, executors, administrators and assigns, forever; He, the said party of the first part, hath bargained, sold, assigned, transferred, and set over to the said party of the second part, his heirs, executors, administrators and assigns, the said principal sum of $, so due and owing to him as aforesaid, and secured by the hereinbefore in part recited Indenture or Mortgage, and also all future and other sums of money which from henceforth shall or may grow due by way of interest for or on account of the said principal sum of $. And also the said messuages and tenements, lands and premises, comprised in the said in part recited Indenture of Mortgage, and all the estate, right, title, interest, claim, and demand whatsoever of him, the said party of the first part, of, in, to, or out of the said premises or any part thereof, or the said principal and interest moneys.

To have and to hold, receive and take, the said principal sum of $ and interest, and all and singular other the premises hereby assigned, and every part thereof, unto the said party of the second part, his heirs, executors, administrators or assigns, to and for his and their own proper moneys, securities, and effects absolutely; And for the more effectually enabling the said party of the second part, his executors, administrators and assigns, to recover and receive the said principal sum of $ and interest, and to have and take the benefit of the security for the same, he, the said party of the first part, hath made, ordained, constituted, and appointed the said party of the second part, his executors, administrators and assigns, his true and lawful attorney or attorneys, to ask, demand, sue for, recover, and receive from the said E. F., his executors, administrators, or assigns, or any other person or persons liable to pay the same, the said sum of $ and interest, and to commence and prosecute any action, suit or other proceeding, either at law or in equity, for the recovery of the same, and on receipt of the said principal moneys and interest, or any part thereof, to give sufficient receipts and discharges, And to make, do and execute all or any other act, matter or thing, for recovering and receiving the said principal sum and interest; And the said party hereto of the first part, for himself, his heirs, executors, administrators and assigns, covenants with the party hereto of the second part, his heirs, executors, administrators and assigns, that the said principal sum of $ is now owing to him, the said party hereto of the first part, under the said security, and that he has done no act or thing whereby the said principal sum of $ is or has been received, released, discharged, or incumbered.

In witness, &c., (*as in General Form of Assignment.*)

Assignment of Mortgage (by Indorsement.)

This Indenture, made the   day of   , one thousand eight hundred and   , Between C. D., within named of the first part, and E. F., of, &c., of the second part, Witnesseth, that the party of the first part, in consideration of the sum of $, to him paid by the party of the second part, the receipt whereof is hereby acknowledged, hath granted, bargained, sold and assigned, and by these presents doth grant, bargain, sell and assign, to the party of the second part, his heirs, executors, administrators and assigns, all the right, title, interest, claim and demand whatsoever of him, the said party of the first part, of, in and to the lands and tenements mentioned and described in the within mortgage, And also to all sum and sums of money secured and payable thereby, and now remaining unpaid, To have and to hold the same, and to ask, demand, sue for, and recover the same, as fully to all intents and purposes as he, the party of the first part, now holds and is entitled to the same.

In Witness, &c. (*As in General Form of Assignment*).

Assignment of Debts.

Know all men by these presents, that I, A. B., of &c., in consideration of the sum of $ paid to me by C. D., of, &c., (the receipt of which is hereby acknowledged) do hereby sell, assign and transfer, unto the said C. D., his executors, administrators and assigns, all my claims and demands against E. F., of, &c., for debt, due to me, and all actions against the said E. F., now pending in my favor, and all causes of action whatsoever against him.

And I do hereby nominate and appoint the said C. D., his executors, administrators and assigns, my attorney or attorneys irrevocable, and do give him and them full power and authority to institute any suit or suits against the said

E. F., and to prosecute the same, and any suit or suits which are now pending, for any cause or causes of action in favor of me, against the said E. F., to final judgment and execution : and such execution to cause to be satisfied by levying the same on any real or personal estate of the said E. F. in due course of law, and the proceeds thereof to take and apply to his or their own use ; but it is hereby expressly stipulated that all such acts and proceedings are to be at the proper costs and charges of the said C. D., his executors, administrators or sssigns, without expense to me.

And I do further empower the said C. D., his executors, administrators and assigns, to appoint such substitute or substitutes as he or they shall see fit, to carry into effect the objects and purposes of this authority, or any of them, and the same to revoke from time to time, at his or their pleasure, I, the said A. B., hereby ratifying and confirming all the lawful acts of the said C. D., his executors, administrators and assigns, in pursuance of the foregoing authority.

In Witness, &c. (*As in General Form of Assignment.*)

Assignment of a Policy of Fire Insurance by Indorsement.

Know all men by these presents, that I, the within named A. B., in consideration of the sum of $ to me paid by C. D., of, &c., (the receipt whereof is hereby acknowledged) have assigned and transferred, and by these presents do absolutely assign and transfer unto the said C. D., his executors, administrators and assigns, All my right, title and interest to and in the within policy of insurance, with full power to use my name so far as may be necessary to enable him fully to avail himself of the interest herein assigned, or hereby intended to be assigned, but at his own costs and charges.

In witness, &c. (*As in General Form of Assignment.*)

AUCTIONS AND AUCTIONEERS.

An auction is a public sale of property of any kind, real or personal, to the highest bidder, by a person who is termed an auctioneer; and who is regularly licensed, or appointed, for the purpose, or receives his authority under some particular Statute, as in the case of bailiffs of a court, or otherwise. In the Province of Ontario the Council of any county, city, or town separated from a county, has power to pass by-laws for licensing, regulating, and governing auctioneers and other persons, who sell goods, wares and merchandize by public auction; and for determining the price of a license, and the length of time it shall be in force.* In that Province, also, the law is such that sales of land shall be without reserve, unless it is stated in the conditions or particulars of sale, that it will be made subject to a reserved price; and if the seller desires to bid that circumstance must also be set out. Unless that is done the auctioneer is forbidden to take any bid from the seller, or from a "puffer" in his behalf.† An auctioneer is usually paid by a commission, or per centage, on the gross amount of sales; and his duty is simply to sell for his employer, or patron; but not to buy for him or any other person whatever. From a primary point of view he is regarded as the agent of the party for whom he sells; but after he makes the sale, by knocking down the article sold to the highest bidder, and writing his name in his sale's book, he becomes in point of law the agent of both parties, and his memorandum is quite sufficient, under the Statute of Frauds, (already referred to under the head of agreements) to bind them firmly to the transaction. An auctioneer has

---

*Vide Revised Statutes of Ontario Chap. 174, Sec. 455.
†Ibid, Chap. 98, Sec's. 12, 13, 14.

a certain special property and pecuniary interest in the goods sold by him, in the shape of a lien on the same, and the proceeds thereof, for his charges and commissions. And he has the right, also, to sue the purchaser at any sale to compel the fulfilment of his contract, in his own name as well as in that of his principal. Although, as already stated, the auctioneer's entry of the sale, or transaction, in his sale's book is a sufficient memorandum to bind both parties thereto; still, in transactions of magnitude, and especially as regards the sale of land, it is advisable to have the agreement of sale and purchase put into writing subsequently, and signed by the auctioneer and buyer.

Auction sales should always be conducted with the most scrupulous honesty and fairness; and every real bid should be accepted. Before the bidding takes place the conditions of sale should be read or announced. These conditions will bind the auctioneer. Due notice of every sale of importance should be given either by written or printed hand-bill.

Memorandum to be Signed by an Auctioneer after a Sale of Land.

I hereby acknowledge that A. B. has been this day declared by me the highest bidder, and purchaser of [describe the land] at the sum of $, [or at the sum of $ per acre or foot], and that he has paid into my hands the sum of $, as a deposit, and in part payment of the purchase money, and I hereby agree that the vendor, C. D., shall in all respects fulfil the conditions of sale hereto annexed.

Witness my hand, the   day of   , 18 .

J. S., Auctioneer.

Memorandum to be Signed by Purchaser.

I hereby acknowledged that I have this day purchased at public auction, all that [describe the land], for the sum of $, [or for the price of $ per acre or foot], and have paid into the hands of J. S., the auctioneer, the sum of $ as a deposit, and in part payment of the said purchase money; and I hereby agree to pay the remaining sum of $ unto C. D., the vendor, at   , on or before the   day of   , and in all other respects on my part to fulfil the annexed conditions of sale.

Witness my hand, this   day of   , 18 .

A. B.

Conditions of Sale of Goods.

1. The highest bidder to be the purchaser; and, if any dispute shall arise as to the last or highest bidder, the property shall be immediately put up again at the former bidding.

2. No person to advance less than $ at a bidding.

3. The purchasers to give in their names, and places of residence (if required), and pay down a deposit of   per cent. in part payment of purchase money; in default of which the lot or lots so purchased will be immediately put up again and re-sold.

4. The lots to be taken away at the buyer's expense, within three days after the sale, and the remainder of the purchase money to be paid on or before delivery.

5. Upon failure of complying with these conditions, the deposit money shall be forfeited; and all lots uncleared within the time aforesaid shall be resold by public auction or private sale, and the deficiency, if any, on such re-sale shall be made good by the defaulter.

Conditions of Sale of Land.

1. The highest bidder shall be declared the purchaser; and, if any dispute shall arise as to the last or best bidder, the property shall be immediately put up again at the former bidding.

2. No person shall advance at any one bidding less than $, or retract his or her bidding; and the vendors, by themselves or their agents, shall be at liberty to bid once for the property.

3. The purchaser shall pay, immediately after the sale, to the vendor's solicitor, a deposit of   per cent. in

part of the purchase money, and sign an agreement for the payment of the remainder on or before the   day of   , 18   . The premises will be sold subject to all defects or imperfections of title subsisting before the commencement of the title of the present vendors, and not occasioned by any act done by them or any person claiming under or in trust for them, and subject also to the several mortgages outstanding appearing on the certificate of the registrar of the County of   , which will be produced at the time of sale.

4. The purchaser shall accept a conveyance from the vendors, to be prepared at his own expense, on payment of the remainder of the purchase money; and possession will be given on completion of the purchase, from which time the purchaser shall be entitled to the rents and profits. But if, from any cause, the remainder of the purchase money shall not be paid on on the   day of 188   , the purchaser shall pay interest for the same at the rate of   per cent from that day to the day of payment. But, nevertheless, this stipulation is without prejudice to the vendor's right of re-sale under the last of these conditions.

5. If any mistake be made in the description of the property, or there be any other error in the particulars of sale, the same shall not annul the sale, but a compensation or equivalent shall be given, or taken as the case may require, according to the average of the whole purchase money (on such error or mis-statement being proved); such compensation or equivalent to be settled by two referees or their umpire—one referee to be chosen by each party, within ten days after notice given of the error, and the umpire to be chosen by the referees immediately after their appointment.

6. The purchaser shall not be entitled to the production of any title deeds other than such as are in the vendor's hands, or in the hands of the several mortgagees.

7. Lastly, upon failure of complying with the above conditions, the deposit shall be forfeited, and the vendor shall be at full liberty (with or without notice) to re-sell the property by public auction or private sale; and if, on such re-sale, there should be any deficiency, the purchaser shall make good such deficiency to the vendor, and all expenses

attending such re-sale; the same to be recoverable as liquidated damages.

[NOTE.—*Special conditions may be necessary to meet particular cases: but the above conditions will meet ordinary cases. Except in very plain and simple cases, the services of a professional man should be procured.*]

Conditions of Sale of the Court of Chancery.

1. No person shall advance less than $10 at any bidding under $500, nor less than $20 at any bidding over $500; and no person shall retract his bidding.

2. The highest bidder shall be the purchaser; and, if any dispute arise as to the last or highest bidder, the property shall be put up at a former bidding.

3. The parties to the suit with the exception of the vendor, and (*naming any parties, trustees, agents, or others, in a fiduciary situation*) are to be at liberty to bid.

4. The purchaser shall, at the time of sale, pay down a deposit in the proportion of $10 for every $100 of his purchase money to the vendor or his solicitor, and shall pay the remainder of the purchase money on the   day of   next, and upon such payment the purchaser shall be entitled to the conveyance, and to be let into possession, the purchaser at the time of such sale to sign an agreement for the completion of the purchase.

5. The purchaser shall have the conveyance prepared at his own expense, and tender the same for execution.

6. If the purchaser fail to comply with the conditions aforesaid, or any of them, the deposit and all other payments made thereon shall be forfeited, and the premises may be re-sold; and the deficiency, if any, by such re sale, together with all charges attending the same or occasioned by the defaulter, are to be made good by the defaulter.

BILLS OF EXCHANGE AND PROMISSORY NOTES.

A Bill of Exchange, or Draft as it is frequently called, is a written order addressed by one party to another to pay to some person, or persons, named therein, a specified sum of money.

A bill of exchange is a negotiable instrument, and is transferable by *endorsement*, if made payable to order; or by delivery, if payable to bearer. If a bill of exchange were founded upon an illegal consideration, such as a gambling debt, an action could not be maintained by the drawer thereof against the acceptor. But if the bill should go into the hands of an innocent third party who knew nothing of the illegality of the original transaction, and had paid fair value therefor, he would be entitled to bring an action thereon, to which the conditions on which the bill was given would not be a sufficient defence. Bills of exchange are a vast convenience in the mercantile world, and give great facilities for the transaction of business between different individuals, as well as between different countries. For example, if JOHN DOE, of Montreal, owes RICHARD ROE, of Toronto, one hundred dollars, and desires to pay him, instead of running the risk of loss by sending him that amount by hand, or through the post, he could go to the nearest bank, and for an eighth or a quarter per cent procure a bill of exchange on its corresponding bank at Toronto for the amount. And if John Doe has that bill made payable to his own order, he can then make it payable to the order of Richard Roe, whose endorsation before he receives payment from the bank at Toronto will operate as a receipt for the money should any dispute occur afterwards about it. In cases where remittances are made to foreign countries, bills of exchange are of still greater convenience and value, as the money of one country will not usually pass current in another. If a Canadian has a debt to pay in England the bank bills of this country would not be a legal tender there. He accordingly goes to some agency of the Bank of Montreal, or other bank, and buys a bill of exchange in sterling money, or pounds, shillings, and pence, and forwards it to his correspondent in England to pay his account. For convenience sake the fictitious standard of $109\frac{1}{2}$ per cent is accepted as the par of exchange, and that standard is the basis of all sterling exchange calculations. When sterling exchange falls below that amount it is said to be below par; if more is paid it is quoted above par. The fluctuations of exchange are sometimes produced by several causes; but the usual cause in this country arises from the results of the commerce between Canada and the United States and Europe. If Canada and the United States export more produce, or other articles of domestic production, to Europe than they import therefrom, there will be a difference, or balance, in their favor which will have to be paid in coin or its equivalent. To bring this coin to this country would involve a considerable outlay for freight and insurance; and to avoid this outlay the balance is allowed to remain in the hands of the debtors, or is deposited in some bank usually located in London, the great money centre of the Old World, and bills of exchange are sold against it to parties who have debts to pay there or elsewhere in Europe. Sometimes the balance of trade is largely in favor of this country, and in consequence of an unusual amount of sterling exchange being in the market for sale it falls below par, or, in other words, becomes cheaper, like any other commodity under similar circumstances. Foreign bills of of exchange are usually drawn in two ways—one payable at three days after sight, and the other at sixty days. Sight bills on London usually sell in this country for one per cent more than sixty day bills. To provide against the contingency of loss, foreign bills of exchange are usually drawn in triplicate. Inland bills of exchange, or drafts as they are more usually called, are not so liable to be lost, and are, as a rule, drawn singly. The person who makes a bill is called the *drawer*, the person to whom it is addressed for payment is called the *drawee*, and the person in whose favor it is made is called the *payee*. If the drawee accepts the bill he is termed the *acceptor*, the person endorsing it is called the *endorser*, and the person to whom it is endorsed the *endorsee*. A bill is usually accepted by the drawee writing his name across its face under the word accepted, and it is endorsed by the endorsee writing his name on its back. Bills of exchange should be presented by the holder or by his authorized agent for acceptance, at the residence or usual place of business of the drawee. If the latter is not to be found, from having changed his domicile or other cause, the holder should endeavor to trace him out, so that the bill may be duly presented for his acceptance. If he should, however, be unsuccessful in his enquiries he has the right to protest the bill as being dishonored. But the temporary absence from his home of the drawee, when a bill is presented for acceptance, is not such a refusal to accept it as would warrant the holder to give notice to the drawer and endorsers. But such an absence when the bill becomes due would be equivalent to a refusal to pay it, and, necessitates a protest. The acceptor of a bill is bound to provide for its payment when it falls due, without any alternative. A bill should be presented to the drawee in person, or to his authorised agent, for acceptance. If there is more than one drawee, and the first drawee refuses to accept, it should be presented to the next in order, and so on, or recourse cannot be had against the drawer or endorsers. If the drawee has left the country it will be sufficient to present the bill at his house; but if he has a known agent it must be presented to him. If the drawee is dead the bill should be presented for acceptance to his heir at law, or his other legal representative. In all cases presentment should be made during the usual days and hours of business. It is optional with the holder of a bill whether he leaves it with the drawee to give time for consideration as to its acceptance or otherwise. When the drawee refuses acceptance of a bill the holder is bound to notify, as soon as possible, the drawer and endorser that he will look to them, or either of them, for payment; and a suit may be at once brought against the drawer for its amount.

Having now given at sufficient length, for all ordinary purposes, the distinctive features of the bill of exchange from promissory notes, we shall proceed to consider the nature of the latter instruments. In ordinary acceptation a promissory note is a written or printed paper acknowledging a debt, and promising payment; but in legal acceptation it is a definite contract in writing by one person to pay a specific sum, named therein, at a fixed date to another or second person, or to the order of that second person, or to the bearer who presents it for payment. The person who signs a note is termed the *maker*, and the person to whom it is made payable the *payee*. If the payee transfers his interest therein by endorsement he becomes the *endorser*, while the new holder is termed the *endorsee*. The person who holds the bill at maturity is termed the *holder*. A legal consideration must be given for a note to make it valid as regards the maker and payee, but any third party who gives fair value therefor before it becomes due, and who is not aware that its making was dishonest or illegal, will be entitled to recover its amount from all or any of the persons whose names appear upon it as makers or endorsers, except only where the latter make some special reservation above their signatures. Although not legally necessary, the consideration for the promise to pay the sum of money expressed in a note is usually set out by the words "for value received." A negotiable note, or note that can be sold, is transferable either by endorsement or simple delivery. If it is desired to have it transferable by endorsement it must be made payable to order, and if by delivery without endorsement payable to bearer. A note made payable to the payee only, without the words to order, or to bearer, is not transferable, and cannot be collected by a new holder. Any holder of a note who desires to transfer it by endorsement without incurring any further liability, may effect this object by writing above his endorsement signature *without recourse to me*. If the holder wishes to make a note or draft payable specially to some person, Richard Roe for example, he can do so by writing over his own name the words pay to Richard Roe or order. A note made by two or more parties may be drawn jointly and severally where it is desired to be collectively and individually liable; but if it is sought to be only jointly liable the words *and not severally* should be used.— A simple promise to pay without specifying the time of payment in a note is equal in law to a promise to pay on demand; but a promise to pay as soon as circumstances will permit is of no value. The altering of a note in any manner by the holder makes it void. A minor is not competent to make a note.

A note disposed of after it becomes due is subject to any offset the maker may have against the person to whom it was originally payable. If a note is to draw interest from its date the words *with interest* should appear on its face, otherwise it will only draw interest after maturity. If a note is payable on demand interest can only accrue after the demand for payment is made. The legal rate of interest is six per cent, which can only be collected unless some higher rate is expressed in the note. Should part-payments be accepted on a note they should be credited on its back, with the date of each payment. Should a note be lost before maturity it should at once be publicly advertised in some newspaper, or other means be taken to prevent its purchase. Should it be, however, purchased by an innocent party in good faith, without the commission of any act of forgery, the holder is entitled to recover its value. Promissory notes like bills of exchange are entitled to three days' grace at maturity, and payment can only be demanded on the last day of grace. A note or bill falling due on a Sunday or statutory holiday is payable on the following day. It should be presented for payment on the day when it falls due, and if payment is refused, and if it is endorsed, it should at once be protested for non-payment, or the endorser will be discharged from his liability. The presentment for payment of a bill of exchange or note must be made by the holder or his agent to the maker or acceptor, at the place appointed therein for payment, or at his house or residence, or to himself personally if no particular place is specified, within reasonable hours. Even the death or insolvency of the maker or acceptor, however well-known, must not prevent the regular presentment for payment at the appointed time and place; and afterwards, if necessary, to the executor or other representative of deceased, and if there be neither at his recent residence. When a bill or note is made payable at a particular place, as at some bank for example, presentment there within regular banking hours is alone necessary; and if not paid protest may follow in due course, and the parties thereto made liable. The presentment of a note or bill for payment at the maker or acceptor's usual place of business during business hours, is good even if the place is shut, and no one there to answer enquiries. But if either removes his place of business or residence between the time when the note was made or the bill accepted and it becomes due, presentment must be made at the new domicile, provided it can with due diligence be found. Should the removal be to some foreign country presentment at the last place of business or residence in Canada is alone necessary. When payment of a note or bill is demanded the holder should have it in his possession ready for delivery. When a note or bill is protested notice next day at furthest must be given to the parties to whom the holder is legally entitled to look for payment. The last endorser thereon should also the next day after he receives his notice notify the drawer, acceptor, or other endorser whom he wishes to hold liable. This notice must be given by the principals to the instrument, or by their authorised agents, for notice by a mere stranger will not be sufficient; and in the event of bankruptcy the notice must be given by the assignee. If all the parties reside in the same locality a verbal notice personally given will be sufficient, or a written notice may be left at their residences or places of business. When the parties to be notified live at a distance the usual and best practice is to notify them of the protest by mail. Proof that the letter containing the notice was duly put into the post office is all that the law requires; proof of actual delivery is not necessary. Notice to one of several parties is equivalent to notice to all, and each party into whose hands a dishonored note or bill comes is allowed one whole day in which to give the necessary notice in his case. Where there is no post a notice of protest may be sent by hand or other available mode.

The protest of a bill of exchange or promissory note must be made if possible by a Notary Public; but if either should be payable at some locality where there is no Notary, the protest may be made by a magistrate, or other substantial inhabitant, in the presence of two witnesses.

A blank endorsement on a bill or promissory note is made by simply writing one's name on the back thus " *John Doe*" : a full endorsement would be " *pay to Richard Roe, or order*" with John Doe signed underneath : a qualified endorsement would be "*pay to Richard Roe without recourse to me*: a restrictive endorsement would be "*pay to Richard Roe*". Notes or bills of exchange executed singly require to be stamped as follows, viz :, for $25 one cent ; $50 and over $25 two cents ; $100 and over $50 three cents ; and each fraction over $100 three cents. Bills of exchange in duplicate for $100 two cents, and each fractional part of $100 two cents.

Form of protest for a Bill of Exchange or Promissory Note.

On this   day of   , in the year of our Lord, one thousand eight hundred and   , at the request of A. B., holder of the (bill of exchange or promissory note) hereunto annexed, I, GEORGE SMITH, a Notary Public for the Province of Ontario, by Royal Authority duly appointed, did exhibit the said (bill of exchange or promissory note) unto   at the   at   , being the place where the same is payable, and speaking to him, did demand (payment or acceptance) of the said (bill of exchange or promissory note), to which demand he answered   .
Wherefore, I, the said Notary, at the request aforesaid, have protested, and do hereby solemnly protest, as well against all the parties to the said (bill or note), as against all other persons whom it may concern, for all interest, damages, costs, charges, expenses, and other losses suffered, or to be suffered, for want of (payment or acceptance) of the said (bill or note). And afterwards, on the day and year mentioned in the margin, I, the said Notary Public, did serve due

Notices mailed the   notice, according to law, of the said pre-
         day of   sentment (non-payment or non-acceptance)
A. D. 188   and protest of the said (bill or note) upon
         G. H.   the several parties thereto, by depositing in Her Majesty's Post Office at   being the nearest Post Office to the place of the said presentment, letters containing such notices, one of which letters was addressed to each of the said parties severally ; the superscription and

address of which letters are respectively copied below, as follows, that is to say:
"A. B., Kingston, Ont.;"   "C. D., London, Ont.;"
"E. F., Belleville, Ont."

In testimony whereof I have hereunto set my hand and affixed my seal of office the day and year first above written.
GEORGE SMITH, Notary Public, Ont. [SEAL.]

Form of Notice of Protest.

day of   18

To
                    Take notice that a (promissory note or bill of exchange), dated on the   day of
18   for the sum of $ made by   and payable to   or order,   after the date thereof, at the   and endorsed by   was this day presented by me for (payment or acceptance) at the said
, and that (payment or acceptance) thereof was refused. And that   the holder of the said (promissory note or bill of exchange), look to you for payment thereof. Also take notice that the same (note or bill) was this day protested by me for (non-payment or non-acceptance.)   Yours &c.,

Inland Bill of Exchange or Draft.

$250.00   BROCKVILLE, January 5th, 1881.

Three days after sight, pay to the order of Mr. George Jones two hundred and fifty dollars, value received, and charge the same to account of
                              BROWN & SMITH.
To Mr. CHARLES ROGERS,
          Toronto.

Another Form of Bill of Exchange or Draft.

$250.00

Sixty days after date, pay to the order of Mr. George Jones two hundred and fifty dollars, value received, and charge the same to our account.
                              BROWN & SMITH.
To Mr. CHARLES ROGERS,
          Toronto.

A Set of Bills of Foreign Exchange.

No. 188.—£300 Ster.　　　　Montreal, April 3, 1881.

Three days after sight of this, my first of exchange, (second and third of the same tenor and date unpaid,) pay to Charles Wignell, or order, three hundred pounds sterling, value received, and charge the same to account of

　　　　　　　　　　　　　　　JOHN SMITH.

To Messrs JONES & ROBINSON,
　　　　London.

No. 188.—£300 Ster.　　　　Montreal, April 3, 1881.

Three days after sight of this, my second of exchange, (first and third of the same tenor and date unpaid,) pay to Charles Wignell, or order, three hundred pounds sterling, value received, and charge the same to account of

　　　　　　　　　　　　　　　JOHN SMITH.

To Messrs JONES & ROBINSON,
　　　　London.

No. 188.—£300 Ster.　　　　Montreal, April 3, 1881.

Three days after sight of this, my third of exchange, (first and second of the same tenor and date unpaid,) pay to Charles Wignell, or order, three hundred pounds sterling, value received, and charge the same to account of

　　　　　　　　　　　　　　　JOHN SMITH.

To Messrs JONES & ROBINSON,
　　　　London.

Ordinary Promissory Notes.

$100　　　　　　　　　　Kingston, January 6th, 1881.

Six months after date I promise to pay John Doe, or order, at the Bank of Montreal here, one hundred dollars for value received.

　　　　　　　　　　　　　　　RICHARD ROE.

Note Payable to Bearer.

$100　　　　　　　　　　Kingston, January 6th, 1881.

Six months after date I promise to pay John Doe, or Bearer, at my office (or residence) here, one hundred dollars for value received.

　　　　　　　　　　　　　　　RICHARD ROE.

BILLS OF EXCHANGE AND PROMISSORY NOTES. 77

Interest Note Payable on Demand.

$100   KINGSTON, January 6th, 1881.

On demand, I promise to pay John Doe, or order, one hundred dollars for value received, with interest, at the rate of eight per cent per annum.

                               RICHARD ROE.

Note with Collateral Security.

$500   KINGSTON, January 6th, 1881.

Three months after date I promise to pay John Doe, or order, at his office in Belleville, five hundred dollars for value received.

I have deposited with him as collateral security six shares of the Merchant's Bank of Montreal, with full authority to sell the same should I fail in the performances of this promise.

                               RICHARD ROE.

Note Payable by Instalments.

$500   KINGSTON, January 6th, 1881.

For Value Received I promise to pay John Doe, or order, five hundred dollars: two hundred dollars of which to be paid in three months, two hundred dollars in six months, and one hundred dollars at nine months, with interest at six per cent per annum on all said sums for use.

     Witness,   RICHARD ROE.
GEORGE JONES.

A Joint and Several Note

$100   KINGSTON, January 6th 1881.

Three months after date we jointly and severally promise to pay John Doe, or order, one hundred dollars for value received.

                               RICHARD ROE.
                               JOHN SMITH.

A Joint Note.

$100   KINGSTON, January 6th, 1881.

Three months after date we jointly, and not severally,

promise to pay John Doe, or order, one hundred dollars for value received.

RICHARD ROE.
JOHN SMITH.

Demand Due Bills.

$100   BROCKVILLE, January 4th, 1881.

Due on demand to Brown & Co. one hundred dollars, for value received.

RICHARD JONES.

$100   BROCKVILLE, January 4th, 1881.

Due on demand to George White, or Bearer, one hundred dollars, payable in goods at my store, value received.

HENRY DODDRIDGE.

$100   BROCKVILLE, January 4th, 1881.

Borrowed and received from Richard Wilson one hundred dollars, which I promise to repay him on demand by him, or to pay to his order.

RICHARD JONES.

BILL OF SALE.

A Bill of Sale is a formal instrument for the conveyance or transfer of goods or chattels from one person to another. Its first requisite is the ability of the vendor to sell. This he derives either from absolute property in the goods or chattels, or from other circumstances which give him a legal right to dispose of them. A bill of sale must be based on a good consideration, and if made without such consideration to John Doe for the purpose of avoiding responsibility to Richard Roe, it is fraudulent and void.— If John Doe is in debt to his creditors, and continues to hold property that he, by a bill of sale, has conveyed to Richard Roe, fraud will be presumed; and the transaction will not stand good in law. It must be shown that the sale was made without secret or implied collusion, and in good faith, for a valuable consideration, or a legitimate debt. In Ontario a person in insolvent circumstances is not competent to give a bill of sale, and if he gives such with intent to defraud a creditor, he becomes guilty of a misdemeanor, and is liable to be punished by fine and imprisonment. Where goods or chattels mentioned in a bill of sale are at once handed over to the purchaser, and an actual and continued change of possession takes place, it does not require to be filed, nor is it necessary to make any affidavit as to the bona-fide nature of the transaction. But when the goods or chattels are allowed to remain in the hands of the seller, affidavits must be made according to the annexed forms, and the bill of sale filed with the clerk of the County, or United Counties, Court as the case may be, who is to produce it for examination at any time on the payment of his legal fee. A bill of sale should have attached thereto a full list, or description, of all the articles which it covers, so that there may be no mistake about their identity at any time.

Bill of Sale of Goods.

This Indenture made the   day of   188 , Between John Doe, of, &c., (*vendor*), of the one part, and Richard Roe, of, &c., (*purchaser*), of the other part.

Whereas, the said John Doe hath contracted with the said Richard Roe for the absolute sale to him of the goods, chattels, furniture and effects comprised in the schedule hereunder written or hereto annexed, and now on the premises situated at, &c., (*describe the place*), at or for the price or sum of $. Now this Indenture witnesseth, that in pursuance of the aforesaid agreement, and in consideration of the sum of $, now paid to the said John Doe, by the said Richard Roe, the receipt whereof is hereby acknowledged, He, the said John Doe, by these presents doth assign and set over unto the said Richard Roe, his executors, administrators and assigns, All and singular the household furniture, goods, chattels and effects comprised and set forth in the schedule hereunder written or hereunto annexed, and all the advantages thereof, and all the right, title, interest, possibility, property, claim and demand of him, the said John Doe, into, out of, or upon the said furniture, goods, chattels and effects, and every part thereof. To have, hold, receive and take the said furniture, goods, chattels and effects hereby assigned or expressed, or intended so to be, unto the said Richard Roe, his executors, administrators and assigns absolutely. And the said John Roe, doth hereby for himself, his heirs, executors and administrators, covenant with the said Richard Roe, his executors, administrators and assigns, that he, the said John Doe, now hath in himself absolute authority to assign the several premises hereby assigned or expressed, and intended so to be, unto the said Richard Roe, his executors, admisistrators and assigns, in manner aforesaid : And that the said John Doe, his executors and administrators, and all persons claiming under him and them, shall at any time or times hereafter, on the request, and at the costs and charges of the said Richard Roe, his executors, administrators and assigns, do and execute all such acts and assurances for more effectually assuring the said premises hereby assigned or expressed, and intended so to be, unto the said Richard Roe, his executors, administrators and assigns, and placing him and them in possession of the same in manner aforesaid, and according to the true intent and meaning of these presents, as by him or them, or his or their counsel in the law shall be devised, advised and required.

In witness whereof the parties to these presents have hereunto set their hands and seals the day and year first above written.

Signed, sealed and delivered
in the presence of   JOHN DOE, [L. s.]
    JOHN SMITH.   RICHARD ROE, [L. s.]

The Schedule referred to in the above written Indenture.

(*Here set out a full and particular description of the goods. They must be described with such detail as to render them easy of identification.*)

Another Form of Bill of Sale.

This Indenture, made the   day of   188 ,
Between John Doe, of, &c., of the first part, and Richard Roe, of, &c., of the second part.

Whereas, the said party of the first part is possessed of the chattels hereinafter set forth and enumerated, and hath contracted with the said party of the second part, for the sale to him of the same, at the sum of $

Now this Indenture witnesseth, that in pursuance of the said agreement, and in consideration of the sum of $
of lawful money of Canada, now paid by the said party of the second part to the said party of the first part, (the receipt whereof is hereby acknowledged), He, the said party of the first part, hath bargained, sold, assigned, transferred and set over, and by these presents, doth bargain, sell, assign, transfer and set over unto the said party of the second part, his executors, administrators and assigns, All those the said chattels and effects following, that is to say, *(here enumerate the several articles intended to be assigned with such certainty as that they may be easily identified).* And all the right, title, interest, property, claim and demand whatsoever, both at law and in equity, or otherwise howsoever, of him the said party of the first part of, in, to and out of the same, and every part thereof.

To have and to hold the said hereinbefore assigned premises, and every part thereof, with the appurtenances, and all the right, title, and interest of the said party of the first part therein as aforesaid, unto and to the use of the said party of the second part, his executors, administrators and assigns, to and for his and their sole and only use forever.

And the said party of the first part doth hereby, for himself, his heirs, executors and administrators, covenant, promise and agree with the said party of the second part, his executors and administrators, in manner following, that is to say :

That he, the said party of the first part, is now rightfully and absolutely possessed of and entitled to the said hereby assigned premises and every part thereof, and that the said party of the first part now has in himself good right to assign the same unto the said party of the second part, his executors, administrators and assigns, in manner aforesaid, and according to the true intent and meaning of these presents; And that the said party hereto of the second part, his executors, administrators and assigns, shall and may from time to time, and at all times hereafter, peaceably and quietly have, hold, possess and enjoy the said hereby assigned premises and every part thereof to and for his and their own use and benefit, without any manner of hinderance, interruption, molestation, claim or demand whatsoever, of, from or by him, the said party of the first part, or any person or persons whomsoever: And that free and clear and freely and absolutely released and discharged or otherwise at the costs of the said party of the first part, effectually indemnified from and against all former and other bargains, sales, gifts, grants, titles, charges, and incumbrances whatsoever: And, moreover, that he, the said party of the first part, and all persons rightfully claiming or to claim any estate, right, title or interest of, in or to the said hereby assigned premises, or any part thereof, shall and will from time to time, and at all times hereafter, upon every reasonable request of the said party of the second part, his executors, administrators, or assigns, but at the costs and charges of the said party of the second part, make, do and execute, or cause to be made, done and executed, all such further acts, deeds, and assurances for the more effectually assigning and assuring the said hereby assigned premises unto the said party of the second part, his executors, administrators and assigns, in manner aforesaid, and according to the true intent and meaning of these presents, as by the said party of the second part, his executors, administrators or assigns, or his counsel, shall be reasonably advised and required.

In Witness whereof, &c. (*as in first form*).

Bill of Sale of Vessel.

Know all men by these presents, that I, A. B. of, &c., owner of the brig or vessel, called the   of the burden of   tons, or thereabouts, now lying at the port of   for and in consideration of the sum of   dollars, lawful money of Canada, to me paid by C. D., of the place aforesaid, the receipt whereof I hereby acknowledge, have bargained and sold, and by these presents do bargain, and sell unto the said C. D., his executors, administrators, and assigns, all the hull or body of said brig, or vessel, together with the masts, bowsprit, sails, boats, anchors, cables, spars, and all other necessaries thereunto appertaining and belonging : the certificate of the registry of which said brig, or vessel, is as follows, to wit : [copy certificate of registry.] To have and to hold the said brig or vessel, and appurtenances thereunto belonging, unto the said C. D., his executors, administrators and assigns, to his and their proper use, benefit, and behoof, forever. And I do, for myself, my heirs, executors, and administrators, covenant and agree, to and with the said C. D., his executors, administrators and assigns, to warrant and defend the said brig, or vessel, and all the before mentioned appurtenances, against all and every person and persons whomsoever.

In Witness whereof, &c., (*as in first form*).

Affidavit of the Bargainee.

Province }
County of }
   To wit : } I, Richard Roe, &c.
in the foregoing bill of sale named, make oath and say : that the sale therein made is an equitable one, and for good consideration, namely, and not for the purpose of holding or enabling me, this deponent, to hold the goods mentioned therein against the creditors of the said John Doe.

Sworn before me at
in the County of
this day of } RICHARD ROE.
A. D. 18 .

A Commissioner, &c.

Affidavit of Execution of Bill of Sale.

Province }
County of }
   To wit : } I, John Smith, &c.
make oath and say that I was personally present and did see the annexed Bill of Sale duly signed, sealed and delivered by John Doe and Richard Roe, the parties thereto ; and that I, this deponent, am a subscribing witness to the same, and that the name John Smith set and subscribed

as a witness to the execution thereof, is of the proper handwriting of me, this deponent; and that the same was executed at

Sworn before me, at in the County of this day of A. D. 18 . } JOHN SMITH.

A Commissioner, &c.

BONDS.

A Bond, or obligation, in Law, is a deed under seal whereby the *obligor*, or person bound, obliges himself, his heirs, executors, and administrators, to pay a certain sum of money to another person, called the *obligee*, at a day appointed. If the simple payment of this money be the only conditions expressed, the bond is termed a single one; but there is generally a condition added that if the obligor does some particular act the obligation shall be void, or else shall remain in full force and virtue. That condition is usually payment of rent, performance of covenants in a deed, repayment of principal sum of money borrowed, with interest, (which principal sum is usually one-half of the penal sum specified in the bond), the appearance for trial in some court of justice, &c. In case this condition is not performed, the bond becomes forfeited, or absolute in law, and binds the obligor while living; and after his death the obligation descends upon his heirs, or other legal representatives, who are bound to discharge the debt out of the personal or real assets of the deceased, if there be any such left.

On the forfeiture of a bond the whole penalty was formerly recoverable at law, but eventually the courts of equity interposed, and would not permit a man to take more than in conscience he ought, viz., his principal, interest, and expenses, in case the forfeiture accrued by non-payment of money borrowed; or a reasonable compensation for damages sustained for the non performance of other covenants. A similar practice also gradually gained some footing in the English Courts of law. At length, in the reign of Queen Anne,* a statute was passed which enacted that even although a bond should be forfeited the tender of the principal sum due, with interest and costs, should be held to be a full satisfaction and discharge. This statute is still in force in this Dominion, and guides the decision of our courts. In cases where the condition of a bond is to perform some collateral act, damages may be recovered beyond the penalty, provided they are sustained by the proper proof; and the Court of Queen's Bench will not stay proceedings, even should the amount of the prescribed penalty be paid into court. But where a specified sum has been agreed upon by parties to a bond, for stipulated or liquidated damages, in case of the non-performance of a collateral act, that specific sum can alone be recovered from the defaulting obligor. And in every case where it is designed that the whole sum mentioned in a bond should be forfeited in the event of failure, care should be taken to state in the clearest terms that the sum agreed upon is for stipulated or liquidated damages, as otherwise the courts will always be inclined to regard the sum as a penalty only.

All persons who are enabled to contract, and who are supposed in law to have sufficient freedom and understanding for that purpose, may bond themselves by bonds and obligations. The bond of a minor, even for necessaries, is void, but if he enters into a bond with a competent person the latter will be held liable. A bond without consideration is obligatory, being a voluntary act and a gift; but a bond

---

*Anne 4 and 5, Chap. 16.

given for fraudulent purposes is not competent to be enforced, and will not hold good in law.

A *bottomry* bond is an obligation founded on the joint security of a ship and its owners, and given for money borrowed, which is to be repaid on the successful termination of a voyage. At home, the bond is executed by the owners, or the master, as their agent. In a foreign country, the master has full authority to bind the owners, and pledge the ship and cargo, by a bottomry bond, in cases of necessity. Any amount of interest may be exacted, so long as the sea risk continues, irrespective of any usury laws; but when that terminates, the obligation will only draw legal interest. *Respondentia* is a contract similar to *bottomry*, except that the loan is made upon the chance of the safe arrival of the cargo. Like bottomry, it is used in cases of emergency.

Single Bond, without Condition.

Know all men by these presents, That I, John Doe, of, &c., am held and firmly bound unto Richard Roe, of, &c., in the penal sum of $1,000 of lawful money of Canada, to be paid to the said Richard Roe or to his certain attorney, executors, administrators or assigns; For which payment to be well and faithfully made, I bind myself, my heirs, executors and administrators, and every of them, firmly by these presents.

Sealed with my seal, dated the 6th day of January, 1880.

Signed, sealed and delivered
in the presence of   JOHN DOE [L. S.]
    JOHN SMITH

Bond, with Condition.

Know all men by these presents, That I, John Doe, of, &c., am held and firmly bound unto Richard Roe, of &c., in the penal sum of $1,000 of lawful money of Canada, to be paid to the said Richard Roe or to his certain attorney, executors, administrators or assigns: For which payment well and truly to be made, I bind myself, my heirs, executors and administrators firmly by these presents.

Sealed with my seal, dated this 6th day of January 1881.

The condition of the above written bond or obligation is such that if the above bounden John Doe, his heirs, executors or administrators, do and shall well and truly pay or cause to be paid unto the said Richard Roe, his executors, administrators or assigns, the just and full sum of $500 of lawful money of Canada, with interest thereon at the rate of ten per cent per annum, on the days and times, and in the manner following, that is to say : The said principal sum of $500 on the 6th day of July, 1882, and the said interest half yearly, on the 6th days of January and July in each year, (the first of such payments of interest on the 6th day of July next) without any deduction, defalcation or abatement whatsoever: Then the above written bond or obligation shall be void and of no effect : otherwise shall be and remain in full force and virtue.

Signed, sealed, &c. (*as in single bond*).

Bond to Convey Land.

Know all men by these presents, That I, John Doe, of &c., am held and firmly bound unto Richard Roe, of, &c., in the penal sum of $1,000 of lawful money of Canada, to be paid to the said Richard Roe, or to his certain attorney, executors, administrators or assigns : For which payment well and truly to be made, I bind myself, my heirs, executors and administrators, and every of them forever, firmly by these presents. Sealed with my seal. Dated this 1st day of May, 1881.

Whereas, the said Richard Roe, hath contracted with the above bounden John Doe, for the absolute purchase of fee simple, free from incumbrances, of the following lands and premises, that is to say : (*here describe the lands to be conveyed*). And whereas, the said Richard Roe hath agreed to pay therefor, the sum of $500 of lawful money of Canada, at the times, and in manner following, that is to say : (*here state the mode of payment*).

Now the condition of the above obligation is such that if the said Richard Roe, his heirs, executors, administrators or assigns, shall well and truly pay, or cause to be paid, to the above bounden John Doe, his executors, administrators or assigns, the sum of $500 at the time and in manner aforesaid; then if the above bounden John Doe, his heirs and assigns, shall, by good and sufficient deed or deeds of conveyance in fee simple, convey and assure, or cause to be conveyed and assured, unto the said Richard Roe, his heirs and assigns for ever, the said premises hereinbefore described, free from all incumbrances; Then the above obligation shall be void: otherwise shall be and remain in full force and virtue.

Signed, sealed, &c., *(as in single bond).*

Bond for Payment of Purchase Money.

Know all men by these presents, That I, Richard Roe, of, &c., am held and firmly bound unto John Doe, of, &c., in the penal sum of $1,000 of lawful money of Canada, to be paid to the said John Doe, or to his certain attorney, executors, administrators or assigns: For which payment well and truly to be made, I bind myself, my heirs, executors and administrators and every of them firmly by these presents.

Sealed with my seal, dated this   day of   18 .

Whereas, the above bounden Richard Roe, hath contracted with the said John Doe, for the absolute purchase in fee simple, free from all incumbrances, of the following lands and premises; that is to say: *(here describe the lands).*

And whereas, the above bounden Richard Roe hath agreed to pay therefor the sum of $500 of lawful money of Canada, at the time and in manner following, that is to say: *(here state the mode of payment).*

And whereas, upon the treaty for the said purchase, it was agreed that the above bounden Richard Roe, should enter into the above bond or obligation for payment of the said purchase money, or the unpaid part thereof, and interest in manner aforesaid; and be let into possession of the said lands and premises and receipt of the rents and profits thereof, from the day of the date hereof.

Now the condition of the above written obligation is such that if the above bounden Richard Roe, his heirs, executors, administrators or assigns, shall well and truly pay or cause to be paid to the said John Doe, his executors, administrators or assigns, the whole of the said purchase money and interest thereon as aforesaid, at the time and in manner aforesaid, without making any deduction, defalcation or abatement thereout on any account whatsoever; Then the above obligation shall be void: otherwise shall be and remain in full force and virtue.

Signed, sealed, &c., (*as in single bond*).

Bond of Indemnity.

Know all men by these presents, That I, John Doe, of &c., am held and firmly bound unto Richard Roe, of, &c., in the penal sum of $5,000 of lawful money of Canada, to be paid to the said John Doe, or to his certain attorney, executors, administrators or assigns : For which payment well and truly to be made, I bind myself, my heirs, executors and administrators, and every of them, firmly by these presents.

Sealed with my seal, dated this   day of   18 .

The condition of the above written bond or obligation is such that if the above bounden obligor, his heirs, executors and administrators, do and shall from time to time, and at all times hereafter, hold and keep harmless and fully indemnified the said obligee, his heirs, executors and administrators, and his and their lands and tenements, goods, chattels and effects, of, from and against all loss, costs, charges, damages and expenses, which the said obligee, his heirs, executors and administrators, may at any time hereafter bear, sustain, be at, or be put to, for, or by reason, or on account of (*here state the particular matters to which the indemnity is to apply*) or any thing in any manner relating thereto ; Then the above written bond or obligation shall be void ; otherwise shall be and remain in full force and virtue.

Signed, sealed, &c., (*as in single bond.*)

Bond for a Leasee and his Surety to pay rent according to Lease.

Know all men by these presents, That we, Richard Roe, of, &c., and John Smith, of, &c., are held and firmly bound unto John Doe, of, &c., in the penal sum of $1,000 of lawful money of Canada, to be paid to the said John Doe, or to his certain attorney, executors, administrators or assigns :

For which payment well and truly to be made we bind ourselves and each of us by himself, our and each of our heirs, executors and administrators, firmly by these presents.

Sealed with our seals. Dated this   day of   18   .

Whereas, the above named John Doe by this Indenture of Lease bearing even date with, but executed before, the above written obligation, for the consideration in the said lease mentioned, hath demised to the above bounden Richard Roe, a certain saw mill situate at &c., (*here describe the premises*), To hold unto the said Richard Roe, his executors, administrators and assigns, for the term of   years from thence next ensuing (determinable nevertheless at the end of the first   years of the said term, if the said Richard Roe, his executors, administrators or assigns, shall give   months' notice thereof, in manner therein mentioned) at and under the yearly rent of $500 payable quarterly in manner as therein expressed: as by the said lease will more fully appear.

Now the condition of the above written obligation is such, that if the above bounden Richard Roe and John Smith, or either of them, their, or either of their heirs, executors or administrators, shall and do during the continuance of the said recited lease, well and truly pay or cause to be paid, the said yearly rent or sum of $500, unto him the said John Doe, his heirs or assigns, by four equal quarterly payments of $125 each, on the several days following, that is to say, the   day of   , the   day of   , the   day of   , and the   day of   , in each and every year during the said demise, or within fourteen days next after any of the said days or times of payment, according to the true intent and meaning of the said recited lease, (the first quarterly payment to be made on the   day of   next); Then the above written obligation shall be void and of no effect: otherwise shall remain in full force and virtue.

Signed, sealed, &c., (*as in single bond*).

Bond, with Interest Condition.

Know all men by these presents: &c., (*As in single Bond, and then add :*) the just and full sum of five hundred

dollars, on the   day of   , in the year of our
Lord, 188 , and the legal interest thereon, to be computed from the day of the date hereof, and to be paid semi-annually, on the second day of January and the first day of July, in each and every year ; then the above obligation to be void; else to remain in full force and virtue. And it is hereby expressly agreed, that should any default be made in the payment of said interest, or of any part thereof, on any day whereon the same is made payable, as above expressed, and should the same remain unpaid and in arrear for the space of sixty days, then, and from thenceforth, that is to say, after the lapse of the said sixty days, the aforesaid principal sum of five hundred dollars with all arrears of interest thereon, shall, at the option of the said Richard Roe, his executors, administrators, or assigns, become and be due and payable, immediately thereafter, although the period above limited for the payment thereof may not then have expired ; any thing herein before contained to the contrary thereof, in any wise notwithstanding.

Signed, sealed, &c., (*as in single bond*).

Bond of Indemnity on paying Lost Note.

Know all men, &c., (*as in single Bond :*) Whereas, the said Richard Roe, on the   day of   188 , did make, execute and deliver unto the above bounden John Doe, for a valuable consideration, his promissory note, for the sum of one hundred dollars, written due and payable, on or before the   day of   , then next, with interest, which said promissory note the said John Doe, since the delivery of the same to him, as aforesaid, has in some manner, to him unknown, lost out of his possession ; and whereas the said Richard Roe, hath this day paid unto the said John Doe the sum of   dollars, the receipt whereof the said John Doe doth hereby acknowledge, in full satisfaction and discharge of the said note, upon the promise of the said John Doe to indemnify and save harmless the said Richard Roe, in the premises, and to deliver up the said note, when found, to the said Richard Roe, to be cancelled : Now, therefore, the condition of this obligation is such, that if the above bounden John Doe, his heirs, executors, or administrators, or any of them, do and shall, at all times hereafter, save and keep harmless the said Richard Roe, his heirs, executors, and administrators, of, from, and against the promissory note aforesaid, and of and from all costs, damages and expenses, that shall or may arise therefrom; and also deliver, or cause to be delivered up the said note, when found, to be cancelled, then this obligation to be void; else to remain in full force and virtue.

Signed, sealed, &c., (*as in single bond*).

Bottomry Bond.

Know all men by these presents, that I, John Doe, master, and one third owner of the ship Isabella, for myself and Richard Roe, who owns the other two thirds of said ship, am held and firmly bound unto John Smith, in the penal sum of two thousand dollars, lawful money, for the payment of which to the said John Smith, his heirs, executors, administrators, or assigns, I hereby bind myself, my heirs, executors and administrators, firmly by these presents.

Sealed with my seal. Dated the   day of   A. D., 18 .

Whereas the above bounden John Doe, hath taken up and received of the said John Smith the just and full sum of one thousand dollars, which sum is to run at respondentia, on the block and freight of the said Isabella, whereof the said John Doe is now master, from the port of   , on a voyage to the port of   , having permission to touch, stay at, and proceed to call, at all ports and places within the limits of the voyage, at the rate of premium of   per cent for the voyage: In consideration whereof, usual risks of the sea, rivers, enemies, fires, pirates, &c., are to be on account of the said John Smith. And for further security of the said John Smith, the said John Doe doth, by these presents, mortgage and assign over to the said John Smith, his heirs, executors, administrators, and assigns, the said ship Isabella and her freight, together with all her tackle, apparel, &c.: And it is hereby declared, that the said ship Isabella, and her freight, is thus assigned over for the security of the respondentia taken up by the said John Doe, and shall be delivered to no other use or purpose whatever, until payment of this bond is first made, with the premium that may become due thereon.

Now, therefore, the condition of this obligation is such, that if the above bounden John Doe, his heirs, executors, or administrators, shall and do well and truly pay, or cause to be paid, unto the said John Smith, or to his attorneys, legally authorized to receive the same, his or their executors, administrators, or assigns, the just and full sum of one thousand dollars, being the principal of this bond, together with the premium which shall become due thereon, at or before the expiration of twenty days after the arrival of the ship Isabella at the port of   ; or, in case of the loss of the said ship, such an average as by custom shall have become due on the salvage, then this obligation is to be void; otherwise to remain in full force and virtue.

Having signed to three bonds of the same tenor and date, the one of which being accomplished, the other two to be void and of no effect.

Signed, sealed, &c., *(as in single bond)*.

CHATTEL MORTGAGES.

In legal acceptation the word *Chattel* means any description of moveable personal property, such as household furniture, farm stock and implements, goods, wares and merchandize of every description, and the like. Accordingly when a deed or conveyance, by way of security, is given for an existing debt, or for money advanced, or for endorsations, or other legal obligation, the instrument is termed a *Chattel Mortgage*. In former times chattel mortgages were sometimes given to prevent a judgment creditor levying for his claim under an execution; but legal enactments in the various provinces of the Dominion have, as a rule, put a stop to practices of this description, and other improper practices of a kindred, or even more questionable, character. In 1857 a special act was passed to prevent practices of this description in the then Province of Upper Canada, which has been incorporated, with some amendments, in the Revised

CHATTEL MORTGAGES.

Statutes of Ontario, Chap. 119, the more important Sections of which we how append :

1. Every mortgage, or conveyance intended to operate as a mortgage, of goods and chattels, made in Ontario, which is not accompanied by an immediate delivery, and an actual and continued change of possession of the things mortgaged, or a true copy thereof, shall, within five days from the execution thereof,* be registered as hereinafter provided, together with the affidavit of a witness thereto, of the due execution of such mortgage or conveyance, or of the due execution of the mortgage or conveyance of which the copy filed purports to be a copy, and also with the affidavit of the mortgagee or of one of several mortgagees, or of the agent of the mortgrgee or mortgagees, if such agent is aware of all the the circumstances connected therewith, and is properly authorized in writing to take such mortgage (in which case a copy of such authority shall be registered therewith).

2. Such last mentioned affidavit, whether of the mortgagee or his agent, shall state that the mortgagor therein named is justly and truly indebted to the mortgagee in the sum mentioned in the mortgage, that it was executed in good faith, and for the express purpose of securing the payment of money justly due or accruing due, and not for the purpose of protecting the goods and chattels mentioned therein against the creditors of the mortgagor, or of preventing the creditors of such mortgagor from obtaining payment of any claim against him.

3 Every such mortgage or conveyance shall operate and take effect upon, from and after the day and time of the execution thereof.

4. In case such mortgage or conveyance and affidavits are not registered as hereinbefore provided, the mortgage or conveyance shall be absolutely null and void as against creditors of the mortgagor, and against subsequent purchasers or mortgagees in good faith for valuable consideration.

5. Every sale of goods and chattels, not accompanied by an immediate delivery and followed by an actual and continued change of possession of the goods and chattels sold, shall be in writing, and such writing shall be a conveyance under the provisions of this Act, and shall be accompanied by an affidavit of a witness thereto of the due execution thereof, and an affidavit of the bargainee, or his agent duly authorized in writing to take such conveyance (a copy of which authority shall be attached to such conveyance), that the sale is *bona fide* and for good consideration, as set forth in the said conveyance, and not for the purpose of holding or enabling the bargainee to hold the goods mentioned therein against the creditors of the bargainor, and such conveyance and affidavits shall be registered as hereinafter provided, within five days from the execution

---

* In a Territorial District Chattel Mortgages are to be registered with the Clerk of its first Division Court within 10 days after its execution. In Nipissing District registration must be made with the Clerk of the County Court of Renfrew within 20 days.

thereof, otherwise the sale shall be absolutely. void as against the creditors of the bargainor and as against subsequent purchasers or mortgagees in good faith.

6. In case of an agreement in writing for future advances for the purpose of enabling the borrower to enter into and carry on business with such advances, the time of repayment thereof not being longer than one year from the making of the agreement, and in case of a mortgage of goods and chattels for securing the mortgagee repayment of such advances, or in case of a mortgage of goods and chattels for securing the mortgagee against the endorsements of any bills or promissory notes, or any other liability by him incurred for the mortgagor, not extending for a longer period than one year from the date of such mortgage, and in case the mortgage is executed in good faith, and sets forth fully by recital or otherwise, the terms, nature and effect of the agreement, and the amount of liability intended to be created, and in case such mortgage is accompanied by the affidavit of a witness thereto of the due execution thereof, and by the affidavit of the mortgagee, or in case the agreement has been entered into and the mortgage taken by an agent duly authorized in writing to make such agreement and to take such mortgage, and if the agent is aware of the circumstances connected therewith, then, if accompanied by the affidavit of such agent, such affidavit, whether of the mortgagee or his agent, stating that the mortgage truly sets forth the agreement entered into between the parties thereto, and truly states the extent of the liability intended to be created by such agreement and covered by such mortgage, and that such mortgage is executed in good faith and for the express purpose of securing the mortgagee repayment of his advances or against the payment of the amount of his liability for the mortgagor, as the case may be, and not for the purpose of securing the goods and chattels mentioned therein against the creditors of the mortgagor, nor to prevent such creditors from recovering any claims which they may have against such mortgagor, and in case such mortgage is registered as hereinafter provided, the same shall be as valid and binding as mortgages mentioned in the preceding sections of this act.

7. The instruments mentioned in the proceeding sections shall be registered in the office of the Clerk of the County Court of the County or Union of Counties where the mortgagor or bargainer, if a resident in Ontario, resides, at the time of the execution thereof, or, if he is not a resident, then in the office of the Clerk of the County Court of the County or Union of Counties where the property so mortgaged or sold, is at the time of the execution of such instrument ; and such Clerks shall file all such instruments presented to them respectively for that purpose, and shall endorse thereon the time of receiving the same in their respective offices, and the same shall be kept there for the inspection of all persons interested therein, or intending or desiring to acquire any interest in all or any portion of the property covered thereby.

8. The said Clerks respectively shall number every such instrument or copy filed in their offices, and shall enter in alphabetical order in books to be provided by them, the names of all the parties

to such instruments, with the numbers endorsed thereon opposite to each name, and such entry shall be repeated alphabetically under the name of every party thereto.

9. In the event of the permanent removal of goods and chattels mortgaged as aforesaid from the County or Union of Counties in which they were at the time of the execution of the mortgage, to another County or Union of Counties before the payment and discharge of the mortgage, a certified copy of such mortgage, under the hand of the Clerk of the County Court, in whose office it was first registered, and under the seal of the said Court, and of the affidavits and documents and instruments relating thereto filed in such office, shall be filed with the Clerk of the County Court of the County or Union of Counties to which such goods and chattels are removed, within two months from such removal, otherwise the said goods and chattels shall be liable to seizure and sale under execution, and in such case the mortgage shall be null and void as against subsequent purchasers and mortgagees in good faith for valuable consideration as if never executed.

23. All the instruments mentioned in this Act, whether for the sale or mortgage of goods and chattels, shall contain such sufficient and full description thereof that the same may be thereby readily and easily known and distinguished.

24. All affidavits and affirmations required by this Act shall be taken and administered by any Judge or Commissioner for taking affidavits in and for the Courts of Queen's Bench or Common Pleas, or a Justice of the Peace, and the sum of twenty cents shall be paid for every oath thus administered.

25. This Act does not apply to mortgages of vessels registered under the provisions of any Act in that behalf.

SCHEDULE.

(Section 13.)

FORM OF DISCHARGE OF MORTGAGE.

To the Clerk of the County Court of the County of

I, A. B., of do certify that has satisfied all money due on, or to grow due on a certain chattel mortgage made by to , which mortgage bears date the day of , A. D. , and was registered in the office of the Clerk of the County Court of the County of , on the , A. D., , as No. *(here mention the day and date of registration of each assignment thereof, and the names of the parties, or mention that such mortgage has not been assigned, as the fact may be)*; and that I am the person entitled by law to receive the money; and that such mortgage is therefore discharged.

Witness my hand, this day of A. D.
One Witness stating residence } A. B.
and occupation

CHATTEL MORTGAGES.

This Statute of the Province of Ontario was amended in 1878 by 41 Vic., Chap. 8, Sec. 12 ; and was further amended in 1880 by 43 Vic., Chap. 15, which Statute materially simplifies the renewal of Chattel Mortgages, and enacts as follows :

2. Section ten of the said Revised Statute is hereby repealed, and the following substituted therefor :

Every mortgage, or copy thereof, filed in pursuance of this Act, shall cease to be valid, as against the creditors of the persons making the same and against subsequent purchasers and mortgagees in good faith for valuable consideration, after the expiration of one year from the filing thereof, unless within thirty days next preceding the expiration of the said term of one year, a statement exhibiting the interest of the mortgagee, his executors, administrators or other assigns in the property claimed by virtue thereof, and showing the amount still due for principal and interest thereon, and showing all payments made on account thereof, is again filed in the office of the clerk of the county court of the county, or union of counties, wherein such goods and chattels are then situate, with an affidavit of the mortgagee, or one of several mortgagees, or of the assignee or one of several assignees, or of the agent of the mortgagee or assignee, or mortgagees or assignees (as the case may be), duly authorized in writing, for that purpose, (a copy of which authority shall be filed therewith,) that such statement is true, and that the said mortgage has not been kept on foot for any fraudulent purpose.

3. The statement and affidavit mentioned in the next preceding paragraph may be in the form given in the schedule to this Act, or to the like effect.

4. The said statement and affidavit shall be deemed one instrument, and be filed and entered in like manner as the instruments mentioned in the said Revised Statute are, by section eight thereof, required to be filed and entered, and the like fees shall be payable for filing and entering the same as are now payable for filing and entering such instruments.

5. Section fifteen of the said Revised Statute is hereby repealed, and the following substituted therefor :

Where a mortgage has been renewed under section ten of this Act, the endorsement or entries required by the preceding section to be made need only be made upon the statement and affidavit filed on the last renewal, and at the entries of such statement and affidavit in the said book.

6. An authority for the purpose of taking or renewing a mortgage or conveyance under the provisions of the said Revised Statute may be a general one to take and renew all or any mortgages or conveyances to the mortgagee or bargainee.

Form of Renewal Statement under Section 3 of 43 Vic. Chap. 15.

Statement exhibiting the interest of C. D. in the property mentioned in a Chattel Mortgage dated the   day of   18   , made between A. B. of   of the one part, and C. D., of   of the other part, and filed in the office of the clerk of the county court of the county of   on the   day of   18   and of the amount due for principal and interest thereon, and of all payments made on account thereof.

The said C. D. is still the mortgagee of the said property, and has not assigned the said Mortgage (*or* the said E. F. is the assignee of the said Mortgage by virtue of an assignment thereof from the said C. D. to him, dated the   day of 18   ,) (*or as the case may be*).

No payments have been made on account of the said mortgage (*or* the following payments, and no other, have been made on account of the said Mortgage:

    1880, January 1, Cash received... ....$100 00

The amount still due for principal and interest on the said Mortgage is the sum of   dollars, computed as follows: [*here give the computation.*]

C. D.

Form of Affidavit to accompany Renewal Statement.

County of   ) I,   of the
    To wit: }   of   in the County of   the mortgagee named in the Chattel Mortgage mentioned in the foregoing (*or* annexed) statement, (*or* assignee of   the mortgagee named in .the Chattel Mortgage mentioned in the foregoing [*or* annexed statement,) (*as the case may be*), make oath and say:

1. That the foregoing (*or* annexed) statement is true.
2. That the Chattel Mortgage mentioned in the said statement has not been kept on foot for any fraudulent purpose.

Sworn before me at the)
    of   in the (
county of   this {
  day of   18 .)

A Chattel Mortgage is a special contract, entered into between two parties, (of whom the party who gives it is termed the Mortgagor, and the party in whose favor it is made the Mortgagee), whereby the mortgagor conditionally sells, assigns and transfers, certain goods and chattels to the mortgagee. The conditional part of the sale is the payment of a certain sum of money at a particular time, or the performance of some stipulated act or acts ; and if the money is paid according to contract, or the act performed, the mortgage becomes void. In the meantime, and until default is made by the mortgagor, he is to have possession and use of the goods and chattels sold, assigned and transferred.— Chattel mortgages can only be made for a good and equitable consideration, and if made with the intention of defrauding creditors or purchasers, are null and void as against them. No one with intent to defraud can legally give or take a chattel mortgage ; and even if a valuable consideration be given therefor, but with some fradulent intent, it will not hold good in law. The transaction must be free from all taint of fraud and collusion whatever.

It is absolutely necessary that the mortgagee, in order to maintain intact his right to the property mortgaged to him, should comply with all the legal provisions required, whether for the renewal of his claim from year to year, or taking possession of the chattels in the event of default. If he fails to do these acts at the proper time, and in the proper way, he must abide the consequences of his own neglect.— All chattel mortgages usually provide that until default is made, the mortgagor is to retain quiet possession of the property mortgaged, but when default is once made the mortgagor breaks the sole condition on which he has the right of possession, and his legal interest in the property terminates. The mortgagee has now the right to actual possession, and he may enter the premises of the mortgagor, at any time by day or night, (unless prevented by some special clause in the mortgage), to get possession of the property mortgaged, provided he does so without committing any breach of the criminal law. But after possession is taken the mortgagor has no right to permit any subsequent act of ownership by the mortgagee. The usual mode of taking possession of chattels by the mortgagee on default is by a warrant under his hand, directed to some bailiff or other responsible person, but he has the right to take personal possession, if he pleases, of what has now become in every sense his own property, and the absolute title to which had been already invested in him by special contract. A chattel mortgage on goods will not, however, bar the right of the landlord to levy thereon for rent due, nor the right of the tax collector to levy taxes.

We may add that a party giving a chattel mortgage who makes any false statement as to previous liabilities on the property mortgaged, with a view of deceiving the mortgagee, renders himself liable to a criminal prosecution for fraud.— Vide 29 Vic. Cap. 28.

Ordinary Chattel Mortgage

This Indenture, made the   day of   , 18 , between John Doe, of, &c., of the first part, and Richard Roe, of, &c., of the second part, Witnesseth, that the said party of the first part, for and in consideration of the sum of one hundred dollars of lawful money of Canada, to him in hand well and truly paid by the said party of the second part, at or before the sealing and delivery of these presents, the receipt whereof is hereby acknowledged, doth bargain, sell and assign unto the said party of the second part, his executors, administrators and assigns, all and every the goods, chattels, furniture and effects in and about the dwelling house (*or store*) of the said John Doe, situate at, etc., and hereinafter particularly mentioned, that is to say (*Here specify the chattels, or you may refer to a schedule saying after the word, etc., "which are particularly specified in the schedule hereunder written."*)

To have, receive and take the said goods and chattels hereby assigned or intended so to be, unto the said party of the second part, his executors, administrators and assigns, as his and their own proper goods and effects.

Provided always, that if the said party of the first part, his executors or administrators, shall pay unto the said party of the second part, his executors, administrators or assigns the full sum of one hundred dollars, with interest thereon at the rate of ten per cent. on the   day of   next, then these presents shall be void.

And the said party of the first part, doth hereby, for himself, his executors and administrators, covenant, promise and agree, to and with the said party of the second part, his executors, administrators and assigns, that he, the said party of the first part, his executors or administrators, or some or one of them, shall and will well and truly pay, or cause to be paid, unto the said party of the second part, his executors, administrators and assigns, the said sum of money in the above proviso mentioned, with interest for the same as aforesaid, on the days and times and in the manner above limited for the payment thereof.

And also, that in case default shall be made in the payment of the said sum of money in the said proviso mentioned, or the interest thereon, or any part thereof, or in case the said party of the first part shall attempt to sell or dispose of, or in any way part with the possession of the said goods and chattels, or any of them, or to remove the same or any part thereof out of the county of   , without the consent of the said party of the second part, his executors, administrators or assigns, to such sale, removal or disposal thereof, first had and obtained in writing ; then and in such case it shall and may be lawful for the said party of the second part, his executors, administrators and assigns, peaceably and quietly to receive and take into his or their absolute possession, and thenceforth to hold and enjoy all and every or any of the goods, chattels and premises hereby assigned or intended so to be, and with his or their servant or servants, and with such other assistant or assistants as he may require, at any time during the day, to enter into and upon any lands, tenements, houses and premises belonging to and in the occupation of the party of the first part, where the said goods and chattels or any part thereof may be, and to break and force open any door, lock bolt, fastening, hinge, gate, fence, house, building, enclosure and place, for the purpose of taking possession of and removing the said goods and chattels, and to sell the said goods and chattels, or any of them, or any part thereof, at public auction or private sale, as to them or any of them may seem meet ; and from and out of the proceeds of such sale in the first place to pay and reimburse himself or themselves all such sums of money as may then be due, by virtue of these presents, and all such expenses as may have been incurred by the said party of the second part, his executors, administrators or assigns, in consequence of the default, neglect or failure of the said party of the first part, his executors, administrators or assigns, in payment of the said sum of money with interest thereon as above mentioned, or in consequence of such sale or removal as above mentioned; and in the next place to pay unto the said party of the first part, his executors, administrators and assigns, all such surplus as may remain after such sale, and after payment of all such sum and sums of money and interest thereon as may be due by virtue of these presents at the time of such seizure, and after payment of the costs, charges and expenses incurred by such seizure and sale as aforesaid.

And the said party of the first part doth hereby further covenant, promise and agree to and with the said party of the second part, his executors, administrators and assigns, that in case the sum of money realized under such sale as above mentioned shall not be sufficient to pay the whole amount due at the time of such sale, then he, the said party of the first part, his executors or administrators, will forthwith pay any deficiency to the said party of the second part, his executors, administrators and assigns.

In witness whereof, the parties to these presents have hereunto set their hands and seals the day and year first above written.

Signed, sealed and delivered   JOHN DOE [L. s.]
  in the presence of
    JOHN SMITH.

Affidavit of Mortgagee.

Province   } I, Richard Roe, of the   of
County of   , in the county of   ,
  To wit :   } the mortgagee in the within bill of sale, by way of mortgage named, make oath and say, that John Doe, the mortgagor in the within bill of sale, by way of mortgage named, is justly and truly indebted to me, this deponent Richard Roe, the mortgagee therein named, in the sum of one hundred dollars mentioned therein.

That the said bill of sale, by way of mortgage, was executed in good faith, and for the express purpose of securing the payment of the money so justly due as aforesaid, and not for the purpose of protecting the goods and chattels mentioned in the said bill of sale, by way of mortgage, against the creditors of the said John Doe, the mortgagor therein named, or of preventing the creditors of such mortgagor from obtaining payment of any claim against him.

Sworn before me, at   RICHARD ROE.
in the County of   this
     day of   188

JOHN BROWN,
    J. P., or a Commissioner, &c.

Affidavit of Witness to Mortgage.

Province,   I, John Smith, of the   of   ,
County of   in the county of   , (*Here insert*
    To wit: *occupation of Witness*) make oath and say, that I was personally present, and did see the within Bill of Sale, by way of mortgage, duly signed, sealed and delivered by John Doe, the party thereto, and that the name John Smith, set and subscribed as a witness to the execution thereof, is of the proper handwriting of me, this deponent, and that the same was executed at   , in the said county of   .

                                           JOHN SMITH.
Sworn before me, &c.

    J. P., or a Commissioner, &c.

Chattel Mortgage by way of Security against Indorsement.

This Indenture, made the   day of   , 18   , between John Doe, of, &c., of the first part, and Richard Roe, of, &c., of the second part: Whereas, the said party of the second part has indorsed the Promissory Note of the the said party of the first part for the sum of five hundred dollars, of lawful money of Canada, for the accommodation of the said party of the first part, which Promissory Note is in the words and figures following, that is to say: [Here copy the note.] And whereas the said party of the first part has agreed to enter into these presents for the purpose of indemnifying and saving harmless the said party of the second part of and from the payment of the said Promissory Note, or any part thereof, or any note or notes hereafter to be indorsed by the said party of the second part, for the accommodation of the said party of the first part, by way of renewal of the said recited note, or otherwise howsoever, within the period of one year from the date hereof.

Now this Indenture Witnesseth, That the said party of the first part, in consideration of the premises, hath bargained, sold and assigned, and by these presents doth bargain, sell and assign, unto the said party of the second part, his executors, administrators and assigns, all and singular the goods, chattels, furniture and household stuff hereinafter particularly mentioned and expressed, that is to say: [*Describe as in preceding form.*]

To have, hold, receive and take the said goods, chattels, furniture and household stuff hereby assigned or mentioned, or intended so to be, unto the said party of the second part, his executors, administrators and assigns, forever: Provided always—and these presents are upon this condition—that if the said party of the first part, his executors or administrators, do and shall well and truly pay, or cause to be paid, the said promissory note so as aforesaid indorsed by the said party of the second part, and all and every other note or notes, which may hereafter be endorsed by the said party of the second part for the accommodation of the said party of the first part, by way of renewal of the said note, and indemnify and save harmless the said party of the second part, his heirs, executors and administrators, from all loss, costs, charges, damages or expenses in respect of the said note or any renewals thereof; then these presents, and every matter and thing herein contained, shall cease, determine and be utterly void to all intents and purposes, anything herein contained to the contrary thereof in any wise notwithstanding. And the said party of the first part doth hereby, for himself, his heirs, executors and administrators, covenant, promise and agree to and with the said party of the second part, his executors and administrators, that he, the said party of the first part, his executors or administrators, or some or one of them, shall and will well and truly pay, or cause to be paid, the said promissory note in the above recital and proviso mentioned, and all future or other promissory notes which the said party of the second part shall hereinafter indorse for the accommodation of the said party of the first part, by way of renewal as aforesaid, and indemnify and save harmless the said party of the second part from all loss, costs, charges, damages or expenses in respect thereof.

And also, that in case default should be made in the payment of the said promissory note, or any renewal note or notes as in the said proviso mentioned, or in case the said party of the first part shall attempt to sell or dispose of, or in any way part with the possession of, the said goods and chattels, or any of them, or remove the same or any part thereof out of the county of   , without the consent of the said party of the second part, his executors or administrators, to such sale, removal or disposal thereof, first had and obtained in writing, then and in such case it shall and may be lawful for the said party of the second part, his executors or administrators, with his or their servant or servants, and with such other assistant or assistants as he or they may require, at any time during the day to enter into and upon any lands, tenements, houses, and premises, wheresoever and whatsoever, belonging to and in the occupation of the said party of the first part, his executors or administrators, where the said goods and chattels, or any part thereof, may be, and for such persons to break and force open any doors, locks, bolts, fastenings, hinges, gates, fences, houses, buildings, enclosures and places, for the purpose of taking possession of and removing the said goods and chattels, and upon and from, and after taking possession of such goods and chattels as aforesaid, it shall and may be lawful, and the said party of the second part, his executors or administrators, and each or any of them, is and are hereby authorized and empowered to sell the said goods and chattels, or any of them, or any part thereof, at public auction or private sale, as to him or them, or any of them, may seem meet, and from and out of the proceeds of such sale in the first place to pay and reimburse himself or themselves all such sums and sum of money as may then be due by virtue of these presents on the said promissory note, or any renewal note or notes, as aforesaid, and all such expenses as may have been incurred by the said party of the second part, his executors or administrators, in consequence of the default, neglect or failure of the said party of the first part, his executors or administrators, in payment of the said note or notes as above mentioned, or in consequence of such sale or removal as above mentioned; and in the next place to pay unto the said party of the first part, his executors, administrators or assigns, all of such surplus as may remain after such sale, and after payment of all such sum or sums of money, and interest thereon, as he, the said party of the second part, shall be called upon to pay by reason of indorsing the said promissory note in the said recital and proviso mentioned, or any renewal note or notes to be indorsed by the said party of the second part for the said party of the first part, as aforeaid, at the time of such seizure, and after payment of such costs, charges and expenses incurred by such seizure and sale, as aforesaid.

Provided always, nevertheless, that it shall not be incumbent on the said party of the second part, his executors or administrators, to sell and dispose of the said goods and chattels, but that in case of default in payment of the said note or notes as aforesaid, it shall and may be lawful for the said party of the second part, his executors, administrators and assigns, peaceably and quietly to have, hold, use, occupy, possess and enjoy the said goods and chattels without the let, molestation, eviction, hindrance or interruption of him, the said party of the first part, his executors, administrators or assigns, or any of them, or any other persons or person whomsoever. And the said party of the first part doth hereby further covenant, promise and agree, to and with the said party of the second part, his executors and administrators, that in case the sum of money realized under any such sale as above mentioned shall not be sufficient to pay the whole amount due on the said note or notes at the time of such sale that he, the said party of the first part his executors or administrators, shall and will forthwith, pay, or cause to be paid, unto the said party of the second part, his executors or administrators, all such sum or sums of money, with interest thereon, as may then be remaining due upon the said note or notes.

In witness, &c., (*as in General Form*).

Affidavit of Mortgagee.

Province, } I Richard Roe, of, &c., the Mortgagee
County of } in the within mortgage named, make
To Wit. : } oath and say : That such mortgage truly
states the extent of the liability intended to be created and
covered by such mortgage, and that the said mortgage was
executed in good faith and for the express purpose of securing me, the said mortgagee therein named, against the payment of the amount of my liability for the said mortgagor
by reason of the promissory note therein recited, or any
note or notes which I may indorse for the accommodation of
the said party of the first part, as renewals of the said note;
And not for the purpose of securing the goods and chattels
mentioned therein against the creditors of the mortgagor,
nor to prevent such creditors from recovering any claims
which they may have against such mortgagor.

RICHARD ROE.

Sworn before me, &c.

J. P., or a Commissioner, &c.

Affidavit of Witness.

Province, } I, John Smith, of, &c., make oath and
County of } and say : That I was personally present
To Wit. : } and did see the annexed Bill of Sale, by
way of Mortgage, duly signed sealed and delivered by John
Doe and Richard Roe, the parties thereto, and that I, this
deponent, am a subscribing witness to the same ; that the
name John Smith, set and subscribed as a witness to the
execution thereof, is of the proper handwriting of me, this
deponent, and that the same was executed at   , in
the said County of

JOHN SMITH.

Sworn before me, &c.

J. P., or a Commissioner, &c.

Chattel Mortgage to secure further advances.

This Indenture, made the   day of   18 ,
Between John Doe, of, &c., of the first part, and Richard
Roe, of, &c., of the second part. Whereas, (*Here set forth*

fully, by way of recital, the terms, nature and effect, of the agreement for the future advances, and the amount of liability to be created, as for instance :) " Whereas the said John Doe, is desirous of entering into and carrying on the business of a dry goods merchant at the City of Belleville, and hath applied to the said Richard Roe to make him future advances, not exceeding in the whole the sum of $5,000, at such times and in such sums as he, the said John Doe, may require the same. And whereas, by an agreement in writing, dated on the   day of 18 , and made between the said John Doe and Richard Roe, the said Richard Roe hath agreed to make such future advances to the extent of $5,000 to the said John Doe for the purpose aforesaid at such times, and in such sums as the said John Doe may require it; the whole to be repaid within one year from the date of the said agreement." Now this Indenture witnesseth that the said party of the first part, in consideration of the premises, and in pursuance of the said agreement hath bargained, sold and assigned, and by these presents doth bargain, sell and assign, unto the said party of the second part, his executors, administrators and assigns, All and singular the goods, chattels, furniture and household effects hereinafter particularly mentioned and described in the schedule hereunto annexed marked A. To have, hold, receive and take, all and singular the goods, chattels, furniture and effects hereinbefore bargained, sold and assigned, or mentioned, or intended so to be, unto the said party of the second part, his executors, administrators and assigns forever. Provided always, that these presents are upon this condition, that if the said party of the first part, his executors or administrators do and shall well and truly pay, or cause to be paid, unto the said party of the second part, his executors, administrators or assigns, the said sum of $5,000 or so much thereof as the said party of the second part shall advance to the said party of the first part, according to the terms of the said agreement, together with interest thereon at the rate of   per cent per annum, within one year from the date of the said agreement, then these presents and every matter and thing herein contained, shall cease, determine and be utterly void to all intents and purposes, anything herein contained to the contrary thereof in any wise notwithstanding. Provided always that in case default shall be made in payment of the said sum of $5,000, or so much thereof as may be advanced as aforesaid, and interest contrary to the last mentioned proviso; or in case the said party of the first part shall attempt to sell or dispose of, or in any way part with the possession of, the said goods and chattels or any of them, or to remove the same or any part thereof out of the City of Belleville, without the consent of the said party of the second part, his executors, administrators or assigns, to such sale, removal or disposal thereof, first had and obtained in writing; then and in such case it shall and may be lawful for the said party of the second part, his executors, administrators or assigns with his or their servant or servants, and with such other assistant or assistants as he or they may require, peaceably and quietly to receive and take into his or their absolute possession, and thenceforth to hold and enjoy all and every, or any of the said goods and chattels; and upon and from and after taking possession of such goods and chattels as aforesaid, it shall and may be lawful, and the said party of the second part, his executors, administrators and assigns, and each or any of them is and are hereby authorized and empowered to sell the said goods and chattels, or any of them, or any part thereof at public auction or private sale, as to him or any of them may seem meet, and from and out of the proceeds of such sale in the first place to pay and reimburse him and them all such sums and sum of money as may then be due by virtue of these presents, and all such expenses as may have been incurred by the said party of the second part, his executors, administrators or assigns, in consequence of the default, neglect or failure of the said party of the first part, his executors, administrators or assigns, in payment of the said sum of money with interest thereon as above mentioned, and in the next place to pay unto the said party of the first part, his executors or administrators, all such surplus as may remain after payment of such sum or sums of money as aforesaid: And the said party of the first part, for himself, his heirs, executors and administrators, doth hereby covenant, promise and agree to and with the said party of the second part, his executors, administrators and assigns, that in case the sum of money realized under any such sale as above mentioned, shall not be sufficient to pay the whole amount due at the time of such sale, he, the said party of the first part, his executors or administrators, shall and will forthwith pay or cause to be paid unto the said party of the second part, his executors, administrators or assigns, all such sum and sums of money, with interest thereon, as may then be remaining due.

And it is hereby also declared and agreed, that until default shall be made in payment of the said principal sum of $5,000 and interest contrary to the aforesaid proviso, it shall be lawful for the said John Doe, his executors or administrators, to make use of (but not to remove from the premises) the said goods, chattels and things hereby assigned or intended so to be without any hindrance or disturbance by the said Richard Roe, his executors, administrators or assigns. And the said John Doe doth hereby, for himself, his heirs, executors and administrators, covenant with the said Richard Roe, his executors and administrators, that he, the said John Doe, hath not heretofore made, done, permitted or suffered, nor will at any time hereafter make, do, permit or suffer any act, deed. matter or thing whereby, or by means whereof, the said goods, chattels and premises hereby assigned are, is, can or may be in any wise impeached, charged, affected, incumbered or prejudicially affected in any manner howsoever; and also that he the said John Doe, his executors and administrators will, so long as any money shall remain due on this security, insure and keep insured the said goods, chattels and premises from damage by fire, in some respectable insurance office, in the names of the said Richard Roe, his executors, administrators or assigns, in the sum of $, and hand the policy for such insurance, and the receipt for the current year's premium, to the said Richard Roe, his executors, administrators or assigns, on demand; and that in default of the said policy being so effected or kept on foot as aforesaid, it shall be lawful for the said Richard Roe, his executors, administrators and assigns, to effect or keep on foot the same, and all the premiums and other expenses incurred by him or them in so doing shall be repaid on demand by the said John Doe, his executors or administrators, and until repayment, the same shall be a charge on the said goods, chattels and premises hereby assigned, and shall bear interest after the rate aforesaid. And also that the said John Doe, his executors and administrators, will, during the continuance of this security, keep the chattels, effects and premises hereby assigned, in good order, repair and condition in all respects, as they are in at the time of the execution hereof.

In witness, &c., (*as in General Form*).

THE SCHEDULE ABOVE REFERRED TO MARKED A.

[*Here set out a full and particular description of the goods as required in the preceding forms.*]

Affidavit of Mortgagee.

Province } I, Richard Roe, of, &c,, the
County of } mortgagee in the within mortgage
To Wit : } named, make oath and say, that the within mortgage truly sets forth the agreement entered into between myself and John Doe, therein named, and truly states the extent of the liability intended to be created by such agreement, and covered by the within mortgage. That the within mortgage is executed in good faith, and for the express purpose of securing to me the re-payment of the advances agreed to be made as within mentioned, and not for the purpose of securing the goods and chattels mentioned therein, and set forth in the schedule attached thereto, marked A, against the creditors of the said John Doe, or to prevent such creditors from recovering any claims which they may have against the said John Doe.

RICHARD ROE.

Sworn before, &c.

J. P., or a Commissioner, &c.

Form of Chattel Mortgage, under the Revised Statutes of Ontario, Chap. 119, Sec. 1.

This Indenture, made (in duplicate) the   day of   one thousand eight hundred and between John Doe, of the   of   in the County of   ,   (hereinafter called "the mortgagor"), of the First Part; and Richard Roe, of the   of   in the County of   ,   (hereinafter called "the mortgagee"), of the Second Part ;

Witnesseth, that the mortgagor for, and in consideration of   dollars of lawful money of Canada, to him in hand, well and truly paid by the mortgagee at or before the sealing and delivery of these Presents (the receipt whereof is hereby acknowledged) hath granted, bargained, sold and assigned, and, by these Presents, doth grant, bargain, sell assign, unto the said mortgagee, his executors, administrators and assigns, all and singular the goods, chattels, personal property and effects, hereinafter particularly mentioned and described, that is to say, (*Here insert a full and accurate description of each article intended to be mortgaged, or refer to schedule attached to mortgage in which they are so described.*) all which said goods, chattels, personal property and effects are now in the possession of the said mortgagor, and are now situate, lying and being on, upon, and about (*Here describe accurately the lot, half lot, parcel of ground or premises upon which are the goods, &c., at the date of the execution of the instrument.*)

To Hold All and Singular the said goods, chattels, personal property and effects unto the mortgagee, his executors, administrators and assigns to the only proper use and behoof of the mortgagee, his executors, administrators and assigns forever, Provided always, and these Presents are upon this express condition that if the mortgagor, his executors or administrators, do and shall, well and truly pay, or cause to be paid, unto the mortgagee, his executors, administrators or assigns, the full sum of   dollars, with interest for the same at the rate of   per centum per annum in manner following, that is to say, (*Here insert time and the mode of payment.*)

Then these Presents and every matter and thing herein contained shall cease, determine and be utterly void to all intents and purposes, anything herein contained to the contrary thereof in anywise notwithstanding :

And the mortgagor for himself, his executors and administrators, shall and will warrant, and for ever defend by these Presents, all and singular, the said goods, chattels and property unto the mortgagee, his executors, administrators, and assigns, against him the mortgagor, his executors and administrators, and against all and every other person and persons whomsoever ;

And the mortgagor, doth hereby for himself, his executors

and administrators, covenant, promise and agree to, and with the mortgagee, his executors, administrators and assigns, that the mortgagor, his executors or administrators, or some or one of them, shall and will well and truly pay, or cause to be paid, unto the mortgagee, his executors, administrators, or assigns, the said sum of money in the above proviso mentioned, with interest for the same as aforesaid, on the days and times, and in the manner above limited for the payment thereof; and also, in case default shall be made in the payment of the said sum of money, in the said proviso mentioned, or of the interest thereon, or any part thereof, or in case the mortgagor shall attempt to sell or dispose of, or in any way part with the possession of the said goods and chattels, or any of them, or shall attempt to remove the same or any part thereof, out of the   of   without the consent of the mortgagee, his executors, administrators, or assigns, to such sale, removal or disposal thereof, first had and obtained in writing, or in case the said mortgagor, shall suffer, allow or permit a judgment to be obtained against him for a debt in any court of law or equity, or shall suffer, allow or permit any taxes, rates, duties or assessments whatsoever, for which he now is, or hereafter, during the currency of these Presents, may be assessed, to remain unpaid and unsatisfied for a period of seven days after demand lawfully made therefor, by the proper officer in that behalf, or in case the said mortgagor shall fail to pay the rent arising out of the land and premises upon which are situate and lying the said goods and chattels at any time during the currency of these Presents, six days at least before the same shall become due, or in case default shall be made in the performance of any of the covenants by the mortgagor in these Presents contained: Then, and in such case, it shall and may be lawful for the mortgagee, his executors, administrators or assigns, with his or their servant or servants, and with such other assistant or assistants, as he or they may require at any time during the day to enter into and upon any lands and tenements, houses and premises, wheresoever and whatsoever, where the said goods and chattels, or any part thereof, may be, and for such persons to break and force open any doors, locks, bars, bolts, fastenings, hinges, gates, fences, houses, buildings, enclosures, and places, for the purpose of taking possession of and removing the said goods and chattels; and upon and from, and after, the taking possession of such goods and chattels, as aforesaid, it shall and may be lawful for the mortgagee, his executors, administrators or assigns, and each or any of them, to sell the said goods and chattels, or any of them, or any part thereof, at public auction or private sale, as to him, them, or any of them may seem meet; and from and out of the proceeds of such sale in the first place to pay and reimburse himself, or themselves, all such sum and sums of money and interest as may then be due by virtue of these Presents, and all costs and expenses as may have been incurred by the mortgagee, his executors, administrators or assigns, in consequence of the default, neglect or failure of the mortgagor, his executors, administrators or assigns, in the payment of the said sum of money, with interest thereon, as above mentioned, or in consequence of such sale or removal as above mentioned; and in the next place to pay unto the mortgagor, his executors, administrators and assigns, all such surplus as may remain after such sale, and after payment of all such sum or sums of money and interest thereon, as may be due by virtue of these Presents at the time of such seizure, and after payment of the costs, charges and expenses incurred by such seizure and sale as aforesaid:

Provided that the mortgagee, his executors, administrators or assigns, may, in default of payment of any of the payments of interest or instalments hereinbefore mentioned, or any part thereof, distrain for the whole principal sum then unpaid:

Provided always, nevertheless, that it shall not be incumbent on the mortgagee, his executors, administrators or assigns, to sell and dispose of the said goods and chattels, but that in case of default of payment of the said sum of money with interest thereon, as aforesaid, it shall and may be lawful for the mortgagee, his executors, administrators or assigns, peaceably and quietly, to have, hold, use, occupy, possess and enjoy the said goods and chattels without the let, molestation, eviction, hinderance or interruption of him, the mortgagor, his executors, administrators or assigns, or any of them, or any other person or persons whomsoever :

And the mortgagor doth hereby, in manner aforesaid, further covenant, promise and agree to and with the mortgagee, his executors, administrators and assigns that, in case the sum of money realized under any such sale, as above mentioned, shall not be sufficient to pay the whole amount due at the time of such sale, then the mortgagor, his executors or administrators, shall, and will forthwith, pay or cause to be paid unto the mortgagee, his executors, administrators and assigns, all such sum or sums of money, with interest thereon at the rate aforesaid, as may then be remaining due, as well also as all costs and expenses as may have been incurred by the mortgagee in and about such seizure and sale :

And the mortgagor doth put the mortgagee in the full possession of said goods and chattels, by delivering to him these Presents in the name of all the said goods and chattels at the sealing and delivery hereof :

And the mortgagor further covenants with the mortgagee, in manner aforesaid, that he will, during the continuance of this mortgage, and any and every renewal thereof, insure the goods and chattels hereinbefore mentioned against loss or damage by fire in some insurance office (authorized to transact business in Canada) in the sum of not less than   dollars, and will pay all premiums and moneys necessary for that purpose, three days at least before the same become due, and will on demand assign and deliver over to the said mortgagee, his executors and administrators, the policy or policies of insurance and receipts thereto appertaining :

Provided, that if no default of payment of said premiums or sums of money by the mortgagor, in manner and at the times aforesaid, the mortgagee, his executors or administrators, may pay the same, and such sum of money shall be added to the debt hereby secured (and shall bear interest at the same rate from the day of such payment) and shall be repayable with the principal sum hereby secured.

In witness whereof, &c., *(as in General Form)*,

Affidavit of Mortgagee.

Province of Ontario, } I, Richard Roe, of the
County of   } of   in the County of
    To Wit :   }   ,   , the
mortgagee in the foregoing Bill of Sale by way of mortgage named, make oath and say :

That John Doe, the mortgagor in the foregoing Bill of Sale by way of mortgage named, is justly and truly indebted to me, this deponent Richard Roe, the mortgagee therein named, in the sum of   dollars mentioned therein ; that the said Bill of Sale by way of mortgage, was executed in good faith, and for the express purpose of securing the payment of the money so justly due, or accruing due, as aforesaid, and not for the purpose of protecting the goods and chattels mentioned in the said Bill of Sale by way of mortgage against the creditors' of the said John Doe, the mortgagor therein named, or of preventing the creditors of such mortgagor from obtaining payment of any claim against him, the said John Doe.

RICHARD ROE.

Sworn before me, &c.

    J. P. or a Commissioner, &c., &c.

Affidavit of Witness.

Province of Ontario, } I, John Smith, of the
County of   } of   in the County of
    To Wit :   }   , *(here insert occupation of the deponent)*, make oath and say :

That I was personally present, and did see the within Bill of Sale by way of mortgage, duly signed, sealed and executed by John Doe, one of the parties thereto, and that the name John Smith, set and subscribed as a witness to the execution thereof, is of the proper handwriting of me, this deponent, and that the same was executed at the of   , in the said County of   .

JOHN SMITH.

Sworn before me, &c.

    J. P., or a Commissioner, &c., &c.

Form of an Assignment of Chattel Mortgage.

(Under Revised Statutes of Ontario, Chap. 119.)

This Indenture made the   day of   one thousand eight hundred and   , Between John Doe of the   of   in the County of   ,   (*hereinafter called the "assignor"*) of the First Part, and Richard Roe of the   of   , in the County of   , (*hereinafter called the "assignee"*), of the Second Part.

Whereas, by a certain Chattel Mortgage dated on the   day of   one thousand eight hundred and   , and duly filed in the office of the Clerk of the County Court of the County of   , one (*the name of the mortgagor in full*) did grant and mortgage the goods and chattels therein mentioned unto the said assignor, his executors, administrators and assigns, for securing the payment of   dollars and interest thereon at the rate of   per cent per annum in manner following, that is to say,

(*Here set out the mode of payment as provided in the mortgage to be assigned.*)

And whereas there is now owing on the said mortgage the sum of   dollars, and interest thereon at the rate aforesaid, from the   day of   A. D. 188 .

And whereas, for the consideration hereinafter mentioned, it is intended to assign, transfer, and set over the said in part recited mortgage to the said assignee, together with all moneys due, or to become due thereon; and, to also grant the goods and chattels therein contained, and hereinafter set out, to the said assignee, and these Presents are intended to carry out such intention:

Witnesseth that in consideration of   dollars of lawful money of Canada, now paid by the said assignee to the said assignor (the receipt whereof is hereby acknowledged), the said assignor doth hereby assign and set over unto the said assignee, his executors, administrators, and assigns, all that the said hereinbefore in part recited mortgage, and also the said sum of   dollars, and the interest thereon, now owing, as aforesaid, together with all moneys that may hereafter become due, or owing, in respect of the said mortgage, and the full benefit of all powers, and of all covenants and provisoes contained in said mortgage; and the said assignor doth hereby grant, bargain, sell and assign unto the said assignee, his heirs and assigns, all and singular the said goods and chattels therein and hereinafter more particularly mentioned and described, that is to say,

(*Here set out a list of the chattels as contained in the mortgage intended to be assigned, or refer to a Schedule of the same, attached to assignment, marked A.*)

And all the right, title, interest, property, claim and demand whatsoever, both at law and in equity, or otherwise, howsoever, of him the said assignor of, in, to and out of the same, and every part thereof:

To Have and to Hold the said hereinbefore recited mortgage, and the moneys secured thereby, and also the said goods and chattels, and every of them, with their appurtenances, unto the said assignee, his executors, administrators and assigns absolutely; subject to the proviso for redemption contained in the said mortgage:

And the said assignor for himself, his executors and administrators doth hereby covenant with the said assignee, his executors, administrators and assigns, that the said sum of   dollars, and interest thereon, at the rate aforesaid, from the   day of   , is now justly due, owing and unpaid, under and by virtue of the said mortgage, and that he has not done or permitted any act, matter or thing to be done whereby the said mortgage has been released or discharged, or the said goods and chattels in anywise incumbered, or whereby the said goods and chattels, or any of them, have been, or may be, removed from the said   , and that he, his executors, and administrators and assigns will do, perform and execute every act necessary for further assuring the said mortgage and money, goods and chattels, to the said assignee, and for enforcing the performance of the covenants and other matters contained in the said mortgage.

In witness whereof the said parties hereto have hereunto set their hands and seals.

Signed, Sealed, &c.

Affidavit of Assignee.

Province of Ontario, ⎫ I, Richard Roe, of the
County of   ⎬ of   in the County of
           To Wit : ⎭   ,   , the assignee in the within assignment of Chattel Mortgage named, make oath and say : That the sale therein made is *bona fide*, and for good consideration, namely, in consideration of the sum of   dollars, as set forth in the said within assignment, and is not for the purpose of holding or enabling me, this deponent, to hold the goods mentioned therein against the creditors of John Doe, the assignor therein named.

RICHARD ROE.

Sworn before me, &c.
  J. P., or a Commissioner, &c.

Affidavit of Execution of an Assignment of Chattel Mortgage.

Province of Ontario, ⎫ I, John Smith, of the
County of   ⎬ of   in the County
           To Wit : ⎭ of

make oath and say :

That I was personally present, and did see the foregoing assignment of Chattel Mortgage duly signed, sealed and executed by John Doe and Richard Roe, the parties thereto; and that I, this deponent, am a subscribing witness to the same; and that the name John Smith set and subscribed as a witness to the execution thereof, is of the proper handwriting of me, this deponent, and that the same was executed at the   of   in the County of   .

Sworn before me, &c.   JOHN SMITH.
  J. P., or a Commissioner, &c.

Warrant of Seizure under Chattel Mortgage.

Province,   ⎫ To William Robinson, of
County of   ⎬ Brockville, my Bailiff in this
    To Wit :   ⎭ behalf.

Whereas by a certain Indenture of Chattel Mortgage (a copy of which marked C, is hereto attached) John Doe, the mortgagor therein named, did grant, bargain, sell and assign, unto me, Richard Roe, the goods and chattels therein specified (*or in the schedule attached thereto marked A*) and whereas the said John Doe has made default in the conditions to be observed on his part, as set forth in the said Chattel Mortgage; and has, therefore, forfeited all claim right and title, to the longer possession and use of the said goods and chattels; you are, therefore, hereby authorized, empowered and required, to take immediate possession on my behalf of the said goods and chattels in the said Chattel Mortgage mentioned, by virtue of the provisions therein contained, and to (*here set out plainly the disposition to be made of the goods and chattels seized; whether they shall be sold at public auction after due notice being given, and the surplus if any to be paid over to the mortgagor; or whether they are to be retained for the benefit of the mortgagee without sale. Care to be taken in every case to comply with the conditions and covenants contained in the mortgage, and with the special applying statute, if any such exists, of the Province in which the seizure takes place.*) And for so doing this shall be your sufficient warrant and authority.

Witness my hand and seal at Brockville, this day of   A. D. 1881.

Witness   RICHARD ROE, [L. S.]
JOHN SMITH.

Subsequent to the greater part of the foregoing, as regards Chattel Mortgages, having been put to press, the following Act, being 44 Vic., Chap. 12 (1881), has been passed by the Ontario Legislature:—

An Act to further amend the Revised Statute respecting Mortgages and Sales of Personal Property.

1. Another statement in accordance with the provisions of the tenth section of the Revised Statute, chaptered one hundred and nineteen, respecting mortgages and sales of personal property, as amended by the Act passed in the forty-third year of Her Majesty's reign, chapter fifteen, duly verified as required by that section, shall be filed in the office of the clerk of the county court of the county wherein the goods and chattels described in the mortgage are then situate, within thirty days next preceding the expiration of the term of one year from the day of the filing of the statement required by the said tenth section, or such mortgage, or copy thereof, shall cease to be valid as against the creditors of the persons

making the same, and as against purchasers and mortgagees in good faith for valuable consideration, and so on from year to year, that is to say, another statement as aforesaid, duly verified, shall be filed within thirty days next preceding the expiration of one year from the day of the filing of the former statement, or such mortgage, or copy thereof, shall cease to be valid as aforesaid.

CONSTABLES:—THEIR POWERS AND DUTIES.

In England the Constable was anciently the head and principal person of his own locality, and was an elective officer, who was charged with most important duties as a conservator of the peace, and a protector of the district in which he lived. Gradually, however, his standing in the community underwent a change, until he eventually came to be regarded in the light of a ministerial officer of the criminal law only, and to owe his appointment to the magistrates of the county assembled in Quarter Sessions, or at the General Sessions of the Peace. In the Dominion of Canada constables are appointed, as a rule, under statutes passed by the various legislatures of the several Provinces. No legislature, however, has framed any complete code to guide them in the performance of their duties; and these duties continue to be executed under the common law of England, various English statutes, statutes of the Dominion Parliament, and statutes of the various Local Legislatures.

At common law the constable is still a conservator, or keeper, of the peace; and in that capacity can act without any warrant, and exercises very great and extensive powers. He can arrest on his own authority all traitors, felons and suspicious persons; and all those whom he shall see on the point of, or committing, treason or felony, or doing any act that would manifestly endanger human life. Where a breach of the peace is committed, or about to be committed, in his presence, as where violent attempts are made by one person to hurt another, a constable may arrest the assailant and take him before the nearest magistrate, or detain him in custody until he can conveniently do so, but no longer. A constable after giving notice that he is one may break open the doors of a house to arrest a felon, if he be concealed therein, and entrance is denied; and if the felon makes resistance, and puts the constable in any serious peril, the latter may kill him in self defence. He may break open a house when entrance is denied to abate an affray, or fight, or to suppress disorderly drinking or noise at an unreasonable hour of the night. He may arrest any one who insults or assaults himself, or opposes him in the execution of his office, and may lawfully beat another in his own defence; but he has no right to handcuff a prisoner except he has attempted to escape, or unless it becomes necessary to prevent his escape. A constable may arrest a stranger guilty of profane cursing and swearing, but if known he must lay an information. He may arrest, on complaint being made to him, any person who threatens the death of another person. He may arrest a person for selling wares or goods, or for being guilty of engaging in any unlawful sports, on the Sabbath. He may also arrest without a warrant any one playing with false dice, or committing any other indictable fraud affecting the public; or for keeping a common gaming house, as such is a nuisance and misdemeanor. He may also arrest on his own view for cock fighting or prize fighting; night-walking women, who behave themselves disorderly, and men who frequent bawdy houses. It will thus be seen the extensive powers which constables have, as conservators of the public peace. But constables should take care that these powers are exercised warily and circumspectly, on good and reasonable grounds, and not tyrannically or capriciously, or for the gratification of personal pique or malice. If a constable is guilty of an overt act, rashly exceeds his duty, or is moved by any corrupt influence, he may render himself liable to be punished for misdemeanor or otherwise. While he should always exercise his great authority with firmness and decision, he should also do so without dishonest or corrupt motive of any kind.

The duties of a constable are of various discriptions. He must execute within the county, or other district, or city, or town, for which he has been appointed, all legal process of the magistrates having jurisdiction which may be directed to him, or given to him, for execution. If he arrests under a warrant he should certify what he has done on the back of it with the date, but he should not give up the warrant as it is his protection. He should make outcry and pursue, until arrested any one resisting his authority by force. He should call out and give warning to the public at any large gathering, if he sees thieves or suspicious characters around. He should see to the welfare and safety of the community during daytime, and keep watch at night. He should use all reasonable force to keep back a crowd from a place to be kept clear, but he should not strike any person to compel him to stand back, when the pressure from behind is so great that he cannot do so. He should carefully observe all the regulations laid down for his guidance by the high constable, or other superior officer. A constable has no right to execute a warrant out of the county or district of the justice who grants it, unless backed by a justice of his own district in which the offender is found. If a warrant be directed generally to "*bring before me or some other justice of the peace,*" he may carry the prisoner before any justice whom he pleases in that district; but not if the warrant directs that the prisoner "*be brought before me.*" A constable is bound to aid and assist in the appraisement and sale of goods, or other chattels, distrained for rent, and may swear the appraiser. He is also to aid landlords in seizing as a distress for rent, goods fraudulently removed to avoid such distress, and to break open any outhouse or enclosure where they may be concealed. But if they are concealed in a dwelling house, oath must first be made before a magistrate as to the fact, or suspicion, of concealment, before the premises can be broken open. A constable making a distress under a justice's warrant is bound to exhibit the same on demand if he is a stranger, but if known to the party on whom the seizure is made, he need only acquaint him with the substance of his warrant. In cases of necessity a constable has the right to command assistance from any person in the vicinity, and such person is bound to give that assistance at his peril, as a good subject of the Queen. But whatever powers he may have to appoint a deputy in England, it appears that he has no such power in this country, in the absence of any local statute giving him authority to do so; and in the event of his not being able to perform his duties in person, from sickness or otherwise, he should procure the assistance of another constable.— When a constable receives a warrant, or other process, to execute, he is bound to do so with all due care and diligence. If he refuses to act under the order of the justice, or to do his duty otherwise, he renders himself liable to be prosecuted for misdemeanor. If a constable duly appointed, and notified of his appointment, refuses to take the necesssary oath, or refuses to go before a justice to take that oath, he is guilty of a misdemeanor, and may be indicted therefor at the Assizes or General Sessions. He is also bound to attend, when ordered to do so by the sitting justice, any court held by him under the Summary Conviction Act, or for any ministerial purpose; and to obey all legal orders issued by such justice as to the good regulation of the court, conveying prisoners to gaol, or doing any other act or acts for promoting the ends of justice, and the requirements of the law. He is also bound to execute all precepts directed to him by coroners, to summons jurors at inquests, to notify the coroner in good time when any death occurs from violent and unfair means in his district, and to attend at any inquest when ordered to do so. Such are the general duties of the ordinary constable, appointed by the magistrates of the district. In cities and towns police constables will have many additional duties to perform under special applying statutes, by-laws, and regulations made by the local authorities, which they will have to acquaint themselves with.— Special constables who are merely called on to perform some particular act, such as to keep the peace in case of expected riot, or to put down an existing riot, or do some other thing for the preservation of life and property, should always receive full instructions as to their special duty from the authorities appointing them. We have merely to say that during the term of their temporary authority, they are armed with all the powers of the regular constable.

We may add that the law provides all reasonable indemnity and protection for any mistakes or overt acts that a constable may unwittingly commit in the honest and faithful execution of his duty, and for any person aiding him. And so long as no corrupt, or unnecessarily cruel or tyrannical act, is committed by him; judges and juries will take the most lenient view of his conduct. Actions against him for anything done in the execution of his duty must be brought within his own district, and within six months; and the law otherwise throws its protecting shield around him in various ways.

With certain exemptions every male of the age of twenty-one years, and under sixty, being an inhabitant of the district, or municipality, for which he is chosen, may be appointed to the office of constable, and is compellable, under certain pains and penalties, to execute its duties. The exemptions from appointment are confined chiefly to persons filling public offices of one kind or another, or who are engaged in occupations incompatible with the duties of a constable. They embrace Judges, Magistrates, Coroners, Ministers of religion, Barristers and Attorneys, Doctors, Army and Militia officers and Non-commissioned officers, Firemen, Volunteer corps, Foreigners, and the Prosecutor of any felon to conviction. No person keeping a public house should be appointed to the office of constable.

In the Province of Ontario, Chapter 82 of the Revised Statutes makes the following provisions as to constables :—

1. The Justices of the Peace may from time to time, at any sitting or adjourned sitting of the Court of General Sessions of the Peace, appoint a County High Constable, and a sufficient number of fit and proper persons to act as Constables in each Township, incorporated Village, Police Village and place within their County, and may, in like manner, from time to time in their discretion, dismiss any Constable so appointed.

2. The persons so appointed shall, before entering on the duties of their office, take and subscribe the following oath, which any Justice of the Peace may administer :

"I   , having been appointed High Constable (or Constable) for the County (or United Counties) of   do solemnly swear that I will truly, faithfully and impartially perform the duties appertaining to the said office, according to the best of my skill and ability : So help me God."

3. Every Constable so appointed, and having taken the aforesaid oath, shall continue in office at least one year, and shall further continue in office from year to year without re-appointment, unless he claims exemption from serving as such Constable, in which case he shall be released at any time after the end of the first year.

4. To prevent injurious delay in appointing County Constables, arising from the long intervals between the sittings of the Courts of General Sessions of the Peace, any Judge of a County Court may, at any time, and from time to time, appoint any person or persons to be a Constable or Constables for the County or United Counties of the County Court of which such Judge is a Judge.

5. The Judge making any such appointment shall forthwith notify the Clerk of the Peace thereof.

6. The Clerk of the Peace shall report every such appointment to the next Court of General Sessions of the Peace which is holden after he receives notice thereof from the said Judge, and unless at such Court such appointment is revoked by order duly passed in Sessions, the same shall continue as if the same had originally been made at such Court.

7. Any Constable so appointed by a Judge as aforesaid shall during the continuance of such appointment, have the same authority and privileges and be subject to the same liability and the performance of the same duties as if originally appointed by the Court of General Sessions of the Peace.

8. The Judge of the County Court may suspend from office any

County Constable for any period, in the discretion of the Judge, but not beyond one week after the time appointed for the next sittings of the General Sessions of the Peace ; such suspension shall be by notice in writing ; and in case the Judge considers the suspended officer deserving of dismissal, such Judge shall, immediately after suspending him, report the case fully to the Clerk of the Peace for submission to the Justices at the next General Sessions of the Peace ; and the Justices may dismiss such officer, or direct him to be restored to his office, after the period of his suspension has expired, or after such further period of suspension as they may order.

9. The Lieutenant-Governor may appoint, either permanently or for such a period as he may think fit, persons to be Provincial Constables, and every person so appointed shall, while he holds office, be a Constable of every County and District in Ontario, and, as such, shall have authority to act in any part of the Province.

10. The Lieutenant-Governor may, from time to time, appoint Constables for any Provisional Judicial, Temporary Judicial or Territorial District, or Provisional County, or for any portion of the territory of Ontario not attached to a County for ordinary municipal and judicial purpose.

The following extracts from Chapter 83 of the Revised Statutes for Ontario, will be found very useful to Special Constables :—

1. In case it is made to appear to any two or more Justices of the Peace of any territorial division in this Province, upon the oath of any credible witness, that any tumult, riot or felony has taken place or is continuing, or may be reasonably apprehended in any territorial division or place situate within the limits for which the said respective Justices usually act, and in case such Justices are of opinion that the ordinary officers appointed for preserving the peace are not sufficient for the preservation of the peace and for the protection of the inhabitants and the security of the property in any such territorial division or place as aforesaid, then and in every such case such Justices or any two or more Justices acting for the same limits may nominate and appoint, by precept in writing under their hands, so many as they think fit of the householders or other persons not legally exempt from serving in the office of Constable, residing in such territorial division or place as aforesaid, or in the neighbourhood thereof, to act as Special Constables for such time and in such manner as to the said Justices respectively seems necessary for the preservation of the public peace and for the protection of the inhabitants, and the security of property in such territorial division or place.

2. The Justices of the Peace who appoint Special Constables by virtue of this Act, or any one of them, or any other Justice of the Peace acting for the same limit, may administer to any person so appointed the following oath, that is to say :

"I, A. B., do swear that I will well and truly serve our Sovereign
" Lady the Queen in the office of Special Constable for the

"of   , without favour or affection, malice or ill-will;
"and that I will to the best of my power, cause the peace to be
"kept and preserved, and will prevent all offences against the per-
"sons and properties of Her Majesty's subjects; and that while
"I continue to hold the said office, 1 will to the best of my skill and
"knowledge discharge all the duties thereof faithfully according to
"law : So help me God."

3. In case it is deemed necessary to nominate and appoint Special Constables as aforesaid, notice of the nomination and appointment, and of the circumstances which rendered it expedient, shall be forthwith transmitted by the Justice making such nomination and appointment to the Secretary of the Province.

4. The Justices of the Peace who appoint any Special Constables under this Act, or any two of them, or the Justices acting for the limit within which such Special Constables have been called out, may, at a special session of such last mentioned Justices, or the major part of such last mentioned Justices, at such special session, make such orders and regulations as may from time to time be necessary and expedient for rendering such Special Constables more efficient for the preservation of the public peace, and may remove any such Special Constable from his office for any misconduct or neglect of duty therein.

5. Every Special Constable appointed under this act shall, not only within the territorial division or place for which he has been appointed, but also throughout the entire jurisdiction of the Justices who appoint him, have, exercise and enjoy all such powers, authorities, advantages and immunities, and be liable to all such duties and responsibilities, as any Constable duly appointed has by virtue of any law or statute whatsoever.

6. Where any Special Constable appointed under this Act are serving within any territorial division or place, and two or more Justices of the Peace of any adjoining territorial division or place, make it appear, to the satisfaction of any two or more Justices of the Peace, acting for the limits within which such Special Constables are serving, that extraordinary circumstances exist which render it expedient that the said Special Constables should act in such adjoining territorial division or place, then and in every such case the said last mentioned Justices may, if they think fit, order all or any of the said Special Constables to act in such adjoining territorial division or place in such manner as to the said last mentioned Justices seems meet.

7. Every such Special Constable, during the time he so acts in such adjoining territorial division or place, shall have, exercise and enjoy all such powers, authorities, advantages and immunities, and be liable to the same duties and responsibilities as if he were acting within the territorial division or place for which he was originally appointed.

8. The Justices of the Peace acting for the limits within which such Special Constable have been called out to serve, may, at a special session to be held for that purpose, or the major part of the Justices at such special session, may from time to time order such reasonable allowances for their trouble, loss of time and expenses,

not exceeding one dollar per diem, to be paid to such Special Constables who have so served or are then serving, as to such Justices or to such major part of them seems proper.

9. The Justices so ordering shall make every order for the payment of such allowances and expenses upon the Treasurer of the territorial division or other municipal division within which such Special Constables have been called out to serve, and such Treasurer shall pay the same out of any moneys in his hands at the time, and the said Treasurer shall be allowed the same in his accounts, and the sum shall be provided for by the Council of the territorial division or other municipal division wherein the expense arises.

12. Every such Special Constable shall, within one week after the expiration of his office, or after he has ceased to hold or exercise the same pursuant to this Act, deliver over to his successor, if any such has been appointed, or otherwise to such person and at such time and place as may be directed by any Justice of the Peace acting for the limits within which such Special Constable has been called out, every staff, weapon and other article which has been provided for such Special Constable under this Act ; and if any such Special Constable omits or refuses so to do, he shall, on conviction thereof before two Justices of the Peace, forfeit and pay for such offence such sum of money, not exceeding eight dollars, as to the convicting Justices seems meet.

13. If any person being appointed a Special Constable as aforesaid refuses to take the oath hereinbefore mentioned when thereunto required by the Justices of the Peace who so appointed him, or by any two of them, or by any other two Justices of the Peace acting for the same limits, he may be convicted thereof forthwith before the said Justices so requiring him, and shall forfeit and pay such sum of money not exceeding twenty dollars as to the convicting Justices seems meet.

14. If any person, being appointed a Special Constable as aforesaid, neglects or refuses to appear for the purpose of taking the said oath at the time and place for which he has been summoned, he may be convicted thereof before the Justices who appointed him, or any two of them, or before any other two Justices of the Peace acting for the same limits, and shall forfeit and pay such sum of money, not exceeding twenty dollars, as to the convicting Justices seems meet, unless such person proves to the satisfaction of the said Justices that he was prevented by sickness or some unavoidable accident which in the judgment of the said Justices is a sufficient excuse.

15. If any person having been appointed a Special Constable as aforesaid, and being called upon to serve, neglects or refuses to serve as such Special Constable, or to obey such lawful orders or directions as may be given to him for the performance of the duties of his office, the person so offending shall, on conviction thereof before any two Justices of the Peace, forfeit and pay for every such neglect or refusal such sum of money, not exceeding twenty dollars, as to the said Justices seems meet, unless such person proves to the satisfaction of the said Justices that he was prevented

by sickness or some unavoidable accident in the judgment of the said Justices constituting a sufficient excuse.

Under the separate heads of Landlord and Tenant and Coroner, Constables will find additional information as to their duties in certain cases.

Chapter 16 of the Revised Statutes of Ontario enacts as follows :—

27. No Sheriff, Deputy Sheriff, Bailiff or Constable shall directly or indirectly purchase any goods or chattels, lands or tenements by him exposed to sale under execution.

28. If any Bailiff or Constable entrusted with the execution of any writ, warrant, process, mesne or final, wilfully misconducts himself in the execution of the same, or wilfully makes any false return to any such writ, warrant or process, unless by the consent of the party in whose favor the process issued, he shall answer in damages to any party aggrieved by such misconduct or false return.

If any Bailiff or Constable entrusted with the execution of any writ, warrant or process, mesne or final, shall wilfully misconduct himself in the execution of the same or wilfully make any false return to such writ, warrant or process, unless by the consent of the party in whose favor the process may have issued, he shall be guilty of a misdemeanor, and upon conviction thereof before any Court of competent jurisdiction, shall be liable to fine and imprisonment, in the discretion of the Court, and shall answer in damages to any party aggrieved by such misconduct or false return.

Constable's Fees in the Province of Ontario; Vide Revised Statutes, Chap. 84.

1. Arrest of each individual upon a warrant, (*to be paid out of the County funds, or by the party, as the case may be*) $1 50
2. Serving summons or subpœna, (*to be paid out of the County funds, or by the party, as the case may be*).... 25
3. Mileage to serve summons, subpœna or warrant, (*to be paid out of the County funds, or by the party, as the case may be*)................................... 10
4. Mileage when service cannot be effected, upon proof of due diligence, (*do.   do.*).................... 10
5. Mileage taking prisoner to gaol, exclusive of disbursements necessarily expended in his conveyance........ 10
6. Attending Justices on summary trials, or on examination of prisoners charged with crime, for each day necessarily employed in one or more cases, when not engaged more than four hours....................... 1 00
7. Do. when engaged more than four hours............. 1 50
8. Attending Assizes or Sessions each day.............. 1 50
9. Mileage travelling to attend Assizes, Sessions, or before Justices, (*when public conveyances can be taken, only reasonable disbursements to be allowed*)............. 10

10. Summoning Jury for Coroner's inquest, including attending at inquest, and all services in respect thereof, if held on same day as Jury summoned...... ...... 2 00
11. Attending each adjournment thereof, if not engaged more than four hours.............................. 1 00
12. Do. if engaged more than four hours.............. 1 50
13. Serving summons or subpœna to attend before Coroner, (subject to No. 10).............................. 25
14. Mileage serving same............................. ... 10
15. Exhuming body under Coroner's warrant.... .... 2 00
16. Reburying same................................. 2 00
17. Serving distress warrant, and returning same.... .... 1 50
18. Advertising under distress warrant................... 1 00
19. Travelling to made distress, or to search for goods to make distress, when no goods are found... 10
20. Appraisements, whether by one Appraiser or more, ...*two cents in the dollar on the value of the goods.*
21. Catalogue sale and commission, and delivery of goods, *five cents in the dollar on the net produce of the goods.*
22. Executing search warrant......................... .. 1 50
23. Serving notices on constables, when personally served 50

CORONERS :— THEIR POWERS AND DUTIES.

The office of Coroner is among the most ancient known to English Law. In the fourth year of the reign of Edward I a statute was passed respecting the duties of coroners, which were then of a much more comprehensive and general character than they are now. The Coroner's Court is one of Record ; and according to the Common Law he is to enquire when any person dies in prison, or comes to a violent or sudden death by accident or mischance, or by his own hand, or by the hands of others ; and this he is only entitled to do upon view of the body, *(super visum corpus.)* The Coroner's duties being partly judicial and partly ministerial cannot be executed by deputy, and must be performed personally. Sudden violent deaths may occur (1) *by the unusual visitation of God*, but not by ordinary sickness ; (2 *by misfortune*, where no other person had a hand in it, as if a man fell from a house; or a horse, or a waggon; (3) by one's own hand as *felo de se*, or suicide; (4) by the hand of another in self defence, or accidentally, or by mischance, or as manslaughter, or as murder.

It is clearly agreed that an inquest can only be held by a Coroner on view of the body; and that an inquest taken otherwise is illegal and void. When a body cannot be found, or is so decomposed as to be unrecognizable, the Coroner without a special commission from the Crown cannot take the inquest. In such cases the enquiry into the cause of death should be made by a Justice, or Justices, of the Peace. When the body of any person coming to a violent death is found, it is an indictable offence at Common Law to bury it without sending for the Coroner. And a Coroner may within convenient time take up a dead body out of the grave in order to view it and hold an inquest, when suspicions of foul play make such a course necessary. The Coroner may enquire of accessories before the fact, but not of accessories after the fact. Where there is no pretence for supposing that the deceased died otherwise than by a natural death, such as fever, appoplexy, or other ordinary visitation of God, an inquest ought not to be held. If a prisoner comes to an untimely death by any act of unnecessary cruelty or violence on the part of a gaoler it would be murder, and should be enquired into; and all deaths in prison should be enquired into. Coroners are not to obtrude themselves into private families unless on well-grounded suspicions of foul play; nor where there are no good grounds for supposing that the deceased died otherwise than by a natural death. If a lunatic kills himself it is not suicide unless it can be shown that he did so in a lucid interval. In addition to their ordinary functions Coroners are empowered to execute, ministerially, civil process upon any disability of the Sheriff of the County.

But as exigencies of this kind very rarely arise in this country, and should only be exercised on the advice of competent counsel, it is unnecessary to allude to them at any length in a popular work of this kind.

At Common Law where any man kills himself, or is by misfortune slain, or is killed by a horse or other animal, a cart or any moving thing, that which causes death becomes forfeited to the Crown as a deodand, or personal chattel, to be devoted to pious uses. (*Deo dandum*). It will accordingly be the duty of the coroner to impound the same, and to advise with the County Attorney, or other proper Crown Officer, as to the proper disposition to be made thereof.

Statutes of the Dominion, and of several of its Provinces, passed at different times, have regulated and modified the duties of Coroners, as prescribed by the Common Law. In 1869, 32-33 Vic., Chap 30,* of the Dominion Statutes, enacts for all Canada touching Coroners as follows:—

60. Every Coroner, upon any inquisition taken before him, whereby any person is indicted for manslaughter or murder, or as an accessory to murder before the fact, shall, in presence of the party accused, if he can be apprehended, put in writing the evidence given to the jury before him, or as much thereof as may be material, giving to the party accused full opportunity of cross-examination; and the Coroner shall have authority to bind by recognizance all such persons as know or declare any thing material touching the manslaughter or murder, or the offence of being accessory to murder, to appear at the next Court of Oyer and Terminer, or Gaol Delivery, or other Court or term or sitting of a Court, at which the trial is to be, then and there to prosecute or give evidence against the party charged; and every such Coroner shall certify and subscribe the evidence, and all the recognizances, and also the inquisition before him taken, and shall deliver the same to the proper Officer of the Court at the time and in the manner specified in the thirty-eighth section of this Act.

61. When any person has been committed for trial by any Justice or Justices, or Coroner, the Prisoner, his Counsel, Attorney or Agent, may notify the committing Justice or Justices, or Coroner, that he will so soon as council can be heard, move one of Her

---

* Subsequently extended to Prince Edward Island by 40 Vic. Chap. 4.

Majesty's Courts of Superior Criminal jurisdiction for the Province in which such person stands committed, or one of the Judges thereof, or in the Province of Quebec, a Judge of the Court of Queen's Bench, or of the Superior Court, or in the Provinces of Ontario or New Brunswick, the Judge of the County Court if it is intended to apply to such Judge under the fifty-third section of this Act, for an order to the Justices of the Peace, or Coroner for the Territorial Division where such Prisoner is confined, to admit such Prisoner to bail, whereupon such committing Justice or Justices, or Coroner, shall, with all convenient expedition, transmit to the office of the Clerk of the Crown, or the Chief Clerk of the Court, or the Clerk of the County Court or other proper officer (as the case may be,) close under the hand and seal of one of them, a certified copy of all informations, examinations, and other evidences, touching the offence wherewith the Prisoner has been charged, together with a copy of the warrant of commitment and inquest, if any such there be, and the packet containing the same shall be handed to the person applying therefor, in order to its transmission, and it shall be certified on the outside thereof to contain the information touching the case in question.

62. Upon such application to any such Court or Judge as in the last preceding section mentioned, the same order touching the prisoner being bailed or continued in custody, shall be made as if the party were brought up upon a *Habeas Corpus*.

63. If any Justice or Coroner neglects or offends in any thing contrary to the true intent and meaning of any of the provisions of the sixtieth and following sections of this Act, the Court to whose Officer any such examination, information, evidence, bailment, recognizance, or inquisition ought to have been delivered, shall, upon examination and proof of the offence, in a summary manner, set such fine upon every such Justice or Coroner as the Court thinks meet.

64. The provisions of this Act relating to Justices and Coroners, shall apply to the Justices and Coroners not only of Districts and Counties at large, but also of all other Territorial Divisions and Jurisdictions.

65. The words "Territorial Division," whenever used in this Act shall mean County, Union of Counties, Township, City, Town, Parish or other Juridical Division or place to which the context may apply.

In the Province of Ontario Coroners are appointed by the Lieutenant Governor for every County, City, Town, or Provisional or other District, under authority of Chapter 79 of the Revised Statutes, which act also provides as follows :—

2. Except as provided in the next section, no inquest shall be held on the body of any deceased person by any Coroner until it has been made to appear to such Coroner that there is reason to believe that the deceased died from violence or unfair means, or by culpable or negligent conduct, either of himself or of others, under

such circumstances as require investigation, and not through mere accident or mischance.

3. Upon the death of any prisoner, the Warden, Gaoler, Keeper or Superintendent of any Penitentiary, Gaol, Prison, House of Correction, Lock-up house, or House of Industry in which such prisoner dies, shall immediately give notice thereof to some Coroner of the County, City or Town in which such death has taken place, and such Coroner shall proceed forthwith to hold an inquest upon the body.

4. If any person, having been duly summoned as a juror to serve, or as a witness to give evidence upon any Coroner's inquest, does not, after being openly called three times, appear and serve as such juror, or appear and give evidence as such witness, the Coroner may impose a fine upon the delinquent person not exceeding four dollars; and shall thereupon make out and sign a certificate, containing the name, residence and trade or calling of such person, the amount of the fine imposed, and the cause of the fine, and shall transmit such certificate to the Clerk of the Peace of the County in which such person resides, on or before the first day of the General Sessions of the Peace then next ensuing, and shall cause a copy of such certificate to be served upon such person by leaving it at his residence, within a reasonable time after the inquest.

5. The fine so certified shall be estreated, levied and applied in like manner, and subject to the like powers, provisions and penalties in all respects, as if it had been part of the fines imposed at such General Sessions.

6. Wherever, upon the summoning or holding of any Coroner's inquest, the Coroner finds that the deceased was attended during his last illness, or at his death, by any legally qualified medical practitioner, the Coroner may issue his order for the attendance of such practitioner as a witness at such inquest in the form following:

Coroner's Inquest at   , upon the body of   .

By virtue of this my order, as Coroner for   , you are required to appear before me and the Jury, at   , on the   day of   , at   o'clock, to give evidence touching the cause of the death of   [*and when the witness is required to make or assist at a* post mortem *examination, add:* and make or assist in making a *post mortem* examination of the body, with (*or* without) an analysis (*as the case may be*), and report thereon at the said Inquest.]

Signed,   C. P.,
Coroner.

7. If the Coroner finds that the deceased was not so attended, he may issue his order for the attendance of any legally qualified medical practitioner being at the time in actual practice in or near the place where the death happened ; and the Coroner may, at any time before the termination of the inquest, direct a *post mortem* examination, with or without any analysis of the contents of the

stomach or intestines, by the medical witness summoned to attend at such inquest; but if any person states upon oath before the Coroner, that in his belief the death was caused partly or entirely by the improper or negligent treatment of a medical practitioner or other person, such medical practitioner or other person shall not assist at the *post mortem* examination.

8. Wherever it appears to the majority of the jurymen sitting at any Coroner's inquest, that the cause of death has not been satisfactorily explained by the evidence of the medical practitioner or other witnesses examined in the first instance, such majority may name to the Coroner, in writing, any other legally qualified medical practitioner or practitioners, and require the Coroner to issue his order in the form hereinbefore mentioned for the attendance of such last mentioned medical practitioner or practitioners, as a witness or witnesses, and for the performance of such *post mortem* examination as in the last preceding section mentioned, and whether before performed or not.

[And if the Coroner refuses to issue such order he is guilty of a misdemeanor, and shall be punishable by a fine not exceeding forty dollars, or by imprisonment not exceeding one month, or by both fine and imprisonment.]

9. Where any legally qualified medical practitioner has attended in obedience to any such order as aforesaid, he shall receive for such attendance, if without a *post mortem* examination, five dollars; if with a *post mortem* examination, without an analysis of the contents of the stomach or intestines, ten dollars; if with such analysis, twenty dollars; together with the sum of twenty cents per mile for each mile he has to travel to and from such inquest, such travel to be proved by his own oath to the Coroner, who may administer the same.   *   *   *   *   *   (Struck out by 42 Vic., Chap. 17)

10. Where any such order for the attendance of any medical practitioner has been personally served, or if not personally served, has been received by him or left at his residence in sufficient time for him to have obeyed such order, and he has not obeyed the same, he shall forfeit the sum of forty dollars upon complaint by the Coroner who held or by any two of the Jury who sat on the inquest, made before any two Justices of the Peace of the County where the inquest has been held, or of the County where such medical practitioner resides; and such Justices shall proceed to hear and adjudicate upon the complaint; and if such medical practitioner does not show a sufficient reason for not having obeyed such order, they shall enforce the said penalty by distress and sale of the offender's goods in the same manner as they are empowered to do by *The Act respecting Summary Convictions before Justices of the Peace.*

11. Nothing herein contained shall effect any power otherwise by law vested in any Coroner for compelling any person to appear and give evidence before him, or for punishing any person for contempt of Court, in not so appearing and giving evidence or otherwise.

12. No inquisition found upon or by any Coroner's inquest, nor any judgment recorded upon or by virtue of any such inquisition,

shall be quashed, stayed or reversed for want of the averment therein of any matter unnecessary to be proved, nor for the omission of any technical words of mere form; and in all cases of technical defect, either of the Superior Courts of Common Law, or any Judge thereof, or any Judge of Assize or Gaol Delivery, may, upon any such inquisition being called in question before them or him, order the same to be amended.

13. Every Coroner shall forthwith after an inquisition found before him return the same and every recognizance taken before him, with the written information (if any) and the depositions and statements (if any) of the accused, to the Crown Attorney of the County in which the inquisition has been found.

14. Every Coroner shall, on or before the first day of January in every year, return to the Provincial Treasurer a list of the inquests held by him during the preceding year, together with the findings of the Juries.

The foregoing act was amended in 1879 by 42 Vic., Chapter 17 (Ontario) as follows :—

Whereas it is expedient that in all cases where inquests are held by County Coroners, upon bodies of deceased persons who have come by their deaths within cities, that the allowance to medical practitioners who have been summoned by the Coroner to attend the inquest, should be borne by the city in which the inquest is held :

Therefore Her Majesty, by and with the advice and consent of the Legislative Assembly of the Province of Ontario, enacts as follows :—

1. The Revised Statutes of Ontario, chapter seventy-nine, section nine, is amended by striking out all the words of the said section after the word "same" in the ninth line, and inserting the following words in lieu thereof, "And the Coroner shall make his order on the treasurer of the county when the inquest is held in the County, and on the treasurer of the city when death occurs and the inquest is held in a city, in favour of such medical practitioner, for the payment of such fees or remuneration, and such treasurer shall pay the sum mentioned in such order to such medical witness, out of any funds he may then have in the County or City Treasury."

In 1880 43 Vic., Chap. 11 (Ontario) enacts respecting Coroners' Inquests :—

1. No fees shall be claimable by any coroner in respect of an inquest, unless, prior to the issuing of his warrant for summoning the jury, he shall have made a declaration in writing under oath (which oath may be administered by any justice of the peace or commissioner for taking affidavits in the Superior Courts, and shall be returned and filed with the inquisition), stating that from information received by such coroner, he is of opinion that there is reason for believing that the deceased did not come to his death from natural causes or from mere accident or mischance, but came to his death from violence or unfair means, or culpable or negligent conduct of

others, under circumstances requiring investigation by a coroner's inquest.

2. The preceding section shall not apply to any inquest held upon the written request of the county attorney; or to any inquest held in the Districts of Muskoka, Parry Sound, Thunder Bay and Nipissing, upon the written request of a stipendiary magistrate; or to any inquest held under the third section of the Revised Statute respecting Coroners, or under other similar provisions.

3. The written request of the jury for a second medical witness referred to in section eight of chapter seventy-nine of the Revised Statutes of Ontario, shall be attached by the coroner to the order given by him on the treasurer of the county for the payment of the fees of such second medical witness.

4. Subject to the provisions of the Revised Statutes of Ontario, chapter one hundred and forty-three, any unclaimed human body found dead within the limits of a city, town, incorporated village or township, shall be buried at the expense of the corporation of such city, town, village or township, but such corporation may recover such expenses from the estate of the deceased.

Under the provisions of Chap. 196 of the Revised Statutes of Ontario, Coroners are empowered to hold investigations into the origin of any fire occurring within their jurisdiction, and to impannel a jury for that purpose. This act provides (Sec. 8) that the party requiring the investigation shall pay the expenses attending it. If required by a Municipality, the requisition must be under the hand and seal of the Mayor or Reeve, or other head officer, or at least of two members of the Council; and such requisition must be based on strong special and public reasons, otherwise the Municipality will not be liable for expenses. The fees of a Coroner under this Act is $10 per day.

Chapter 143 Sec. 2, of Revised Statutes of Ontario, provides that Coroners shall deliver unclaimed bodies on which inquests have been held, to public teachers of Anatomy or Surgery. Chapter 84 provides for fees of Coroners as follows:

1. Precept to summon Jury.................................... $ 50
2. Empanelling a Jury.. 1 00
3. Summons for witnesses each............................ 25
4. Information or examination of each witness...... 25
5. Taking every recognizance................................ 50
6. Necessary travel to take an inquest, per mile.... 20
7. Taking inquisition and making return................ 4 00
8. Every warrant.. 1 00

Jurors' Fees.

The law makes no provision for the payment of any fees to jurors.

Proceedings by the Coroner.

When the Coroner receives notice of a violent death, casualty, or misadventure, which regularly ought to be given by the constable of the parish, place or township, where the body lies dead, he is then to issue his precept, or warrant, to summon a jury to appear at a particular time and place named, to enquire when, how, and by what means the deceased came by his death; which warrant is directed to the constables or constables of the parish, place or precinct, where the party lies dead.

Form of a Warrant.

Province,
County of
To Wit :
} To the constables and peace officers of the township of
in the County of   .

By virtue of my office, these are in her Majesty's name to charge and command you, that on sight hereof, you summon and warn twenty-four able and sufficient men of your township, personally to be and appear before me, on the   day of   at   o'clock in the forenoon of the same day, at the house of A. B., called or known by the name or sign of the   , situate in the said township, then and there to do and execute all such things as shall be given them in charge, on behalf of our sovereign lady the Queen, touching the death of R. F., (*) and for so doing, this shall be your sufficient warrant; and that you also attend at the time or place above mentioned, to make a return of the names of the persons whom you shall have so summoned, and further, to do and execute such other matters as shall be then and there enjoined on you. And have you then and there this war-

---

(*) Or if unknown they say "of a man (or woman), male, or female, infant child, whose name is unknown."

rant. Given under my hand and seal, this   day
of   , 18 .

G. H.,   [L. S.]
Coroner.

If there be not sufficient jurors in the place, the coroner may summon them from the adjoining township or parish.

The coroner shall furnish a sufficient number of blank summonses to the constable, for service by him upon the jurors, pursuant to the above warrant.

Form of the Summons.

Province,   } To R. M. of the township of
County of   }   , in the County of   ,
   To Wit: } yeoman.

By virtue of a warrant, under the hand and seal of G. H., gentleman, one of Her Majesty's Coroners for the said county, you are hereby summoned to be and appear before him as a juryman, on the   day of   at   of the clock in the forenoon of the same day, at the house of   , known by the sign of the   in the township of   in the said county, then and there to enquire in Her Majesty's name touching the death of R. F., and further to do and execute such other matters and things as shall be then and there given you in charge, and not to depart without leave. Herein fail not, at your peril. Dated the   day of   18 .

E. F., Constable.

On the day appointed, the coroner attends, and having received the return of the jurors, and precept, &c., the first thing he does, is to direct the officer to open the court by proclamation, viz., by proclaiming "Oyez" three times, and to repeat after him as follows :—

"You, good men of this county, summoned to appear here this day, to inquire for our sovereign lady the Queen, when, how and by what means R. F. came to his death, answer to your names as you shall be called, every man at the first call, upon the pain and peril that shall fall thereon."

The coroner then proceeds to call over the jury by name, marking the names of such as appear in the list. There must be twelve at the least to constitute a jury, but it is usual to swear thirteen or more; the jurors then proceed to elect their foreman; when done, he is called to the book and sworn first, the coroner at the same time saying to the rest of the jurors, " Gentlemen, hearken to your foreman's oath: for the oath he is to take on his part you are severally to observe and keep on your part."

Foreman's Oath.

" You shall diligently inquire and true presentment make of all such matters and things as shall be here given you in charge on behalf of our sovereign lady the Queen, touching the death of R. F. now lying dead, of whose body you shall have a view; you shall present no man for hatred, malice or ill-will, nor spare any through fear, favour or affection; but a true verdict give according to the evidence. So help you God."

The rest of the jurors are then sworn thus, four at a time.

" The same oath your foreman has taken on his part, you and each of you are severally well and truly to observe and keep on your part. So help you God."

After they are sworn it is usual for the coroner to give a charge acquainting them with the purpose of the meeting, as thus:

" Gentlemen, you are sworn to enquire on behalf of the Queen, how and by what means R. F. came to his death; your duty is to take a view of the body of the deceased, wherein you will be careful to observe if there be any marks of violence thereon, from which and on the examination of the witnesses intended to be produced before you, you will endeavour to discover the cause of his death, so as to be able to return me a true verdict on this occasion."

When the charge is finished the coroner goes with the jury to take a view, and examine the body of the deceased. As soon as the view is taken it is usual for the coroner again to call them over, and add to his former charge some necessary observations he has made on view of the body; and add, " that he shall now proceed to hear and take down the evidence respecting the fact, to which he must crave particular attention." Particular charges are not necessary, but in particular cases arising from the fact or in the course of evidence, such as lunacy, *felo de se*, deodand, flight, forfeiture, &c. The deodand requires no other charge than of a value to be put upon what caused the death, and of whose property and in whose possession. As to the particular charge in case of a flight, which induces a forfeiture, where the party charged is not forthcoming, it may be necessary to add something to the general charge, as thus :—

"Your charge will be further to inquire in what degree the party charged is guilty, whether of murder or manslaughter, or of a killing in his own defence ; if you find him guilty of murder or manslaughter, you are then to enquire what goods and chattels, lands and tenements he had at the time of the act committed or at any time since; if you find the fact to be a justifiable homicide, from inevitable necessity, or in defence of his own person, life, or property, or where a suspected person doth fly and resist the proper officer, and is from necessity slain because he could not be be otherwise taken : this flight and resistance presumes a guilt, and will incur a forfeiture ; and therefore you are to inquire whether, in either of the instances the party fled for it, this is a presumptive confession of the charge ; and you are then to enquire of his goods and chattels, but not lands or tenements, in the same manner as if you had found him guilty.

The latter charge may be given after the evidence taken, so as to have a perfect verdict.

If the inquiry be of the death of one man by another, and it be doubtful whether the wound be mortal or not, a surgeon should be present, to examine and show the wound.

After the general charge is given to the coroner, the officer then calls silence, and repeats after the coroner thus :—

"If any one can give evidence on behalf of our sovereign lady the Queen, when, how and by what means R. F. came to his death, let them come forth and they shall be heard."

The witness appearing, the coroner takes down his name, place of abode and occupation, and then the officer tenders to him the following oath :—

"The evidence you shall give to this inquest on behalf of our sovereign lady the Queen, touching the death of R. F., shall be the truth, the whole truth, and nothing but the truth, So help you God."

The evidence shall be taken down in writing, (*) and as nearly as possible in the words of the witness.

The examinations shall be entitled thus :—

Province, } Informations of witnesses severally taken and acknowledged on the behalf of our sovereign lady the Queen, touching the death of R. F. at the dwelling house of J. B., known by the name or sign of the   , in the township of   , in the county of   , on the   day of   in the   year of the reign of our sovereign lady Queen Victoria, &c. before G. H. Esquire, one of the coroners of the said county, on an inquisition then and there taken on view of the body of the said R. F., then and there lying dead, as follows, to wit :

A. B., of the township of   in the said county, yeoman, being sworn, saith, &c.

Before the witness signs his examination it should be read over to him, and he should be asked "if that is the whole of the evidence he can give." He then signs it to the right hand of the paper. The coroner generally asks the jurors before the witness signs, whether they have any questions for him to ask the witness ; and if any be asked, and the answer prove material, it should be added to the deposition. When the witness has signed his name to the examination taken, the coroner writes thus, to the left hand side : " taken and acknowledged the day, year, and at the place above mentioned, before G. H., coroner ;" or if there are several witnesses, then at the end of the last information, thus, "all the above informations were severally taken and acknowledged on the day and year and at the first place above mentioned, before G. H., coroner."

If the evidence be not all taken, the coroner may adjourn the jury to another day, to the same or another place, to take and receive other evidence, first binding the jurors in a recognizance to appear at the adjournment, thus :—

" Gentlemen, you acknowledge yourselves severally to owe to our sovereign lady the Queen, the sum of ten pounds, to be levied on your goods and chattels, lands and tene-

---

(*) And in case of "murder" or "manslaughter," in the presence of the party accused, if apprehended.

ments, for her Majesty's use, *upon condition* that you and each of you do personally appear here again (or other appointed place) on the   day of   instant, at   of the clock in the forenoon precisely, then and there to make further enquiry on behalf of our said lady the Queen, touching the death of the said R. F., of whose body you have already had the view. Are you all content?"

The coroner then adjourns the court, thus :

Gentlemen, the court doth dismiss you for this time : but requires you severally to appear here again (or at the adjourned place) on   the   day of   instant, at   of the clock in the forenoon precisely, upon a pain of £10 a man, on the condition contained in your recognizance entered into.

The coroner may in his discretion grant his warrant to bury the body of the deceased to prevent infection. Then the officer adjourns the court by making proclamation, thus :

"Oyez! oyez! oyez! all manner of persons who have any thing more to do at this court before the Queen's coroner for this county, may depart hence and give their attendance here again (*or other adjourned place*) on   the   day of   instant, at   of the clock in the forenoon precisely. God save the Queen.

The coroner will make a proper entry in his minutes of the recognizance and the adjournment, &c.

When the jury are met at the adjourned time and place, the officer opens the court by proclamation as in the first instance, with this addition :—

"And you, gentlemen of the jury, who have been empannelled and sworn on this inquest to enquire touching the death of R. F., severally answer to your names, and save your recognizance."

If foreigners are examined as witnesses, the coroner is to have an interpreter, who is to be sworn, thus :—

"You shall well and truly interpret unto the several witnesses here produced on behalf of our sovereign lady the Queen, touching the death of R. F., the oath that shall be administered to them, and also the questions and demands which shall be made to the witnesses by the court or jury, concerning the matters of this enquiry, and you shall well and truly interpret the answers which the witnesses shall thereunto give. *So help you God.*

He then interprets the oath to the witnesses, and their answers, which the coroner takes down in writing in the same way as other depositions.

After the additional evidence has been taken down in writing and subscribed by the witnesses, the coroner then sums up the whole of the evidence to the jury, at the same time explaining to them the law upon the case when necessary. He then desires the jury to consider their verdict. If they withdraw to consider their verdict, the officer is sworn to take care of them, thus:—

"You shall well and truly keep the jury upon this enquiry without meat, drink, or fire: you shall not suffer any person to speak to them, nor you yourself, unless it be to ask them whether they be agreed to their verdict, until they shall be agreed. So help you God."

The officer then takes them to a convenient room, and attends the door on the outside until they are agreed; when agreed they return, and the coroner calls over their names, and afterwards asks them if they be agreed in their verdict; if the foreman replies in the affirmative, the coroner asks them "who shall say for you?" to which they reply "our foreman." Then the coroner says, "Mr. Foreman, how do you find that R. F. come to his death, and by what means?"

The foreman then delivers the verdict, which the coroner records.

It seems that twelve at least must agree if there be no division; but if there be a division, the coroner then collects their voices, beginning with the last on the panel and rising upwards to the foreman, who declares last. The coroner collects the numbers and declares the majority into which the minority sinks, and the finding (which is to be given by the foreman) is from necessity taken and considered as the verdict of all. When the verdict is given, the coroner then draws up his inquisition in form, and at the foot affixes a seal for himself and each of the jurymen. The coroner and jurors then sign their names opposite the seals; to the coroner's name he adds "the office" thus, G. H. "*coroner.*"

The inquisition being thus completed, the coroner then addresses the jury as follows:—

"Gentlemen, hearken to your verdict, as delivered by you, and as I have recorded it. You find, &c." (*Here repeat the substance of the verdict.*)

If it is a case that will come to the assizes, the coroner binds all proper persons over in a recognizance to appear, prosecute and give evidence.

He should in the first place bind over one of the parties (generally the next of kin to the deceased) to appear and prosecute.

If the grand jury should return, "no bill," the party may still be arraigned and tried on the coroners inquisition.

The usual manner of taking a recognizance is by calling the parties by name and thus addressing them:

"You J. R., E. D., and G. B., severally acknowledge to owe to our sovereign lady the Queen, the sum of   each of good and lawful money of this province, to be made and levied upon your respective goods and chattels, lands and tenements, by way of recognizance, to Her Majesty's use if default shall be made in the condition following."

(*For condition see annexed form.*)

The coroner then says " are you content ?"

Form of Recognizance to appear and prosecute.

Province,   ⎫ Be it remembered that on the
County of   ⎬   day of   in the
  To wit :   ⎭ year of our Lord   J. R. of
yeoman, personally came before me one of Her Majesty's coroners for the said county, and acknowledged himself to owe to our sovereign lady the Queen, the sum of   , of good and lawful money of this province, to be made and levied on his goods and chattels, lands and tenements, by way of recognizance to her Majesty's use, if default shall be made in the condition following :

The condition of this recognizance is such, that if the above bounden J. R. do personally appear at the next session of general gaol delivery to be holden in and for the county of   , and shall then and there prefer, or cause to be preferred, to the grand jury, a bill of indictment against C. D. late of   , labourer, and now in custody for the wilful murder of, A. B. late of, &c., and that the said J. R. do then and there personally appear and give evidence upon such bill of indictment to the said grand jury, and in case the said bill of indictment be found by the grand jury a true bill, that then the said J. R. do personally appear at

the said general gaol delivery, and there prosecute the said
C. D. on such indictment, and do then and there give
evidence to the jury that shall pass on the trial of the said
C. D. touching the premises, and in case the said bill of indictment shall be returned not found, that then the said J.
R. do personally appear at the said general gaol delivery,
and then and there prosecute and give evidence to the jury
that shall pass on the trial of the said C. D. upon an
inquisition taken before me, one of Her Majesty's coroners
for the said county, on the view of the body of the said A.
B., and not depart the court without leave, then this recognizance to be void, otherwise to remain in full force. Taken
and acknowledged this   day of   before me.

G. H. Coroner.

Form of a Recognizance to appear and give Evidence.

Province,   ) Be it remembered that on the
County of   }   day of   in the year
        To Wit :) of our Lord   , S. R. of
yeoman, E. D. of   blacksmith, and G. B. of
mason, personally came before me, one of Her Majesty's
coroners for the said county, and severally acknowledge
themselves to owe to our sovereign lady the Queen the sum
of   of good and lawful money of this province, to be
made and levied on their respective goods and chattels,
lands and tenements, by way of recognizance, to Her
Majesty's use, if default shall be made in the condition
following :

"The condition of this recognizance is such, that if the
above bounden S. R., E. D. and G. B. do severally appear
at the next session of general gaol delivery to be holden in
and for the said county, and then and there give evidence
upon a bill of indictment to be then and there preferred to
the grand jury against C. D., late of the township of
in the said county, labourer, for the wilful murder of R. F.
late of   &c. And in case the bill of indictment be
found by the grand jury a true bill, then if they the said S.
R., E. D. and G. B. do severally appear and give evidence
to the jury that shall pass on the trial of the said C. D.
upon the said indictment ; and in case the said indictment

shall be returned by the grand jury aforesaid " not found," then if they the said S. R.; E. D. and G. B. do severally appear at the said session of general gaol delivery, and then and there give evidence to the jury that shall pass on the trial of the said C. D. upon an inquisition taken before me, one of Her Majesty's coroners for the said county, on the view of the body of the said R. F., and not depart the court without leave, then this recognizance to be void, otherwise to remain in full force.

Taken and acknowledged this   . day of before me

G. H., Coroner.

If one of the witnesses be a married woman, and the husband not present to enter into a recognizance for her, she is not to be bound in any sum penal, but, " on pain of imprisonment," thus : S. the wife of J. S. of, &c., labourer, on pain of imprisonment, in case she shall make default in such condition ; but if the husband be present, he is also to be bound for the appearance of his wife ; and if the witness happen to be an infant, (*or minor under the age of twenty-one years,*) the parent or master should be bound in a recognizance for his appearance.

Form of Recognizance by Husband and Wife.

Province   } Be it remembered that J. P. of
County of   } the township of   in the
      To Wit : } county of   , yeoman,
and E. P., his wife, severally acknowledged themselves to be bound by recognizance to our sovereign lady the Queen, as follows, that is to say, the said J. P. the sum of £20 of lawful money of the Dominion of Canada to be levied on his goods and chattels, lands and tenements, by way of recognizance, to Her Majesty's use, and the said E. P. his wife, on pain of imprisonment, in case of default shall be made in the condition following :—The condition of this recognizance is such, that if the said E. P., the wife of the said J. P., do and shall personally appear, &c. (*as in the former Recognizance page 147.*

Form of Recognizance by a Master, (parent or guardian,) for the appearance of an apprentice or minor.

Province, County of To Wit : } Be it remembered, that on the day of in the year of our Lord J. P., of the township of in the said county, shopkeeper the *mainpernor* of J. J. his apprentice (*or son*), an infant, personally came before me, one of Her Majesty's coroners for the said county and acknowledged himself to owe to our sovereign lady the Queen, the sum of good and lawful money of Canada, to be levied on his goods and chattels, lands and tenements, by way of recognizance, to Her Majesty use, if default shall be made in the condition following :

The condition of this recognizance is such that if the above named J. J. the apprentice (*or son*) of the said J. P., do appear at the next session of general gaol delivery to be holden in and for the said county, and then and there give evidence upon a bill of indictment to be then and there preferred to the grand jury, against C. D. late of the township of in the said county, labourer, for the wilful murder of R. F. late of &c. And in case the bill of indictment be found by the grand jury a true bill, then if the said J. J. do appear and give evidence to the jury that shall pass on the trial of the said C. D. upon the said indictment ; and in case the said indictment shall be returned by the grand jury aforesaid "not found," then if the said J. J. do appear at the said session of general gaol delivery, and then and there give evidence to the jury that shall pass on the trial of the said C. D. upon an inquisition taken before me, one of Her Majesty's coroners for the said county, on the view of the body of the said R. F., and not depart the court without leave, then this recognizance to be void, otherwise to remain in full force.

Taken and acknowledged this day of before me

G. H. Coroner.

The business of the court being concluded, the officer then makes proclamation thus :—

"You good men of this township, (*city or town*) who have been impannelled and sworn of the jury to enquire for our sovereign lady the Queen, touching the death of R. F., and who have returned your verdict, may now depart hence and take your ease. God save the Queen."

The following forms of inquisitions, summonses, warrants, &c., are transcribed from *Impey's Office of Coroner.*

Form of an Inquisition on a Lunatic.

Province, County of   To Wit : } An inquisition indented, taken for our sovereign lady the Queen, at the township of   in the county of   the   day of   in the   year of the reign of our sovereign lady Queen Victoria, &c., before G. H., gentleman, one of the coroners of our said lady the Queen for the said county, on view of the body of R. F., then and there lying dead, upon the oath of A. B., &c., (*here insert the names of all the jurors sworn,*) good and lawful men of the said township, duly chosen, and who being then and there duly sworn and charged to enquire for our said lady the Queen, when, where, how, and after what manner, the said R. F. came to his death, do upon their oath say, that the said R. F. not being of sound mind, memory and understanding, but lunatic and distracted, on the   day of   in the year aforesaid, at the township aforesaid, in the county aforesaid, to wit, into the river Humber, there did cast and throw himself, by means of which said casting and throwing, he the said R. F., in the waters of the said river was then and there suffocated and drowned : of which said suffocation and drowning, he the said R. F. then and there instantly died ; and so the jurors aforesaid, upon their oath aforesaid, do say that the said R. F. in manner and by the means aforesaid, not being of sound mind, memory, and understanding, but lunatic and distracted, did drown and kill himself.

In witness whereof, as well the said coroner as the jurors aforesaid, have to this inquisition set their hands and seals, on the day and year, and at the place first above mentioned.

>   G. H., Coroner. [L. S.]
>   A. B. [L. S.]
>   C. D. [L. S.]
>   E. F. [L. S.]
>   &c.

Felo de se, by Drowning.

That the said R, F., not having the fear of God before his eyes, but being moved and seduced by the instigation of the devil, on   , with force and arms, at the township aforesaid, in the county aforesaid, in and upon himself, in the peace of God, and of our said lady the Queen, then and there being, feloniously, wilfully, and of his malice aforethought, did make an assault, and that the said R. F. into a certain river or stream of water, commonly called   , at the township aforesaid, in the county aforesaid, did violently cast and throw himself, by means of which said casting and throwing, he, the said R. F., in the waters of the said river, was then and there suffocated and drowned, of which said suffocation and drowning, he the said R. F. then and there instantly died. And so the jurors aforesaid, upon their oath aforesaid, do say, that the said R. F. in manner and by means aforesaid, feloniously, wilfully, and of his malice aforethought, did kill and murder himself, against the peace of our said lady the Queen, her crown and dignity; and that the said R. F., at the time of the said felony and murder, so as aforesaid done and committed, had no goods or chattels, lands and tenements, within the said county, or elsewhere, to the knowledge of the said jurors;—(or that the said R. F. at the time of doing and committing of the felony and murder aforesaid, had goods and chattels contained in the inventory to this inquisition annexed, which remain in the custody of C. D., who claims the same).

In witness, &c., (*as in first Form*).

Upon an Accidental Death occasioned by a Cart.

That W. C., late of the township aforesaid, in the county aforesaid, carman, on   , at the township aforesaid, in the county aforesaid, in a certain public street or highway, there called   , being negligently driving in a cart, drawn by one horse, and loaded with twelve barrels of flour; it so happened, that the said A. P. being in the street and highway aforesaid, was then and there accidentally, casually, and by misfortune, forced to the ground by the horse so drawing the said cart as aforesaid, and the said cart so loaded as aforesaid, was then and there, by the said horse violently and forcibly drawn to and against the said A. P., and the wheel of the said cart, so drawn and loaded as aforesaid, did then and there accidentally, casually and by misfortune, violently go upon, and pass over the breast and body of the said A. P., by means whereof the said A. P. from the weight and pressure of the said cart, so loaded and drawn as aforesaid, did then and there receive one mortal bruise in and upon his said breast and body, of which said mortal bruise, he the said A. P. then and there instantly died; and so the jurors aforesaid, upon their oath aforesaid, do say that the said A. P., in manner and by the means aforesaid, accidentally, casually, and by misfortune came to his death, and not otherwise; and that the said horse, cart, and loading were the cause of the death of the said A. P., and that the said twelve barrels of flour are of the value of   ' the said cart of the value of   , and the said horse of the value of   , amounting in the whole, to the sum of   of lawful money of the the Dominion of Canada, and are the property and in the possession of D. E. of   yeoman, or of his assigns.

In witness, &c., (*as in first Form*).

(*) If it be intended to impose a nominal fine or deodand only, then say:

"And that the said horse, cart, and loading are of the value of five shillings of lawful money, &c." (*as before*).

By a Fire.—That on   , at, &c., the warehouse of C. D., situate in the same township and county, casually took fire, and the said A. B., being then and there present, aiding and assisting to extinguish the said fire; it so happened, that a piece of timber, by the force and violence of the said fire, then and there accidentally, casually, and by misfortune, fell from the top of the said warehouse, in and

---

(*) The amount is generally regulated by the nature of the case; if purely accidental the deodand is nominal: but in cases of gross or culpable **negligence** the amount is accordingly.

upon the head of him, the said A. B., by reason whereof, he the said A. B. then and there received a mortal fracture on the head of him, the said A. B., of which said mortal fracture, he, the said A. B., from the said   day of   , in the year aforesaid, until the   day of   , in the year aforesaid, there did languish, and languishing did live ; on which [said   day of   , in the year aforesaid, at the township aforesaid, in the county aforesaid, he, the said A. B., of the mortal fracture aforesaid, did die. And so the jurors aforesaid, &c., and that the said piece of timber was the occasion of the death of the said A. B., and is of no value : (or it is of the value of, &c.,) and in the possession, &c.

In witness, &c. (*as in first Form*).

By Drowning.—That the said A. B. on   ✦ aforesaid, in a certain river, called   , at the township, and in the county aforesaid, accidentally, casually, and by misfortune, was in the waters of the said river, then and there suffocated and drowned ; of which said suffocation and drowning, he, the said A. B. then and there instantly died. And so the jurors, &c.

Natural Death.—That the said A. B., on   and for a long time before, at, &c., did labour and languish under a grievous disease of body, to wit, an asthma ; and that on the said   day of   in the year aforesaid, at, &c., she the said A. B. departed this life, by the visitation of God, in a natural way, to wit, of the disease and distemper aforesaid, and not by any hurt or injury received from any person, to the knowledge of the said jurors.

In witness, &c., *(as in first Form).*

Found Dead.—That the said A. B., on, &c., at, &c., in a certain brick-field, in the possession of one C. D., was found dead. That he the said A. B., for some time before, had been very ailing and infirm, and not able to work ; that he had no marks of violence appearing on his body, and departed this life by the visitation of God, in a natural way, to wit, of his said ailment and infirmity, and not by any violent means whatsoever, to the knowledge of the said jurors.

In witness, &c., (*as in first Form.*)

Stranger found Dead.—That the said man, unknown, on, &c., at, &c., to wit, in a certain wood, there called the long wood, was found dead. That the said man, unknown, had no marks of violence appearing on his body; but how, or by what means he came to his death, no evidence thereof doth appear to the said jurors.

In witness, &c., (*as in first Form*).

By Excessive Drinking.—That the said A. B., on, &c., at, &c., departed this life by excessive drinking of ardent spirits, and not from any hurt, injury or violence done or committed by any person or persons whatsoever to the knowledge of the jurors.

In witness, &c., (*as in first Form*).

Inclemency of the Weather.—That the said man, unknown, was found dead in a certain lane, situate in the said township, commonly called   , that the said man unknown, had no marks of violence appearing on his body, but died through want and inclemency of the weather, and by no violent ways or means whatsoever, to the knowledge of the said jurors.

In witness, &c., (*as in first Form*).

Death in Prison.—That the said A. B. being a prisoner for debt in the gaol of   , at, &c., in the gaol aforesaid, departed this life by the visitation of God, in a natural way, to wit, of a fever, and not otherwise.

In witness, &c., (*as in first Form*).

Falling out of a Boat.—That the said C D., on, &c., being in a certain boat with a certain sail and oars, the property of him, the said C. D. at, &c., it so happened, that by the violence of the wind and waves, the said boat was then and there accidentally, casually, and by misfortune, upset, by means whereof the said C. D., was then, and accidentally, casually and by misfortune, cast and thrown into the waters of the said river, and in the waters of the said river was then and there suffocated and drowned, of which said suffocation and drowning, he the said C. D. then and there instantly died. And so the jurors, &c., and that the said boat, and the sail and oars thereof, did occasion the death of the said C. D., and are of the value of   , and in the possession of   , or his assigns.

In witness, &c., (*as in General Form*).

Murder.—That C. D., late of, &c., labourer, not having the fear of God before his eyes, but being moved and seduced by the instigation of the devil, on, &c., with force and arms, at, &c., in and upon the said A. B., in the peace of God, and of our said lady the Queen, then and there being, feloniously, (*wilfully and of his malice aforethought,*) did make an assault, and that the said C. D. with a certain iron poker of the value of , the said C. D. then and there had and held in both his hands, him the said A. B., in and upon the head of him the said A. B., then and there, divers times, feloniously, (*wilfully and of his malice aforethought,*) did strike and beat, then and there giving unto him, the said A. B., in and upon the back part of the head of him, the said A. B., with the iron poker aforesaid, one mortal fracture of the length of two inches, of which said mortal fracture he the said A. B. then and there instantly died. And so the jurors aforesaid upon their oath aforesaid, do say, that the said C. D. him, the said A. B. in manner, and by the means aforesaid, feloniously, (*wilfully, and of his malice aforethought,*) did (*kill and murder,*) against the peace of our lady the Queen, her crown and dignity, and that the said C. D. after the doing and committing of the said felony and (*murder*) aforesaid, withdrew and fled for the same, and that neither at the time of the doing and committing thereof, nor at any time since, he the said C. D. had any goods or chattels, lands or tenements within the said county or elsewhere, to the knowledge of the said jurors.

In witness, &c., (*as in first Form*).

Manslaughter.—The form is precisely the same, except that the words "wilfully and of malice aforethought," are to be left out, and the words "feloniously did *kill and slay*," substituted for "kill and murder," and the word "manslaughter," for "murder," in another part.—See the parts marked with brackets.

Se Defendendo.

That on the day of in the year aforesaid, at the township aforesaid, in the county aforesaid, the said A. B. being in a certain common drinking room belonging to a public house there situate, known by the name or sign of , in which said common drinking room one C. D., late of the township aforesaid, in the county aforesaid, labourer, and divers other persons was and were then and there present ; and that the said A. B., without any cause or provocation given by the said C. D., did then and there menace and threaten the said C. D. to turn him the said C. D. out of the said common drinking room, and for that purpose did then and there lay hold of the person of him the said C. D., and on him the said C. D., in the peace of God and of our said lady the Queen, then and there being, violently did make an assault, and him the said C. D., without any cause or provocation whatsoever, did then and there beat, abuse and evilly entreat, whereupon the said C. D. for the preservation and safety of his person, and of inevitable necessity, did then and there with the hands of him the said C. D. defend himself against such the violent assault of him the said A. B. as it was lawful for him to do ; and the said A. B. did then and there receive against the will of him the C. D., by the falls and blows which he the said A. B. then and there sustained by him the said C. D. so defending himself as aforesaid, divers mortal bruises, in and upon the head, back and loins of him the said A. B., of which said mortal bruises he the said A. B. from the said   day of   , in the year aforesaid, until the   day of the same month in the same year, at the township aforesaid, in the county aforesaid, did languish, &c., (*as in former precedent*) ; and so the jurors aforesaid, upon their oath aforesaid, do say that the said C. D. him the said A. B. in the defence of himself the said C. D. in manner and by means aforesaid, did kill and slay ; but what goods or chattels the said C. D. had at the time of the doing and committing the said manslaughter in his own defence as aforesaid, the said jurors know not.

In witness, &c., (*as in first Form*).

By Suffocating a Bastard.—That A. B., late of, &c.   , single woman, on &c.   , being then and there big with a female child, afterwards, to wit, on the same day and year, at the township aforesaid, in the county aforesaid, the said female child, alone and secretly from her body, by the providence of God, did bring forth alive, which said female child by the laws of this   was a bastard ; and that the said A. B. not having the fear of God, &c., (*as before*), afterwards, to wit, on the same day and year aforesaid, with force and arms, at the township aforesaid, in the county aforesaid, in and upon the said new-born female bastard child so alive, and in the peace of God and of our said lady the Queen then and there being, feloniously, wilfully, and of her malice aforethought, did make an assault, and that the said A. B., her the said newborn female bastard child with both her hands, in a certain linen cloth of no value, then and there feloniously, wilfully and of her malice aforethought, did wrap up and fold, by means of which said wrapping up and folding of her the said new-born female bastard child, in the linen cloth aforesaid, she the said new-born female bastard child was then and there suffocated and smothered, of which said suffocation and smothering she the said new-born female bastard child then and there instantly died; and so the jurors aforesaid, do say that the said A. B. her, the said new-born female child, in manner and by the means aforesaid, feloniously, wilfully and of her malice aforethought, did kill and murder. against the peace of our said lady the Queen, her crown and dignity, (*flight, forfeiture,—as before*)

In witness, &c., (*as in first Form*).

By throwing down a Privy.—And that the A. B. him, the said new-born male child, did then and there take into both her hands, and him the said new-born male child into a certain privy, or necessary house, there situate, then and there feloniously, wilfully and of her malice aforethougt, did violently cast and throw down, by means whereof he, the said new-born male child, in the soil or filth then and there contained in the said privy or necessary house, was then and there suffocated and smothered, of which said suffocation and smothering he the said new-born male child then and there instantly died; and so the jurors, &c., (*as before*) *flight, forfeiture—as before*).

In witness, &c., (*as in first Form*).

Against Aiders and Abettors, in murder or manslaughter.—And the jurors aforesaid, upon their oath aforesaid, do further say that S. W. late of &c. labourer, and G. W., late of the same place, labourer, at the time of the doing and committing of the felony and murder (*or felony and manslaughter*) aforesaid, were present, aiding abetting, assisting, comforting and maintaining the said C. D. to kill and murder (*or kill and slay*) the said A. B., in manner aforesaid; and so the jurors aforesaid, upon their oath aforesaid, do say that the said C. D. and E. F. him, the said A. B., in manner and by the means aforesaid, feloniously, wilfully and of their malice aforethought, did kill and murder, (*and in cases of manslaughter say, feloniously did kill and slay*), against the peace, &c., (*conclude with flight and forfeiture*).

In witness, &c., (*as in first Form*).

Form of the Warrant to Summon a Jury.

Province,   To the constables of the township of   , in the county of   , and all other of Her Majesty's officers of the peace in and for the said county.

County of
    To Wit:

By virtue of my office, these are in Her Majesty's name to charge and command you, that on sight hereof you summon and warn twenty-four able and sufficient men of your township, personally to be and appear before me, on the   day of   at   o'clock in the forenoon, at the house of A. B., called or known by the name or sign of the   situate at   in the said township, then and there to do and execute all such things that shall be given them in charge on behalf of our sovereign lady the Queen's Majesty, touching the death of R. F., and for so doing this shall be your sufficient warrant: and that you also attend at the time and place above mentioned, to make a return of the names of the persons whom you have so summoned, and further to do and execute such other matters as shall be then and there enjoined you, and have you then and there this warrant.

Given under my hand and seal, this day of   188 .

                            G. H. Coroner.

Form of the Constable's Summons.

Province,   By virtue of a warrant under the hand and seal of G. H., gentleman, one of Her Majesty's coroners for this county, you are hereby summoned personally to be and appear before him as a juryman, on the   day of   at   of the clock in the forenoon, precisely, at the house of   known by

County of
    To Wit:

the sign of the   in the township of   in the said county, then and there to enquire in her Majesty's behalf, touching the death of R. F., and further to do and execute such other other matters and things as shall be then and there given you in charge, and not to depart without leave. Herein fail not at your peril.

Dated the   day of   in the year of our Lord, 188   .

Constable.

N. B.—The Coroner should furnish a sufficient number of printed or written summonses to the constable for service on the Jurors.

Warrant to Bury after a View.

Province,   } To the minister and church-
County of   } wardens of the township of
            To Wit : } in the county of   , and to all others whom it may concern.

Whereas I, with my inquest, the day and year hereunder written, have taken a view of the body of J. D., who not being of sound mind, memory and understanding, but lunatic and distracted, shot himself, (*or agreeably to the finding of the jury*), who now lies dead in your township, and have proceeded therein according to law. These are therefore to certify that you may lawfully permit the body of the said J. D. to be buried : and for so doing this shall be your warrant.

Given under my hand seal the   day of

G. H., Coroner.

Warrant to Bury a felo de se, after Inquisition found.

Province,   } To the church wardens and
County of   } constables of the township of
            To Wit : }   , in the county of   .

Whereas by an inquisition taken before me, one of Her Majesty's coroners for the said county, this   day of   , in the   year of the reign of her present Majesty Queen Victoria, at the township of   , in the said county, on view of the body of J. D., then and there lying dead, the jurors in the said inquisition named have found that the said J. D. feloniously, wilfully and of his malice aforethought killed and murdered himself (*as the finding may be*); these are therefore, by virtue of my office, to will and require you forthwith to cause the body of the said J. D. to be buried according to law; and for your so doing this is your warrant.

Given under my hand and seal this   day of

G. H., Coroner.

N. B.—The last form of warrant should not be directed to the minister.

The Return thereto.

By virtue of the within warrant to us directed, we have caused the body within named to be buried according to law.

C. D. } Church Wardens.
E. F. }
I. D. Constable.

Warrant to Bury without a View, where no effectual Inquest can be taken.

Province,   }
County of   } To the minister and church-
    To Wit :   } wardens in the township of

Whereas I am credibly informed that on the   day of   , the body of a new-born male child was found dead in a coffin, in the churchyard of the said township, and that there is not any evidence to be found to make appear to the jury either by what means the said male child was there laid, or who was the mother thereof, or how it came to his death, nor are there any marks of violence appearing on its body. These are therefore to certify that in the county charge you may permit the body of the said new-born male child to be buried: and for so doing this is your warrant.

Given under my hand and seal this   day of

G. H., Coroner.

Another form of Warrant to Bury without a view.

Province,   } To the minister and church-
County of   } wardens in the township of   ,
    To Wit :   } in the county of   .

Whereas I am credibly informed, that on the day of   instant, A. B. died suddenly in the street, to wit, *(name the street)* in the township of   in the said county, as supposed by a fit of an apoplexy or other sudden visitation of God, and that he came not to his death by any violent means whatsoever. These are therefore to certify that in ease of the county charge you may permit the body of the said A. B. to be buried : and for so doing this shall be your warrant.

Given under my hand and seal this   day of
G. H., Coroner.

Warrant to Bury without a View when the body was found Drowned.

Province,   } To the minister and church-
County of   } wardens of the township of
      To Wit : } in the county of   .

Whereas I am credibly informed that on the   day of   , the body of a man unknown was taken up dead, and floating in the river   , in the township of   in the said county, and that no marks of violence do appear on the body of the said man unknown ; and whereas there is no evidence to make appear to a jury how or by what means the said man unknown came to his death. These are therefore to certify that in ease of the county charge you may permit the body of the said man unknown to be buried ; and for so doing this is your warrant.

Given under my hand and seal, this   day
G. H. Coroner.

A Warrant to take up a Body interred.

Province,   } To the minister and church
County of   } wardens of the township of   ,
      To wit : } in the county of   .

Whereas, complaint hath been made unto me, one of Her Majesty's coroners for the said county, on the   day of   that the body of one G. R. was privately and secretly buried in your township, and that the said G. R. died not of a natural but violent death : and whereas no notice of the violent death of the said G. R. hath been given to any of Her Majesty's coroners for the said county, where-

by, on Her Majesty's behalf, an investigation might have been taken on view of the body of the said G. R. before his interment, as by law required. These are therefore, by virtue of my office, in Her Majesty's name to charge and command you, that you forthwith cause the body of the said G. R. to be taken up and safely conveyed to
in the said township, that I with my inquest, may have a view thereof, and proceed therein according to law. Herein fail not, as you will answer the contrary at your peril.

Given under my hand and seal, the   day of   .

G. H., Coroner.

N. B.—In Canada, where no State Church exists, these warrants may be directed to persons controlling or having charge of any cemeteries, Church of England or otherwise.

Warrant to Apprehend a Person for Murder.

Province, } To the constables of the town-
County of } ship of   , in the county
   To wit: } of   , and all other Her
Majesty's peace officers in the said county.

Whereas, by an inquisition taken before me
one of Her Majesty's coroners for the said county, this
day of   , at   , in the said county, on view of the body of G. R., then and there lying dead, one C. D., late of   , in the said county, labourer, stands charged with the wilful murder of the said G. R., these are, therefore, by virtue of my office, in Her Majesty's name, to charge and command you, and every of you, that you or some one of you, without delay, do apprehend and bring before me   the said coroner, or one of Her Majesty's justices of the peace of the said county, the body of the said C. D., of whom you shall have notice, that he may be dealt with according to law. And for your so doing, this is your warrant.

Given under my hand and seal, this   day of

G. H., Coroner.

Commitment for Murder

Province, } To the constables of the town-
County of } ship of   in the county of
   To wit: }   , and all other Her

Majesty's officers of the peace for the said county, and to the keeper of Her Majesty's gaol at   , in the said county.

Whereas, by an inquisition taken before me, one of Her Majesty's coroners for the said county, the day and year here under-mentioned, on view of the body of R. L., lying dead in the said township of   , in the county aforesaid, J. K., late of the township of   , in the said county, labourer, stands charged with the wilful murder of the said R. L. These are, therefore, by virtue of my office, in Her Majesty's name to charge and command you, the said constables and others aforesaid, or any of you, forthwith safely to convey the body of the said J. K. to Her Majesty's gaol at   , aforesaid, and safely to deliver him to the keeper of the said gaol; and these are likewise by virtue of my said office, in Her Majesty's name, to will and require you, the said keeper, to receive the body of the said J. K. into your custody, and him safely to keep in the said gaol, until he shall be thence discharged by due course of law, and for you so doing this shall be your warrant.

Given under my hand and seal, the   day of
G. H., Coroner.

Summons to a Witness.

Province,   } To A. P., of the township of
County of   }   , in the county of   ,
To wit: } yeoman.

Whereas I am credibly informed that you can give evidence on behalf of our sovereign lady the Queen, touching the death of A. P., now lying dead in the township of   , in the said county. These are, therefore, by virtue of my office, in Her Majesty's name, to charge and command you personally to be and appear before me, at the dwelling-house of J. R., known as the sign of   , situate at   , in the said township, at   o'clock in the afternoon, on the   day of   instant, then and there to give evidence and be examined on Her Majesty's behalf before me and my inquest touching the premises: herein fail not, as you will answer the contrary at your peril.

Given under my hand and seal, this   day of
G. H., Coroner.

Warrant for Contempt against a Witness for not appearing to give evidence.

Province, ⎱ To the constable of the town-
County of ⎰ ship of , in the county
      To Wit : ⎰ of , and to all other Her Majesty's officers of the peace in and for the said county.

Whereas I have received credible information that A. P. of the township of , in the said county, can give evidence on behalf of our sovereign lady the Queen, touching the death of C. D., now lying dead in the said township ; and whereas the said A. P. having been duly summoned to appear and give evidence before me and my inquest touching the premises, at the time and place in the said summons specified, of which oath hath been duly made before me, hath refused and neglected so to do, to the great hindrance and delay of justice. These are, therefore, by virtue of my office, in Her Majesty's name, to charge and command you, or one of you, without delay to apprehend and bring before me, one of Her Majesty's coroners of the said county, now sitting at the township aforesaid, by virtue of my said office, the body of the said C. D.,: that he may be dealt with according to law : and for your so doing this is your warrant.

Given under my hand and seal, the   day of
                                      G. H., Coroner.

Warrant to Commit a Witness refusing to give Evidence.

Province, ⎱ To the constables of the town-
County of ⎰ ship of in the county of
      To Wit : ⎰ , and all other Her Majesty's officers of the peace in and for the county aforesaid, and also to the keeper of the gaol in the said county.

Whereas I heretofore issued my summons under my hand, directed to A. P. of, &c., requiring his personal appearance before me, then and now one of Her Majesty's coroners for the said county, at the time and place therein mentioned, to give evidence and be examined on Her Majesty's behalf, touching and concerning the death of C. D., then and there lying dead, of the personal service of which said summons oath hath been duly made before me; and whereas the said A. P. having neglected and refused to appear pursuant to the contents of the said summons, I thereupon afterwards issued my warrant, under my hand and seal, in order that the said A. P., by virtue thereof, might be apprehended and brought before me to answer the premises. And whereas the said A. P., in pursuance thereof, hath been apprehended and brought before me, now duly sitting by virtue of my office, and hath been duly required to give evidence, and be examined before me and my inquest on her said Majesty's behalf, touching the death of the said C. D., yet the said A. P. notwithstanding, hath absolutely and wilfully refused, and still doth wilfully and absolutely refuse to give evidence and be examined touching the premises, or to give sufficient reason for his refusal, in wilful and open violation and delay of justice : these are, therefore, by virtue of my office, in Her Majesty's name, to charge and command you, or any one of you, the said constables and officers of the peace in and for the said township and county, forthwith to convey the body of the said A. P. to the gaol of the said county, at the city of   , in the said county, and him safely to deliver to the keeper of the said gaol : and these are likewise by virtue of my said office, in Her Majesty's name, to will and require you, the said keeper to receive the body of the said A. P. into your custody, and him safely to keep until he shall consent to give his evidence, and be examined before me and my inquest on Her Majesty's behalf, touching the death of the said C. D., or until he shall be from thence otherwise discharged by due course of law, and for so doing this is your warrant.

Given under my hand and seal, the   day of
G. H., Coroner.

Commitment of a Witness for refusing to sign his Information.

Province,   ⎫ To the constables of the town-
County of   ⎬ ship of   , in the County
         To Wit : ⎭ of   , and all other Her
Majesty's officers of the peace in and for the said county, and also to the keeper of the gaol of the said county.

Whereas A. B. of   , is a material witness on

behalf of our sovereign lady the Queen, against J. P., late of the township of, in the county aforesaid, labourer, now charged before me, one of Her Majesty's coroners for the said county, and my inquest, with the wilful murder of C. D., there now lying dead; and whereas the said A. B. at the time of my inquiry, on view of the body of the said C. D., how and by what means he the said C. D. came by his death, hath personally appeared before me and my said inquest, and on Her Majesty's behalf hath given evidence and information on oath touching the premises, which said information having by me been reduced into writing, and the contents thereof by me, in the presence of the said inquest, openly and truly read to him the said A. B., who doth acknowledge the same to be true, and that the same doth contain the full substance and effect of the evidence by him given before me to my said inquest, and the said A. B. having by me been requested and desired to sign and set his hand to his said testimony and information, and to acknowledge the same as by law is required, yet, notwithstanding, the said A. B. doth wilfully and absolutely refuse so to do, in open defiance of law, and to the great hindrance of justice. These are, therefore, by virtue of my office, in Her Majesty's name to charge and command you, or some one of you, the said constables and other Her Majesty's officers of the peace in and for the said county, forthwith to convey the body of the said A. B. to the gaol of the said county, at   in the said county, and him safely to deliver to the keeper of the said gaol; and these are likewise by virtue of my said office, in Her Majesty's name to will and require you the said keeper to receive the body of the said A. B. into your custody, and him safely to keep in prison until he shall duly sign and acknowledge his said information, or shall be from thence otherwise discharged by due course of law: and for so doing this is your warrant.

Given under my hand and seal, this   day of

G. H., Coroner.

Commitment of a Witness for refusing to enter into Recognizance to appear to give evidence.

Province, } To the constables of the town-
County of } ship of   , in the county
  To Wit : } of   , and all other Her

Majesty's officers of the peace in and for the same county, and also to the keeper of the gaol of the said county.

Whereas upon an inquisition this day taken before me, one of Her Majesty's coroners for the county aforesaid, at   , in the said county, on view of the body of C. D. then and there lying dead, one J. U., late of the township aforesaid, in the county aforesaid, labourer, was by my inquest then and there sitting, found guilty of the wilful murder of the said C. D. ; and whereas one U. B. of the township and county aforesaid, yeoman, was then and there examined and gave information in writing before me and my inquest touching the premises, and which said information he, the said U. P., then and there before me and my inquest duly signed and acknowledged, and by which said information it appears that the said U. P. is a material witness on Her Majesty's behalf against the said J. U. now in custody, and charged by my inquest with the said murder, and the said U. P. having wilfully and absolutely refused to enter into the usual recognizance for his personal appearance at the next general gaol delivery to be holden in and for the county of   , aforesaid, and then and there to give evidence on Her Majesty's behalf against the said J. U., to the great hindrance and delay of justice. These are, therefore, by virtue of my office in Her Majesty's name to charge and command you, or one of you, the said constables and other Her Majesty's officers of the peace in and for the said county, forthwith to convey the body of the said U. P. to the gaol of the said county, at   in the said county, and him safely to deliver to the keeper of the said gaol there ; and these are likewise by virtue of my said office in Her Majesty's name to will and require you the said keeper to receive the body of the said U. P. into your custody, and him safely to keep in prison until he shall enter into such recognizance before me, or before one of Her Majesty's justices of the peace for the said county, for the purposes aforesaid, or in default thereof, until he shall be from thence otherwise discharged by due course of law : and for so doing this is your warrant.

Given under my hand and seal, this   day of

G. H., Coroner.

Recognizance by Husband for Wife's appearance, and by Master, &c., for the appearance of an Apprentice, &c.

Province,   }   J. P. of the township of
County of   } in the said county, blacksmith;
           To wit: } T. P. of the same place, victualler;
J. R. of the same place, whitesmith, the husband of S. R.; J. B. of the same place, shopkeeper, the *mainpernor* of J. J. his apprentice, an *infant*; J. S. of the same place, yeoman, the *mainpernor* of G. S. his son, an infant, do severally acknowledge to owe to our sovereign lady the Queen the sum of   pounds, of lawful money of Canada, to be levied on their respective goods and chattels, lands and tenements, by way of recognizance, to Her Majesty's use, in case default shall be made in the condition following: And S., the wife of J. P. of the same place, labourer, on pain of imprisonment, in case she shall make default in such condition.

The condition of this recognizance is such, that if the above bounden J. P., T. R., S. R. the wife of the said J. R., J. J., G. S., and S. R. the wife of the said J. P., do severally and personally appear at the next general gaol delivery to be holden in and for the county of   , and there give evidence on a bill of indictment to be preferred against W. T. now at large for the wilful murder of S. his wife, and in case the said bill of indictment shall be returned by the grand jury a true bill, then that they do severally personally appear at the session of general gaol delivery for the said county next after the apprehending or surrender of the said W. T., and then and there severally give evidence to the jury that shall pass upon the trial of the said W. T. touching the premises, and in case the said bill of indictment shall be returned by the grand jury not found, that then they do severally personally appear at such session of general gaol delivery to be then and there holden for the said county, and then and there give evidence to the jury that shall pass upon the trial of the said W. T. upon an inquisition taken before me, one of Her Majesty's coroners for the said county, on view of the body of the said S. T., and not depart the court without leave, then this recognizance to be void, otherwise to be and remain in full force. Taken and acknowledged this   day of   G. H., Coroner.

DEEDS.

A Deed, in a legal point of view, is a written instrument signed, sealed and delivered. The writing must be either on parchment or paper, and not on any other substance, such as linen or wood. The written instrument must also be sealed, as that is an indispensable part of every deed, and so also is the delivery. To constitute delivery it is not absolutely necessary that the executing party should take the instrument into his hand, and give it to the person for whose benefit it is intended. A deed, according to Lord Coke, may be delivered by words without actual touch, or by touch without words. But it is always the safest and best way to follow the ordinary and regular course in matters of this important nature, which is to cause the person who gives the deed, after writing his signature thereon, or making his mark if he cannot write, to place his finger on the seal, and acknowledge the seal to be his, and to state that he delivers the instrument as his act and deed.* A deed executed in this way without any condition is held to be legally delivered ; and valid and effectual even if it should still remain in the hands of the executing party. Sometimes a conditional delivery of a deed is made to a third party when all the money is not paid over, or something else remains to be done ; but when the condition is performed the deed becomes absolute, and takes effect from the date of its original delivery. Under old English law deeds are divided into two classes, to wit, *Deeds Poll* and *Indentures*. A deed poll is an instrument executed by one person only ; an indenture by several contracting parties. The term deed poll was derived from the circumstance that it was shaved, or polled, as the ancient term was, at the edges ; whereas the parchment of the indenture was cut or indented with teeth

---

* Vide Smith on Contracts page 20.

like a saw. In old times when deeds were usually very short, it was the custom to write both deed and duplicate on the same skin of parchment, and to write a word in large letters between the parts, and then this word being cut through, saw fashion, each party took away his or her half ; and if afterwards it became necessary to establish the identity of the instrument, the halves were put together, whereupon the word became legible. Bonds, assignments, chattel mortgages, and other instruments of a kindred nature, being writings sealed and delivered, are all deeds ; but the general and popular idea of a deed is that of an instrument which transfers lands or tenements from one party to another, and it is in this restricted sense that we now speak of it.

A deed of land, then, is a writing upon parchment or paper signed, sealed and delivered by the parties thereto, by which one party called the *grantor*, conveys lands, tenements, or hereditaments to another party called the *grantee*. A deed may be either written or printed, or partly written and partly printed. In drafting a deed figures should be avoided in the body of the instrument, and all words written in full therein, without abbreviation or contraction. The name, residence, and occupation, or addition, of every party to the instrument should be carefully inserted therein, as well as its date of execution as the better way, although a deed may be legally dated on one day, and executed on some subsequent day. Great care should always be used in giving an accurate description of the lands or tenements conveyed, in order to prevent future difficulty and expense. If a full township lot is to be conveyed, it will be sufficient to describe it as lot number so and so, in such a concession, township and county, containing so many acres. If a part of a lot only is to be conveyed, state clearly whether it is the North or South half, or North-East or South-West quarter, as the case may be. Where a part of a lot only is conveyed, if possible the premises should be described by its boundaries, magnetic bearings, and the exact surveyor's measurement of each side. A well and carefully prepared deed will have neither alterations nor interlineations of any kind therein, but if these cannot be avoided, they should all be made before its execution, and the witness should put his initials in every case opposite thereto, in the margin, or above them in brackets, so that he may be able to prove to them afterwards if required to do so. When once signed and executed, a deed must not be altered or added to, as any such alteration or addition may wholly vitiate the instrument, and in some cases would amount to a forgery. Where the grantor or party giving the deed is a married man, care should always be taken that his wife should join therein, and bar her dower, as otherwise should her husband die before her she would be entitled to the use of one-third of the land or tenement conveyed during her life-time. When a deed is to be executed by an illiterate person, it should be fully read over and explained to him, clause by clause, so that he may understand fully what he is about to do. Before a deed is executed care should always be taken that a proper investigation should be made as regards the title, and the extent of the incumbrances, if any, clearly ascertained ; and these incumbrances should be recited in the instrument. This search should be made in the registry office of the district, where such legally exists, or in such other place as may be designated by any statute of the particular Province for the safe keeping and inspection of public records.

In Ontario when a married woman is the owner of land in her own right, and of the full age of twenty-one years, she has power to convey her estate by an ordinary deed, provided her husband joins with her therein, and is a party to its execution. But if from any cause the husband is incapacitated from executing the deed with her, or is in prison, or living apart from his wife by mutual consent, or if the husband refuses to join therein, she may apply to a

Judge of one of the Superior Courts, or to a Judge of the County Court, who has power to grant her an order, on sufficient cause being shown, which will enable her to execute the deed alone, just as if she were a single woman.*

Deeds of land should always be placed on record in the proper registry office or other place appointed by law. In Ontario deeds used formerly to be registered by means of abstracts or memorials, but in 1865 this mode of registration was abolished, and the much better plan of lodging the deed itself, or a duplicate of it, in the registry office adopted.†— In order to facilitate this mode of registration, a statute was passed providing for short forms of conveyances, ‡ under which nearly all the deeds now given in this Province are made. The Revised Statutes of Ontario, Chap. 111, make the following provisions for the Registration of Deeds and other legal instruments :—

38. In the case of an instrument other than a will, grant from the Crown, Order in Council, by-law or other instrument under the seal of any Corporation, or certificate of judicial proceedings, a subscribing witness to such instrument shall in an affidavit setting forth his name, place of residence, and addition, occupation or calling, in full, swear to the following facts :

(a) To the execution of the original and duplicate if any there be ;

(b) To the place of execution ;

(c) That he knew the parties to such instrument, if such be the fact ; or that he knew such one or more of them, according to the fact ;

(d) That he is subscribing witness thereto.

2. The affidavit may be in the form of Schedule E. to this Act, or to the like effect.

39. The said affidavit shall be made on the said instrument or securely attached thereto, and such instrument and affidavit shall be copied at full length in the Registry Book.

40. Where any instrument is executed by one or more grantors, but not by all of them, in presence of the same witness or witnesses, and by one or more of the other parties thereto in presence

---

* Vide Revised Statutes Ontario Chap. 127.

† Vide Revised Statutes of Ontario Chap. 111, Sec's. 38 to 61.

‡ Vide Chap. 102. (An Act respecting short forms of conveyances.)

of another witness or other witnesses, then and in such case the witness or one of the witnesses, whether the same be so executed in the same or in different places, shall make an affidavit in accordance with the thirty-eighth section as to each separate and distinct execution of the instrument before the same is registered.

41. No registration under this Act of any instrument shall be deemed or adjudged void, or defective by reason of the name, place of residence, addition, occupation or calling of the subscribing witness thereto not being set forth in full, or being improperly or insufficiently given or described in the affidavit mentioned in and required by section thirty-eight, nor by reason of any clerical error or omission of a merely formal or technical character in such affidavit.

42. Any instrument may be registered under this Act, notwithstanding that the Christian name or names of the subscribing witness making such affidavit is or are only set forth therein by initial letter or letters, or abbreviation or abbreviations, and not in full.

42. Every affidavit made under the authority of this Act shall be made before some one of the following persons :

1. If made in Ontario, it shall be made before—
    The Registrar or Deputy Registrar of the County in which the lands lie,
    Or, before a Judge of any of the Superior Courts of Law or Equity,
    Or, before any Judge of a County Court within his County.
    Or, before a Commissioner authorized by any of the Superior Courts to take affidavits.
    Or, before any Justice of the Peace for the County in which such affidavit is sworn.

2. If made in Quebec, it shall be made before—
    A Judge or Prothonotary of the Superior Court or Clerk of the Circuit Court,
    Or, before a Commissioner authorized under the laws of Ontario to take, in Quebec, affidavits in and for any of the Courts of Record in the Province of Ontario,
    Or, before any Notary Public in Quebec, certified under his official seal.

3. If made in Great Britain or Ireland, it shall be made before—
    A Judge of the Supreme Court of Judicature in England, or of the Court of Session or the Justiciary Court in Scotland, or of the High Court of Chancery, or of the Court of Queen's Bench, Common Pleas, or Exchequer, in Ireland,
    Or, before a Judge of any of the County Courts within his County,
    Or, before the Mayor or Chief Magistrate of any City, Borough or Town corporate therein, and certified under the common seal of such City, Borough or Town corporate,

Or, before a Commissioner authorized to administer oaths in the Supreme Court of Judicature in England or before a Commissioner authorized by the laws of Ontario to take, in Great Britain or Ireland, affidavits in and for any of the Courts of Record in the Province of Ontario,

Or, before any Notary Public certified under his official seal.

4. If made in any British Colony or Possession, it shall be made before—

A Judge of a Court of Record, or of any Court of Supreme Jurisdiction in the Colony,

Or, before the Mayor of any City, Borough or Town corporate, and certified under the common seal of such City, Borough or Town,

Or, before any notary Public, certified under his official seal,

Or, if made in the British Possessions in India, before any Magistrate or Collector, certified to have been such under the hand of the Governor of such Possession,

Or, before a Commissioner authorized by the laws of Ontario to take, in such British Colony or Possession, affidavits in and for any of the Superior Courts of the Province of Ontario.

5. If made in any Foreign Country it shall be made before—

The Mayor of any City, Borough or Town corporate of such country, and certified under the common seal of such City, Borough or Town corporate,

Or, before any Consul, Vice-Consul, or Consular Agent of Her Majesty, resident therein,

Or, before a Judge of a Court of Record or a Notary Public, certified under his official seal,

Or, before a Commissioner authorized by the laws of Ontario to take, in such country, affidavits in and for any of the Courts of Record of the Province of Ontario.

Deed of Bargain and Sale. (Absolute Covenants.)

This Indenture made (In duplicate) the   day of   , 18 , Between John Doe, of, &c., of the first part, Sarah Doe, wife of the said party of the first part, of the second part, and Richard Roe, of, &c., of the third part; Witnesseth, that the said party of the first part, in consideration of the sum of $500, of lawful money of Canada, to him, by the said party of the third part, in hand well and truly paid, at or before the sealing and delivery of these presents (the receipt whereof is hereby acknowledged), doth grant unto the said party of the third part, his heirs and assigns, All and singular that certain parcel or tract of land and premises situate, lying and being in the (*here describe the lands*), Together with the appurtenances : To have and to hold the same lands, tenements, hereditaments, and all and singular other the premises hereby conveyed or intended so to be, with their and every of their appurtenances, unto the said party of the third part, his heirs and assigns, to the sole and only use of the said party of the third part, his heirs and assigns, forever. Subject, nevertheless, to the reservations, limitations, provisoes and conditions expressed in the original grant thereof from the Crown.

And this Indenture further witnesseth, that the said party of the second part, with the privity and full approbation and consent of her said husband, testified by his being a party to these presents, in consideration of the premises, and also in consideration of the further sum of one dollar of lawful money of Canada aforesaid, to her by the said party of the third part in hand well and truly paid at or before the sealing and delivery of these presents (*the receipt whereof is hereby acknowledged*), hath granted and released, and by these presents doth grant and release, unto the said party of the third part, his heirs and assigns, all dower, and all right and title thereto, which she, the said party of the second part, now hath or in the event of surviving her said husband might or would have in, to or out of the lands and premises hereby conveyed or intended so to be.

And the said party of the first part doth hereby, for himself, his heirs, executors and administrators, covenant, promise and agree with and to the said party of the third part, his heirs and assigns, in manner following, that is to say : That he, the said party of the first part, now hath, in himself, good right, full power and absolute authority to convey the said lands and other the premises hereby conveyed or intended so to be, with their and every of their appurtenances, unto the said party of the third part, in manner aforesaid and according to the true intent and meaning of these presents ; And that it shall be lawful for the said party of the third part, his heirs and assigns, from time to time and at all times hereafter peaceably, and quietly to enter upon, have, hold, occupy, possess and enjoy the said lands and premises hereby conveyed or intended so to be, with their and every of their appurtenances, and to have, receive and take the rents, issues and profits thereof, and of every part thereof to and for his and their use and benefit, without any let, suit, trouble, denial, eviction, interruption, claim or demand whatsoever of, from or by him, the said party of the first part, or his heirs, or any other person or persons whomsoever; And that free and clear, and freely and absolutely acquitted, exonerated and forever discharged or otherwise by the said party of the first part or his heirs, well and sufficiently saved, kept harmless, and indemnified of, from and against any and every former and other gift, grant, bargain, sale, jointure, dower, use, trust, entail, will, statute, recognizance, judgment, execution, extent, rent, annuity, forfeiture, re-entry and any and every other estate, title, charge, trouble and incumbrance whatsoever; And lastly, that he, the said party of the first part, his heirs, executors or administrators, and all and every other person whomsoever having or claiming, or who shall or may hereafter have or claim, any estate, right, title or interest whatsoever, either at law or in equity, in, to or out of the said lands and premises hereby conveyed or intended so to be, or any of them, or any party thereof, by, from, under or in trust for him, them or any of them, shall and will from time to time and at all times hereafter, upon every reasonable request, and at the costs and charges of the said party of the third part, his heirs or assigns, make, do or execute, or cause to be made, done or executed, all such further and other lawful acts, deeds, things, devises, conveyances and assurances in the law whatsoever, for the better, more perfectly and absolutely conveying and assuring the said lands and premises hereby conveyed, or intended so to be, and every part thereof, with their appurtenances, unto the said party of the third part, his heirs and assigns, in manner aforesaid, as by the said party of the third part, his heirs and assigns, his or their counsel in the law, shall be reasonably devised, advised or required : so as no person who shall be required to make or execute such assurances shall be compellable, for the making or executing thereof, to go or travel from his usual place of abode.

In witness whereof, the said parties to these presents have hereunto set their hands and seals, the day and year first above written.

Signed, sealed and delivered
in the presence of JOHN DOE [L. S.]
JOHN SMITH. SARAH DOE [L. S.]
RICHARD ROE [L. S.]

Received, on the day of the date of the within Indenture, the sum of $500, of lawful money of Canada, being the full consideration therein mentioned.

JOHN DOE.

Witness,
JOHN SMITH.

Deed with Qualified Covenants.

This Indenture, made (in duplicate) the   day of   18 , Between John Doe, of, &c., of the first part, Sarah Doe, wife of the said party of the first part, of the second part, and Richard Roe, of, &c., of the third part : Witnesseth, that the said party of the first part, in consideration of the sum of $500, of lawful money of Canada, to him by the said party of the third part in hand well and truly paid at or before the sealing and delivery of these presents (the receipt whereof is hereby acknowledged), doth grant unto the said party of the third part, his heirs and assigns, All and singular that certain parcel or tract of land and premises situate, lying and being in the (*here describe the lands*), together with the appurtenances : To have and to hold the same lands, tenements and hereditaments, and all and singular other the premises hereby conveyed or intended so to be, with their and every of their appurtenances, unto the said party of the third part, his heirs and assigns, to the sole and only use of the said party of the third part, his heirs and assigns, forever. Subject, nevertheless, to the reservations, limitations, provisoes, and conditions expressed in the original grant thereof from the Crown.

And this Indenture further witnesseth, that the said party of the second part, with the privity and full approbation and consent of her said husband, testified by his being a party to these presents, in consideration of the premises, and also in consideration of the further sum of one dollar of lawful money of Canada aforesaid, to her by the said party of the third part in hand well and truly paid at or before the sealing and delivery of these presents (*the re-*

ceipt whereof is hereby acknowledged), hath granted and released, and by these presents doth grant and release, unto the said party of the third part, his heirs and assigns, all dower, and all right and title thereto, which she the said party of the second part, now hath, or in the event of surviving her said husband might or would have in, to or out of the lands and premises hereby conveyed, or intended so to be.

And the said party of the first part doth hereby, for himself, his heirs, executors and administrators, covenant, promise and agree with and to the said party of the third part, his heirs and assigns, in manner following, that is to say: That for and notwithstanding any act, deed, matter or thing by the said party of the first part done, executed, committed or knowingly or wilfully permitted or suffered to the contrary, he, the said party of the first part, now hath in himself good right, full power and absolute authority to convey the said lands and other the premises hereby conveyed, or intended so to be, with their and every of their appurtenances, unto the said party of the third part, in manner aforesaid, and according to the true intent of these presents: And that it shall be lawful for the said party of the third part, his heirs and assigns, from time to time, and at all times hereafter, peaceably and quietly to enter upon, have, hold, occupy, possess and enjoy the said lands and premises hereby conveyed, or intended so to be, with their and every of their appurtenances, and to have, receive and take the rents, issues and profits thereof, and of every part thereof, to and for his and their use and benefit, without any let, suit, trouble, denial, eviction, interruption, claim or demand whatsoever of, from or by him, the said party of the first part or his heirs, or any person claiming or to claim by, from, under or in trust for him, them or any of them : And that free and clear, and freely and absolutely acquitted, exonerated and forever discharged or otherwise by the said party of the first part, or his heirs, well and sufficiently saved, kept harmless, and indemnified of, from and against any and every former and other gift, grant, bargain, sale, jointure, dower, use, trust, entail, will, statute, recognizance, judgment, execution, extent, rent, annuity, forfeiture, re-entry, and any and every other estate, title, charge, trouble and incumbrance whatsoever, made, executed, occasioned or suffered by the said party of the first part, or his heirs, or by any person claiming or to claim by, from, under or in trust for him, them or any of them : And lastly, that he, the said party of the first part, his heirs, executors or administrators, and all and every other person whomsoever having or claiming, or who shall or may hereafter have or claim, any estate, right, title or interest whatsoever, either at law or in equity, in, to or out of the said lands and premises hereby conveyed or intended so to be, or any of them, or any part thereof, by, from, under or in trust for him, them or any of them, shall and will from time to time, and at all times hereafter, upon every reasonable request, and at the costs and charges of the said party of the third part, his heirs or assigns, make, do or execute, or cause to be made, done or executed, all such further and other lawful acts, deeds, things, devices, conveyances and assurances in the law whatsoever, for the better, more perfectly and absolutely, conveying and assuring the said lands and premises hereby conveyed, or intended so to be, and every part thereof, with their appurtenances, unto the said party of the third part, his heirs and assigns, in manner aforesaid, as by the said party of the third part, his heirs and assigns, his or their counsel in the law, shall be reasonably devised, advised or required, so as no such further assurances contain or imply any further or other covenant or warranty than against the acts and deeds of the person who shall be required to make or execute the same, and his heirs executors, or administrators, only, and so as no person who shall be required to make or execute such assurances shall be compellable, for the making or executing thereof, to go or travel from his usual place of abode.

In witness whereof, &c., (*as in first Form.*)

Deed of Land belonging to Married Woman. (Ontario).

This Indenture made (in duplicate) the   day of   , 18   , in pursuance of an Act respecting Short Forms of Conveyances :

Between Sarah Doe, of, &c., wife of John Doe, of the same place,   of the first part, the said John Doe, of the second part, and Richard Roe, of, &c., of the third part.

Witnesseth, that in consideration of   dollars of lawful money of Canada now paid by the said party of the third part to the said parties of the first and second parts, (*the receipt whereof is hereby by them acknowledged*), They the said parties of the first and second parts, do grant unto the said party of the third part, his heirs and assigns for ever, All and singular that certain parcel or tract of land and premises situate, lying and being, &c., (*here describe the land, &c.*). To have and to hold unto the said party of the third part, his heirs and assigns, to and for his and their sole and only use for ever, subject, nevertheless, to the reservations, limitations, provisoes and conditions expressed in the original grant thereof from the Crown.

The said party of the second part covenants with the said party of the third part, that she, the said party of the first part jointly with the said party of the second part, hath the right to convey the said lands to the said party of the third part, notwithstanding any act of the said parties of the first and second parts.

And that the said party of the third part shall have quiet possession of the said lands, free from all incumbrances, and that the said parties of the first and second parts will execute such further assurances of the said lands as may be requisite.

And that the said parties of the first and second parts have done no act to incumber the said lands.

And the said parties of the first and second parts release to the said party of the third part all their claims upon the said lands.

In witness whereof, &c., (*as in first Form*).

Short Form Deed with Dower. (Ontario).

This Indenture, made (in duplicate) the   day of   , 18   , in pursuance of the Act respecting Short Forms of Conveyances :

Between   of the first part ;   wife of the said part   of the first part of the second part ; and   of the third part.

Witnesseth, that in consideration of   of lawful money of Canada, now paid by the said part   of the third part, to the said part   of the first part, (*the re-*

*ceipt whereof is hereby by   acknowledged),   the said part   of the first part do   grant unto the said part   of the third part   , heirs and assigns, for ever :

All and singular that certain parcel or tract of land and premises, situate, lying and being *(Here describe the land, &c.)*

To have and to hold unto the said part   of the third part,   heirs and assigns, to and for   their sole and only use for ever : subject, nevertheless, to the reservations, limitations, provisoes and conditions expressed in the original grant thereof from the Crown.

The said part   of the first part covenant with the said part   of the third part, that   ha   the right to convey the said lands to the said part   of the third part notwithstanding any act of the said part   of the first part.

And that the said part   of the third part shall have quiet possession of the said lands, free from all incumbrances.

And the said part   of the first part, covenant with the said part   of the third part, that   will execute such further assurances of the said lands as may be requisite.

And the said part   of the first part covenant with the said part   of the third part, that   ha   done no act to incumber the said lands.

And the said part   of the first part release to the said part   of the third part all   claims upon the said lands.

And the said party of the second part, wife of the said party of the first part, hereby bars her dower in the said lands.

In witness whereof &c., *(as in first Form).*

Statutory Deed. (Ontario).

This Indenture, made (in duplicate) the   day of   18 . in pursuance of the Act respecting Short Forms of Conveyances : Between *(Here state fully the names, additions and residences of the several parties to deed).*

Witnesseth, that in consideration of   of lawful money of Canada, now paid by the said part   of the   part, to the said part   of the first part, (the receipt whereof is hereby by   acknowledged),   the said part   of the first part do grant unto the said part   of the   part,   heirs and assigns, for ever :

All and singular that certain parcel or tract of land and premises, situate, lying and being *(Here describe the land, &c.)*

To have and to hold unto the said part   of the part,   heirs and assigns, to and for   their sole and only use for ever : subject nevertheless, to the reservations, limitations, provisoes and conditions expressed in the original grant thereof from the Crown.

The said part   of the first part covenant with the said part   of the   part, that   ha   the right to convey the said lands to the said part   of the   part notwithstanding any act of the said part   , of the first part.

And that the said part   of the   part shall have quiet possession of the said lands, free from all incumbrances.

And the said part   of the first part covenant with the said part   of the   part, that   will execute such further assurances of the said lands as may be requisite.

(Any reference to previous deeds to be made here).

And the said part   of the first part covenant with the said part   of the   part, that   ha   done no act to incumber the said lands.

And the said part   of the first part release to the said part   of the   part all   claims upon the said lands.

(If the grantor is married and dower to be barred, insert here : And the said party of the second part, wife of the said party of the first part, hereby bars her dower in the said lands).

In witness whereof, &c., *(as in first Form).*

Deed of Right of Way.

This Indenture, made this   day of   , 18 , Between   of   of the first part, and   of   aforesaid, of the second part.

Witnesseth, that the said   for and in consideration of the sum of   lawful money of Canada, unto him well and truly paid by the said   at and before the ensealing and delivery hereof, (the receipt whereof is hereby acknowledged) hath granted, bargained and sold, and by these presents doth grant, bargain and sell unto the said   his heirs and assigns, the free and uninterrupted use, liberty and privilege of, and passage in and along a certain alley or passage, of   feet in breadth by   feet in depth, extending out and from (*describing the direction of the way*); together with free ingress, egress and regress to and for the said   his heirs and assigns, and his and their tenants, under tenants (*if for a carriageway, here add, " with carts, vehicles, carriages, horses or cattle, as by him or them shall be necessary and convenient*"), at all times and seasons forever thereafter, into, along, upon and out of the said alley or passage-way, in common with him the said   his heirs and assigns, and his and their tenants or under-tenants : To have and to hold all and singular the privileges aforesaid to him the said   his heirs and assigns, to his and their only proper use and behoof, in common with him, the said   his heirs and assigns, as aforesaid. (*Here add if desired, " subject, nevertheless, to the moiety or equal half part of all necessary charges and expenses, which shall from time to time accrue, in paving, amending, repairing and cleansing the same alley or passage-way.*")

In witness &c., (*as in first Form.*)

Deed of Gift of Personal Property.

Know all men by these presents, that I John Doe, of the   of   in the province of   merchant, for and in consideration of the natural love and affection which I bear unto my daughter Clara Doe, and for her better preferment in marriage, and the increase of her portion ; and also, in consideration of the sum of one dollar to me paid by my said daughter Clara Doe, at and before the sealing and delivery hereof (*the receipt whereof I do hereby acknowledge*), have given, granted, bargained, sold, and by these presents do give, grant, bargain and sell, unto my said daughter Clara Doe, all the goods and chattels following, to wit, &c., *(or, all those goods and chattels mentioned and expressed in the schedule or writing hereunto annexed.)*

To have and to hold, all and singular, the premises hereby given and granted unto the said Clara Doe, my daughter, her executors and administrators forever, as her and their own proper goods and chattels.

In witness whereof I have hereunto set my hand and seal this   day of   18 .

In witness whereof, &c., *(as in first Form.)*

Deed of Gift of Lands.

This Indenture, made the   day of   18 ,
Between John Doe, of the township of   in the county of   yeoman, of the first part, and Robert Doe *(eldest son and heir apparent of the said John Doe)* of the second part,

Witnesseth, that the said John Doe, as well for and in consideration of the natural love and affection which he hath and beareth unto the said Robert Doe, as also for the better maintenance, support, livelihood, and preferment of him the said Robert Doe, hath given, granted, aliened, enfeoffed and confirmed, and by these presents doth give, grant, alien, enfeoff and confirm unto the said Robert Doe, his heirs and assigns, all that parcel or tract of land, &c., *(describing the land, &c.)* together with all and singular, houses, out-houses, edifices, buildings, barns, stables, courts, curtilages, gardens, orchards, woods, underwoods, ways, waters, water-courses, advantages and appurtenances, whatsoever, to the said parcel or tract of land and premises belonging, or in anywise appertaining, and the reversion and reversions, remainder and remainders, rents, issues and profits of the same, and all the estate, right, title, interest, property, claim and demand whatsoever, of him the said John Doe, of, in and to the said parcel or tract of land and premises, and of, in and to every part and parcel thereof, with their and every of their appurtenances, and all deeds, evidences and writings, concerning the said premises. To have and to hold the said parcel and tract of land, and all and singular other the premises hereby granted and confirmed unto and to the only proper use and behoof of the said Robert Doe his heirs and assigns for ever. *(Add cove-*

nant against incumbrances and otherwise as the donor pleases).

In witness whereof, &c., (*as in first Form*).

Affidavit of Execution of Deed in Ontario.

County of   , to wit : I John Smith, of, &c., (*state here the name in full of the witness, his place of residence and occupation*) make oath and say :

1. That I was personally present and did see the within instrument and duplicate (*if any according to the fact*) duly signed, sealed and executed by John Doe and Richard Roe, the parties thereto.
2. That the said instrument and duplicate were executed at the   of   .
3. That I know the said parties.
4. That I am a subscribing witness to the said instrument and duplicate.

Sworn before me at }   JOHN SMITH.
in the County of   , this
    day of   , 18 .
              W. W.
    J. P., or a Commissioner, &c.

DIVISION COURTS. (ONTARIO).

Division Courts have been established in the Province of Ontario for the inexpensive recovery of small claims. The number of them held in the different counties varies from three to twelve, at least one of which must be held in each City and County Town. They are presided over by the County Judge, or in some of the larger and more populous Counties by the Junior or a Deputy Judge. The Judge of every such court may hold plea of, and may determine in a summary way, for or against persons, bodies coporate or otherwise, as follows : (1) All personal actions where the amount claimed, and all actions of replevin where the value of the goods or other property or effects distrained, taken or detained, does not exceed the sum of sixty dollars; (2) all claims and demands of debt, account or breach of contract, or covenant or money demand, whether payable in money or otherwise, where the amount or balance claimed does not exceed one hundred dollars; (3) all claims for the recovery of a debt or money demand, the amount or balance of which does not exceed two hundred dollars, and where the amount or original amount of the claim is ascertained by the signature of the defendant or of the person whom, as executor or administrator, the defendant represents. This "signature" must be affixed before action brought. Where the sum in dispute exceeds (exclusive of costs) one hundred dollars, an appeal lies to the Court of Appeal, unless before the opening of the court at which the suit is to be tried and without the intervention of the Judge before the commencement of the trial, there shall be filed with the Clerk of the court an agreement in writing not to appeal, signed by both parties or their attornies or agents.

The Division Courts have no jurisdiction in any of the following cases: (1) Actions for any gambling debt; (2) actions for spirituous or malt liquors drunk in a tavern or ale-house; (3) actions on notes of hand given wholly or partly in consideration of a gambling debt or for such liquors; (4) actions of ejectment, or actions in which the right or title to any corporeal or incorporeal hereditaments, or any toll, custom or franchise comes in question; (5) actions in which the validity of any devise, bequest or limitation under any will or settlement may be disputed; (6) actions for malicious prosecution, libel, slander, criminal conversation, seduction, or breach of promise of marriage.; or (7) actions against a Justice of the Peace for anything done by him in the execution of his office, if he objects thereto.— These Courts possess no common law authority as the courts of the Sovereign, but on the contrary their authority is defined and restricted by the statutes creating them.

A minor may sue in the Division Court for any sum not exceeding one hundred dollars due to him for wages in the same manner as if he were of full age. A cause of action shall not be divided into two or more parts for the purpose of bringing the same within the jurisdiction of a Division Court, nor can any greater sum than one hundred dollars be recovered in an action for the balance of an unsettled account, and no action for such balance can be maintained in this court where the unsettled account in the whole exceeds four hundred dollars.

A suit is properly entered in the court holden for the Division in which the cause of action (*i. e.*, the *whole* cause of action, all those things necessary to give a right of action) arose, or in that in which the defendant resides or carries on business ; or it may be entered and tried in the court the place of sitting whereof is the nearest to the residence of the defendant, in which case the plaintiff must in his claim set out that he enters the suit and desires to have it tried there because the place of sitting thereof is the nearest to the defendant's residence. Where the debt or money payable exceeds one hundred dollars, and is made payable by the contract of the parties at any place named therein, the action may be brought thereon in the court holden for the Division in which such place of payment is situate, subject, however, to the place of trial being changed on the application of the defendant to any other Division in which the court holden therein has jurisdiction in the particular case. If a person desires to bring his action in any other Division, the County Judge before whom the action is to be tried, may by special order authorise the suit to be entered and tried in the court of any Division in his County adjacent to the Division in which the defendant resides. A suit may on consent of the parties thereto be tried in any Division. A suit entered by mistake or inadvertence in a wrong Division Court, may by order of the Judge be transferred to the proper Division Court.

When entering an action, the plaintiff brings to the Clerk of the Court a copy (and, if necessary, copies) of his account, claim or demand. The claim should show the names in full, and the present or last known place of abode of the parties to the suit. In every case admitting thereof it should show the particulars in detail, and in other cases it should contain a statement of the particulars of the claim, or the facts constituting the cause of action, in ordinary and concise language. If, however, the plaintiff is not acquainted with the defendant's christian name, he (the defendant) may be described by his surname, or by his surname and the initials of his christian name, or by such name as he is generally known by.

The clerk thereupon issues his summons, which is the first process in the Division Court. Summonses are of two kinds, ordinary and special. The former may be used in every case; the latter can be used only where the action is for a debt or money demand, and where the particulars of the plaintiff's claim are given with reasonable certainty and detail. There is also a summons in replevin, used in actions of that nature.

This summons is, when defendants reside in the county, returnable on the eleventh day after service. When they reside in an adjoining county, it is returnable on the sixteenth day; and when they reside elsewhere, on the twenty-first day.

If the defendant, who is served with a special summons, disputes the plaintiff's claim in the whole or in part, he must leave with the clerk of the court a notice to that effect within eight days after service, when the summons is returnable on the eleventh day, and within twelve days in other cases. If he does not do so, judgment will be entered by default on the return of the summons, and execution may at once be issued. The judge has, however, a discretion to let a defendant dispute a claim at any time before judgment is entered, although such notice may not have been given ; and he may set aside a judgment already entered on sufficient grounds being shown. Judgment by default must be entered within one month after the return of a summons. Where a special summons has been issued against several defendants, but all have not been served, the plaintiff may take judgment against those served ; but in this case his claim against the others will be lost. If he does not wish to abandon his right of action against those not served, he must proceed in the ordinary way. When the claim exceeds eight dollars, the service must be personal on the defendant ; but when the amount does not exceed eight dollars, the service may be on the defendant, his wife or servant, or some grown person being an inmate of the defendant's dwelling house or store.

On the day named in the summons for the sitting of the court, the Judge proceeds in a summary way to try the cause and give judgment. If the defendant does not appear or sufficiently excuses his absence, the Judge, on proof of due service of the summons and copy of the plaintiff's claim, may proceed to the trial of the cause on the part of the plaintiff only, and the judgment thereupon will be as valid as if both parties had attended. If the plaintiff fails to establish his cause, judgment will be given for the defendant, or he (the plaintiff) will be non-suited. The plaintiff may, before verdict in jury cases, and before judgment pronounced in other cases, insist on bring non-suited. When he is non-suited, he is at liberty to bring his case again into court, on a new summons ; but if judgment against him be given he cannot do so. He may, however, within fourteen days thereafter, apply to the judge for a new trial. The judge may adjourn the hearing of any case in order to permit either party to summon witnesses or to produce further proof;

or to serve or give any notice necessary to enable such party to enter more fully into his case or defence, or for any other cause which the judge thinks reasonable, upon such conditions as to the payment of costs or other equitable terms as to him seems meet.

If the defendant desires to plead a tender, before action brought, of a sum of money in full satisfaction of the plaintiff's claim, he may do so on filing his plea with the clerk of the court before which he is summoned to appear at least six days before the day appointed for the trial of the cause, and at the same time paying into court the amount of the money mentioned in such plea. The defendant may, at any time not less than six days before the day appointed for the trial, pay into court such sum as he thinks a full satisfaction for the plaintiff's demand, together with the plaintiff's costs up to the time of such payment. When the defendant desires to avail himself of the law of set off, or of the statute of limitations, or of any defence under any other statute having force of law in Ontario, he must at least six days before the trial give notice thereof in writing to the plaintiff, or leave the same for him at his usual place of abode if within the Division; or if living without the Division, deliver the same to the clerk of the court in which the action is to be tried; and in case of a set-off, he must also deliver two copies of the particulars thereof to the clerk, one to be kept with the papers of the suit, and the other for the plaintiff. No evidence of set-off can be given by the defendant at the trial other than that specified in the particulars of set-off delivered. If the defendant's set-off, as proved, exceeds the plaintiff's claim, the plaintiff shall be non-suited, or the defendant may elect to have judgment for such excess, provided such excess be an amount within the jurisdiction of the court, and if such excess be greater in amount than the jurisdiction of the court, the judge may adjudicate that an amount of such set-off equal to the amount shown to be due to the plaintiff be satisfied by such claim, but the defendant may take proceedings for the recovery of the balance.

If a party to a suit is not certain that his witnesses will voluntarily attend and give evidence, he should subpœna them. The subpœna (with or without a clause for the production of books, papers and writings, and in which any number of names may be inserted) with copies for service may be obtained from the clerk of any Division Court in the county. A Division Court subpœna has no efficacy out of the county in which it is issued. If the witnesses be resident in Ontario, but out of the county, the subpœna must be obtained from one of the Superior Courts of Common Law. The party served with such subpœna, and to whom at the same time a tender of payment of his lawful expenses is made, and also every person in court called upon to give evidence who refuses to be sworn or affirm and give evidence, is liable to a fine of eight dollars and to imprisonment for ten days. If the plaintiff or defendant is desirous of having at the trial the testimony of any witness residing out of Ontario, the judge of the county court wherein such suit is pending may, if in the opinion of such judge a saving of expense will be caused thereby, or if it is clearly made to appear that such person or persons are aged or infirm, or otherwise unable from sickness to appear and give evidence, order the issue of a commission or commissions to take the examination of such person or persons.

In any suit for a debt or demand not exceeding twenty dollars, the judge, on being satisfied of their general correctness, may receive the plaintiff's books as evidence; or in case of a set off or of payment, so far as the same extends to twenty dollars, he may receive the defendant's books as evidence, and he may also receive as evidence the affidavit of any party or witness in the suit resident without the limits of his county. This, however, does not apply to torts, that is actions founded upon violations by one person of any of the rights possessed by another person, independently of any agreement with the wrong-doer.

The judge may openly in court, and immediately after the hearing, pronounce his decision, or he may postpone judgment and name a subsequent day and hour for the delivery thereof in writing at the clerk's office, and the clerk shall then read the decision to the parties or their agents if present, and forthwith enter the judgment. All applications for a new trial must be made within fourteen days from the day of trial, except in garnishee matters (McLean *vs.* McLeod, 5 P. R. 467) or when the delivery of judgment has been postponed by the judge and then within fourteen days from its delivery. Except in cases where a new trial is granted, the issue of execution shall not be postponed for more than fifty days from the service of the summons, without the consent of the party entitled to the same, but if it at any time is made to appear to the satisfaction of the judge that any defendant is unable, from sickness or other sufficient cause, to pay the debt or damages recovered against him or any instalment thereof ordered to be paid, the judge may stay judgment or execution for such time and on such terms as he thinks fit.

Either party to a suit may require a jury in actions of tort or replevin where the sum or the value of the goods sought to be recovered exceeds twenty dollars, and in all other cases where the amount sought to be recovered exceeds thirty dollars. In case the plaintiff requires a jury to be summoned, he shall give notice thereof in writing to the clerk at the time that he enters his suit and shall pay to the clerk the proper fees for the expenses of such jury; and if the defendant requires a jury, he shall within five days after he is served with the summons give to the clerk or leave at his office the said notice in writing and pay the proper fees for their expenses. Five jurors are impannelled and sworn to do justice between the parties whose cause they are required to try. Their verdict must be unanimous. On either side three of the jurors can be peremptorily challenged without assigning any cause. The challenge of a juror must take place before the oath is commenced. The judge may, if he thinks proper, have any disputed fact in a cause tried by a jury.

When any debt or money demand of the proper competence of the Division Court, and not being a claim strictly for damages, is due and owing to any party from any other party, either on a judgment of any Division Court or otherwise, and any debt is due or owing to such debtor from any other party, the party to whom such first mentioned debt or money demand is so due and owing (called the primary creditor) may attach the debt so due or owing to his debtor (called the primary debtor) from that other party (called the garnishee), or so much thereof as is sufficient to satisfy the primary creditor's claim. The claim of the primary creditor must be due *and* owing—that is, past due—before he can proceed; but the debt of the garnishee to the primary debtor need only be due *or* owing—that is due or accruing due—at the time that proceedings for garnishment are taken. No debt due or accruing due to a mechanic, workman, labourer, servant, clerk or employee for or in respect of his wages or salary shall, however, be liable to be seized or attached in this manner unless such debt exceeds the sum of twenty-five dollars, and then only to the extent of such excess.

The judge may in any case, with the consent of both parties to the suit, or of their agents, order the same with or without other matters in dispute between such parties, being within the jurisdiction of the Court, to be referred to arbitration to such person or persons, and in such manner and on such terms as he thinks reasonable and just. Such reference cannot be revoked by either party without the consent of the judge. The award of the arbitrator is to be entered as the judgment in the cause, and shall be as binding and effectual as if given by the judge. The judge, on application to him within fourteen days after the entry of such award, may, if he thinks fit, set aside the award; or he may, with the consent of both parties, revoke the reference and order another reference to be made in the manner aforesaid. Any of such arbitrators may administer an oath or affirmation to the parties and to all other persons examined before such arbitrator.

Any bailiff or clerk, before or after suit commenced, may take a confession or acknowledgement of debt from any debtor or defendant desirous of executing the same. A confession taken before suit must show therein, or by statement annexed, the particulars of claim with the same fulness and certainty as in a special summons.

In case the judge makes an order for the payment of money, and in case of default of payment of the whole or of any part thereof, the party in whose favor such order has been made may sue out execution against the goods and chattels of the party in default. If there are cross-judgments between the parties, the party only who has obtained judgment for the larger sum can have execution, and then only for the balance over the smaller judgment; and if both amounts are equal, satisfaction will be entered upon both judgments. Where a party against whom a judgment has been entered up removes to another county without satisfying the judgment, the county judge of the county to which such party has removed may, upon the production of a copy of the judgment duly certified by the Judge of the county in which the judgment has been entered, order an execution for the debt and costs awarded by the judgment to issue against such party. The clerk shall upon the application of any plaintiff or defendant (or his agent) having an unsatisfied judgment in his favor, prepare a transcript of the entry of such judgment and send the same to the clerk of any other Division Court, and all proceedings may then be taken for enforcing and collecting the judgment in such last mentioned Division Court by the officers thereof that could be had or taken for the like purpose upon judgments recovered in any Division Court. In case of the death of either or both of the parties to a judgment in any Division Court, the party in whose favor the judgment has been entered or his personal representative in case of his death, may revive such judgment against the other party, or his personal representative in case of his death, and may issue execution thereon. Every execution shall be returnable within one month from the date thereof, but may from time to time be renewed by the clerk at the instance of the execution creditor for six months from the date of such renewal. In case a judge is satisfied that a party will be in danger of losing the amount of a judgment in his favour if he is compelled to wait till the day appointed for the payment thereof before any execution can issue, he may order an execution to issue at such time as he thinks fit. Under a Division Court execution, goods and chattels only can be seized. If an execution is returned nulla bona, and there remains the sum of forty dollars still unsatisfied on the judgment, the plaintiff or defendant may obtain a transcript of the judgment from the clerk, file the same in the office of the clerk of the County Court in the county where such judgment has been obtained or that wherein the defendant's or plaintiff's lands are situate. The same shall then become a judgment of the County Court upon which execution against the lands of the debtor may be issued. Goods taken in execution are not to be sold until the expiration of eight days at least after the seizure thereof unless upon the request in writing under the hand of the party whose goods have been seized.

Any party having an unsatisfied judgment may procure from the court wherein the judgment has been obtained if the defendant resides or carries on business within the county in which the Division is situate, or from any Division Court in any other county into which the judgment has been removed and within the limits of which the defendant resides or carries on his business, a judgment summons, provided that before such summons shall issue, the plaintiff, his attorney or agent shall make and file with the clerk of the court from which the summons may issue an affidavit stating (1) That the judgment remains unsatisfied in the whole or in part; (2) That the deponent believes that the defendant sought to be examined is able to pay the amount due in respect of the judgment or some part thereof; or, that the defendant sought to be examined has rendered himself liable to be committed to gaol under the Division Courts Act. This Summons is to be served either personally upon the person to whom the same is directed, or by leaving a copy thereof at the house of the party to be served, or at his usual or last place of abode, or with some grown person there residing. If the defendant appears in pursuance thereof, he may be examined upon oath touching his estate and effects, and the manner and circumstances under which he contracted the debt or incurred the damages or liability which formed the subject of the action, and as to the means and expectation he then had, and as to the property and means he still has of discharging the said debt, damages or liability, and as to the disposal he has made of any property.

If the party so summoned (1) does not attend as required by the summons or allege a sufficient reason for not attending; or (2) if he attends and refuses to be sworn or to declare any of the things aforesaid; or (3) if he does not make answer touching the same to the satisfaction of the judge; or (4) if it appears to the judge, either by the examination of the party or by other evidence, that the party obtained credit from the plaintiff, or incurred the debt or liability under false pretences, or by means of fraud or breach of trust, or that he wilfully contracted the debt or liability without having had at the time a reasonable expectation of being able to pay or discharge the same, or that he has or caused to be made any gift, delivery or transfer of any property, or has removed or concealed the same with intent to defraud his creditors or any of them; or (5) if it appears to the satisfaction of the judge that the party had, when summoned, or since the judgment was obtained against him has had, sufficient means and ability to pay the debt or damages or costs recovered against him, either altogether or by the instalments which the court in which the judgment was obtained has ordered, and if he has refused or neglected to pay the same at the time ordered, whether before or after the return of the summons, the judge may if he thinks fit, order such party to be committed to the common gaol of the county in which the party so summoned is resident for any period not exceeding forty days. Such imprisonment will not extinguish the debt, nor protect the defendant from being summoned anew if on affidavit the judge is satisfied that the party did not then make a full disclosure of his estate, effects and debts, or that since such examination the party has acquired the means of paying.

In case any person being indebted in a sum not exceeding one hundred dollars nor less than four dollars for any debt or damages arising upon any contract, express or implied, or upon any judgment, (1) absconds from Ontario leaving personal property liable to seizure under execution for debt in any county in Ontario; or (2) attempts to remove such property either out of Ontario or from one county to another therein; or (3) keeps concealed in any county to avoid service of process; and in case any creditor of such person his servant (*i. e.* one who from the nature of his employment would have an express or implied authority to protect the interests of his master) or agent makes and produces an affidavit or affirmation proving the debt, and the debtor had absconded leaving personal property liable to seizure, then on such affidavit or affirmation being filed with the clerk of any Division Courts, such clerk upon the application of such creditor, his servant or agent, shall issue a warrant to his Bailiff or to any constable of the county commanding such Bailiff or Constable to attach, seize, take and safely keep all the personal estate and effects of the absconding, removing or concealed person within such county liable to seizure under execution for debt, or a sufficient portion thereof to secure the sum mentioned in the warrant with the costs of the action. The judge or a justice of the peace for the county may take the affidavit and issue the warrant. If the person against whom an attachment has been issued, or any person on his behalf, at any time prior to the recovery of judgment in the cause executes and tenders to the creditor who sued out the attachment, and files in court a bond with good sureties to be approved of by the judge or clerk, in double the amount claimed, that the debtor will, in the event of the claim being proved and judgment recovered, pay the same or the value of the property taken to the claimant, or produce such property whenever required, the clerk may supersede the attachment, and the property attached shall be restored. If within one month from the seizure, the party against whom the attachment issued, or some one on his behalf, does not appear and give such bond, execution may be issued as soon as judgment has been obtained, and the property seized upon the attachment, or enough thereof to satisfy the judgment and costs, may be sold for the satisfaction thereof, or if the property has been previously sold as perishable (which at the request of the plaintiff who sued out the warrant of attachment may be done on giving at least eight day's notice of the sale) enough of the proceeds thereof may be applied to satisfy the **judgment and costs.**

In case a claim be made to or in respect of any goods or chattels, property or security, taken in execution or attached in any Division Court, or in respect of the proceeds or value thereof by any person not being the party against whom such process issued, interpleader proceedings may be instituted upon the application of the officer charged with the execution of such process, for the purpose of determining whether the goods, &c., so taken in execution were at the time of the seizure the property of the claimant as against the creditor. A landlord (if there is an existing tenancy at a fixed rent) has a prior claim for any rent then due him not exceeding the rent of four weeks where the tenement has been let by the week, and not exceeding the rent accruing due in two terms of payment, where the tenement has been let for any other term less than a year, and not exceeding in any case the rent accruing due in one year, of which he or his agent should give notice in writing to the Bailiff making the levy, which should state the terms of holding, and the rent payable for the same.

If goods are illegally distrained for rent, or are wrongfully detained from the owner, a replevin summons may be issued. Before the Bailiff will replevy the goods, he will require a bond to produce the goods replevied if judgment be given against the party replevying, or to pay the value thereof with all costs.

As this work is not prepared for the use of professional persons but for the information of ordinary business men, and of the yeoman class generally, it would be useless to append any Division Court forms. The foregoing explanations will enable any intelligent person to understand what that court can do for him in his particular case: the clerk of the court will tell him how it should be done.

GUARANTEES.

From a legal point of view to Guarantee means to answer for the payment of some debt, about to be incurred for the future performance of a contract, or duty, in case of the failure of another person, who is primarily liable; so that a third party may be saved harmless and indemnified in case of loss. There is much popular misconception with regard to the matter of guarantees, and as to what extent they bind those who make them. A brief review of their nature is, therefore, necessary in a work of this kind.

The 4th Section of the "Statute of Frauds," as 29 Charles II, Chap. 3, is usually termed, enacts "That no action shall be brought to answer for the debt, default, or miscarriage of another person, unless the agreement upon which the action shall be brought, or some memorandum or note thereof, shall be in writing and signed by the party (*or guarantor*) to be charged therewith, or by some person authorized by him to sign it. It will thus be seen that all guarantee promises to answer for the debt of another person, or for his good conduct in any way, or for his ability to perform some special undertaking, must be in writing, which writing should also set out, or show, the reason, or consideration, why the guarantee was given; and that a verbal guarantee is of no value whatever. Thus, if John Smith goes to a store or shop, and says to the owner let Richard Roe have what goods he pleases to order, and if he does not pay you I will, that is a promise to answer for a debt for which Richard Roe himself is liable; and, if it be sought to enforce it, it must be shown to have been reduced to writing, or no action will lie: but if John Smith had said, let Richard Roe have goods on my account, or let him have goods and charge me with them, no writing would be necessary, as the goods would be supplied on John Smith's credit and responsibility, and Richard Roe would not be liable at all.

In determining whether a guarantee has been properly reduced to writing to satisfy the provisions of the Statute of Frauds, the question which most frequently arises is whether the consideration, or reason, for giving it appears sufficiently on the written instrument. It is not absolutely necessary that the consideration should be set out in express terms, as its nature may be arrived at by the probable and fair inference deducible from the guarantee itself, on its perusal by any person of fair ordinary capacity or by extraneous evidence. Hence, if John Smith were to write to a merchant thus:—" I guarantee the payment of any goods which you may deliver to Richard Roe," he would be held liable in law for the debt contracted, as it might fairly be collected from the terms of the memorandum, that Smith intended the consideration of his own liability to be the delivery by the merchant of the goods to Roe.*

In Ontario the consideration provision of the Statute of Frauds has been modified by Chap. 111, Sec. 10, of its Revised Statutes, which provides that a promise in writing to answer for the debt, default or miscarriage, of another person, shall not be invalid because the consideration does not appear in the instrument, or be necessarily inferred therefrom. In Ontario, therefore, it would be competent for a plaintiff in an action on a guarantee promise, to prove the consideration in court, independent of the written instrument altogether.

Guarantee for a fixed sum.

To *Thomas White, Grocer, Brockville.*

The bearer hereof, Henry Johns, wishes to purchase a quantity of groceries from you. If you will supply him

---

*Vide Smith's Law of Contracts on Guarantees.

with them I will guarantee that you shall be paid therefor to the extent of thirty ($30) dollars and no more.

RICHARD ROE.

Township of Elizabethtown, July 1st, 1881.

Continuing Guarantee.

To Messrs. H. Shepherd & Co., Merchants, Brockville.

If you will furnish George Smith, the bearer hereof, with such articles of Dry Goods and Groceries as he may require from time to time, during the next six months, and no longer, I guarantee that you shall be paid therefor to the extent of eighty ($80) dollars, and no more.

WILLIAM YOUNG.

Township of Kitley, July 6th, 1881.

Guarantee for a Servant.

To Mr. John Newbury, of the City of Hamilton.

SIR,—I the undersigned do hereby bind myself to you in the sum of Two Hundred Dollars, to make good any default by Samuel Corcoran, should you take him into your employment as porter, and while he continues in such employment for the term hereinafter mentioned, and to make good any loss which he may occasion by default or neglect during the said term to the extent of the said sum of two hundred dollars and no more. This Guarantee to extend to, and cover, a period of three years from this date.

RICHARD ROE.

Hamilton, January 16th, 1881.

Guarantee for a Clerk.

To Messrs. Jones & Forest, General Merchants, London, Ont.

GENTLEMEN,—My nephew, George Smith, is desirous of entering into your employment as a clerk. Should you engage him I guarantee that he will well and honestly serve you, and faithfully account to you for all money, property and securities, which may be committed to his care from time to time; and I further agree to make good any losses which he may cause to you by misconduct on his part. It is to be understood, however, that I shall be at liberty to terminate this guarantee at any time by giving you one calendar month's notice, and at the expiration of such notice all further responsibility on my part will cease.

MARK ROBINSON.

London, Oct. 10th, 1881.

EXEMPTION FROM SEIZURE UNDER WRITS OF EXECUTION.

In the United States Exemption Laws, of one kind or another, exist in the various States. In some cases these laws only cover articles of personal property, while in other cases they extend to the family homestead, averaging in value from two hundred to five thousand dollars. In Canada none of its Provinces have a homestead exemption law, but in all of them certain goods and chattels of the debtor are exempted from seizure under writs of execution out of any court of law. In the Province of Ontario, Chap. 66 of its Revised Statutes, termed "The Execution Act," makes the following provisions as to exemption from seizure :—

2. The following chattels are hereby declared exempt from seizure under any writ, in respect of which this Province has legislative authority, issued out of any Court whatever in this Province, namely :

1. The bed, bedding and bedsteads in ordinary use by the debtor and his family ;

2. The necessary and ordinary wearing apparel of the debtor and his family ;

3. One stove and pipes, and one crane and its appendages, and one pair of andirons, one set of cooking utensils, one pair of tongs and shovel, one table, six chairs, six knives, six forks, six plates, six teacups, six saucers, one sugar basin, one milk jug, one tea pot, six spoons, all spinning wheels and weaving looms in domestic use, and ten volumes of books, one axe, one saw, one gun, six traps, and such fishing nets and seines as are in common use ;

4. All necessary fuel, meat, fish, flour and vegetables, actually provided for family use, not more than sufficient for the ordinary consumption of the debtor and his family for thirty days, and not exceeding in value the sum of forty dollars ;

5. One cow, four sheep, two hogs, and food therefor, for thirty days ;

6. Tools and implements of, or chattels ordinarily used in, the debtor's occupation to the value of sixty dollars.

7. Bees reared and kept in hives to the extent of fifteen hives.

3. The said chattels so exempt from seizure as against a debtor shall, after his death, be exempt from the claims of creditors of the deceased, and the widow shall be entitled to retain the said exempted goods for the benefit of herself and the family of the debtor, or, if there is no widow, the family of the debtor shall be entitled to the said exempted goods; and such goods so exempt as aforesaid shall not be liable to seizure under an attachment against the debtor as an absconding debtor.

4. The debtor or his widow or family, or, in the case of infants, their guardian may select out of any larger number the several chattels exempt from seizure under this act.

5. Nothing herein contained shall exempt any article enumerated in sub-divisions three, four, five, six and seven of the second section of this Act from seizure in satisfaction of a debt contracted for such identical chattel.

In the Province of Quebec the exemptions from seizure for debt are the same as in Ontario, with the exceptions that the food for the debtors family must not be of greater value than twenty dollars, nor the tools or implements worth more than thirty dollars.

In the Province of New Brunswick, wearing apparel, and kitchen utensils to the value of sixty dollars, are exempt from seizure.

In the Province of Nova Scotia wearing apparel is exempt, and kitchen utensils to the value of forty dollars.

JUSTICES OF THE PEACE.

General Observations.

The important office of Justice of the Peace, as it now exists, has been known to English law for the long space of five hundred and fifty-four years. In 1327 the Statute of Edward III, Chap 1, first ordained the assignment of justices of the peace by the king's commission, but without any other power than to keep the peace. It was, however, very soon determined to increase their authority, and to clothe them with judicial as well as ministerial functions, and accordingly in the following year the form of the commission was enlarged, and continued to be further enlarged, both in the reign of Edward III, and in the reign of almost every succeeding sovereign of England until the 30th year of the reign of Elizabeth. In that year it was found that the form of the commission had become so overloaded with the number of statutes given in charge to justices of the peace to be enforced, and many of which had been repealed, and that the commission had otherwise become so cumbersome and blemished by the lapse of time, and the mistakes of clerks in copying it, that it was absolutely necessary to revise it. On becoming aware of this condition of affairs Sir Christopher Wrey, then Lord Chief Justice of the Queen's Bench, consulted with other judges and barons, and after a general conference the form of the commission was revised. At the Michaelmas term of 1590 the new form was presented to the Lord Chancellor, who commanded the same to be used.* This form, with very little alteration, is the one used at the present day in all parts of the British Empire.

It will thus be seen that from the very first statutory creation of justices of the peace, until the present generation, they have always been appointed by a Royal Commission directly emanating from the Crown, or from its immediate representative, and that no inferior authority has power to issue such a commission. Before Canada became a Dominion the governors of its various provinces, being appointed directly by the crown, had the right to issue the royal commission for the appointment of justices of the peace. But these governors, or rather lieutenant governors, being now no longer appointed by the crown, and not representing it in any way, have no legal right to make any appointments which have their source in royal prerogative.

---

*Lamb. Chap. 9.

No individual of the community is capable of rendering more valuable services to the state and to the people generally than a justice of the peace, whether considered in relation to his ministerial or judicial functions. In a large number of cases he forms the connecting link between the law, as a mere passive enactment, and the enforcement of its provisions, and is in fact the mainspring by which the criminal law is put in motion, and made subservient to the ends of justice and the protection of the community. He is emphatically a conservator of the peace, and without his authority and oversight the public at large would be continually exposed to acts of violence and outrage. The peaceable and well-disposed confide in his vigilance and presence amongst them; and in his neighborhood offenders pause before the commission of the crime meditated, and are no doubt often deterred from doing that which but for the proximity of a watchful magistrate they might otherwise be tempted to do. Under these circumstances it should always be the especial care and duty of members of parliament or others, who present the names of individuals for justices of the peace, to see that they are men of honesty, of personal respectability and moral worth, and possessed of sufficient educational attainments to enable them to discharge the duties of the office intelligently and efficiently. In Great Britain these essential qualifications are almost always to be found in every person appointed to fill the office of a justice of the peace. There the magistrate is usually a man of good standing in his neighborhood, possessed of a liberal education, and fully competent, as a rule, to discharge the duties of his most important office. But in new countries like Canada we cannot look for this high standard of qualifications in the magistrate, who must here of necessity be mostly furnished from the yeoman class or not at all. But that class in this country has now abundant materials for a most respectable and efficient magistracy, were the selection to be made solely in the interests of the public, and with a single eye to the proper discharge of the duties of the office; instead of too often being made, as at present, to subserve political ends, and as a sort of reward for political support. The appointment of political commissions of the peace, by one Canadian government after another, has lowered the character and standing of the magistracy of the Dominion very seriously; and has greatly tended also to corrupt the administration of justice at its source. The writer has been a Canadian justice of the peace for nearly a quarter of a century, and has had the most abundant opportunities for noting the great disorders which resulted, from time to time, from the appointment of illiterate and improper persons otherwise to the magistracy; and now that education is more widely diffused, and a higher standard of qualification, can always be found if sought for, it is to be hoped, for the welfare of the country, that more care will be exercised in the selection of magistrates in the future.

In Canada persons are frequently named in royal commissions as justices of the peace who, aware of their own educational deficiencies, or other unfitness for the office, decline to take the oath of qualification, and thus refuse to accept the position. This conduct at once gives evidence of honesty and good sense, and is unquestionably the best and wisest course to pursue under the circumstances. There are other persons, however, who accept the office and duly qualify, although purposing, at the same time, to avoid the performance of the grave duties which it entails, and to assume as little responsibility as possible on every occasion when their services may be required. We may state that conduct of this kind is not only dishonest but criminal. It is opposed, in the first place, to the tenor of the commission, and, in the second, to the justice's oath of office, which binds him "well and truly" to perform the duties connected therewith. If any person is aggrieved by another, and applies to the *nearest* justice of the peace for redress, and that justice refuses to act in the case, and supposing the application to be based on fair and reasonable grounds, he becomes guilty of an indictable offence at common law, and may be prosecuted therefor by information before another justice of the peace and subsequent trial at the assizes; or the aggrieved party, should he be a resident of the Province of Ontario,* may apply to the county judge who has power to compel the magistrate to act in the case, and to pay all costs of the application against him. Under those circumstances persons who qualify as justices of the peace should do so with the honest determination to perform the duties of the office faithfully, in the sight of God and man, so far as in them lie. While endeavoring by moderate and prudent counsel to reconcile neighbors who disagree, and to prevent litigation of every kind as much as possible, every justice should always be prepared to administer the law with firmness and decision when such a course becomes necessary. It should always be remembered that the law should not be put in motion on every trifling pretence, and that a justice of the peace, from the very nature of his authority, and the influence which it gives him, may do much to promote the harmony and good order of a community by his example and advice alone. On the other hand if he foments quarrels by hasty and ill-advised conduct, and grants legal proceedings too readily on every trivial occasion, he lays himself open to the charge of promoting litigation for the purpose of increasing his fees, and becomes a source of positive injury instead of benefit to the community.

But while the justice of the peace who refuses to do his duty, when properly called on to perform it, renders himself liable to be prosecuted therefor, the justice who performs his duty corruptly also lays himself open to punishment in various

---

* Revised Statutes of Ont., Chap. 73, Sec. 6.

ways. When he so far forgets his office, and his duty to his Maker as well as to the state, and corruptly decides in opposition to the evidence laid before him, or does any overt act to prevent the due administration of the law, or is guilty of extortion by taking directly or indirectly larger fees than the law allows him, or takes money for his time to sit on any case, or to favour any person who may be brought before himself or any other magistrate, or does any other corrupt act in connection with his office, he is guilty of a misdemeanor at common law, and renders himself liable to be indicted therefor. The law can be easily set in motion against him by the ordinary mode of information before another justice of the peace, or a rule may be applied for to the superior courts for leave to file a criminal information against him. The corrupt magistrate can be very speedily made to understand that his office does not place him above the law in any way, while on the other hand the honest and upright magistrate will find that the law gives him every possible protection in case of his unwittingly committing an error in the execution of his duty.

When a justice of the peace has qualified by taking the oaths of qualification and of office, he should apply himself as soon as possible to learn the duties he has so solemnly undertaken to perform, and the nature of the very important authority with which he has been invested. He should, if possible, provide himself, in the first place, with a full set of the statutes of the Dominion, from 1867 to the time of his appointment, and also with the statutes of the particular province in which he resides up to the date of the last revision. A careful scrutiny of these will enable him to ascertain the various statutes under which he will have to act, and make him acquainted, to some extent at least, with their subject matter. While engaged in this way he could sit occasionally with some of his experienced brother justices when trying cases, and thus make himself familiar with the proper mode of holding court, and preserving due order and decorum therein. He should next provide himself with a minute book, of say 200 foolscap pages, in which to keep the record of all trials which come before him under the Summary Convictions Act. In every case tried by him he should plainly write down in this minute book the names of the plaintiff, (or complainant) and the defendant, the nature of the information or charge, a synopsis of the evidence, and a clear statement of the conviction or order made. The name of the acting constable should also be stated at the end of the proceedings, and a sufficient space left to take his receipt for his fees when they are paid over to him.— When the justice makes a return of the conviction to the clerk of the peace he should make an entry of the circumstances on the margin of the record of the particular case. A record of proceedings kept in this careful way will be of great value to the magistrate, will enable him to ascertain, if necessary, in a few moments whether his return of convictions has been properly made at the right time or not, and to be as accurate as possible at all times in his money transactions with complainants, constables and others; while it will also form an excellent book of reference for him afterwards. The young magistrate will also find it a very great convenience to have a supply of printed forms always by him. With the aid of these forms he can draw up the necessary papers in any case in a quarter of the time it would take him to write them out in full, and with much greater accuracy.

Having qualified himself in the way described, for the due performance of his duties, we will suppose that a person comes before the new justice of the peace to lay an information or complaint. The first thing for the justice to do is to ascertain whether he has authority to act in the matter either by common law, statute law, or by-law, as the case may be. Having satisfied himself on that point the information should be drawn to correspond as closely as possible to the language of the authority or applying clause of the statute or by-law. This is a safe rule to follow, and cannot possibly lead to any mistakes. It should next be read carefully over to the informant so that he may fully understand its contents, and so that no mistake may be made. When the case comes on for trial the justice should always have one or two constables in attendance to preserve good order in court, and to do any other act that may be necessary for the furtherance of the ends of justice. A decorous and orderly court is an essential element of the proper administration of the law, and magistrates should never forget this fact. In cases where a magistrate is apprehensive that the bench may be packed by partisan justices of the peace for improper purposes, he may make the summons or warrant specially returnable before himself, and afterwards try the case alone, presuming he has authority to act singly, and any two justices may also pursue the same course. But if the ordinary statutory form is used all the justices present in court when the case commences will have a right to take part in its trial, and cannot be excluded; but no justice coming into court after the case has commenced has a right to interfere. When a magistrate makes a summons special before himself it may be desirable to invite some discreet brother justice or justices to sit with him. If there is much feeling about the case, as sometimes happens, this proceeding will relieve him of a part of the responsibility; and show that he desires to act with impartiality, and with the true ends of justice solely in view. Where the magistrate has doubts of any kind about a case he can, in Ontario, always have the benefit of the county attorney's advice free of charge, and in writing if desired, a privilege he should not hesitate to avail himself of at any time. In other provinces he can seek advice from the proper public officer or from his own legal adviser.

Nature and Powers of the Office of Justice of the Peace.

The Office of a Justice of the Peace is partly ministerial and partly judicial. His ministerial duties extend to all cases which may be brought before him, which are properly the subjects of indictment at the sessions of the peace or at the assizes, and cannot therefore be tried by him. In these cases he has authority to determine whether the evidence laid before him is sufficient to warrant him in committing the accused person for trial, to admit him to bail, when the law permits him to do so, or to discharge him from custody where the evidence is insufficient. In all such cases the justice of the peace is the minister of the law, and by or through whom the accused party is compelled to appear and take his trial before the proper tribunal. His judicial duties extend to all those cases which, under the authority of various statutes, he has the power to try and determine summarily. But his decisions are always open to appeal, unless the right of appeal is taken away by the particular statute under which he may be acting. His decision or judgment is termed a conviction. In any proceeding before him in which he has authority to fine and imprison a justice of the peace is a Judge of Record, and has power to imprison for contempt of court committed before him.* While in the discharge of his duty the justice of the peace has full power to protect himself from insult and to repress disorder, by committing for contempt any person who shall violently interrupt his proceedings, or use abusive or insulting language to himself; and may on his own view, and without any formal proceedings, forthwith order into custody any

---

* Dalton Chap. 2. Owens *v* Taylor 19 C. P. Ont. 53.

person disturbing his court, or obstructing the course of justice; or he may commit the offender until he find sureties to keep the peace. But this must be done at the time when the disturbance or obstruction takes place, and not afterwards. If the matter is allowed to stand over until next day, or even until the court has been closed, a summons should be issued against the offending party, and a hearing accorded him in which he should be permitted to make his full defence, after which a minute should be made of his sentence in the usual way, and the formal committal of the offender for a specified time then made out.

In England justices of the peace are of three classes; (1) those created by special act of Parliament, as some of the bishops; (2) by charter or grant made by the crown under the great seal, as mayors and the chief officers in corporate cities and towns; (3) and by the Queen's Commission. In Canada, however, justices of the peace only appear under two clases, those appointed by royal commission, and those who have authority as such for the time being in consequence of holding some other statutory office. For example, in the Province of Ontario, mayors of cities and towns, reeves of towns, townships and villages, and police magistrates, are *ex-officio* justices of the peace, not only for their own particular municipalities but also for the whole county or united counties in which those municipalities are situated.

The position of a justice of the peace, the office itself, and his official duties, have their foundation in his commission, and in the several statutes which have set out, or described, the various criminal and civil matters which come under his jurisdiction. His commission makes him a conservator of the peace, and thus clothes him with all the authority of ancient conservators of the peace at common law, as regards suppressing riots and affrays, taking securities to keep the peace from disorderly persons, and to commit to prison felons and other inferior criminals. It also empowers any

two or more justices of the peace to hear and determine felonies and misdemeanors, which form the foundation of their jurisdiction at Quarter or General Sessions. His name being put in the commission will not, however, give a justice full authority to act until he has duly qualified by taking the oaths of property qualification and of office. His property qualification must represent an interest in real estate amounting to $1200 over and above any or all incumbrances thereon.* The objects of this qualification are (1) that the justice should be a respectable person who had a solid stake in the country, and (2) have sufficient property to satisfy any claim or action at law of parties who might be wronged by his proceedings and sought redress by civil suit in the courts. The oath of qualification may be taken before a justice or before the clerk of the peace for the district or county set out in the commission, and a certificate of such oath having been taken and subscribed must be deposited with the latter to be filed among the records of the sessions.† In cases, however, when a person is an ex-officio justice of the peace by virtue of some civic office, such as mayor or reeve, which he holds, he is only obliged to take the municipal oath or declaration which qualifies him to fill such civic office,‡ and is not required to qualify in the same way as magistrates appointed by the royal commission. As a general rule the authority of a justice is limited to the city, or county, or union of counties, for which the commission appoints him. But in some special cases statute law enlarges his authority, and gives him jurisdiction over offences of a serious character committed elsewhere. §
With respect to the performance of the statutory duties of a

---

* Vide Consolidated Statutes of Canada Chap. 100., Sec. 3, and Revised Statutes of Ont. Chap. 74 Sec. 7.

† Vide 29 Vic. (Can.) Chap. 12, Sec. 1.

‡ Revised Statutes Ontario Chap. 174, Sec. 397.

§ 32–33 Vic. (Can.) Chap. 29, Sec. 8 9 10, and Chap. 21, Sec. 121.

justice of the peace he can best learn their nature by a careful perusal of the "act respecting the duties of justices of the peace out of sessions, in relation to persons charged with indictable offences,* and of the act relating to summary convictions and orders. † The Statutes of the Dominion, and of its various provinces, can, as a rule, be readily understood by any intelligent justice; and in cases where any doubt may arise as to their meaning the county attorney or other competent counsel should be at once consulted. No magistrate's guide or manual of any kind will give the justice as clear a knowledge of his duties as the study of the statutes themselves. As new statute books come into his hands, each year, he should examine them at the earliest leisure opportunities, to see if any amendments to the laws affecting his duties have been made, and to note such on the margin of the amended statute or statutes for his future guidance.‡

The justice of the peace acts judicially or as a judge in all cases of summary jurisdiction, and while trying them his court is one of record. His conviction drawn up in due form, and unappealed against, is final and conclusive, and cannot be disputed or set aside by any action at law. It is not an unusual practice for persons on conviction for some offence to ask time for the payment of the fine, or of part of the fine. Such applications cannot be safely granted, as the law does not design that a conviction should be enforced in

---

*32 33 Vic. (Can.) Chap. 30. † Ibid Chap. 31.

‡ All *we* propose to do in this volume is to supply him with information which he cannot acquire in this direction, and with such advice as a long experience with a magistrate's duties enable us to offer. Nearly every magistrate's manual now in use is better adapted for a reference book for the legal profession than for the ordinary justice of the peace; and is of very little practical value to him. Under those circumstances we consider it to be much the better way to leave the justice of the peace to learn the proper mode of conducting his court, and of transacting his official business, from the applying statutes.

part. The committal in default of payment must always set out the full amount of the fine in accordance with the conviction. When a justice has given judgment in a case, made a minute thereof on the record, and the court is closed, he has no power to re-open the case again. His judgment can then only be impeached by appeal to the sessions, or by writ of *certiorari*. A justice is not obliged to declare the penalty at the time of conviction, and may defer his decision on this point until he can consider the matter more fully or get legal advice. Nor is he obliged to supply a copy of the evidence given before him in his judicial capacity, or when he commits in default of sureties to keep the peace; but in indictable cases he must furnish copies of the depositions, while they remain in his hands, at the rate of five cents for every one hundred words.* A justice should always refrain from taking part in any case in which he has a direct or even indirect interest. A pecuniary interest in the result, however small, disqualifies a justice from sitting on any case; and so does a manifest bias or disposition to unduly favor one of the parties to the suit. It has been held by the courts that a justice is interrested in the prosecution for selling liquor illegally, if he should be a member of the temperance lodge which prosecutes; that he is therefore incompetent to try the case, and that a conviction before him is bad.†

While in the performance of their official duties justices should be careful not to abuse their position, and inflict a wrong upon either principals or witnesses in any case pending before them, by the use of maliciously insulting or improper language. Where language of this kind is used

---

* 32–33 Vic. (Can.) Chap 30 Sec. 53.
† R. c. s. Simmons 1, Pugsley 159.

without any legal justification exemplary damages will be given against the justice.‡

When a fair and reasonable right to property or title is shown the jurisdiction of a justice terminates, and he has no power to either try or convict summarily under the circumstances. But if the claim of right does not appear to be a fair and reasonable one to the justice, he is bound to proceed with the case of trespass, or whatever else it may be, and convict if the evidence warrants him in doing so.

When a justice acts in the execution of his office with a partial, malicious, or corrupt motive, he is guilty of a misdemeanor, and may be proceeded against by indictment or information; and the courts will grant a rule for a criminal information against him for any gross act of oppression committed by him in the exercise or pretended exercise of his duty, whenever there can be shown any vindictive or corrupt motive. 32–33 Vic. (Can.) Chap. 31, Sec. 82, does not prevent the prosecution by indictment of a justice of the peace for any offence, the commission of which would subject him to indictment previous to the coming into force of that act.

On the other hand justices who perform their duty honestly and fairly, to the best of their knowledge and ability, are protected by special statutes; and the law of the empire, as well as of this country, shields them in every reasonable way when they commit errors unwittingly. In this connection we may state that Chap. 73 of the Revised Statutes of Ontario makes the most ample provisions to protect the justice of the peace from vexatious actions as regards this province.

Oath of Qualification.

"I, A. B. do swear, that I truly and *bona fide* have to

---

‡ 26, Q. B., Ont. 422.

" and for my own proper use and benefit, such an Estate
" (*specifying the same by its local description, rents, or any
" thing else*) as doth qualify me to act as a Justice of the
" Peace for the District or County of   , according
" to the true intent and meaning of the Act respecting the
" qualification of Justices of the Peace ; (*nature of such
" Estate, whether land, and if land, designating*) and that
" the same is lying and being (*or* issuing out of lands, tene-
" ments and hereditaments, situate) within the Township,
" (*Parish, or Seigniory*) of   , (*or*) in the several
" Townships, (*Parishes, or Seigniories*) of   (*or as
" the case may be.*)—So help me God."

4. A certificate of such oath having been so taken and subscribed as aforesaid, shall be forthwith deposited by the Justice of the Peace, who has taken the same, at the Office of the Clerk of the Peace for the District or County, and shall, by the said Clerk, be filed among the records of the Sessions of the said District.

5. Every such Clerk of the Peace shall, upon demand, forthwith deliver a true and attested copy of the said Oath in writing to any person paying the sum of twenty cents for the same ; which copy being produced as evidence on the trial of any issue in any action or suit brought upon this Act, shall have the same force and effect as the record of the said Oath would have, if produced.*

Oath of Office.

Ye shall swear, that as justices of the peace, in the county of   , in all articles in the Queen's commission to you directed, you shall do equal right to the poor and to the rich, after your cunning, wit, and power, and after the laws and customs of the Dominion of Canada, and statutes thereof made ; and ye shall not be of counsel of any quarrel hanging before you ; and that ye hold your sessions after the form of the statutes made ; and the issues, fines, and americaments, that shall happen to be made, and all forfeitures which shall fall before you, ye shall cause to be entered without any concealment, (or embezzling) and truly send them to the Queen's exchequer ; ye shall not let, for gift or other cause, but well and truly you shall do your office of justice of the peace in that behalf; and that you take nothing for your office as justice of the peace to be done, but of the Queen, and fees accustomed, and costs limited by

---

* Consolidated Statutes of Canada, Chap. 100, Sec's 3, 4 and 5.— For Ontario see Revised Statutes, Chap. 71.

statute; and ye shall not direct, nor cause to be directed, any warrant (*by you to be made*) to the parties, but ye shall direct them to the bailiffs of the said county, or other the Queen's officers or ministers, or other indifferent persons, to do execution thereof.—So help you God.

Form of the Commission of the Peace.

Victoria, by the grace of God, of the United Kingdom of Great Britain and Ireland, Queen, defender of the faith, &c.

To (*the names of the justices being here inserted*), esquires, *greeting:* KNOW YE, that we have assigned you, jointly and severally, and every one of you, our justices, to keep the peace in our county of   , and to keep, and cause to be kept, all ordinances and statutes for the good of the peace, and for the preservation of the same, and for the quiet rule and government of our people, made in all and singular their articles in our said county, according to the force, form and effect of the same; and to chastise and punish all persons that offend against the form of those ordinances and statutes; and to cause to come before you, or any one of you, all those who to any one or more of our people concerning their bodies, or the firing of their houses, have used threats, to find security for the peace or their good behaviour towards us and our people; and if they shall refuse to find such security, then them in our prisons, until they shall find such security, to cause to be safely kept. We have also assigned you, and every two or more of you, our justices, to enquire more fully the truth, by the oaths of the good and lawful men of the county aforesaid, by whom the truth of the matter may be better known, of all and all manner of felonies, poisonings, trespasses, forestallings, regratings, engrossings and extortions whatsoever; of all and singular the crimes and offences of which the justices of the peace may and ought lawfully to enquire, by whomsoever, and after what manner soever, in the said county, had done or perpetrated, or which hereafter shall there happen to be done or attempted. And also, of all those who in the aforesaid county, in companies, against our peace in disturbance of our people, with armed force have gone or rode, or hereafter shall presume to go or ride. And also, of all those who shall have lain in wait, or hereafter shall presume to lie in wait, to maim, or cut, or kill our people. And also, of all victuallers, and all and singular other persons who in the abuse of weights and measures, or in selling victuals, against the form of the ordinances and statutes, or any one of them, therefore made for the common benefit of our Dominion of Canada, and our people thereof, have offended or attempted, or hereafter shall presume, in our said county, to offend or attempt. And also of the sheriffs, bailiffs, stewards, constables, keepers of gaols, and other officers who, in the execution of their offices about the premises, or any of them, have unduly behaved themselves, or hereafter shall presume to behave themselves unduly, or have been, or hereafter shall happen to be careless, remiss or negligent, in our said county; and of all and singular articles and circumstances, and all other things whatsoever that concern the premises, or any of them, by whomsoever, and after what manner soever, in our aforesaid county, done or perpetrated, or which shall hereafter happen to be done or attempted in what manner soever. And to inspect all indictments whatsoever before you or any of you taken or to be taken, or before others, late our justices of the peace in our aforesaid county made or taken and not yet determined; and to make and continue process thereupon against all and singular the persons so indicted, or who before you hereafter shall happen to be indicted, until they can be taken, surrender themselves, or be outlawed. And to hear and determine all and singular the felonies, poisonings, trespasses, forestallings, regratings, engrossings, extortions, unlawful assemblies and indictments, aforesaid, and all and singular other the premises according to the laws and statutes of our said Dominion of Canada, or form of the ordinances and statutes aforesaid, it has been accustomed or ought to be done to chastise and punish: *provided always*, that if a case of difficulty upon a determination of any of the premises before you, or any two or more of you, should happen to arise, then let judgment in nowise be given before you or any two or more of you unless in the presence of one of our justices of our court of our bench, or one of our justices appointed to hold the assizes in the said county; and therefore we command you, and every of you, that to keeping the peace, ordinances, and statutes, and all and singular other the premises, you diligently apply yourselves, and that at certain days and places which you, or any such two or more of you as is aforesaid, shall appoint for the purpose, into the premises, you make enquiries, all and singular the premises you hear and determine, and perform and fulfil them in the aforesaid form, doing therein what to justice appertains according to the law and custom of Canada ; saving to us our americaments and other things thereupon belonging. And we command, by the tenor of these presents, our sheriff of our said county, that at certain days and places which you, or any such two or more of you, shall make known unto him, he cause to come before you, or any such two or more of you as is aforesaid, such and so many good and lawful men of his county, by whom the truth of the matter in the premises shall be better known and inquired into.

In testimony, &c.

Explanatory Notes to the Commission of the Peace.

Victoria, by the grace of God, &c.—This manner of issuing the Commission in the Queen's or King's name, as the case may be, appears to have been used at the time of the creation of the office of justice of the peace in the reign of Edward III. The Statute of 27 Henry VIII, Chap. 24, more clearly defines this manner of issuing the Commission, and enacts, in Sections 2, 6 and 19, that all justices of the peace shall be made by letters patent under the king's great seal, in the name and by authority of the king, but reserves to all cities and towns corporate the liberties which they already enjoyed in that behalf.

Know ye that we have assigned you. This clause in the commission is founded on the Statute of 1 Edward III, Chap. 16, which sets out that "for the better keeping and maintenance of the peace, the king wills, that in every county, good men and lawful, which be no maintainers of evil, shall be assigned to keep the peace." From this statute dates that great alteration in the English constitution whereby the election of conservators of the peace was taken from the people, and transferred to the assignment of the crown.— The commission, it will be observed, has two parts, or rather two assignments. Under the first part, any one or more justices have all the ancient power touching the preservation of the peace which the conservator of the peace had at common law, as also the whole authority which various statutes, passed from time to time, have added thereto. The second part defines the powers of justices as regards the general sessions of the peace.

Jointly and severally and every one of you. Under this clause whatever official act one justice alone may do, can be performed conjointly by any two or more justices; but where the law giveth only authority to two justices to do an act it cannot be performed by one alone. One justice, however, may issue a warrant or summons, but two justices must determine the case where any statute so prescribes.

Our Justices. In that the Queen calls them *our* justices, their authority in England would terminate with her death, were it not for the Statute of 1 Anne, Chap. 8, Sec. 2, which provides that the commission, like all other patents of office or employment, shall continue for six months after the death of the Sovereign, unless made void by some Act of the successor to the throne. The commission may also be terminated by express writ under the great seal, or by a new commission which virtually, although silently, discharges all the former justices not included in it. But these provisions do not affect mayors, reeves, or police magistrates, or other ex-officio justices of the peace for the time being, whose tenure of office is not disturbed in any way by the demise of the sovereign. In Canada the act 31 Vic., Chap. 36 provides that commissions shall not terminate by demise of the Crown, but that, on a proclamation made by the Governor General, new oaths of allegiance and of office shall be taken by all proper functionaries—justices of the peace among the rest.

In our county of, &c. By this clause the powers of the justice are limited to the county or union of counties for which he is appointed; but, as already explained elsewhere, certain statutes give him jurisdiction, although under special and occasional circumstances only, outside the boundary prescribed in the commission.

And to cause to come before you, or any one of you, all those who to any one or more of our people, concerning their bodies, or the firing of their houses, have used threats, &c.— It is under this clause of the commission that justices have authority to bind over to keep the peace those who make threats to injure their neighbors, and commit such to prison if they cannot find the required sureties. Justices have also authority, as well from the tenor of their commission as from the Statute 34 Edward III, Chap. 1, to require sureties to keep the peace and be of good behaviour, from a person who uses violent language to another calculated to provoke a breach of the peace; or who seeks to deter an officer of any court from doing his duty; or who is a dangerous, quarrelsome, or scandalous person; or who prowls about at night with evident evil intent; or is a common drunkard and thus a nuisance to his neighbors, or is a suspected person who lives idly and cannot give a good account of himself, or is likely to commit murder, robbery, or any other serious crime; or is a common gambler, or a frequenter of bawdy houses; or charges another before a justice with a felony or misdemeanor, and afterwards refuses to prosecute; or who is likely to do any other act or acts to endanger the life or property of any of Her Majesty's subjects, or disturb the public peace. Great latitude is allowed to the justice in the matter of requiring sureties to keep the peace, but if he commits one for want of sureties he must show the cause with sufficient certainty in the committal.* As to his

---

* Hawkins 132.

authority otherwise under this head, it will be fully treated elsewhere under the head of "Articles of the Peace."

We have also assigned to you and every one of you, &c.—This clause begins the second part, or second assignment, of the commission, which refers solely to the duties of justices at the general sessions of the peace. An explanation of this part of the commission would be of no practical value to the ordinary justice, and its careful perusal will give him all the information he can possibly need. We may add, however, that when he commits any person for trial, it is always best not to commit to the Sessions or Assizes, but to the next court of competent jurisdiction, as otherwise he may ignorantly send a case case to the sessions which cannot legally be tried there.

Articles of the Peace.

Whenever a person has just cause to fear that another will burn his house, or do himself or his wife or children any bodily injury, or cause such act or acts to be done by others, he has the right to exhibit what is termed in law "Articles of the Peace" against the person, from whom he apprehends such mischief, either in the Court of Chancery or Queen's Bench, or before a justice of the peace; and such court or justice is bound to require the party complained against to keep the peace towards whoever makes the application.—But the latter must first make oath that he is actually under such fear as regards the other person, that he has just cause to be so from certain threats or expressions, or from some other overt act, which must be set out plainly in the sworn information, and that he does not require surety from him out of malice or vexation, but solely with the view to preserve his person, or his wife or children, or his property, from injury. All persons whatsoever under the Queen's protection, subjects or aliens, have a right to demand surety of the peace; and a wife may demand it against her husband, and a husband against his wife. Persons under age and married women should not be bound themselves, and ought to find sureties by their friends.*

When a person appears before a justice to prefer articles of the peace against another, the latter should carefully hear the statement of such person, and then consider whether the facts or circumstances stated by him were of such a grave nature as to warrant further steps being taken. If they appear to be of a trivial character, or to result from malice, or ill-will, or vexation, on the part of the complainant, he should decide to refuse proceedings in the case, and his decision in that respect will be final. But if on the contrary he decides to grant proceedings, he will then take an information according to the annexed form, and afterwards issue his warrant for the arrest of the accused party. This warrant may be special or general.— The justice makes it a special instrument by directing that the accused shall be brought before himself, or general by using the words to bring the said A. B. before me or some other justice of the peace. If the warrant is general the acting constable can take the accused, when arrested, before any magistrate he pleases. A peace warrant can only be executed by the constable to whom it is directed, who is authorized to break open any door to make an arrest after having been refused admittance, and stating the cause of making the demand.†

Justices should be careful not to require sureties of the peace without sufficient grounds, for if they do so from an error of judgment they render themselves liable to an action, to which their general jurisdiction in the matter would not be a sufficient answer. As soon, therefore, as the accused party is brought before a justice the latter should first

---
* 1 Hawkins, Chap. 60, Sec's. 2, 4, 5, 6, 7.
† 2 Hawkins, Chap. 14, Sec. 2.

carefully read to him the information laid against him, and then ask him if he can show any good reason why he should not be ordered to find sureties to keep the peace. The accused person cannot be allowed to controvert or dispute the truth of the facts sworn to in the complaint.* All he is allowed to do is to show that the complaint was preferred from malice only,† or explain any parts of it that may be ambiguous. If the justice decides that the statement of the accused is not a sufficient defence to the complaint, he orders him to find bail to keep the peace, usually himself in a certain sum and two good and solvent sureties in so much each, taking care at the same time that the amounts named should not be excessive or unreasonable. The justice may bind the accused over to appear at the sessions, and to keep the peace in the meantime towards the complainant; or he may, in his discretion, bind him to keep the peace for a reasonable specified time, which time must not however exceed two years. The latter is held to be the better way, rather than to appear at the sessions, where the offender would be obliged to find fresh sureties without any new offence being alleged, and for non-appearance his recognizance would be forfeited unless good cause of excuse should be shown. * If the offender fails or refuses to find the sureties ordered, the justice must commit him to prison until the next general sessions, or for the time specified in his order during which he is to keep the peace.

A recognizance may be forfeited by doing any actual violence to the person of another aside from the original complainant, or causing it to be done. † But a justifiable assault (as in one's own defence) is no forfeiture. ‡ The recognizance may be discharged on the release of the complaining party. § If the recognizance runs to keep the peace

---

* R. *v* Doherty 13 East 171. † R. *v* Parnell 2 Burr 806.
* 2 B. & A. 278. † Dalton Chap. 121.
‡ 1 Hawkins, Chap. 60, Sec. 23-24. § Ibid Sec. 17.

towards the Queen and all her subjects the sessions may discharge it, unless on proclamation made some person appears to demand sureties upon warrantable cause; but if it is made to keep the peace with some particular person the sessions will not discharge it, though the complainant requiring it does not appear; and the court may bind over the defendant to the next sessions.* If an accused person is in prison for want of sureties he must be released on the death of the party demanding the peace against him, or if he offers sufficient bail.

Canadian judges have heretofore been in the habit, during their semi-annual assize circuits, of ordering persons committed to gaol on peace warrants to be brought before them, and directing that they should be discharged. As magistrates have the same jurisdiction as judges of the Court of Chancery and Queen's Bench in the matter of taking sureties to keep the peace, no judge has a right to review their decision, or to discharge persons committed by them under peace warrants.† Nor has he that right at the present day under the common law. In 1878, however, Chap. 19 of the Dominion Statutes was expressly passed to give authority to county judges, and to other judges in some of the provinces (but not in Ontario) to have persons committed to gaol under peace warrants, and who have been there for two weeks, brought before them. After inquiring into their cases the judge may direct their discharge from custody, or make such order concerning them as might be made by the court of general sessions.

Complaint of the party threatened for Sureties for the Peace.

Canada,
Province of,
County of
  To Wit :
} The information (*or* complaint) of C. D. of the township of in the said District (or County, United Counties, *or as the*

---

* Dalton Chap. 120.   † Willis *v* Bridges 2 B & A. 278,

case may be,) of   , (*laborer*).   (*If preferred by an Attorney or Agent, say:*) "D. E. his duly authorized Agent (*or Attorney*), in this behalf, taken upon oath, before me, the undersigned, one of Her Majesty's Justices of the Peace, in and for the said District (*or* County, United Counties, *or as the case may be*) of   , at N., in the said District, County, *or as the case may be*) of   this day of   , in the year of our Lord, one thousand eight hundred and   , who saith that A. B. of the (*Township*) of   , in the District (County, *or as the case may be*, of   , did, on the   day of   (instant *or* last past, *as the case may be*), threaten the said C. D. in the words, or to the effect following, that is to say, (*Set them out with the circumstances under which they were used*) and that from the above and other threats used by the said A. B. towards the said C. D., he, the said C. D., is afraid that the said A. B. will do him some bodily injury, and therefore prays that the said A. B. may be required to find sufficient Sureties to keep the peace and be of good behaviour towards him, the said C. D. ; and the said C. D also saith, that he doth not make this complaint against, nor require such Sureties from the said A. B., from any malice or ill will, but merely for the preservation of his person from injury.

A. B. or (*or* C. D.)

Taken and Sworn before me, the day and year and at the place above mentioned.

J. S.

Form of Peace Warrant.

Canada,
Province of,   } To the constables of
County of   } in the county of   .
  To Wit :

Whereas John Doe, of   , yeoman, hath on this   day of   personally come before me, John Smith, Esq., one of Her Majesty's justices of the peace in and for the said county, and hath this day made information and complaint upon oath that Richard Roe, of   , yeoman, did on the   day of   , at   , threaten to beat, &c., (*here follows the information*) and that from the above and other threats used by the said Richard Roe towards the said John Doe, he, the said John Doe, is afraid that the said Richard Roe will do him some bodily harm, and hath therefore prayed of me the said justice, that the Richard Roe may be required to find sufficient sureties to keep the peace and be of good behaviour towards him the said John Doe. These are therefore to require you immediately upon sight hereof, to apprehend and bring the said Richard Roe before me, to find sufficient sureties as well for his appearance at the next general quarter sessions of the peace to be holden in and for the said county, then and there to answer to the premises, and to do and receive what shall be then and their enjoined him by the court, as also to keep the peace and be of good behaviour towards Her Majesty and all her liege people, and especially towards the said John Doe.

Given under my hand and seal, at   in the said county, the   day of   .

JOHN SMITH, J. P. [L. S.]

Form of Recognizance for the Sessions.

Be it remembered, that on the   day of   in the year of our Lord   , A. B. of   *(labourer)*, L. M. of   *(grocer)*, and N. O. of *(butcher)*, personally came before *(us)* the undersigned, *(two)* of Her Majesty's Justices of the Peace for the said District (*or* County, United Counties, *or as the case may be*, of   and severally acknowledged themselves to owe to our Lady the Queen the several sums following, that is to say : the said A. B. the sum of   and the said L. M. and N. O. the sum of   , each, of good and lawful money of Canada, to be made and levied of their goods and chattels, lands and tenements respectively, to the use of our said Lady the Queen; Her Heirs and Successors, if the said A. B. fail in the condition endorsed.

Taken and acknowledged the day and year first above mentioned, at   , before us.

J. S.
J. T.

The condition of the within written Recognizance is such, that if the within bounden A. B. (of, &c.) shall appear at the next Court of General or Quarter Sessions of the Peace (*or other Court discharging the functions of the Court of General Quarter Sessions, as the case may be,*) to be holden in and for the said District (*or* County, United Counties, *or as the case may be*) of   to do and receive what shall be then and there enjoined him by the Court ; and in the meantime shall keep the peace, and be of good behaviour towards Her Majesty and all Her liege people, and especially towards C. D. (of &c.) for the term of   now next ensuing, then the said Recognizance to be void, or else to stand in full force and virtue.

Condition of the Recognizance to keep the Peace, &c., without appearing at the Sessions.

The condition of the above recognizance is such that if the above bounden Richard Roe shall keep the peace, and be of good behaviour towards Her Majesty and all her liege people, and especially towards John Doe of   , for the space of one year, (*or longer if need be,*) then this recognizance to be void, or else to remain in full force and virtue.

Form of Commitment in Default of Sureties.

Canada, Province of County of   To Wit : } To all or any of the Constables or other Peace Officers   in the District (*or* County) (*or* one of the United Counties, *or as the case may be*) of   and to the Keeper of the Common Gaol of the said District, (County *or* United Counties, *or as the case may be*) at   , in the said District (*or* County, &c.,   )

Whereas, on the   , day of   instant, complaint on oath was made before the undersigned (*or* J. L., Esquire,) (*one*) of Her Majesty's Justices of the Peace in and for the said District (*or* County, United Counties, *or as the case may be*) of   , by C. D. of the township of   , in the said District (County, *or as the case may be*) (*laborer,*) that A. B. of, &c., on the   day of   , at the township of   aforesaid, did threaten (*&c., follow to end of complaint, as in form above, in the past tense, then*) : And whereas the said A. B. was this day brought and uppeared before me the said Justice, (*or* J. L., Esquire, one of Her Majesty's Justices of the Peace in and for the said District (*or* County, United Counties, *or as the case may be*) of   , to answer unto the said complaint : And having been required by me to enter into his own Recognizance in the sum of   , with two sufficient sureties in the sum of   each, as well for his appearance at the next General or Quarter Sessions of the Peace, (*or other Court discharging the functions of the Court of General or Quarter Sessions, as the case may be,*) to be held in and for the said District (*or* County, United Counties, *or as the case may be,*) of   , to do what shall be then and there enjoined him by the Court, as also in the meantime to keep the Peace and be of good behaviour towards Her Majesty and all Her liege people, and especially towards the said C. D., hath refused and neglected, and still refuses and neglects to find such sureties) ; These are therefore to command you and each of you to take the said A. R., and him safely to convey to the (*Common Gaol*) at   aforesaid, and there to deliver him to the Keeper thereof, together with this precept ; And I do hereby command you the said Keeper of the (*Common Gaol,*) to receive the said A. B. into your custody, in the said (*Common Gaol,*) there to imprison him until the said next General *or* Quarter Sessions of the Peace, (*or the next term or sitting, the said Court discharging functions of the Court of General or Quarter Sessions, as the case may be,*) unless he, in the meantime, find sufficient sureties as well for his appearance at the said Sessions (or Court), as in the meantime to keep the peace as aforesaid.

Given under my hand and seal this   day of   in the year of our Lord, 18 , at   in the District (*or* County, *or as the case may be*) aforesaid.

The form of a Supersedeas to be used where the defendant finds surety before the warrant is executed upon him.

Province,	John Smith, Esq., one of the
County of	justices of our lady the Queen,
To Wit :	assigned to keep the peace within

the said county, to the sheriff of the said county, and to the

---

(*a*) A neglect or inability to find sureties is the same as a *refusal* at law.

constables and others, the faithful ministers and subjects of our said lady the Queen within the said county, and to every of them, greeting.

Forasmuch as Richard Roe, of   , in the said county, yeoman, hath personally came before me at   , in the said county, and hath found sufficient surety, that is to say, Frank Brown, of   yeoman, and James King, of   yeoman, either of whom hath undertaken for the said Richard Roe, upon the pain of $, and he the said Richard Roe hath undertaken for himself, under the pain of $, that he, the said Richard Roe, shall personally appear at the next general (or quarter) sessions of the peace to be holden in and for the said county, then and there to do and receive what shall be then and there enjoined him by the court, and in the meantime to keep the peace and be of good behaviour towards Her Majesty and all her liege people, and especially towards John Doe, of   , therefore, I do command you and every of you, that you utterly forbear and do cease to arrest, take, imprison, or otherwise by any means, for the said cause, to molest the said Richard Roe, and if you have for the said occasion and for none other taken and imprisoned him the said Richard Roe, that then him you deliver or cause to be delivered and set at liberty without further delay.

Given under my hand and seal, this   day of   &c.

JOHN SMITH, J. P. [L. S.]

Release of the Surety of the Peace, &c.

Province,   ⎫ Be it remembered, that John
County of   ⎬ Doe, of   , in the said
To Wit: ⎭ county, yeoman, on the
day of   , in the   year of the reign of our sovereign lady Victoria, came before me, John Smith, Esq., one of the justices of our said lady the Queen assigned to keep the peace within the said county, and there remised and freely released to Richard Roe, of   , in the said county, yeoman, the surety of the peace and good behaviour by him the said John Doe before me prayed against the said Richard Roe.

Given under my hand and seal, the   day of   , in the year of our Lord, 18   .

JOHN SMITH, J. P. [L. S.]

Or, if it is before another Justice, then say—

The surety of the peace and good behaviour which he has against Richard Roe of   , in the said county, yeoman.

Given under my hand and seal, &c.

Discharge of one Committed for want of Sureties.

Province, ⎱ John Smith, Esq., one of the
County of ⎰ justices of our lady the Queen as-
   To Wit: ⎱ signed to keep the peace in the county of   , to the keeper of Her Majesty's common gaol at   in the said county, greeting.

Forasmuch as Richard Roe, in the prison of our said lady the Queen, in your custody now being, at the suit of John Doe, of   , in the said county yeoman, for the want of his finding sufficient sureties, &c. (*as in the former precedent of a supersedeas*). Therefore, I do command you that if the said Richard Roe do remain in the said gaol for the said cause, and none other, then you forbear to grieve or detain him any longer, but that you deliver him thence and suffer him to go at large, and that upon the pain which will fall thereon.

Given under my hand and seal, this   day of   , 18 .

JOHN SMITH, J. P. [L. S.]

Form of Articles of the Peace in the Courts of Chancery or Queen's Bench.

Province, ⎱ Sarah Roe, wife of Richard Roe,
County of ⎰ of   in the said county,
   To Wit: ⎱ labourer, prays surety of the peace against the said Richard Roe, her said husband, for fear of death or bodily injury.

First—This informant, on her oath, saith, that she intermarried with her said husband about   years ago, since which time he hath often in a cruel, barbarous, and inhuman manner, beat, abused, and ill-treated this informant, and frequently threatened to take away her life.

Secondly—This informant saith, that on the   day of   last past, her said husband in a violent passion, (*state the particular acts of cruelty.*)

Lastly—This informant saith, that she is actually afraid

her said husband will do her some bodily injury, if not murder her, should she return home again to him; and saith that she did not make this complaint against her said husband out of any hatred, malice, or ill-will which she hath or beareth towards him, but purely for the preservation of her life and person from further danger.

N. B.—Articles of the peace should have the signature of counsel appended thereto.

Commitment for Contempt.

Province, }
County of } To the keeper of
To Wit: }

Receive into your custody the body of Richard Roe herewith sent you by me John Smith, Esquire, one of Her Majesty's justices of the peace in and for the said county, and convicted (or charged, as the case may be) by me, the said justice, with contempt and indecent behaviour in my presence, by insulting and obstructing me, the said justice, in the due execution of my office, as such justice as aforesaid, (*and for saying &c., in the presence and hearing of me, the said justice,*) [*here set forth the particulars, if the justice shall think it necessary,*] and him the said Richard Roe detain in your custody, in the gaol aforesaid, for the space of hours, to be computed from the hour of o'clock, in the forenoon of this present day of instant, for his contempt aforesaid, (or until he find two sufficient sureties for his appearance at the next general (or quarter) sessions of the peace for the said county, to answer to the charge aforesaid, or be otherwise discharged by the due course of law.)

Given under my hand and seal, at , in the said county, the , day of .

JOHN SMITH, J. P. [L. S.]

Public Statutes of the Dominion of Canada under which Justices of the Peace are empowered to perform some official act.

31 VICTORIA, 1867–8.

CHAP. 15. *To prevent the unlawful Training of persons to the use of arms.* This act comes into force by proclamation only of the Governor-General in Council, and gives certain powers to justices of the peace.

CHAP. 36. *Respecting Commissions, and Oaths of Allegiance and of Office.* This act provides that it shall not be necessary to renew any commission (such as that of justices of the peace or otherwise) on the death of the Sovereign.— The oaths of office and allegiance, however, must be taken anew, for which see Sec's 3 and 4.

CHAP. 40. *Respecting Militia and Defence of the Dominion of Canada.* Sec. 27 provides that two magistrates may call out active militia to aid civil power. Justices have jurisdiction under this act for various offences.

CHAP. 47. *Respecting the Unlawful Manufacture or importation of copper coins or tokens.* Gives jurisdiction to justices of the peace, singly and before two justices.

CHAP. 55. *Respecting Trade Marks and industrial designs.* Gives jurisdiction to a justice of the peace in several cases. Sec. 9 repealed by 35 Vic., Chap. 32, Sec. 24.

CHAP. 60. *The Fisheries Act of 1868.* (Sec. 7 repealed by 33 Vic., Chap. 33). This Act repeals all former Fisheries Acts by Sec. 20, except those of New Brunswick and Nova Scotia, as set out in Sec. 21. Gives jurisdiction to one justice of the peace.

CHAP. 63. *Quarantine and Health Act of 1868.* (Sec. 15 repeals certain acts), Sec. 12 gives jurisdiction to two justices of the peace.

CHAP. 65. *Respecting Inspection of Steamboats.* (Repeals all former acts by Sec. 50). Sec. 38 gives jurisdiction to two justices of the peace.

CHAP. 66. *Respecting Aliens and Naturalization.* Sec. 4 prescribes certain duties for justices of the peace. Sec. 13

makes false swearing perjury. Sec. 14 repeals certain acts and parts of acts.

CHAP. 70. *Respecting Riots and Riotous Assemblies.* (Repeals all former Canadian Acts). Sec. 1 provides that twelve persons may be termed riotously assembled. Sec. 2 provides form of "Riot Act" proclamation. Prescribes the various duties of justices of the peace under this act.

CHAP. 71. *Respecting Forgery, Perjury and Intimidation in connection with the Provincial Legislatures and their Acts.* This act makes the crimes recited in its title felonies.

CHAP. 72. *Respecting Accessories to, and Abettors of, indictable offences.* This statute makes accessories before and after the act liable to be tried for the same offence as the principals, as regards felonies. Sec. 9 makes the same provision as to misdemeanors.

CHAP. 75. *Penitentiary Act, 1868.* (Repeals all former Acts). Sec. 43 gives jurisdiction to one justice of the peace for trespass on premises.

32-33 VICTORIA, 1869.

CHAP. 10. *The Immigration Act 1869.* (Amended by 35 Vic., Chap. 28). Sec. 25 gives jurisdiction to one justice to enforce penalties in certain cases. Sec. 26 gives jurisdiction to two justices up to eighty dollars. Sec. 27 empowers one justice to take complaint and issue process.

CRAP. 11. *The Patent Act of 1869.* Sections 50 and 51 make certain acts, such as countefeiting marks and false entries, misdemeanors.

CHAP. 18. *Respecting Coinage Offences.* (Repeals all coinage acts of the several Provinces). Provides various penalties for counterfeiting coin, &c., and prescribes the duties of justices of the peace under the act.

CHAP. 19. *Respecting Forgery.* (Repeals all Forgery Acts of the several Provinces). Sec's 30 and 31 of this act repealed by 35 Vic., Chap. 32, as to trade marks. This act deals with the various kinds of forgery, and prescribes the duties of justices thereunder.

CHAP. 20. *Respecting Offences against the Person.*— (Repeals all former acts of same nature of the various Provinces). Provides for the various offences against the person.

Sec. 49 of this act relating to rape, &c., is amended by 36 Vic., Chap. 50. It is further amended by 37 Vic., Chap. 37, which adds five new sections thereto after Sec. 81.

CHAP. 21. *Respecting Larceny and similar offences.*— (Repeals all former acts of the several Provinces). Provides for the various offences under this head. Gives summary jurisdiction to justices in certain cases of petty theft. Sec. 111 is amended by 38 Vic., Chap. 40.

CHAP. 22. *Respecting Malicious Injuries to property.* (Repeals all similar laws of the several Provinces). Defines the various offences under this head, and prescribes the duties jutices have to perform under act.

CHAP. 23. *Respecting Perjury.* (Repeals all acts as to perjury of the several Provinces). Makes perjury a misdemeanor. Justices of the peace have now primary jurisdiction.

CHAP. 24. *To preserve the Peace on Public Works.*— (Amended by 38 Vic., Chap. 38). Gives jurisdiction to a justice of the peace.

CHAP. 25. *Respecting certain offences in the Army and Navy.* Provides penalties for enticing to desert, &c., and gives jurisdiction to one justice of the peace in certain cases.

CHAP. 26. *For the better protection of Military and Naval Stores,* Gives jurisdiction to two justices of the peace.

CHAP. 27. *Respecting Cruelty to Animals.* Sec's 1 and 2 of this act are repealed by 43 Vic., Chap. 38, Sec's 2 and 3. Amended act gives jurisdiction to two justices only, instead of one as before.

CHAP. 28. *Respecting Vagrants.* Gives jurisdiction to two justices. Amended by 37 Vic., Chap. 43, which permits imprisonment to be for six months in place of two.

CHAP. 29. *Respecting procedure in Criminal Cases.*— For duties of justices under this act see Sec's 2 to 6, also 111.

CHAP. 30. *Respecting the duties of Justices of the Pence out of Sessions, in relation to persons charged with indictable offences.* (Repeals all similar acts of the various Provinces). This act gives the clearest and most explicit instructions as to duties of the justice of the peace, where he is the minister of the law only, and sends persons to trial to higher courts than his own. Every justice should carefully study this act, and comply with its provisions when investigating criminal cases.

CHAP. 31. *Respecting the duties of Justices of the Peace in relation to Summary Convictions and orders.* (Repeals all similar former acts of the several Provinces). This act gives the clearest and most ample instructions to justices of the peace as to how they shall proceed in relation to all cases brought before them in their judicial capacity. In these cases the justice sits as a judge. Every justice should study this act up fully for himself, and carefully conform to its provisions. Sec. 65 of this act has been repealed, and a new Section substituted as to right of appeal, by 33 Vic., Chap. 27, Sec. 1. Sec. 71 also repealed by Sec. 2 of same act, which likewise supplies a new form of notice of appeal.

CHAP. 32. *Respecting the prompt and Summary Administration of Criminal Justice in certain cases.* Sec. 19 provides that a justice may send for trial before a competent magistrate, as defined in Section 1. This act is amended by 40 Vic., Chap. 31, Sec. 3.

CHAP. 33. *Respecting the trial and punishment of Juvenile Offenders.* Sec. 1 gives jurisdiction to two justices of the peace. Sec. 7 provides that one justice may issue process to arrest, &c. See also Sec's 9 to 12.

CHAP. 38. *Respecting inquiries and investigations into Shipwreck and other matters.* Gives jurisdiction to one justice in certain cases.

33 VICTORIA, 1870.

CHAP. 27. *To amend the Summary Conviction and Order Act of 1869.* Sec. 1 repeals Sec. 65 of 32-33 Vic., Chap. 31, and substitutes a a new Sec. therefor. Further amended by 40 Vic., Chap. 27.

CHAP. 31. *The Queen's Seaman's Clothing Act 1870.* Provides penalties for the purchase of sailor's clothing, and gives jurisdiction to one justice of the peace.

CHAP. 35. *Respecting Dominion Ferries.* Gives jurisdiction to one justice of the peace.

CHAP. 36. *Respecting the Marking of Timber.* Sec. 8 makes using another person's mark a misdemeanor.

CHAP. 37. *To Amend the law relating to Inspection of Raw Hides and Leather.* (Amends 27-28 Vic., Chap. 21 and 29-30 Vic., Chap. 24,) Sec. 5, gives jurisdiction to two justices of the peace up to forty dollars penalty.

34 VICTORIA, 1871.

CHAP. 11. *For the prevention of corrupt practices in relation to the Collection of the Revenue.* This act makes receiving bribes or offering them and other offences misdemeanors.

CHAP. 22. *To Amend 31 Vic. Chap. 66, Respecting Aliens and Naturalization.* Provides that certain oaths or affirmations may be taken by justices of the peace.

35 VICTORIA, 1872.

CHAP. 28. *To amend the Immigration Act of 1869.* Sec. 4 provides that breach of contract may be sued for before one justice. Sec. 11 makes seduction by any of the crew a misdemeanor. Sec. 12 provides against intercourse by crew with female passengers under penalty of loss of wages for voyage.

CHAP. 29. *The Trade Unions Act 1872.* Sec. 19 gives jurisdiction to two justices.

CHAP. 31. *To amend the Criminal Law relating to Violence, Threats and Molestation.* (Amended by 39 Vic., Chap. 37.) Gives jurisdiction to two justices.

CHAP. 32. *To amend the Law relating to the fraudulent marking of merchandize.* Sec. 2 makes counterfeiting a trade-mark a misdemeanor. Other sections create various offences under the act. Sec. 16 provides that certain penalties shall be recoverable by proceedings before two justices of the peace. Repeals Sections 30 and 31 of 32-33 Vic., Chap. 19, and 31 Vic., Chap. 55, Sec. 9.

CHAP. 33. *For the avoidance of doubt respecting the Larceny of Stamps.* This act makes the stealing of postal cards and stamps of all kinds a larceny.

36 VICTORIA, 1873.

CHAP. 48. *Inspection of Gas and Gas Meters.* Sec's 39, 40, 41 and 42, provide various penalties under this act for certain offences. Sec. 44 provides that penalty up to twenty dollars may be enforced by one justice; above that amount by two justices.

CHAP. 55. *The Wreck and Salvage Act, 1873.* This statute declares various acts to be felonies and misdemeanors. Sec. 20 provides that two justices can imprison for certain misdemeanors for six months, or impose a fine of four hundred dollars.

CHAP. 57. *To provide for keeping order on board Passenger Steamers.* Gives jurisdiction to one justice up to ten dollars fine: over that amount to two justices.

CHAP. 58. *Amends the Acts to prevent the Desertion of Seamen.* This act amends Chap. 43 of Consolidated Statutes of Canada, and 34 Vic., Chap. 32, and takes away right of appeal in certain cases.

37 VICTORIA, 1874.

CHAP. 129 of 36 Vic. (Reserved Act). *The Seamen's Act of 1873.* Sec. 114 gives jurisdiction to one justice of the peace.

CHAP. 37. *For the suppression of Voluntary and Extra-Judicial Oaths by Justices of the Peace and others.* Sec. 1 prohibits justices from administering such oaths. Sec. 2 provides that they be liable to a penalty of fine or imprisonment. Provides form of declaration instead of such oath.

CHAP. 38. *Crime of Libel.* Sec. 1 makes threats to publish or to refrain from publishing to extort money a misdemeanor. Sec. 2 makes publication a misdemeanor. Justice of the peace have the same ministerial jurisdiction as in other cases of misdemeanor.

CHAP. 45. *The General Inspection Act, 1874.* Sec. 16 gives jurisdiction to two justices of the peace over all penalties up to forty dollars.

38 VICTORIA, 1875.

CHAP. 7. *The Post Office Act, 1875.* (Repeals former acts), Sec 72 relates to offences and penalties in subsections, 2 to 30. Sec. 73 makes embezzlement, &c., a felony. Sec. 74 provides, that only licensed persons can sell stamps. Sec. 82 provides that all penalties not exceeding forty dollars may be recovered before one justice of the peace. If above that amount may be indicted for misdemeanor.

CHAP. 29. *The Seamen's Agreement Act, 1875.* Sec. 3 sets out the nature of agreement to be made with every sailor. Sec. 5 provides twenty dollars penalty on master if he does not make such agreement. Sec. 7 makes fraudulently altering agreement a misdemeanor. Sec. 16 makes misconduct endangering life or limb a misdemeanor. Sec. 17 provides punishment for desertion and other offences. Sec. 27 provides punishment for enticing to desert, or harbouring deserters. Sec. 30 gives jurisdiction to one justice of the peace. See also Sec's 32 & 33.

CHAP. 30. *Act to amend 36 Vic., Chap. 9, and 37 Vic., Chap. 34, respecting the appointment of Harbour Masters.* Sec. 4 gives jurisdiction to one justice of the peace to enforce any penalty prescribed by order of the Governor General in council.

CHAP. 41. *For Suppressing Gaming Houses.* (Amended by 40 Vic., Chap. 33) gives jurisdiction to one justice of the peace.

CHAP. 42. *To prevent Cruelty to Animals while in transit.* Gives jurisdiction to one justice of the peace.

39 VICTORIA, 1876.

CHAP. 31. *An act to amend the Criminal Law relative to Violence, Threats and Molestation.* Sec. 2 repeals Sec. 1 of 35 Vic., Chap. 31, and substitutes other provisions therefor. Two justices have jurisdiction.

40 VICTORIA, 1877.

CHAP. 10. *An Act respecting the Customs.* (Repeals former acts). Sec. 30 directs that affidavit of appraiser be taken before a justice of the peace. Sec. 76 makes smuggling or making false entries a misdemeanor. Sec. 77 makes penalty for offering pretended smuggled goods for sale recoverable before one justice. Sec. 79 makes having goods liable to forfeiture in possession, where five persons or more are in company, a misdemeanor. Sec. 88 makes penalty for counterfeiting marks or brands recoverable before two justices, and false swearing to be perjury. Sec. 89 makes falsifying certain papers a misdemeanor. Sec's 91, 92, 94, 96, 98, 101 and 104, provide how certain duties shall be performed by justices. Sec. 116 provides for right of appeal from their decisions.

CHAP. 27. *To amend the law as to appeals from Convictions by Justices of the Peace.* Sec. 1 repeals 39 Vic., Chap. 23. Sec. 2 repeals Sec. 65 of Summary Convictions Acts of 1868, (32 33 Vic., Chap. 31), and substitutes a new section therefor. Sec. 3 defines who shall be regarded as Clerk of the Peace.

CHAP. 28. *To amend the act respecting Offences against the Person.* (32-33 Vic. Chap. 20). Repeals Sec's 10 and 51 of this act, and substitutes new sections.

CHAP. 30. *To make provision against the Improper use of Firearms.* Under this act persons carrying a pistol or air-gun without cause, may be ordered to find sureties to keep the peace for six months, or in default be imprisoned for thirty days. It provides other penalties for certain offences, and gives jurisdiction to one justice of the peace.

CHAP. 31. *For the Repression of Betting and Pool Selling.* Makes offence a misdemeanor.

CHAP. 32. *To prevent Gambling Practices in certain Public Conveyances.* Makes the offence an indictable one for which the examining justice must commit for trial to the next competent court.

CHAP. 33. *To amend the Act for the Suppression of Gaming Houses.* Sec. 3 provides that gaming instruments be destroyed. Sec. 4. provides that lookers on shall be punished.

CHAP. 34. *To amend the Post Office Act, 1875.* Makes wilful obstructing or delaying the passage of mails in any way a misdemeanor.

CHAP. 35. *The Breaches of Contract Act, 1877.* This act completely changes the character of all the master and servants acts throughout the Dominion, and in ordinary cases leaves the employer without any remedy save the civil one for breach of contract. It provides, however, that servants or persons who by breaking any contract might endanger life or property, or maliciously withhold gas or water, or refuses to serve a railway company after contract, shall be guilty of malicious injury to property, and be punishable by fine or imprisonment. (For jurisdiction of two justices see 35 Vic., Chap. 31, Sec. 2.) Sec, 7 provides that copies of the act be posted up by certain corporations under a penalty of twenty dollars for each day in default.

41 VICTORIA, 1878.

CHAP. 7. *Public Accounts Audit Act.* Sec's 67, 68 & 69 make certain offences misdemeanors or felonies. For repealing clauses see Sec. 77.

CHAP. 15. *Territories Homestead Exemption Act.* Sec. 7 makes certain false statements perjury.

CHAP. 16. *The Canada Temperance Act 1878.* Sec. 64 makes certain offences misdemeanors. Sec 103 gives jurisdiction to two justices of the peace. Sec. 108 authorizes one justice to issue search warrant under act.

42 VICTORIA, 1879.

CHAP. 9. *Consolidated Railway Act.* (Repeals all former Railway Acts.) Sec. 13 is explanatory as to what justice is meant by act. Sec. 25, Sub-Sec. 11 provides that an engine driver or conductor who is intoxicated is guilty of a misdemeanor. Sec. 26 provides that over-due trains must be announced on a blackboard at each station, and in default a penalty of five dollars may be recovered before two justices. Sec. 27, Sub-Sec. 2, provides how fines under first part of act are to be recovered, (3) how applied, (4) and as to misdemeanor. Sec. 61 provides that justices at General Sessions may appoint Railway Constables. (2) One justice may administer oath. (3) Two justices may dismiss constable for misconduct. (5) Railway Constables liable to a penalty of eighty dollars or two months' imprisonment for certain acts. Sec's 83 & 84 provide that railway companies must keep weeds cut down along track after 20 days' notice by chief officer of municipality, or by a justice of the peace therein. In default can order weeds to be cut, and sue for amount of expenditure for labor, and in addition for two dollars penalty for each day in default after notice. Sec's 86 to 96 are classed under the head of "Penal Clauses," and apply to various offences, in which a justice has either ministerial or judicial authority.

CHAP. 16. *Weights and Measures Act.* (Repeals all former acts.) For penalties under this act see Sec's 21, 24, 25, 26, 28, 29, 30, 44, 46, 47. Sec. 53 provides that all penalties up to fifty dollars may be recovered before one justice; above that amount before two justices; and how penalty is to be applied.

CHAP. 17. *Stamps on Notes and Bills.* (Repeals all former acts.) Sec. 24 makes counterfeiting stamps or stamped paper a forgery. Sec. 26 makes using cancelled stamps a misdemeanor.

CHAP. 18. *Inspection, Safe Keeping, and Storage of Petroleum.* (Repeals former act.) For penalties see Sec's 10, 12, 13 & 14. Sec. 15 provides that penalties shall be recoverable before two justices of the peace. Sec. 16 provides that suits must be brought within six months after offence has been committed.

CHAP. 21. *Respecting Census and Statistics.* (Repeals all former acts.) Sec. 13 makes wilful neglect by any census officer a misdemeanor. Sec. 15 compels every person to fill up schedule under a penalty of forty dollars. Sec. 16 provides that persons who do not answer questions shall be liable to a penalty of twenty dollars. Sec. 17 provides that penalties, as described, may be recovered before one justice.

CHAP. 22. *Trade Mark and Design Act.* (Repeals all former acts.) Sec. 16 provides that the illegal use of trade marks is a misdemeanor.

CHAP. 23. *The Animal Contagious Diseases Act.* (Repeals former act.) Sec's 27 and 38 gives certain powers to justices of the peace. The act, however, does not very clearly explain the nature of these powers and justices should have legal advice before acting on them. Some order in council may possibly more clearly define them.

CHAP. 31. *Dominion Lands Act. 1879.* (Repeals all former acts.) Sec. 58 gives power to one justice to order, on information sworn, timber cut without authority to be seized. Sec. 60 makes carrying away illegally such timber a felony. Sec's 112 and 113 give power to justices to aid surveyors. See also Sec's 115 and 116 as to protection of surveyors. Sec. 126 gives power to a justice to take affidavits, &c.

CHAP. 45. *Transfer of Bank Shares.* (Amends the act relating to banks and banking, 31st Vic., Chap. 5.) Sec. 5 provides that any broker inserting a false number or share in any agreement shall be guilty of a misdemeanor.

42-43 VICTORIA, 1880.

CHAP. 3. *An Act to amend an Act (31 Vic., Chap. 37) respecting the Security to be given by Officers in Canada.* Sec. 3 provides that sureties in the bond shall make the required affidavit before a justice of the peace.

CHAP. 19. *An Act to Consolidate and Amend the Acts Respecting the Island Revenue.* Sec. 140, Sub-Sec. 4, gives jurisdiction to a police or stipendiary magistrate or to two justices of the peace to enforce certain provisions. See also Sec. 141.

CHAP. 21. *The Petroleum Inspection Act.* Sec. 27 gives jurisdiction to police or stipendiary magistrate or two justices of the peace.

CHAP. 25. *The North-West Territories Act.* Sec. 76, Sub-Sec. 5, gives authority to a stipendiary magistrate and one justice of the peace, with the aid of a jury of six to try murder and all other felonies. See also Sec. 90 as to prohibition of intoxicants in the N. W. Territories, and the schedule extending various statutes thereto.

CHAP. 28. *Respecting Indians.* (Repeals all former acts.) Sec. 24, 27, 65, 74, 85 give jurisdiction to one justice for various offences: Sec. 92 to two justices.

CHAP. 29. *Navigation of Canadian Waters.* Sec. 9 provides that penalties under act, unless otherwise provided, may be sued for before two justices of the peace.

Public Statutes of the Province of Ontario, under which Justices of the Peace are empowered to perform some Ministerial or Judicial Act.

REVISED STATUTES OF ONTARIO, 1877.

CHAP. 10. *The Election Act.* Sec. 146 provides for secrecy at polling places. For violation of this section two justices may imprison for six months.

CHAP. 29. *The General Mining Act.* Sec. 40 gives jurisdiction to two justices to try offenders under this act.

CHAP. 31. *Respecting Riots near Public Works.* Provides that one justice may perform alone certain official acts. Sec. 11 provides that two justices must commit for penalties.

CHAP. 32. *Respecting the Sale of Intoxicating Liquor near Public Works.* This act prohibits the sale of liquor within a certain distance of public works in progress. Sec. 4 gives jurisdiction to a single justice to commit.

CHAP. 36. *Respecting the Registration of Births, Marriages and Deaths.* Sec's 7 to 12 provide who shall register. Sec's 17, 24 and 25 gives jurisdiction to one justice to enforce penalties for offences under this act.

CHAP. 47. *The Division Courts Act.* Sec. 19 provides that a justice may issue warrant to attach the effects of absconding debtors, where the debt is over four and under one hundred dollars. Sec's 217 and 224 gives jurisdiction to one justice to enforce certain penalties.

CHAP. 74. This act provides for appeals against magistrate's convictions under any Ontario Statute.

CHAP. 75. This act provides for the appeal to judge of a County Court, in certain cases, from justices' decisions.

CHAP. 76. *Respecting Returns of Convictions and Fines by Justices of the Peace.*

CHAP. 77. *An act Respecting the Fees of Justices of the Peace.* Amended by 41 Vic., Chap. 4, Sec. 6.

CHAP. 82. *Respecting Constables.* Provides how to be appointed and otherwise

CHAP. 83. *Respecting Special Constables.* Gives jurisdiction to appoint and control to two justices.

CHAP. 90. *Respecting the Administration of Justice in Unorganized Tracts.* Sec's 35, 44, 50 and 51, prescribe the duties and powers of justices of the peace under this act.

CHAP. 96 *Respecting the rights of property in swarms of Bees.* See addition to Sec. 5 for misdemeanor.

CHAP. 112. *Respecting Ferries.* Sec. 10 gives jurisdiction to one justice.

CHAP. 113. *Respecting Mills and Mill-Dams.* Sec. 4 provides that owners and occupiers of mill-dams must keep timber slides (if there are any) in repair. Sec. 7 provides the penalty in default, and gives two justices jurisdiction.

CHAP. 115. *Respecting Rivers and Streams.* To prevent the obstruction of floatable rivers and streams. Sec. 8 provides that penalties may be sued for before one justice.

CHAP. 118. *Respecting Fraudulent Preferences by Creditors in Insolvent circumstances.* This act makes certain offences misdemeanors.

CHAP. 131. *Respecting the Support of Illegitimate children.* Provides that an action may be maintained against the father of an illegitimate child for necessaries for its use. Sec. 3 provides that an affidavit of affiliation must first be made before a justice of the peace.

CHAP. 133. *Respecting Master and Servant.* Gives jurisdiction to one justice.

CHAP. 135. *Respecting Apprentices and Minors.* Sec. 17 gives jurisdiction to one justice in certain cases.

CHAP. 142. *Respecting the Profession of Medicine and Surgery.* Sec. 46 gives jurisdiction to one justice.

CHAP. 143. *Respecting the Study of Anatomy.* Sec. 21 gives jurisdiction to one justice.

CHAP. 144. *Respecting Dentistry.* Sec. 21 gives jurisdiction to one justice.

CHAP. 145. *Respecting Pharmacy.* Sec. 29 gives jurisdiction to two justices.

CHAP. 146. *Respecting Land Surveyors.* Sec. 78 makes certain offences misdemeanors.

CHAP. 148. *Respecting Pawnbrokers.* A justice of the peace has various ministerial and judicial duties to perform under this act.

CHAP. 149. *Respecting Joint Stock Companies.* Sec. 30 provides that making false entries in books of account is a misdemeanor.

CHAP. 151. *Respecting Telegraph Companies.* One justice has jurisdiction.

CHAP. 152. *Respecting Joint Stock Road Companies.* Sec. 130 gives jurisdiction to one justice. See also Sec. 142.

CHAP. 153. *Respecting Joint Stock Companies as regards floating Timber down Rivers and Streams.* Sec's 65 to 69 give one justice jurisdiction in various cases.

CHAP. 157. *Respecting Gas and Water Companies.*—Sec. 79 gives jurisdiction to one justice.

CHAP. 159. *To Protect Cheese and Butter Manufacturers.* Sec. 3 gives jurisdiction to two justices.

CHAP. 165. *Respecting Railways.* Sec. 34 gives one justice jurisdiction.

CHAP. 174. *Respecting Municipal Institutions.* Sec 162 gives jurisdiction to two justices of the peace over certain offences under this act. See Sec. 593 as regards police villages.

CHAP. 177. *Respecting Public Meetings.* Justices of the peace have various duties to perform under this act.

CHAP. 180. *Assessment of Property.* Sec. 215 gives jurisdiction to one justice.

CHAP. 181. *Liquor License Act.* Sec. 65 provides that one justice may take information : Sec. 68 that two justices must convict.

CHAP. 182. *The Temperance Act of Ontario.* Sec. 16 gives jurisdiction to two justices.

CHAP. 183. *To regulate Travelling on Public Highways and Bridges.* Sec. 10 gives jurisdiction to one justice.

CHAP. 185. *Respecting Double Tracks in Snow Roads.* County Councils may pass by-laws to have double tracks in Winter. Penalties Sec's 7 and 8. By-law to prescribe mode of levying penalties.

CHAP. 186. *To authorize the use of Traction Engines on Highways.* See Sec's 16 to 19 as to penalties. One justice has jurisdiction.

CHAP. 187. *To encourage the Planting of Trees along Highways.* Sec. 5 gives jurisdiction to one justice.

CHAP. 188. *To prevent the spread of Canada Thistles.* Sec. 11 gives jurisdiction to one justice.

CHAP. 189. *To prevent the Profanation of the Lord's Day.* Sec. 8 gives jurisdiction to one justice.

CHAP. 190. *Respecting the Public Health.* Sec. 32 gives jurisdiction to two justices.

CHAP. 191. *Respecting Vaccination and Inoculation.* Sec. 13 gives jurisdiction to two city justices.

CHAP. 192. *Respecting Egress from Public Buildings.* Sec. 1: Doors must open outwards. Sec. 3 gives jurisdiction to two justices.

CHAP. 193. *To guard against Threshing Machine accidents.* Machines to be protected to prevent injuries. Sec. 2 gives jurisdiction to one justice.

CHAP. 194. *To impose a tax on Dogs and protect Sheep.* Sec's 6 and 12 gives jurisdiction to one justice.

CHAP. 195. *Respecting Pounds.* One justice has jurisdiction.

CHAP. 201. *For the Protection of Insectivorous Birds.* Sec. 5 gives jurisdiction to one justice. (Amended by 41 Vic., Chap. 22).

CHAP. 204. *Public School Act.* Sec. 250 gives jurisdiction to one justice.

CHAP. 205. *High School Act.* Sec. 87 gives jurisdiction to one justice.

CHAP. 219. *Prohibiting the sale or use of Spirituous Liquors in Gaols.* Sec. 3 gives jurisdiction to one justice.

CHAP. 220. *Respecting Lunatic Asylums.* Sec's 12 to 24. One justice may commit Dangerous Lunatics. See forms appended to act.

CHAP. 221. *Private Lunatic Asylums.* Sec. 22 states that three justices may license: Sec. 85 that one justice can impose penalties under act.

41 VICTORIA, 1878.

CHAP. 4. *Respecting the Magistracy.* Defines various powers of justices. Sec. 6 amends Schedule A of Chap. 77 of Revised Statutes, as to fees of justices.

42 VICTORIA 1879.

CHAP. 33. *To Protect Plum and Cherry Trees from Black Knot.* Sec. 2 gives jurisdiction to one justice.

43 VICTORIA, 1880.

CHAP. 31. *For the protection of Game and Fur-bearing*

animals. (Repeals former Act). Sec. 9 gives jurisdiction to one justice.

44 VICTORIA, 1881.

CHAP. 27. *To amend the Liquor Act of Revised Statutes, Chap. 181.* Sec. 26 gives jurisdiction to two justices.

CHAP. 28. *To protect Peach, Nectarine and other Trees from the Yellows.* Sec. 8 gives jurisdiction to one justice.

Dictionary of the Criminal Law of the Dominion of Canada not treated of otherwise.

ABDUCTION. *Forcibly taking away a Woman over twenty-one,* for the purpose of marriage or carnal knowledge. Alluring a woman under twenty-one for the same purpose. Vide 32-23 Vic., Chap. 20, Sec's 54 and 55.

ABORTION. *Child Murder before Natural Birth.* Vide 32-33 Vic., Chap. 20, Sec's 59 and 60, and 40 Vic., Chap. 28, for the several offences of principals and accessories under this head.

ADULTERATION of Food, Drink, and Drugs. *The Admixing* improper, deleterious, or poisonous substances therewith. Vide 37 Vic., Chap. 8, as amended by 40 Vic., Chap. 13.

AGENTS, BANKERS, FACTORS *and* ATTORNEYS. For frauds and misdemeanors by persons under these heads see 32-33 Vic., Chap. 21, Sec. 76.

APOSTACY. *Departure from one's Christian Faith.* The Imperial Statute 9-10 William III, Chap. 32, Sec. 1, provides that persons educated in the Christian religion, who apostatizes therefrom, and is afterwards found writing or speaking against it shall suffer three years' imprisonment, without bail. Information must be laid before a justice four days after the offence has been committed.

ARSON. *Maliciously Setting Fire to Houses, Ships, &c.* Vide 32-33 Vic., Chap. 22, Sec's 3, 7, 66 and 67.

ASSAULT AND BATTERY. *An Assault is any Hostile or Threatening Act* committed within a distance which permits of personal injury to the person threatened, such as angrily shaking one's fist at another, menacing him with a stick or any other weapon, raising a stone to throw within pelting distance, or pointing a pistol or gun within shooting distance. A Battery is effected by the party threatened being struck by the fist or some substance propelled by the assailant. For common assault see 32-33 Vic., Chap. 20, Sec. 36 and following Sections: for indecent assault see 32-33 Vic., Chap. 29, Sec. 28, as amended by the 40 Vic., Chap. 26: for felonious assault see same Chap. Sec. 51. Using necessary force in the performance of some legal act is not an assault. Thus a conductor may use sufficient force to put a person off a train who refuses to pay his fare, or a person may use all necessary force to protect himself if attacked. A parent may punish a child with discretion, a master an apprentice, a school teacher a pupil.

ATTEMPT TO MURDER. 32-33 Vic., Chap. 20, creates various felonies under this head. Sec. 10 of this act changed by 40 Vic., Chap. 28.

BETTING AND POOL SELLING. Prohibited by 40 Vic., Chap. 31, which makes these offences misdemeanors.

BARRATRY. *Frequently Exciting and Stirring up Suits and Quarrels between Her Majesty's Subjects.* A misdemeanor at common law. More than one offence must be proved or no case.

BIGAMY. *Marrying a Second Time while the Person doing so has a former Wife or Husband Living.* Vide 32-33 Vic., Chap. 20, Sec. 58, which makes this offence a felony. The first marriage must be shown to be a valid one. When a person leaves Canada and commits the offence in the United States it must be shown on trial, by circumstances or otherwise, that he or she left with that intent.

BRIBERY. *To Influence or Corrupt by some Gift, Money or otherwise.* For bribery at elections, see 37 Vic., Chap. 9, Sec. 92.

BURGLARY. *Breaking and Entering a Dwelling House between the hours of 9 p. m. and 6 a. m.* Vide 32-33 Vic., Chap. 21, Sec. 50.

CHILD ABANDONING, *Child Stealing, &c.* Vide 32-33 Vic., Chap. 20, Sec's 26 and 57.

CLERGYMAN. 32-33 Vic., Chap. 20, Sec. 36 makes obstructing or assaulting a clergyman while performing his duties a misdemeanor.

COINAGE OFFENCES. Vide 32-33 Vic. Chap. 18 for crimes under this head.

COMPOUNDING OFFENCES. *Forbearing to Prosecute on Account of Receiving a Bribe, or being Benefitted in some other way.* Vide 32-33 Vic., Chap. 21, Sec's 115, 116, and the Amending Act 35 Vic., Chap. 35.

COMPULSION. *The Commission af a Crime when a Person is not a Free Agent,* as by force or threats of present bodily injury, or where a person does an illegal act by force of circumstances, as when two persons are in danger of drowning and one pushes another off a plank that would not support both. This is held not to be a crime at common law.

CONCEALMENT OF BIRTH. *A Secret Disposition of the Dead Body of a Child to Conceal the fact of its Birth.* Vide 32-33 Vic., Chap. 20, Sec. 21.

CONSPIRACY. *An agreement by two Persons or more to do any Unlawful or Felonious act.* As to raising wages see 32-33 Vic., Chap. 20, Sec. 42 : to commit murder, same Chap., Sec. 3 : to intimidate a Provincial Legislative body, see 31 Vic., Chap. 71 : for other offences see 32-33 Vic., Chap. 29, Sec. 28, as amended by 40 Vic., Chap. 26, and 35 Vic., Chap. 31.

COPYRIGHT. *The Legal Property in Books, Pictures, Engravings, &c.* Vide 38 Vic., Chap. 88, and Reserved Act of 1876 in Statutes of 38-39 Vic.

CRUELTY TO ANIMALS. *The Wanton, Cruel, or Unnecessary Beating or Abuse of any Dumb Animal.* Vide 32-33 Vic., Chap. 27, as amended by 33 Vic., Chap. 29.

DRIVING WANTONLY AND FURIOUSLY SO AS TO INJURE, OR INJURING BY NEGLECT. A misdemeanor punishable by two years' penitentiary at discretion of court. Vide 32-33 Vic., Chap. 20, Sec. 34.

EMBRACERY. *The Attempt to Influence a Jury to give a Corrupt Verdict,* whether by bribes, promises, threats, or otherwise. A misdemeanor at common law.

ENTICING SOLDIERS TO DESERT. 32-33 Vic., Chap. 25, makes this offence a crime punishable before two justices of the peace.

ESCAPE. Escaping from lawful custody, or assisting another to do so, is a misdemeanor. Vide 32-33 Vic., Chap. 29, Sec. 84.

EMBEZZLEMENT. *The act of Converting to one's own use* money or property entrusted to his care by another person, or a breach of trust. Vide 32-33 Vic., Chap. 21, Sec's 69, 70, and 74.

FALSE PERSONATION. *Doing an act in the name of another person, and pretending to be such person.* As regards Elections to Parliament, see 37 Vic., Chap. 9, Sec. 74. As to personating the ownership of stocks, see 32-33 Vic., Chap. 19, Sec. 6.

FALSE PRETENCES. *Obtaining money or some other property by false representations.* 32-33 Vic. Chap. 21 makes this offence a larceny.

FIRE ARMS, &c. The Act 40 Vic., Chap. 20, prohibits the carrying of pistols or air-guns without sufficient cause, defined to be the fear of probable injury to person, property or family. See also 32-33 Vic., Chap. 20, Sec's 74 and 76.

FISHERIES. To protect the same. Vide 31 Vic., Chap. 60, and 38 Vic., Chap. 33, and 37 Vic. Chap. 28.

FORCIBLE ENTRY OR DETAINER. *Violently and illegally taking possession of lands and tenements.* See 32-33 Vic., Chap. 29, Sec. 28, which makes this an indictable offence. See also 40 Vic., Chap, 26, Sec. 2.

FOREIGN ENLISTMENT. The offences under this head are created by, and will be found in the Imperial Act, published in the Dominion Statutes of 1872.

FORGERY. *The fradulent making or alteration* of any writing or signature to the injury of another person.—Vide 32-33 Vic., Chap. 19, and 31 Vic., Chap. 71.

FRAUDULENT MARKING *of Merchandize.* Vide 35 Vic. Chap. 32.

GAMING AND GAMING HOUSES. To prevent Gaming in certain public conveyances, see 40 Vic. Chap. 32, and 38 Vic., Chap. 41, as amended by 40 Vic., Chap. 33, which provides for the suppression of gambling houses. See also 32-33 Vic., Chap 29, Sec. 28.

INFANTS. Not responsible in law until seven years

old : Nor between seven and fourteen unless a mischievous and bad disposition be shown. Cannot be convicted of rape under fourteen ; but can for being an accessory to the offence.

LARCENY. *The wrongfully obtaining possession* of money or any chattel being the property of another. Vide 32-33 Vic., Chap. 21, Sec's 10 to 14 as regards stealing cattle, &c. : Sec's 15 to 19 as to stealing written documents : Sec's 22 to 27 as to stealing things attached to or growing on land :— Sec's 28 to 37 as to mines or minerals : Sec. 39 as to stealing from the person. See also amending acts, 35 Vic., Chap's 33 and 35 ; 38 Vic. Chap 40 ; and 40 Vic. Chap. 29.

LIBEL. An indictable offence in its restricted legal sense signifying a malicious defamation of any person living or dead, made public either by printing, writing, signs or pictures, in order to provoke to wrath or expose one to public hatred, contempt and ridicule. In a general sense all publications blaspheming the Almighty, or turning the Christian religion into ridicule, or tending to corrupt the minds and morals of the people, or defaming the Sovereign, are libels. Vide 37 Vic., Chap. 38. At common law words spoken calculated to provoke a breach of the peace are libellous, as well as seditious, blasphemous, or grossly immoral language, or abusive words to a magistrate while in the execution of his duty. Words spoken of private individuals, however abusive, are simply slander, for which the only remedy is by civil action, or punishment under some by-law if such exists. Municipal councils have usually the right to pass such by-laws.

LOTTERIES. These are prohibited under Consolidated Statutes of Canada, Chap. 95. No person is to make, print or publish anything connected with a lottery, or sell or offer for sale any ticket or otherwise, under a penalty of twenty dollars, recoverable before one justice of the peace.

MAINTENANCE. *The officious intermeddling in a law suit that in no wise belongs to one, by maintaining or assisting either party thereto.* This is a misdemeanor, and punishable by fine or imprisonment or both, at the discretion of the court. Champerty is a species of maintenance, the champertor seeking to derive some benefit from another person's suit.

MALICIOUS INJURIES TO PROPERTY. These embrace numerous offences, from the crime of arson downwards to petty injuries ; for which various punishments are provided by 32-33 Vic., Chap. 22, as amended by 35 Vic., Chap. 34, and by 40 Vic., Chap. 29.

MASTER AND SERVANT. The law on this head has been materially altered as regards ordinary cases, and the penal remedy against servants entirely abolished (unless in cases where their conduct might endanger public safety), by the Breaches of Contract Act of 1877, being 40 Vic., Chap. 35. For Ontario, see Revised Statutes, Chap. 133. For other Provinces see their local statutes.

MENACES AND THREATS. For offences under this head see 32-33, Chap. 20, Sec. 15 ; Chap 21, Sec's 43 to 48, Chap. 22, Sec. 58.

MISPRISION OF FELONY. A misdemeanor at common law. This offence consists of concealing some felony committed by another person.

MURDER AND MANSLAUGHTER. These offences are governed by 32-33 Vic., Chap. 20.

NUISANCE. A nuisance is a misdemeanor at common law, and must be of the nature of some damage or annoyance to all persons in its neighborhood.

PERJURY. *Swearing or Affirming falsely in a court of justice*, or before some person, such as a magistrate, commissioner, &c., who has the legal right to administer an oath or affirmation. For offences under this head see 32-33 Vic., Chap. 23, as amended by 33 Vic., Chap. 26.

PIRACY. *Act of Robbery and depredation on the high seas.* See Imperial Statute, 12-13 Vic., Chap 96, and 32-33 Vic., Chap. 29, Sec. 136.

PRINCIPALS AND ACCESSORIES. For offences under this head see 31 Vic., Chap. 72 ; 32-33 Vic., Chap. 19, Sec. 48 ; and 38 Vic., Chap. 7, Sec 79.

PROFANE SWEARING. By the Imperial Statute 19 George II, Chap. 21, it is enacted : The following penalties are imposed on offenders who shall profanely curse or swear, and be convicted thereof on confession, or oath of one witness, before one justice, viz. : every day-labourer, common soldier or common seaman, *one shilling ;* every other person under the degree of a gentleman, *two shillings*; and every person of or above the degree of a gentleman, *five shillings*; and for a second offence after conviction, *double;* and for every subsequent offence after conviction, *treble;* which said penalties shall go to the poor of the parish. If such person shall curse or swear in the presence and hearing of a justice, he shall convict him without any other proof.

In Ontario municipal councils of cities, towns, townships, and villages, have power to pass by-laws for the prevention of profane swearing, and other indecent conduct.

RAPE. This offence in common law is the unlawful and carnal knowledge of a woman by force and against her will; of a child under ten years of age whether she consents or not; or of an idiot who is incapable of expressing assent or dissent. See 32-33 Vic., Chap. 20, Sec's 57 and 65.

RECEIVING STOLEN GOODS. 32-33 Vic., Chap. 21, Sec. 100 makes it felony for any person to receive stolen goods, knowing them to have been stolen. See also Sec. 103 of same act, and 40 Vic., Chap. 26.

RIOTS, ROUTS AND UNLAWFUL ASSEMBLIES. For offences under this head see 32-33 Vic., Chap. 22, Sec's 15 and 16; and 31 Vic., Chap. 70.

SESSIONS. The Court of General (or Quarter) Sessions of the Peace has no jurisdiction in certain cases. See 32-33 Vic., Chap. 20, Sec's 1 and 49, and Chap. 29, Sec. 12; 40 Vic., Chap. 28, Sec. 1. To avoid any question of doubt magistrates should always commit to the next court of competent jurisdiction.

SMUGGLING. This offence which consists in importing or exporting goods or other articles without paying the legal duties thereon, is made a misdemeanor by 40 Vic., Chap. 10, Sec's 76 and 81.

SODOMY. *An Unnatural Crime.* 32-33 Vic., Chap. 20, Sec's 53 and 54 prescribe the penalties in connection with this offence.

SUICIDE. *The taking one's own Life or Self Murder.* The attempt to commit suicide is a misdemeanor at common law.

SUNDAY. The seventh or Sabbath day. Laws relative to the due observance of this day come only within the province of the various local Legislatures. For Ontario see Revised Statutes, Chap. 189.

TREASON. *Compasssng the death of the Sovereign*, or doing certain acts of aggression against the State. The Imperial Act of 25 Edward III, and 31 Vic., Chap. 69, govern these offences.

UNLAWFUL TRAINING *to the use of arms*, Prohibited by 31 Vic., Chap. 15.

VAGRANCY. The legal condition of certain idle and disorderly persons. For penalties see 32-33 Vic., Chap. 28, as amended by 37 Vic., Chap. 43.

VIOLENCE, *Threats and Molestation*. See 35 Vic., Chap. 31, as amended by 39 Vic., Chap. 37.

VOLUNTARY OATHS. Must not be administered by justices of the peace or other official persons. See 37 Vic., Chap. 37.

Revised Statutes of Ontario, Chap. 77, an Act [respecting the Fees of Justices of the Peace.

1. The fees mentioned in Schedule A to this Act, and no others, shall be and constitute the fees to be taken by Justices of the Peace, or by their Clerks, for the duties and services therein mentioned.

2. The costs to be charged in all cases of convictions, where the fees are not expressly prescribed by any statute, shall be those contained in Schedule B to this Act.

3. This Act shall not authorize any claim being made by the Justices aforesaid, for fees of any description connected with cases above the degree of misdemeanor.

4. Any Justice or Justices wilfully receiving a larger amount of fees than by law are authorized to be received, shall forfeit and pay the sum of eighty dollars, together with full costs of suit, to be recovered by any person who sues for the same by action of debt or by information in any Court of Record in the Province, one moiety whereof shall be paid to the party suing, and the other moiety to the Treasurer of the Province, to and for the public uses of the Province.

SCHEDULE "A."

(*Section 1.*)

Table of Fees to be taken by Justices of the Peace or their Clerks in the the cases mentioned in Section 1.

1. For an Information and Warrant for apprehension, or for an Information and Summons for assault, tres-

pass, or other misdemeanor	$0 50
2. For each copy of Summons to be served on defendant or defendants	0 10
3. For a *Subpœna*, (*only one Subpœna on each side to be charged for in each case, which may contain any number of names.*) (*If the justice of the case requires it, additional Subpœnas shall be issued without charge.*)	0 10
4. For every Recognizance, (*only one to be charged in each case*)	0 25
5. For Information and Warrant for surety of the peace for good behaviour, (*to be paid by Complainant*)	0 50
6. For Warrant of Commitment for default of surety to keep peace or good behaviour, (*to be paid by Complainant.*)	0 50
7. For hearing and determining, (*Vide amen't 41 Vic., Chap. 4, Sec. 6.*)	0 50

SCHEDULE "B."

(*Section 2.*)

Table of Fees to be taken by Justices of the Peace or their Clerks in Cases of Convictions where Fees are not prescribed by any other Statute.

1. For Information and Warrant for apprehension, or for Information and Summons for service	$0 50
2. For every copy of Summons to be served upon defendant or defendants	0 10
3. For every *Subpœna* to a Witness, (*only one Subpœna on each side to be charged for in each case, which may contain any number of names.*) (*If the justice of the case requires it, additional Subpœnas shall be issued without charge.*)	0 10
4. For hearing and determining the case	0 50
5. For Warrant to levy penalty	0 25
6. For making up every Record of Conviction where the same is ordered to be returned to the Sessions, or on *certiorari*	1 00
7. For copy of any other paper connected with any trial, and the minutes of the same if demanded—per folio of one hundred words	0 10
8. For every Bill of Costs, (*when demanded to be made in detail.*)	0 10

9. But in all cases which admit of a summary proceeding before a single Justice of the Peace, and wherein no

higher penalty than twenty dollars can be imposed, there only shall be charged for the conviction not more than....................... .... 0 50

And for the warrant no levy the penalty 0 25

10. And in all cases where persons are subpœnaed to give evidence before Justices of the Peace in cases of assault, trespass or misdemeanor, the witness shall be entitled, in the discretion of the Justice, to receive for every day's attendance, where the distance travelled in coming to and returning from such adjudication does not exceed ten miles............ ..... 0 50

And for each mile above ten 0 05

LANDLORD AND TENANT.

General Observations.

The Law of Landlord and Tenant, as it prevails in the Dominion of Canada, may be said to spring from three sources, namely, (1) the common law of England, (2) various acts of the Imperial Parliament, passed from time to time up to nearly the close of the last century, (3) and the applying acts of our own Provincial Legislatures. In dealing, therefore, with this law we have first to review it from a common law and Imperial enactment standpoint, and afterwards show how it has been affected or modified by the local legislation of some of the Provinces.

The Landlord may be described as the owner of houses or lands, and the Tenant as the person to whom he grants, or, in other words, rents the occupation and use of them. The relation of landlord and tenant may be created, or brought about, by a written contract such as a lease or an agreement for a lease, or by a verbal agreement to let by the week, or month, or year, as the case may be. In this way the owner of the property, who is termed the landlord or lessor, grants the occupation and use of his property to the other party, who is termed the tenant or lessee, for a specified time, at a stipulated sum which is called rent. A lease may be made for any period of time. It may be drawn for the life of either the landlord or tenant, or for the life or lives of some other person or persons; or it may be drawn for a certain number of years, or so that it may terminate at any time at the will of either of the parties thereto. Under the Statute of Frauds an agreement for a lease must be in writing.* A lease in writing and not under seal is only good for three years, and really amounts in law to an agreement for a lease for the time specified. But when leases are made for a longer period than three years, they must be executed as a deed under seal, and if they extend over seven years they require to be registered to make them valid.

The relation of landlord and tenant may, however, arise in another way, for a year or for a shorter period, by what is known as implication of law, or, in other words, from the relative situations of the parties towards one another, and the fair deduction to be drawn from their actions and conduct, although there may be no express words or stipulations. Where one man occupies the house or lands of another, under circumstances of this nature, the presumption in law is that the use and occupation are to be paid for; and the landlord would have a right to sue and recover a reasonable rent unless the tenant could show that it was tacitly understood on both sides that no rent was to be paid. Where a landlord has permitted a tenant to occupy property and accepted rent from him therefor, he cannot treat him afterwards as a trespasser; and if he requires possession he must give the tenant the legal notice to give up the premises.

Like other deeds leases may be drawn to take effect from a date either before or after their execution as may be desired. Where a tenant continues to occupy after the expiration of his lease without any further understanding, and

---

* Vide 29, Charles II, Chap. 3, Sec. 4.

the landlord continues to receive rent from him, he becomes a yearly tenant upon the terms of the original demise or agreement. A tenantcy from year to year is created by the payment and acceptance of rent at certain half-yearly periods, unless it can be shown that this rent was paid or received by mistake. If the payment of an annual rent is set out in the lease or agreement, the holding is a yearly one, although it may be stipulated that the tenant should leave at a quarter's notice, and such notice can have no effect until within three months of the end of the year's occupation. This stipulation would have the effect simply of reducing the regular six months' notice to quit to three months. But if it is expressly agreed on that a tenant must quit at any time at six months' notice, this virtually constitutes a half-yearly tenantcy; and the leasee can only hold from six months to six months from the date of occupation or from the commencement of the agreement. A quarterly tenantcy would arise in the same way by an agreement to leave at three months' notice, presuming that no annual rent was reserved or expressed. When an annual rent is reserved it may be made payable monthly, or quarterly, or otherwise, as the parties themselves may agree on, no matter how long the lease has to run. Rent also may be made payable in advance, so that the landlord may distrain at the commencement of each quarter instead of at the end. Thus there may be a yearly tenantcy with an annual rent payable quarterly, or a quarterly tenantcy with the rent payable by the week or month.

When rent is permitted by the tenant to run in arrear the landlord may recover by action or by distress. Where the rent to be paid has been agreed on, as to amount and date of payment, the landlord can distrain. But if no certain rent has been covenanted for (or agreed to be paid) the landlord cannot distrain, and must bring an action to recover what would be a fair rental for the use and occupation of the premises. The power of distress can only be exercised by the immediate owner or landlord, and by no other person. Should the landlord, after making the lease, transfer his interest in the property to another person he would have no right to distrain. Nor can a landlord distrain twice for the same rent, unles the distress has been withdrawn at the request of the tenant, or unless a mistake is made in the value of the cattle or other articles distrained, and they are found not to amount to the rent, in which event the execution may be completed.* But if any distress and sale shall be made for rent when none is in fact due the owner shall recover double value with full costs of suit. § Distress for rent must be for rent in arrear, therefore it may not be made on the same day on which the rent becomes due. Nor can distress for rent be made after tender of payment until a fresh demand has first been made. It should be always understood, however, that the tenant is obliged to go to the landlord to make a tender of payment. Where a lease has expired and rent is due thereunder, the landlord can distrain for the same at any time within six months, provided that his title or interest remains undisturbed, and that the tenant is still in occupation. † A landlord must not make an unreasonable distress, and if he does so he renders himself liable for damages. If ten dollars were due for rent it would be illegal to seize two cows therefor, when one cow would be more than sufficient to meet the demand. The distress should always be proportioned to the amount due, with a fair margin for necessary attendant fees and other expenses. ‡ Should a landlord distrain before rent has become due, the tenant may legally resist the entry and seizure by force if necessary, and may

---

* Vide 17, Charles II, Chap. 7. Burrow Mansfield 589.
§ 2 William III, Chap. 5, Sec. 5.
† 8 Anne, Chap. 14, Sec's 6 & 7; and 6 William IV, Chap. 3, Sec. 28
‡ 52 Henry III, Chap. 4, See also 3, Blackstone's Com. 12.

rescue his goods at any time before they are impounded, but as soon as the goods have been impounded they are in the custody of the law, and cannot be retaken by the tenant. As soon as the person making the distress has made out and delivered to the tenant, or left upon the premises, a statement in writing of the goods or chattels distrained, they are said to be impounded. A landlord or his bailiff cannot legally break open gates, enclosures, or the outer doors of any dwelling house or other building to make distress, but he may draw a staple or undo a fastening which is usually opened from the outside of the house or enclosure. A distress cannot be made during the night time, that is after the sun has set nor before sunrise, nor upon lands or tenements which do not form part of the premises on which the arrears of rent are due, except in cases where the goods have been removed in the view or presence of the person making the distress. But where a tenant removes goods from the leased premises clandestinely, and with the evident purpose of avoiding distress and defrauding the landlord out of his just claim, the landlord may at any time within thirty days of their removal seize such goods wherever they may be found, unless they should have, in the meantime, been sold for their fair value to some third person, who had no knowledge of their fraudulent removal to avoid distress. If it be necessary to break open any door to make the seizure the landlord must procure the assistance of a constable, and must force the fastenings in his presence between sunrise and sunset.* To constitute a fraudulent removal of goods it is not necessary that the rent should be actually in arrear, and the right to distrain existing. Should the goods be removed either the day before or after the rent becomes due to avoid distress, the removal becomes fraudulent. But if sufficient goods be left on the premises to pay the landlord's claim

---

* Vide 2 George II, Chap. 19.

the removal is not a fraudulent one, and the goods removed cannot be seized.

In making a distress for rent in arrear it is not necessary that the landlord or his bailiff should take bodily possession of the articles seized. It is sufficient in law if the landlord personally, or by his agent or bailiff, should enter upon the premises of the tenant and announce the distress to the latter or to his servants, or to some other person or persons who may at the time be in actual occupation of the property. When a landlord distrains by an agent or bailiff authority to do so must be in writing, and is called a distress warrant. As soon as the distress is made by the landlord or other person an inventory of the goods or articles seized should be made as quickly as possible, and served upon the tenant together with the notice of the distress. This notice should describe, or set out, the amount of rent distrained for, and the inventory of the particular things taken. After service of this notice upon him the tenant has five clear days (or six inclusive of the days of seizure and last day) in which to pay the rent, or replevy the goods distrained; after which the landlord may sell them for the highest price he can get for them, and apply the money thus received for his rent account and the costs of making the distress and sale. Should there be any overplus he must pay it to the tenant, who has the right to get a copy of the charges from the distrainor signed by him, no matter whether the rent exceeds the sum of eighty dollars or not. Where the rent distrained for exceeds that amount the costs are not limited to any particular sum, but they must still be fair and reasonable.

With regard to the question of repairs, it may be stated, that in the absence of an express agreement to repair, the tenant is still obliged to use the property occupied in a fair and proper manner. The simple fact of his tenantcy alone, without any other stipulation, will compel him in law to take reasonable care of the property demised to him, and renders it obligatory on him to restore it at the end of his term in the same state of good repair or condition in which he received it, subject only to the ordinary wear and tear of occupation, and of the use for which it was understood to be required.

When the lease is terminated by some agreed-upon event, or contingency, or at a particular date expressed therein, no notice to quit is necessary. Hence, a lease granted for a term of years or for one year only terminates absolutely at the specified time without any notice to quit, and the landlord is entitled to possession. Where a tenantcy at will subsists, no formal notice to quit need be given, but the landlord must make a formal demand for possession or give notice of the determination, or end of the will or contract, on his part before he becomes entitled to possession or to bring an action of ejectment. The tenant, if he desires to give up possession must formally notify the landlord of his decision to rescind the agreement and terminate his tenantcy, otherwise he will still be liable for the rent of the premises whether he occupies them or not. If the tenant holds from year to year at the pleasure of either party, six months' notice is required, which may be given either at the beginning or end of the year at pleasure, but in the case of a yearly tenantcy without any stipulation, to expire say on the 1st of November, six clear months' notice must be given before that date. This notice may be a verbal or written one. But it is always better to have it in writing and a true copy made of it before it is served upon the tenant or landlord as the case may be. A service of this notice upon a wife or grown-up child or servant in the dwelling house of the party served is equally as good as a personal one.

What Goods are liable to be Distrained, and what are not.

Distress for rent must be of a thing whereof a valuable property is in some body; and therefore dogs, bucks, does, conies, and the like, that are *feræ naturæ*, cannot be distrained. Although it be of valuable property, as a horse, yet, if when a man or woman is riding on him, or an axe in a man's hand, cutting of wood, and the like, they are for that time privileged, and cannot be distrained.—1 *Inst.* 47. And it hath been held, that the horses joined to a cart, with a man upon it, cannot be distrained for rent (although they may for damage feasant), but both cart and horses may, if the man be not upon the cart.—*Vent.* 36. Valuable things shall not be distrained for rent if brought to the premises for the benefit and maintenance of trades, which by consequence are for the commonwealth, and are there by the authority of law, as the horse in a smith's shop; nor the cattle or goods of a guest at an inn; nor the materials in a weaver's shop for making cloth; nor cloth or garments in a tailor's shop; nor sacks of corn or meal in a mill; nor any thing distrained for damage feasant; for it is in the custody of the law and the like.—2 *Burr.* 1498. But a chariot or horses standing at livery are not exempt. Beasts belonging to the plough shall not be distrained (which is the ancient common law of England, for no man shall be distrained by the utensils or instruments of his trade or profession, as the axe of the carpenter, or the books of a scholar), while goods or other beasts may be distrained.—1 *Inst.* 47. But this rule holds only in distresses for rent in arrear, and the like; but doth not extend to cases where a distress is given in the nature of an execution, by any particular statute, as for poor rates, and the like.—3 *Salk.* 136. Implements of trade may be distrained when they are not in actual use and no other sufficient distress can be found on the premises.—2 *Chitty's R.* 167. Furnaces, cauldrons or other things fixed to the freehold, or the doors or windows of a house, or the like, cannot be distrained.—1 *Inst.* 47. Things for which a replevin will not lie, so as to be known again, as money out of a bag, cannot be distrained.—2 *Bac. Abr.* 109. But money in a bag sealed, may be distrained, for that the bag sealed may be known again. By the 2 W. & M. sess. 1, chap. 5, § 3, persons having rent in arrear, on any demise, lease or contract, may seize and secure any sheaves or cocks of corn, or corn loose, or in the straw, or hay being in any barn or granary, or upon any hovel, stack or rick, or otherwise, upon any part of the land charged with rent, and may lock up or detain the same, in the place where found, in the nature of a distress, so as the same be not removed, to the damage of the owner, out of the place where found and seized, but kept there (as impounded) till replevied or sold. Also by the 11 Geo. II., ch. 19, § 8, the landlord may take and seize corn, grass, hops, roots, fruits, pulse or other products growing, as a distress; and the same may cut, gather, make, cure, carry, and lay up, when ripe, in the barns or other proper place, on the premises; and if there shall be no barn or proper place on the premises, then in any other barn or proper place which he shall procure so near as may be to the premises; the appraisement whereof shall be taken when cut, gathered, cured, and made, and not before. And notice of the place where the goods so distrained shall be lodged, shall in one week after the lodging thereof be given to the tenant or left at the last place of his abode. § 9. And generally, whatever goods and chattels the landlord finds upon the premises, whether they in fact belong to the tenant or a stranger, are distrainable by him for rent, (with the exceptions in favour of trade) above specified; for otherwise a door would be opened to infinite frauds upon the landlord; and the stranger hath his remedy over by action on the case against the tenant, if by the tenant's default the goods are distrained.—3 *Blackstone*, 8. With regard to a stranger's beasts, if they are put in by consent of the owner of the beasts they are distrainable immediately afterwards for rent-arrere by the landlord; so also if the stranger's cattle break the fences, and commit a trespass by coming on the land, they are distrainable immediately by the lessor for his tenant's rent. But if the lands were not sufficiently fenced so as to keep out cattle, the landlord cannot distrain them, till they have been *levant* and *couchant* on the land; that is, have been long enough there to have lain down, and rose up to feed; which in general is held to be one night at least; and then the law presumes that the owner may have notice whether his cattle have strayed, and it is his own negligence not to have taken them away: yet if the lessor or his tenant were bound to repair the fences, and did not, and thereby the cattle escaped into their grounds, without the negligence or default of the owner, in that case, though the cattle may have been *levant* and *couchant*, yet they are not distrainable for rent, till actual notice is given to the owner that they are there and he neglects to remove them: for the law will not suffer the landlord to take advantage of his own or his tenant's wrong.—3 *Bl. Com.* 8, 9. But cattle put into a field by a drover with the consent of the occupier to graze only one night, on their way to a fair or market, are not liable to distress for rent.—2 *Vern.* 130.

Goods of a principal in the hands of a factor are privileged from distress, being for the benefit of trade.—6 *Moore Rep.* 243; so goods landed at a wharf, and consigned to a broker as agent of the consignor, for sale, and placed by the broker in the wharfinger's warehouse as they were brought there in the course of trade.—1 *Bing.* 283. So goods carried to be weighed, even at a private house, if in the way of trade, are exempt: so is a horse that has carried corn to a mill to be ground.—*Cro. Eliz.* 548, 596. Goods in possession of a carrier are also exempt, and this though the carrier was not a public one.—1 *Salk.* 249. But horses or cattle sent to agist (or pasture) may be immediately distrained by the landlord for rent in arrear, and the owner must seek his remedy by action against the tenant. The principle of this rule extends to public livery stables, to which if horses and carriages are sent to stand, they are distrainable by the landlord.—3 *Burr.* 1498. So upon the same principle the goods of lodgers, or any other person on the premises, are liable to be distrained; and to exempt goods being at an inn, they must be within the very precincts of the inn, and not on other premises at a distance belonging to it.—*Barnes*, 472.

By statute 2 W. & M., sess. 1, chap. 5, where any goods shall be distrained for rent, and the tenant or owner shall not, within *five* days after such distress, and notice thereof left at the premises, replevy the same, the person distraining, with the sheriff, under sheriff, or *constable* of the peace, shall cause the goods distrained to be appraised by two sworn appraisers (whom such sheriff or constable shall swear), to appraise the same truly, and after such appraisement, the same shall be sold for the best price that can be got, for satisfaction for the rent and charges of the distress, appraisement and sale; leaving the overplus (if any) with the sheriff or constable, for the owner's use. The *five* days are reckoned inclusive of the day of sale; as if the goods are distrained on the 1st, they must not be sold before the 6th.—*H. Bla.* 13. But by consent of the tenant the landlord may continue in possession longer than the five days without incurring any liability.—7 *Price*, 690.

Concerning Replevin.

Where the tenant disputes the validity of the distress, his remedy is by action of replevin. The tenant may replevy the goods seized at any time within the five days, or at any time before the sale.—5 *Taunt.* 451. The party intending to replevy sues out a writ of *replevin.* If the distress exceed £15, the writ is sued out from the Queen's Bench (or Common Pleas); if not exceeding £15 then from the county court.—*4 William IV., Chap. 7, Sec. 7. The writ is directed to the sheriff, commanding him to replevy the goods to the plaintiff, and to summons the defendant (the landlord). The statute requires that before the sheriff shall proceed to replevy he shall take pledges from the plaintiff by bond (with sureties), in the form prescribed, conditioned for the prosecution of the action, and the return of the goods, if such return be adjudged. The statute 11 G. II., chap. 19, requires that the sheriff shall take bond, with two sureties, in double the value of the goods distrained. The sheriff on receiving such security, is then immediately, by his officers, to cause the chattels distrained to be restored to the party distrained upon, and the action of replevin proceeds in the ordinary way of other actions.

Fraudulent removal of Goods, &c.

If any tenant for life, years, at will, sufferance, or otherwise, shall fraudulently, or clandestinely, convey off the premises his goods or chattels, to prevent the landlord from distraining, such landlord, or any person by him lawfully empowered, may, in thirty days next after such conveying away, seize the same wherever they shall be found, and dispose of them in such manner as if they had been distrained on the premises. Sec. 3. And if any tenant shall so fraudulently remove and convey away his goods or chattels, or if any person or persons shall wilfully and knowingly aid or assist him in such fraudulent conveying away or carrying off any part of his goods or chattels, or in concealing the same, any person so offending shall forfeit to the landlord *double the value* of such goods, to be recovered in any court of record. Sec. 4. But if the goods and chattels so fraudulently carried off or concealed shall not exceed the value of £50, the landlord or his agent may exhibit a complaint in writing before *two* justices of the peace of the same county or division, residing near the place where such goods and chattels were removed, or near the place where the same were found, not being interested in the lands or tenements whence such goods were removed; who may summon the parties concerned, examine the fact, and all proper witnesses, upon oath (or if a Quaker, upon affirmation), and in a summary way determine whether such person or persons be guilty of the offence with which he or they are charged; and to enquire in like manner of the value of such goods and chattels, and upon full proof of the offence, by order under their hands and seals, the said justices shall adjudge the offender or offenders to pay *double the value* of the said goods and chattels to such landlord, his bailiff, servant or agent, at such time as the said justices shall appoint; and if the offender or offenders, having notice of such order, shall refuse or neglect so to do, they shall, by their warrant, levy the same by distress; and for want of such distress, may commit the offender or offenders to the house of correction, there to be kept to hard labour, without bail or mainprise, for the space of six months, unless the money so ordered to be paid as aforesaid shall be sooner satisfied. Sec. 5. Persons aggrieved by order of such justices may appeal to the next general quarter sessions, who may give costs to either party. Sec. 6. And where the party appealing shall enter into recognizance, with one or two sureties, in double the sum so ordered to be paid, with condition to appear at such sessions, the order of the justices shall not be executed against him in the meantime. Sec. 7. Where any goods or chattels, fraudulently or clandestinely conveyed or carried away, shall be put, placed or kept in any house, barn, stable, outhouse, yard, close, or place locked up, fastened, or otherwise secured, so as to prevent such goods or chattels from being taken and seized as a distress for arrears of rent, it shall be lawful for the landlord, or his stewart, bailiff, receiver, or other person or persons empowered, to take and seize, as a distress for rent, such goods and chattels (first calling to his assistance the constable, headborough, or other peace officer of the district, &c.); and in case of a dwelling-house (oath being first made before a justice of the peace of a reasonable ground to suspect that such goods or chattels are therein), in the day time, to break open and enter into such house, barn, stable, out-house, yard, close or place, and to take and seize such goods and chattels for the said arrears of rent, as he might have done if they had been in any other place.

Case of Tenant Holding Over.

By 4 George II., Chap. 28, it is enacted that if any tenant for life, or years, or other person who shall come into possession by, from, or under him, shall wilfully hold over any lands after the determination of such term, and after demand made, and notice in writing given for delivering the possession thereof, he shall, for the time he shall so hold over, pay double the yearly value, to be recovered by action of *debt* in any court of record.—Sec. 1.

By 11 G. II., ch. 19, sec. 18, if any tenant shall give notice of his intention to quit the premises at a time mentioned in such notice, and shall not accordingly deliver up possession at the time in such notice contained, he, his executors or administrators, shall from thenceforward pay *double rent*, to be recovered in like manner as the single rent.

By 4 William IV., ch. 1, it shall be lawful for any landlord, whose tenant shall, after the expiration of any tenantcy by parol or writing) wrongfully refuse, upon demand made in writing, to go out of possession, to apply to the Court of King's Bench in term, or to a judge in vacation, upon affidavit, who shall order a writ to issue for summoning a jury of twelve men, before the commissioner named to determine the matter; and if in favor of the landlord, a writ of possession shall be issued.

Deserting the Premises.

By 11 George II., Chap. 19, Sec. 16, it is enacted that if any tenant at rack-rent, or where the rent reserved shall be full *three-fourths* of the yearly value of the demised premises, who shall be in arrear for *one year's rent*, shall desert the premises and leave the same uncultivated or unoccupied, so as no sufficient distress can be had, two justices (having no interest in the premises) may at the request of the landlord go upon and view the same, and affix on the most notorious part of the premises notice in writing what day (at the distance of *fourteen* days at the least) they will return to take a second view, and if on such *second view*, the tenant shall not appear and pay the rent, or there shall not be sufficient distress on the premises, then the justices may put the landlord into possession, and the lease as to such demise shall from thence be void. Sec. 17. But the tenant may appeal to the next justice or justices of assize, who may award costs to either party.

Rent Recoverable by Executors.

By 32 Henry VIII., Chap. 37, it is enacted that the executors and administrators of any person to whom any such rent shall be due and not paid at the time of his death, may distrain upon the premises, so long as they shall continue in the possession of such tenant, or of any other person claiming under him. See also 7 W. IV., c. 3, Sec. 17.

Form of a Complaint upon oath to be made before two Justices, in case of a dwelling-house where goods and chattels are fraudulently and clandestinely removed, and conveyed away and secured, so as to prevent them from being taken and seized as a distress for rent.

Province,   } The information and complaint
County of   } of A. J., of   taken upon oath
    To Wit :   } before us the undersigned, two of
her Majesty's justices of the peace in and for the said county of   at   in the said county of   this   day of   in the year of our Lord one thousand eight hundred and   , who saith that A. O. of   , is justly and truly indebted to this informant in the sum of   for arrears of rent, for a [house and lot situate at   ] due to this informant by the said A. O. on the   day of   , and that the said A. O. hath fraudulently and clandestinely conveyed and carried away, or caused to be so conveyed or

carried away, certain goods and chattels of him the said A. O. from the said [house and lot] after the said arrears had so become due; in order to prevent the said goods and chattels from being seized and distrained by this informant for the said arrears of rent, and that the said goods and chattels are, as this informant hath good cause to suspect, and doth suspect and verily believe, put, placed, or kept, in the dwelling house, barn, stable, out-house, yard, close, or other place, of   at   locked up, fastened or otherwise secured, so as to prevent the said goods and chattels from being taken and seized by this informant as a distress for such arrears of rent as aforesaid; wherefore the said A. J. prayeth our warrant in the premises.

Taken and sworn at   the   A. J.
      day of   before   .

Warrant upon the preceding Complaint and Oath.

Province,   ) To all or any of the constables
County of   } or other peace officers in the said
  To Wit :   ) county.

Whereas A. J. of   , yeoman, hath this   day of   exhibited his complaint, and made oath before us the undersigned, two of her Majesty's justices of the peace for the said county, that A. O. of   has fraudulently and clandestinely conveyed and carried away or caused to be so conveyed and carried away, certain goods and chattels of him the said A. O., from a certain house and lot, situate at   , to prevent the said A. J. from distraining the said goods and chattels for $ arrears of rent due to the said A. J. for the said   , and that the said goods and chattels are, as the said A. J. hath good cause to suspect, and doth suspect and verily believe, put, placed or kept in the dwelling-house, barn, stable, out-house, yard, close or other place of   at   , locked up, fastened, or otherwise secured, so as to prevent the said goods and chattels from being taken and seized by the said A. J. as a distress for such arrears of rent, as aforesaid. These are therefore to command you, and each and every of you, to aid and assist the said A. J., his steward, bailiff, receiver or other persons empowered by him to take and seize, as such distress for rent, as aforesaid, the said goods and chattels, in the day time to break open and enter into the said dwelling-house, barn, stable, out-house, yard, close or other place of the said   at   , and to take and seize the said goods and chattels for the said arrears of rent, according to law.

Given under our hands and seals at   , the   day of   .

Information and Complaint under the 11 George II., ch. 19, of Tenant having deserted the Premises.

Province,   ⎫   The information and complaint
County of   ⎬ of A. B., of   , in the said
To Wit: · ⎭ county, taken this   day of
 , 188 , who saith that he the said A. B. did, in and by a certain indenture bearing date the   day of   in the year of our Lord 185   (or, by written or verbal agreement, *as the case may be*), demise unto A. S., of   in the county aforesaid a certain messuage (or other premises, *as the case may be*), situate and being at   , in the county aforesaid, at rack rent (or three-fourths of the yearly value); that is to say, at the yearly rent of   , payable quarterly (*if so*) on the   day of   &c.; and that the said A. B. further complaineth, that on the   day of   now last past there was in arrear and due unto him the said A. B., from the said A. S., the tenant of the said demised premises, one whole year's rent thereof, and that the said A. S. hath deserted the said demised premises, and left the same uncultivated and unoccupied, so as no sufficient distress can be had to countervail the said arrears of rent, and that the said arrears of rent have been duly demanded according to law. Wherefore the said A. B. doth request J. C. and S. R. esquires, two of her Majesty's justices of the peace for the said county, to go and view the said demised premises, and affix on the most notorious part thereof a notice in writing, what day they will return and take a second view thereof, and that a remedy may be given to the said A. B. according to the form of the statute in that case made and provided.

Taken before us, the said justices, the   day of   188 .

Notice to be affixed on the Premises so deserted. (*Burns.*)

Mr. Abraham Sutcliff:

Take notice, that upon the complaint of A. B., of   yeoman, made under us, J. C. and S. R., esquires, two of

her Majesty's justices of the peace for the county of   ,
that you the said A. S. have deserted the messuage and tenement, situate, lying and being at   , unto you demised, at rack-rent, by him the said A. B., and that there is in arrear and due from you the said A. S., unto him the said A. B., one whole year's rent for the said demised premises, and that you have left the said premises uncultivated and unoccupied, so that no sufficient distress can be had to countervail the said arrears of rent: we the said justices (having no interest, nor either of us having any interest in the said demised premises), on the said complaint as aforesaid, and at the request of him the said A. B., have this day come upon and viewed the said demised premises, and do find the said complaint to be true; and on the   day of this present month of   we will return to take a second view thereof, and if upon such second view you or some person on your behalf shall not appear and pay the said rent in arrear, or there shall not be sufficient distress on the said premises, then we the said justices, will put him the said A. B. into the possession of the said demised premises, according to the form of the statute in such case made and provided. In witness whereof we have hereunto set our hands and seals, and have caused this notice to be affixed on the outdoor of the dwelling-house, the same being the most notorious part of the said premises, this   day of   , in the year of our Lord 188   .

Record of putting the Landlord into Possession.

Province,   ⎱ Be it remembered, that on the
County of   ⎰   day of   in the
    To Wit: year of the reign of our sovereign lady Victoria, at   in the said county of   A. B., of   complaineth unto us J. C. and S. R., esquires, two of her Majesty's justices of our said lady the Queen assigned to keep the peace within the said county, and also to hear and determine divers felonies, trespasses, and other misdemeanors, in the said county committed, that he the said A. B. did demise, at rack-rent, unto A. S., of   yeoman, a certain messuage, tenement, or dwelling-house, lying and being at   aforesaid; and that on the said   day of   in the year aforesaid, there was in arrear and due unto him the

said A. B. from him the said A. S. tenant of the said demised premises, one whole year's rent thereof, and that he the said A. S. had deserted the said premises and left the same uncultivated and unoccupied, so as no sufficient distress could be had to countervail the said arrears of rent, whereupon the said A. B. then and there, to wit, on the said day of   in the year aforesaid, at   aforesaid, in the county aforesaid, requested of us, so as aforesaid being justices, that a due remedy should be provided to him in this behalf, according to the form of the statute in that case made, which complaint and request by us the aforesaid justices being heard, we the said J. C. and S. R., justices aforesaid (having no interest in the said demised premises), on the said   day of   in the year aforesaid, at   aforesaid, did personally go and view the said demised premises, and then and there upon our own proper view, did find the said complaint to be true, and did then and there affix on the most notorious part of the said premises, to wit, upon the out-door of the dwelling-house aforesaid, a notice in writing, under our hands and seals, that we, the said justices, on the   day of the same   month of   in the year aforesaid, would return to take a second view thereof, upon which said   day of   in the year aforesaid, we, the said justices, do now return and take a second view of the premises aforesaid, and there upon our own proper view do find, that he the said A. S. doth not appear, nor doth any person on his behalf appear and pay the said rent in arrear, and that there is no sufficient distress upon the premises aforesaid, nor upon any part thereof, to countervail the said arrears of rent; therefore we, the said justices, at   aforesaid, on the   day of   in the year aforesaid, do put the said A. B. into the possession of the said demised premises, according to the form of the statute aforesaid. In witness whereof, we, the said justices, unto this record do set our seals, at   aforesaid, in the county aforesaid, on the said   day of   in the year of our Lord 188 .

Form of Notice to Quit.

Sir,—I hereby (as agent of Mr. Nokes, your landlord, on his behalf,) give you notice to quit and deliver up possession of the [house, lands, and premises, with the appurtenances] situate at   , in the   county, which you hold of [him] as tenant thereof, on the   day of   next, or at the expiration of the current year of your tenancy, which shall expire next after the end of one-half year from the date of this notice. Dated the   day of   , 1881.

JAMES NOKES.

Distraining for Rent.

In case of distress for rent, the constable of the Township in which the goods are taken, may be called to appraise them before sale; and he should attend with two appraisers, and having sworn them, proceed to appraise the goods. The appraisers employed by the constable should be disinterested parties. It would be illegal to swear the person who distrains, as one of the appraisers, for he has an interest in the business; moreover the Statute says that he with the constable, &c., shall cause the goods to be appraised by two sworn appraisers. In a case where a broker who distrained goods for rent, was afterwards sworn one of the appraisers, and together with another broker valued them to a party who became the purchaser according to such valuation, it was held that the sale was irregular under the Statute.

The proper constable to swear the appraisers is the constable of the parish, or place where the distress is taken, and not the constable of the place where the distress is impounded.

The constable must attend with the appraisers at the time of the appraisement, and obtain the inventory of the goods distrained. Having received the goods, the constable administers to the appraisers the following oath:

"You and every of you shall well and truly appraise the goods and chattels mentioned in this Inventory, *(the constable holding in his hand the Inventory and showing it to the appraisers)* according to the best of your Judgment. So help you God."

The constable should then indorse upon the inventory, or annex to it, a memorandum in the following form:—

Memorandum, that on the   day of   in the Year of Our Lord, 18—,   of the Township of   in the County of   and   of the Township of   in the said County of   , two sworn appraisers were sworn upon the Holy Evangelists, by me   of   constable, well and truly to appraise the goods and chattels mentioned in this (*or the annexed*) Inventory, according to the best of their judgment.

Present at the time of swearing the } As witness my hand, above named   and   , } as above, and witness thereto,   }   , Constable.

After the appraisers have valued the goods, add to the foregoing, the following memorandum of valuation :—

We the above named   and   being sworn upon the Holy Evangelist by   , constable, above named, well and truly to appraise the goods and chattels mentioned in the within (*or annexed*) Inventory according to the best of our judgment, and having viewed the said goods and chattels do appraise the same at the sum of   dollars and   cents, and no more.

As witness our hands the   day of   A. D. 18 .

Witness :   } Sworn appraisers.

When the goods are sold, the product of the sale as far as necessary is applied in satisfaction of the rent, and the expenses of the distress; if the product is more than sufficient for the purpose, the residue is to be given to the constable, for the use of the owner of the goods distrained,— and it should be handed over by the constable whenever demanded.

The landlord himself, or any other person, as his bailiff, by an authority from him in writing, may make the distress. The warrant or authority may be in the following form :—

To Mr.   my bailiff:

I do hereby authorize and require you to distrain the goods and chattels of   [*the tenant*] in the house he now dwells in [*or* "on the premises in his possession,"] situate in the Township of   , in the County of   , for   dollars, being one year's rent, due to me for the same, on the   day of   last, and to proceed thereon for the recovery of the said rent as the law directs.

Dated the   day of   , A. D. 18   .

Being legally authorized to distrain, you enter on the premises, and make a seizure of the distress. It it be made in a house, seize a chair or other piece of furniture, and say, "I seize this chair in the name of all the other goods on the premises for the sum of   dollars, being one year's rent due to me [*or* " to   your landlord] on the   day of   last, [" by virtue of an authority to me from the said   your landlord for that purpose," *provided you distrain as bailiff.*]

Then take an inventory of so many goods as you judge will be sufficient to cover the rent distrained for, and also the charges of the distress. Make a copy thereof as follows:

An Inventory of the several goods and chattels distrained by me   [*or, if as bailiff, say* "   as bailiff to Mr.   "] this   day of   in the year of our Lord 18   , in the dwelling-house, out-houses, and lands [*as the case may be*] of   situate in the Township of   in the County of   [*and if as bailiff, say,* " by the authority and on the behalf of the said   "] for the sum of   dollars, being one year's rent due to me [*or* " to the said   "] for the said house and premises, on the   day of   last, and as yet in arrear and unpaid.

In the Dwelling-house.

1. In the Kitchen.

Two tables, six chairs, one cooking stove, &c.

2. In the Parlour.

(Describing the various articles seized.)

3. In the Dining-room.

(Describing minutely the various articles.)

In the Outhouses.

1. Barn.

One fanning mill, fifty bushels of wheat, &c.
2. *Stable, &c.*
One horse, one waggon, &c.

And so on, describing the things according to where they are taken from. At the bottom of the Inventory, subscribe the following notice to the tenant, according as the case may be:—

Mr.   ,

Take notice, that I have this day distrained [*or* " that I, as bailiff, to   , your landlord, have this day distrained "] on the premises above mentioned, the several goods and chattels specified in the above Inventory, for the sum of   dollars, being one year's rent due to me [*or* " to the said   "] on the   day of   last, for the said premises;* and that unless you pay the said arrears of rent, with the charges of distraining for the same, or replevy the said goods and chattels within five days from the date hereof, the said goods and chattels will be appraised and sold according to law.

Given under my hand, the   day of   in the year of our Lord one thousand, eight hundred and   ,

The notice of distress of growing crops, under Stat. 2. Geo. II., chap. 19, sec. 8, is as follows:

Mr.   ,

Take notice, that I have this day taken and distrained (*or* " that as bailiff to   , your landlord, I have taken and distrained,") on the lands and premises above mentioned, the several growing crops specified in the Inventory, for the sum of   dollars, being two quarters' rent due to me (*or* " to the said   ") on the   day of   last, for the said lands and premises, and unless you previously pay the said rent, with the charges of distraining for the same, I shall proceed to cut, gather, make, cure, carry, and lay-up the crops when ripe, in the barn or other proper place on the said premises, and in convenient time sell and dispose of the

---

* If the goods are secured on the premises, under the authority of the Statute 11 Geo. II., ch. 19, sec. 10, insert the following: "And having secured the said goods and chattels in the Stable, &c., on the said premises."—1 Dougl., 279.

same towards satisfaction of the said rent, and of the charges of such distress, appraisement and sale, according to the form of the Statute in such case made and provided.

Given under my hand, the   day of   in the year of our Lord one thousand, eight hundred, and

Upon such notice and immediately following the above should be made a memorandum to the effect that a true copy had been delivered to the tenant.

A true copy of the above Inventory and notice must either be given to the tenant himself, or to the owner of the goods, or left at the tenant's house, with any person dwelling therein; or, if there be no person in the house, on some notorious part of it, or, if there be no house, on the most notorious place on the premises. And it is proper to have a person with you when you make the distress, and also when you serve the Inventory and notice, to examine the same, and to attest the regularity of the proceedings, if there should be occasion.

The goods may be removed immediately, and in the notice the tenant may be made acquainted where they are removed to, but it is now most usual to put a man in possession, and let him remain on the premises till you are entitled by law to sell them, which is the sixth day inclusive, after the distress made; *i. e.* goods distrained on the Saturday, may be removed on the Thursday afternoon following. —*Wallace* vs. *King*. 1, H. Black, 13.

If the tenant require further time for the payment of the rent, and the landlord choose to allow it, it is best to take a memorandum in writing from the tenant to the following effect, so as to prevent the landlord from being deemed a trespasser, which after the expiration of five days he otherwise would be, and might have an action of trespass brought against him for staying longer upon the premises.

Mr.

I hereby desire you will keep possession of my goods, which you have this day distrained for rent due (or alleged to be due) from me to you, in the place where they now are, being in the back room of the house in which I now reside, said house being situated in and upon Lot Number   , in the   Concession of the Township of   , in the County of   (*being the premises where the distress was made*) for the space of seven days from the date hereof, on your undertaking to delay the sale of the said goods and chattels for that time, to enable me to discharge the said rent; and I will pay the man for keeping the said possession.

Witness my hand, this   day of   , A. D., 18
Witness, }

Under the Act of 1st Victoria, chap. 16, entitled, "An Act to regulate the costs of levying distresses for small rents and penalties," the following schedule of fees can alone be demanded for any sum under £20:—

Levying distress under ten pounds,—five shillings.

Man keeping possession, per diem—three shillings and nine pence.

Appraisement, whether by one appraiser or more,—four pence in the pound on the value of the goods.

If any printed advertisement,—not to exceed in all five shillings.

Catalogues, Sale and Commission, and delivery of goods, —one shilling in the pound on the net produce of sale.

Laws of the Province of Ontario in relation to Landlord and Tenant.

REVISED STATUTES OF ONTARIO CHAP. 65.

An Act respecting the Costs of Levying Distresses for small Rents and Penalties.

1. No person making any distress for rent or for any

penalty when the sum demanded and due does not exceed the sum of eighty dollars, in respect of such rent or penalty, and no person employed in making such distress, or doing any act in the course of such distress, or for carrying the same into effect, shall take or receive, from any person or out of the produce of the chattels distrained upon and sold, any other costs in respect of such distress, than such as are set forth in Schedule A hereunto annexed, and no person shall make any charge for anything mentioned in the said Schedule, unless such thing has been really done.

2. If any person offends against any of the provisions in the foregoing section contained, the party aggrieved thereby may apply to any Justice of the Peace for the County, City or Town where the offence was committed, for the redress of such grievance, whereupon such Justice shall summon the person complained of to appear before him, at a reasonable time to be fixed in the summons, and the Justice shall examine into the matter of such complaint, and also hear the defence of the person complained of; and if it appears to the Justice that the person complained of has so offended, such Justice shall order and adjudge treble the amount of the money unlawfully taken and full costs to be paid by the offender to the party aggrieved.

3. In case of non-payment of any money or costs so adjudged to be paid, the Justice shall forthwith issue his warrant to levy the same by distress and sale of the goods and chattels of the party convicted, rendering to him the overplus, if any.

4. In case no sufficient distress can be had, the Justice shall by warrant under his hand and seal, commit the party to the Common Gaol within the limits of his jurisdiction, there to remain until the order or judgment is satisfied.

5. The Justice, at the request of the party complaining, or complained against, may summon all persons as witnesses, and may administer an oath to them touching the matter of such complaint, or the defence against it.

6. If any person so summoned neglects to obey the summons without any reasonable or lawful excuse, or refuses to be examined upon oath (or affirmation, as the case may be), he shall forfeit a sum not exceeding eight dollars, to be

adjudged, levied and paid in such manner, and by such means, and with such power of commitment, as hereinbefore directed with respect to orders and judgments made or given at the instance of original complaints, excepting as regards the form thereof, which may be made in such form as the Justice thinks fit.

7. If the Justice finds that the complaint of the party aggrieved is not well founded, he may order and adjudge costs, not exceeding four dollars, to be paid by the complainant to the party complained against, which order shall be carried into effect and levied and paid in the manner hereinbefore directed with respect to orders and judgments made or given at the instance of original complainants.

8. Nothing hereinbefore contained shall empower the Justice to make any order or judgment against the landlord for whose benefit any such distress has been made, unless the landlord personally levied the distress.

9. Every person who makes and levies any distress shall give a copy of demand, and of all the costs and charges of the distress, signed by him, to the person on whose goods and chattels the distress is levied, although the amount of the rent or penalty demanded exceeds the sum of eighty dollars.

10. No person aggrieved by any distress for any rents or penalty, or by any proceedings had in the course thereof, or by any costs or charges levied upon him in respect of the same, shall be barred from any suit or remedy which he might have had before the passing of this Act, excepting so far as any complaint preferred under this Act has been determined by the order and judgment of the Justice before whom it has been heard and determined; and in case the matter of such complaint is made the subject of an action, the order and judgment may be given in evidence, under the plea of the general issue.

11. Orders and judgments on such complaints shall be made in the words or to the effect of the forms given in Schedule B hereunto annexed; and may be proved before any Court, by proof of the signature of the Justice to such orders and judgments.

SCHEDULE "A."

(Section 1.)

Costs and Charges on Distresses for Small Rents and Penalties.

Levying distresses under eighty dollars..................	$1 00
Man keeping possession, per diem.......................	0 75
Appraisement, whether by one appraiser or more—*two cents in the dollar on the value of the goods;*	
If any printed advertisement, not to exceed in all...........	1 00
Catalogues, sale and commission, and delivery of goods—*five cents in the dollar on the net produce of the sale.*	

SCHEDULE "B."

(Section 11.)

FORM 1.

Form of the Order and judgment of the Justice before whom complaint is preferred when the order and judgment is for the Complainant.

In the matter of complaint of A. B. against C. D., for the breach of the provisions of the Act Chapter Sixty-five of *The Revised Statutes of Ontario,* entitled "*An Act respecting the Costs of levying Distresses for small Rents and Penalties,*" I, E. F., a Justice of the Peace for the   , do order and adjudge that the said C. D. shall pay to A. B. the sum of   , as a compensation and satisfaction for unlawful charges and costs levied and taken from the said A. B., under a distress for (*as the case may be*), and the further sum of   for costs in this complaint.

(Signed)   E. F.

FORM 2.

Form of the Order and Judgment of the Justice when he dismisses the Complaint as unfounded, with or without costs, as the case may be.

In the matter of complaint of A. B. against C. D., for the breach of the provisions of the Act Chapter Sixty-five of *The Revised Statutes of Ontario,* entitled "*An Act respecting the Costs of levying Distresses for small Rents and Penalties,*" I, E. F., a Justice of the Peace in and for the   , do order and adjudge that the complaint of the said A. B. is unfounded; (*if costs are given* add and I do further order and adjudge that the said A. B. shall pay unto the said C. D. the sum of   .)

(Signed)   E. F.

Length of Notices to Quit.

15. In the case of tenancies from week to week and from month to month, a week's notice to quit and a month's notice to quit, respectively, ending with the week or the month, as the case may be, shall be deemed sufficient notice to determine, respectively, a weekly or monthly tenancy. Revised Statutes, Ont., Chap. 136, Sec. 15.

REVISED STATUTES OF ONTARIO CHAP. 137.

Respecting Overholding Tenants.

1. In the construction of this Act—

(*a*) "Tenant" shall mean and include an occupant, a sub-tenant, under-tenant, and his and their assigns and legal representatives.

(*b*) "Landlord" shall mean and include the lessor, owner, the person giving or permitting the occupation of the premises in question and the person entitled to the possession thereof, and his and their heirs and assigns and legal representatives.

2. In case a tenant, after his lease or right of occupation, whether created by writing or by verbal agreement, has expired, or been determined, either by the landlord or the tenant, by a notice to quit or notice pursuant to a proviso in any lease or agreement in that behalf, or has been determined by any other act whereby a tenancy or right of occupancy may be determined or put an end to, wrongfully refuses, upon demand made in writing, to go out of possession of the land demised to him, or which he has been permitted to occupy, his landlord, or the agent of his landlord, may apply to the County Judge of the County, or Union of Counties, in which such land lies, in Term or in Vacation, and wherever such Judge then is, setting forth, on affidavit, the terms of the demise or right of occupation, if verbal, and annexing a copy of the instrument creating or containing such demise or right of occupation, if in writing, (or if a copy cannot be so annexed by reason of the said writing being mislaid, lost or destroyed, or being in the possession of the tenant, or from any other cause, then

annexing a statement setting forth the terms of the demise or occupation, and the reason why a copy of the said writing cannot be annexed), and also annexing a copy of the demand made for the delivering up of possession, and stating also the refusal of the tenant to go out of possession, and the reasons given for such refusal if any were given, adding such explanation in regard to the ground of such refusal as the truth of the case may require ; and this section shall extend and be construed to apply to tenancies from week to week, from month to month, from year to year, and tenancies at will, as well as to all other terms, tenancies, holdings or occupations.

3. If, upon such affidavit, it appears to such County Judge that the tenant wrongfully holds, without colour of right, and that the landlord is entitled to possession, such Judge shall appoint a time and place at which he will inquire and determine whether the person complained of was tenant to the complainant for a term or period which has expired, or has been determined by a notice to quit or otherwise, and whether the tenant, without any colour of right, holds the possession against the right of the landlord, and whether the tenant does wrongfully refuse to go out of possession, having no right to continue in possession, or how otherwise.

4. Notice in writing of the time and place so appointed by the County Judge for holding such inquiry, shall be, by the landlord, served upon the tenant or left at his place of abode, at least three days before the day so appointed, if the place so appointed is not more than twenty miles from the tenant's place of abode, and one day in addition for every twenty miles above the first twenty, reckoning any broken number above the first twenty as twenty miles, to which notice shall be annexed a copy of the affidavit on which the appointment was obtained, and of the papers attached thereto.

5. If at the time and place appointed, as aforesaid, the tenant, having been duly notified, as above provided, fails to appear, the County Judge, if it appears to him that the tenant holds without colour of right, may order a writ to issue to the Sheriff, in the Queen's name, commanding him forth-

with to place the landlord in possession of the premises in question; but if the tenant appears at such time and place, the County Judge shall, in a summary manner, hear the parties, and examine into the matter, and shall administer an oath or affirmation to the witnesses adduced by either party, and shall examine them; and if after such hearing and examination it appears to the County Judge that the case is clearly one coming under the true intent and meaning of the second section of this Act, and that the tenant holds without colour of right against the right of the landlord, then he shall order the issue of such writ, as aforesaid, otherwise he shall dismiss the case; and the proceedings, in any such case, shall form part of the records of the County Court; and the said writs may be in the words or to the effect of Form 1 or Form 2, in the Schedule to this Act, according as the tenant is ordered to pay costs or otherwise.

7. The Judges of the Superior Courts of Common Law may from time to time, make such orders respecting costs, in cases under this Act, as to them seem just; and the County Judge before whom any such case is brought may, in his discretion, award costs therein, according to any such order then in force, and if no such order is in force, reasonable costs, in his discretion, to the party entitled thereto; and in case the party complaining is ordered to pay costs, execution may issue out of the County Court for such costs as in other cases in the County Court, wherein an order is made for the payment of costs.

EJECTMENT BY LANDLORDS.

Extracts from Revised Statutes of Ontario, Chap. 51.

WHERE A HALF-YEAR'S RENT IS IN ARREAR.

59. In all cases between landlord and tenant, as often as it happens that one half year's rent is in arrear, and the landlord or lessor to whom the same is due has the right by law to re-enter for non-payment thereof, such landlord or lessor may, without any formal demand or re-entry, serve a writ in ejectment for the recovery of the demised premises; or in case the same cannot be legally served or no tenant is in actual possession of the premises, then such landlord or

lessor may affix a copy thereof upon the door of any demised messuage, or in case such action of ejectment is not for the recovery of any messuage, then upon some notorious place of the lands, tenements or hereditaments comprised in the writ; and such affixing shall be deemed legal service thereof, which service or affixing of the writ shall stand instead and in place of a demand and re-entry.

60. In case of judgment against the defendant for non-appearance, if it is shown by affidavit, to the Court wherein the action is depending, or is proved upon the trial in case the defendant appears, that half a year's rent was due before the said writ was served, and that no sufficient distress was to be found on the demised premises countervailing the arrears then due, and that the lessor had power to re-enter, the lessor shall recover judgment and have execution in the same manner as if the rent in arrear had been legally demanded and a re-entry made; but if a verdict passes for the defendant, or if the plaintiff is non-suited, the defendant shall recover his costs.

61. In case the lessee or his assignee, or other person claiming or deriving title under the said lease, permits and suffers judgment to be had on such trial and execution to be executed thereon, without paying the rent and arrears together with full costs, and without proceeding for equitable relief within six months after execution executed, then and in every such case the said lessee and his assignee and all other persons claiming and deriving under the said lease, shall be barred and foreclosed from all relief or remedy in Law or Equity, other than by proceedings by way of appeal from such judgment, and the said landlord or lessor shall from thenceforth hold the demised premises discharged from such lease.

62. Nothing hereinbefore contained shall bar the right of any mortgagee of such lease or any part thereof who is not in possession, if such mortgagee, within six months after such judgment obtained and execution executed, pays all rent in arrear and all costs and damages sustained by such lessor or person entitled to the remainder or reversion, and performs all covenants and agreements which on the part and behalf of the first lessee are to be or ought to be performed.

Where lease is determined and tenant refuses to go out.

65. In case (1), the term or interest of any tenant of any lands, tenements or hereditaments, holding the same under a lease or agreement in writing for any term or number of years certain, or from year to year, expires or is determined either by the landlord or tenant by regular notice to quit; and (2), in case a lawful demand of possession in writing, made and signed by the landlord or his agent, is served personally upon the tenant or any person holding or claiming under him, or is left at the dwelling house or usual place of abode of such tenant or person; and (3), in case such tenant or person refuses to deliver up possession accordingly, and the landlord thereupon proceeds by action of ejectment for recovery of possession, he may, at the foot of the writ in ejectment, address a notice to such tenant or person, requiring him to find such bail, if ordered by the Court or a Judge, and for such purposes as are hereinafter next specified.

CLAIMS OF LANDLORDS AS TO GOODS TAKEN IN EXECUTION.

Extracts from Division Courts Act, Revised Statutes Ontario, Chap. 47.

210. In case a claim be made to or in respect of any goods or chattels, property or security, taken in execution or attached under the process of any Division Court, or in respect of the proceeds or value thereof, by any landlord for rent, or by any person not being the party against whom such process issued, then, subject to the provisions of *The Act respecting Absconding Debtors*, the Clerk of the Court, upon application of the officer charged with the execution of such process, may, whether before or after the action has been brought against such officer, issue a summons calling before the Court out of which such process issued, or before the Court holden for the Division in which the seizure under such process was made, as well the party who issued such process as the party making such claim, and thereupon any action which has been brought in any of Her Majesty's Superior Courts of Record, or in a local or inferior Court in respect of such claim, shall be stayed,

(b) The Court in which such action has been brought, or any Judge thereof, on proof of the issue of such summons, and that the goods and chattels or property or security were so taken in execution or upon attachment, may order the party bringing such action to pay the costs of all proceedings had upon such action after the issue of such summons out of the Division Court.

(c) The County Judge having jurisdiction in such Division Court shall adjudicate upon the claim, and make such order between the parties in respect thereof, and of the costs of the proceedings, as to him seems fit, and such order shall be enforced in like manner as an order made in any suit brought in such Division Court, and shall be final and conclusive between the parties, except that upon the application of either the attaching or execution creditor, or the claimant within fourteen days after the trial, the Judge may grant a new trial upon good grounds shown, as in other cases under this Act, upon such terms as he thinks reasonable, and may in the meantime stay proceedings.

211. So much of the Act passed in the eighth year of the reign of Queen Anne, entitled "*An Act for the better security of Rents and to prevent Frauds committed by Tenants,*" as relates to the liability of goods taken by virtue of any execution, shall not be deemed to apply to goods taken in execution under the process of any Division Court, but the landlord of any tenement in which any such goods are so taken may, by writing under his hand or under the hand of his agent, stating the terms of holding and the rent payable for the same, and delivered to the Bailiff making the levy, claim any rent in arrear then due to him, not exceeding the rent of four weeks when the tenement has been let by the week, and not exceeding the rent accruing due in two terms of payment where the tenement has been let for any other term less than a year, and not exceeding in any case the rent accruing due in one year.

212. In case of any such claim being so made, the Bailiff making the levy shall distrain as well for the amount of the rent claimed, and the costs of such additional distress, as for the amount of money and costs for which the warrant of execution has issued, and shall not sell the same, or any part

thereof, until after the end of eight days at least next following after such distress made.

213. For every additional distress for rent in arrear, the Bailiff of the Court shall be entitled to have as the costs of the distress, instead of the fees allowed by this Act, the fees allowed by *The Act respecting Distresses for small Rents and Penalties.*

214. If any replevin is made of the goods distrained, so much of the goods taken under the warrant of execution shall be sold as will satisfy the money and costs for which the said warrant issued, and the costs of the sale, and the surplus of such sale and the goods so distrained, shall be returned as in other cases of distress for rent and replevin thereof.

215. No execution creditor under this Act shall have his debt satisfied out of the proceeds of such execution and distress, or of execution only, where the tenant replevies, until the landlord who conforms to the provisions of this Act has been paid the rent in arrear for the periods hereinbefore mentioned.

Misconduct of Clerks, Bailiffs, &c.

218. If any Bailiff or officer, acting under colour or pretence of process of the Court, is guilty of extortion or miscorduct, or does not duly pay or account for all money levied or received by him by virtue of his office, the Judge, at any sitting of the Court, if a party aggrieved thinks fit to complain to him in writing, may enquire into the matter in a summary way, and for that purpose he may summon and enforce the attendance of all necessary parties and witnesses, and may make such order thereupon for the repayment of any money extorted, or for the due payment of any money so levied or received, and for the payment of any such damages and costs to the parties aggrieved, as he thinks just ; and in default of payment of the money so ordered to be paid by such Bailiff or officer within the time in such order specified for the payment thereof, the Judge may, by warrant under his hand and seal, cause such sum to be levied by distress and sale of the goods of the offender, together with the reasonable charges of such distress and sale, and in default of such distress (or summarily in the

first instance) may commit the offender to the Common Gaol of the County for any period not exceeding three months.

43 VIC. CHAPTER 16, (ONTARIO.)

An Act to protect the goods of Lodgers and Boarders against distresses for rent due to the Superior Landlord.

Whereas lodgers and boarders are subjected to great loss and injustice by the exercise of the power possessed by the superior landlord to levy a distress on their furniture, goods and chattels for arrears of rent due to such superior landlord by his immediate lessee or tenant :

Therefore Her Majesty, by and with the advice and consent of the Legislative Assembly of the Province of Ontario, enacts as follows :—

1. If any superior landlord shall levy or authorize to be levied a distress on any furniture, goods or chattels of any boarder or lodger for arrears of rent due to such superior landlord by his immediate tenant, such boarder or lodger may serve such superior landlord, or the bailiff or other person employed by him to levy such distress, with a declaration in writing, made by such boarder or lodger, setting forth that such immediate tenant has no right of property or beneficial interest in the furniture, goods or chattels so distrained or threatened to be distrained upon, and that such furniture, goods or chattels are the property or in the lawful possession of such boarder or lodger ; and also setting forth whether any and what amount by way of rent, board or otherwise is due from such boarder or lodger to the said immediate tenant ; and such boarder or lodger may pay to the superior landlord, or to the bailiff or other person employed by him as aforesaid, the amount, if any, so due as last aforesaid, or so much thereof as shall be sufficient to discharge the claim of such superior landlord : and to such declaration shall be annexed a correct inventory, subscribed by the boarder or lodger, of the furniture, goods and chattels referred to in the declaration.

2. If any superior landlord, or any bailiff or other person employed by him, after being served with the before mentioned declaration and inventory, and after the boarder or

lodger shall have paid or tendered to such superior landlord, bailiff or other person, the amount, if any, which by the last preceding section, such boarder or lodger is authorized to pay, shall levy or proceed with a distress on the furniture, goods or chattels of the boarder or lodger, such superior landlord, bailiff or other person shall be deemed guilty of an illegal distress, and the boarder or lodger may replevy such furniture, goods or chattels in any court of competent jurisdiction and the superior landlord shall also be liable to an action at law at the suit of the boarder or lodger, in which action the truth of the declaration and inventory may likewise be inquired into.

3. Any payment made by a boarder or lodger pursuant to the first section of this Act shall be deemed a valid payment on account of any amount due from him to the said immediate tenant mentioned in section one of this Act.

4. The declaration hereinbefore referred to shall be made under and in accordance with the "Act for the suppression of voluntary and extrajudicial oaths."

Lease of House.

This Indenture made the   day of,   18 . Between A. B., of, &c., of the first part, and C. D., of, &c., of the second part, Witnesseth, that in consideration of the rents, covenants and agreements hereinafter reserved and contained on the part of the said party of the second part, his executors, administrators and assigns, to be paid, observed and performed, He, the said party of the first part, hath demised and leased, and by these presents doth demise and lease, unto the said party of the second part, his executors, administrators and assigns, all that messuage or tenement situate, lying and being, &c., (*here describe the premises*), Together with all houses, out-houses, yards and other appurtenances thereto belonging, or usually known as part or parcel thereof, or as belonging thereto: To have and to hold the same for and during the term of   years, to be computed from the   day of   , 18 , and from thenceforth next ensuing, and fully to be complete and ended.

Yielding and paying therefor yearly and every year during the said term hereby granted unto the said party of the first part, his heirs, executors, administrators or assigns, the sum of $, to be payable quarterly on the following days and times, that is to say, (*here state the days of payment*), the first of such payments to become due and be made on the   day of   next.

Provided always, and these presents are upon this express condition, that if the said yearly rent, hereby reserved, or any part thereof, shall at any time remain behind or unpaid for the space of twenty-one days next over or after any of the days on which the same shall become due and payable, then, and in every such case, it shall be lawful for the said party of the first, his heirs, executors, administrators, or assigns, into and upon the said premises, or any part thereof, in the name of the whole, to re-enter, and the same to have again, repossess and enjoy, as if these presents had never been executed.

And the said party of the second part, for himself, his heirs, executors, administrators and assigns, doth hereby covenant, promise and agree to and with the said party of the first part, his heirs, executors, administrators and assigns, in manner following, that is to say :

That he, the said party of the second part, his executors, administrators and assigns, shall and will well and truly pay, or cause to be paid, to the said party of the first part, his heirs, executors, administrators or assigns, the said yearly rent hereby reserved at the times and in manner hereinbefore appointed for payment thereof.

And also shall and will, from time to time, and at all times during the said term, keep in good and sufficient repair the said premises hereby demised, (reasonable wear and tear and accident by fire excepted), and the same so kept in repair shall and will, at the end, expiration or other sooner determination of the said term, peaceably and quietly yield and deliver up to the said party of the first part, his heirs, executors, administrators or assigns.

And also shall and will well and truly pay, or cause to be paid, all taxes, rates, levies, duties, charges, assessments and impositions whatsover, whether parliamentary, local or otherwise, which now are, or which during the continuance of this demise shall at any time be rated, taxed or imposed on, or in respect of the said demised premises, or any part thereof.

And also that it shall be lawful for the said party of the first part, his heirs, executors, administrators and assigns, and their agents respectively, either alone or with workmen or others, from time to time at all reasonable times in the daytime, during the said term, to enter upon the said demised premises, and every part thereof, to view and examine the state and condition thereof; and in case any want of reparation or amendment be found on any such examination, the said party of the second part, his executors, administrators or assigns, shall and will from time to time cause the same to be well and sufficiently repaired, amended, and made good, within one month next after notice in writing shall have been given to them or left at or upon the said demised premises for that purpose. And if the said party of the second part, his executors, administrators or assigns, fail in making the necessary repairs in manner hereinbefore described, that it shall be lawful for the said party of the first part, his heirs, executors, administrators and assigns, and their agents, to enter into and upon the said hereby demised premises, and have the same repaired in a proper manner, and to render the account for such repairs to the said party of the second part, his executors, administrators and assigns, and demand payment for the same, and if default is made, to sue for the same in any Court of Law having jurisdiction over the same.

And the said party of the second part, his executors, administrators or assigns, shall not, nor will at any time or times during the continuance of this demise, sell, assign, let or otherwise part with this present lease, or the said premises hereby demised, or any part thereof, to any person or persons whomsoever, for the whole or any part of the said term, nor alter, change or remove any part of the said premises, yards or offices, externally or internally, without the license and consent in writing of the said party of the first part, his heirs, executors, administrators or assigns, from time to time, first had and obtained.

And the said party of the first part, for himself, his heirs, executors and administrators or assigns, covenants with the said party of the second part, his executors, administrators and assigns, that he, the said party of the second part, his executors, administrators and assigns, well and truly paying the rent hereinbefore reserved, and observing, performing, and keeping the covenants hereinbefore contained, shall and may, from time to time, and at all times during the said term, peaceably and quietly enjoy the said premises hereby demised, without molestation or hindrance.

In witness whereof, the said parties to these presents have hereunto set their hands and seals, the day and year first above written.

Signed, sealed and delivered
in the presence of   A. B. [L.S.]
   Y. Z.   C. D. [L.S.]

Lease of Land.

This Indenture, made the   day of   , 18 , Between A. B., of, &c., of the first part, and C. D., of, &c., of the second part, Witnesseth, that for and in consideration of the rent, covenants, conditions and agreements hereinafter reserved and contained, and to be paid, observed and performed by the said party of the second part, his executors, administrators and assigns, He, the said party of the first part Hath demised and leased, and by these presents Doth demise and lease, unto the said party of the second part, his executors, administrators and assigns, All that certain parcel or tract of land and premises situate, lying and being (*here describe the lands.*) To have and to hold the said parcel or tract of land, with the appurtenances, unto the said party of the second part, his executors, administrators and assigns, from the   day of   , 18 , for the term of   , from thence next ensuing, and fully to be complete and ended, Yielding and paying therefor, unto the said party of the first part, his executors, administrators and assigns, the yearly rent or sum of $, of lawful money of Canada, by equal yearly payments, on the   day of   , in each and every year during the said term, the first payment to be made on the   day of   , next ensuing the date hereof. (*The times of payment may be quarterly or half-yearly, if desired.*)

And the said party of the second part doth hereby for himself, his heirs, executors, administrators and assigns, covenant, promise and agree with and to the said party of the first part, his executors, administrators and assigns, that he, the said party of the second part, his executors, administrators and assigns, shall and will well and truly pay, or cause to be paid, to the said party of the first part, his executors, administrators or assigns, the said yearly rent hereby reserved, at the times and in manner hereinbefore mentioned for payment thereof, without any deduction or abatement whatsoever thereout for or in respect of any rates, taxes, assessment, or otherwise : And also shall and will, on or before the   day of   , now next, at his own costs and charges, fence in the premises hereby demised in a good and substantial manner, (*add here such covenants as to the mode of cultivation, &c., as may be agreed on.*)

And it is hereby agreed, on the part of the said party of the first part, his heirs, executors, administrators and assigns, that if at any time within the said term of   the said party of the second part, his heirs, executors, administrators or assigns, shall desire to purchase the fee simple of the land hereby demised, he shall be allowed to do so by paying the sum of $, of lawful money aforesaid, provided the said rent shall have been regularly paid up to the time when he may so desire to purchase ; and provided he gives to the party of the first part, three months previous notice of his intention to purchase.

And it is hereby agreed, on the part of the said party of the second part, his executors, administrators and assigns, that if at any time or times during the said term, the said rent, or any part thereof, shall be in arrear and unpaid for the space of thirty days after any of the days or times whereon the same ought to be paid, as aforesaid, then it shall be lawful for the said party of the first part, his heirs, executors, administrators or assigns, to enter into and take possession of the premises hereby demised, whether the same be lawfully demanded or not, and the same to sell and dispose of, either by public auction or private sale, as to him or them may seem best, without the let, hindrance or denial of him the said party of the second part, his heirs, executors, administrators and assigns : And further, that the non-fulfilment of the covenants hereinbefore mentioned, or any of them, on the part of the lessee or lessees, shall operate as a forfeiture of these presents, and the same shall be considered null and void to all intents and purposes whatsoever; And also, that the said party of the second part, his executors, administrators and assigns, shall not, nor will, during the said term, grant or demise, or assign, transfer, or set over, or otherwise, by any act or deed, procure or cause the said premises hereby demised, or intended so to be, or any part thereof, or any estate, term, or interest therein, to be granted, assigned, transferred, or set over, unto any person or persons whosoever, without the consent in writing of the said party of the first part, his heirs or assigns, first had and obtained.

In witness whereof, the said parties to these presents have hereunto set their hands and seals, the day and year first above written.

Signed, sealed and delivered
in the presence of   A. B. [L.S.]
   Y. Z.   C. D. [L.S.]

Lease of a House and Farm.

This Indenture made the   , day of   , 18   , Between A. B., of, &c., of the one part, and C. D., of, &c., of the other part, Witnesseth, that for and in consideration of the rent, covenants, conditions and agreements hereinafter reserved and contained, and which, on the part and behalf of the said C. D., his executors, administrators and assigns, are or ought to be paid, done and performed, the said A. B. hath demised, leased, set and to farm let, and by these presents doth demise, lease, set and to farm let, unto the said C. D., his executors and administrators, All that parcel or tract of land, &c., [describing the lot] together with the frame dwelling house, barns, stables, and other out-houses thereupon erected, standing and being, together with all ways, paths, passages, waters, water-courses, privileges, advantages, and appurtenances whatsoever, to the same premises belonging, or in any wise appertaining. To have and to hold the said parcel or tract of land, dwelling-house, buildings and premises hereby demised unto the said C. D., his executors, administrators and assigns, from the day of the date of these presents, for, and during, and until the full end and term of   years from thence next ensuing, and fully to be complete and ended: Yielding and paying therefor yearly, and every year during the said term hereby granted, unto the said A. B., his heirs and assigns, the yearly rent or sum of $, of lawful current money of Canada by two equal half-yearly payments, to be made on the   day of   , and the   day of   in each and every year during the said term, without any deduction or abatement thereout for or upon any account or pretence whatsoever. Provided always, nevertheless, that if it shall happen that the said yearly rent hereby reserved, or any part thereof, shall be behind and unpaid for the space of twenty-one days next over or after either of the said days hereinbefore mentioned and appointed for payment of the same (being lawfully demanded) or if the said C. D., his executors or administrators, shall assign over, underlet or otherwise part with this indenture, or the premises hereby leased, or any part thereof, to any person or persons whomsoever, without the consent of the said A. B., his heirs or assigns, first had and obtained in writing, under his or their hands, for that purpose; then, and in either of the said cases, it shall and may be lawful to and for the said A. B., his heirs or assigns, into the said premises hereby demised, or any part thereof, in the name of the whole, to re-enter and the same to have again, retain, repossess and enjoy, as in his and their first and former estate or estates, any thing herein contained to the contrary thereof in any wise, notwithstanding. And the said C. D. doth hereby, for himself, his heirs, executors, administrators and assigns, covenant, promise and agree to and with the said A. B., his heir and assigns, in manner following, that is to say: That he, the said C. D., his executors, administrators and assigns, shall and will well and truly pay, or cause to be paid, unto the said A. B., his heirs and assigns, the said yearly rent of $, by equal half-yearly payments, on or at the days or times and in the manner hereinbefore mentioned and appointed for payment thereof. Also that he, the said C. D., his executors, administrators and assigns, shall and will, at his and their own costs and charges, well and sufficiently repair and keep repaired the dwelling-house, buildings, fences and gates now erected, or which shall at any time or times hereafter during the said term be erected, upon the said demised premises, he, the said A. B., his heirs and assigns, upon request and notice to them made, finding and allowing on the said premises, or within   miles' distance thereof, all rough timber, brick, lime, tiles, and all other materials whatsoever, (except straw), for doing thereof, to be carried to the said hereby demised premises at the charge of the said C. D., his executors, administrators or assigns, or otherwise permitting and allowing him or them, at their like costs and charges, to cut and fell such and so many timber-trees upon some part of the premises hereby demised as shall be requisite and necessary for the purpose (damage happening by accidental fire, tempest, or other inevitable accident being always excepted): And further, that he, the said C. D., his executors, administrators and assigns, shall and will at all times during the said term cultivate and farm such part or parts of the said lands and premises as now are or shall hereafter be brought into cultivation during the said term in a proper husbandlike manner. And shall and will at the expiration or other sooner determination of this lease peaceably and quietly leave, surrender and yield up unto the said A. B., his heirs and assigns, the whole of the said premises hereby demised in such good and sufficient repair as aforesaid, (reasonable use and wear thereof, and damage by accidental fire, tempest or other inevitable accident, as aforesaid, always excepted) : And also, that it shall and may be lawful to and for the said A. B., his heirs or assigns, after six days' previous notice in writing, twice or oftener in every year during the said term, at seasonable and convenient times in the day, to enter and come into and upon the said demised premises, or any part thereof, to view the condition of the same, and of all defects and wants of reparation and amendment which shall then and there be found, to leave notice in writing at the said demised premises to or for the said C. D., his executors, administrators or assigns, to repair and amend the same within the space of three calendar months. And the said C. D., doth hereby, for himself, his executors, administrators and assigns, covenant, promise and agree, to and with the said A. B., his heirs and assigns, that he, the said C. D., his executors, administrators or assigns shall and will within three calendar months next after every and any such notice shall have been so given or left as aforesaid, well and sufficiently repair and amend the same accordingly (except as before excepted, and upon being provided or allowed materials for the same, as aforesaid), and also that he, the said C. D., his executors, administrators or assigns, shall not, nor will at any time during the said term, pull down, or cause or permit to be pulled down, or make, or cause or permit to be made, any alteration by cutting new door-ways or otherwise in the said dwelling-house, or in any of the buildings upon the said demised premises, without the consent in writing of the said A. B., his heirs, or assigns, for that purpose first had and obtained; And moreover shall not, nor will at any time during the continuance of this demise, bargain, sell, assign, transfer or set over this Indenture of Lease, or let, set, demise, underlease, or underlet the said dwelling-house and premises hereby demised, or any part thereof, or in any other manner part with this Indenture of Lease, or the possession or occupation of the premises hereby demised, without such license and consent as aforesaid. Provided always, nevertheless, and these presents are upon this express condition, that if the said yearly rent or sum of $, hereby reserved, or any part thereof, shall be unpaid in part or in all by the space of twenty one days next after either of the days on which the same ought to be paid as aforesaid, being lawfully demanded; or in case the said C. D., his executors or administrators, shall at any time during the said term hereby granted, without such license as aforesaid, assign, transfer or set over, underlease or underlet, the premises hereby demised, or any part thereof; or in other manner part with the possession or occupation of the same, or any part thereof: or if all or any of the covenants, conditions or agreements in these presents contained, on the part and behalf of the said C. D., his executors, administrators and assigns, shall not be performed, fulfilled, and kept according to the true intent and meaning of these presents, then and from thenceforth, in any or either of the said cases, it shall and may be lawful to and for the said A. B., his heirs and assigns, into and upon the said demised premises, or any part thereof, in the name of the whole, wholly to re-enter and the same to have again, retain, repossess and enjoy as in his or their first and former estate, and thereout and from thence the said C. D., his executors, administrators and assigns, and all other occupiers of the said premises, to expel, put out and remove, this indenture or any thing hereinbefore contained to the contrary thereof in any wise notwithstanding. And the said A. B. doth hereby, for himself, his heirs, executors, administrators and assigns, covenant, promise and agree with and to the said C. D., his executors, administrators and assigns, that he, the said C. D., his executors, administrators and assigns, well and truly paying the said yearly rent hereby reserved on the days and in the manner hereinbefore appointed for payment thereof, and observing, keeping and performing all and singular the covenants and agreements in these presents contained, and which, on his and their parts and behalves, are and ought to be paid, kept, done and performed, shall and may lawfully, peaceably and quietly have, hold, use, occupy, possess and enjoy the said demised premises, and every part and parcel thereof, with the appurtenances, during all the said term of   years hereby granted, without any lawful let, suit, trouble, interruption, eviction, molestation, hindrance or denial of or by him, the said A. B., his heirs or assigns, or of, from or by any other person or persons claiming or to claim from, by, or under him, them, or any or either of them.

In witness whereof, the said parties to these presents have hereunto set their hands and seals.

Signed, sealed and delivered
in the presence of   A. B. [L.S.]
  Y. Z.   C. D. [L.S.]

Short Form of Lease, (Ontario.)

This Indenture, made the   day of   , in the year of our Lord one thousand eight hundred and   , in pursuance of *The Act respecting Short Forms of Leases;* between   , of the first part, and   of the second part, Witnesseth, that in consideration of the rents, covenants and agreements, hereinafter reserved and contained on the part of the said party (*or* parties) of the second part, his (*or* their) executors, administrators and assigns, to be paid, observed and performed, he (*or* they) the said party (*or* parties) of the first part hath (*or* have) demised and leased, and by these presents do (*or* doth) demise and lease unto the said party (*or* parties) of the second part, his (*or* their) executors, administrators and assigns, all that messuage or tenement situate (*or* all that parcel or tract of land situate) lying and being (*here insert a description of the premises with sufficient certainty.*)

To have and to hold the said demised premises for and during the term of   to be computed from the   day of   , one thousand eight hundred and   , and from thenceforth next ensuing and fully to be complete and ended.

Yielding and paying therefor yearly and every year during the said term hereby granted unto the said party (*or* parties) of the first part, his (*or* their) heirs, executors, administrators or assigns, the sum of   , to be payable on the following days and times, that is to say (on, &c.,) the first of such payments to become due and be made on the   day of   next.

In witness whereof, &c.

Simple Agreement for the yearly Tenancy of a House.

This agreement made this first day of May, one thousand eight hundred and eighty, between John Jones, of the Town of Prescott, in the County of Grenville, and Province of Ontario, gentleman, of the first part; and George Smith, of the same place, merchant, of the second part.

1. The said John Jones agrees to let, and the said George Smith agrees to take, the dwelling house and premises on George Street, the property of the said John Jones, at the yearly rental of one hundred dollars, commencing from this day, rent payable quarterly.

2. The said George Smith agrees not to sublet the whole or any part of the said house and premises, and to use the same only as a dwelling house for himself and family.

3. The said George Smith agrees to pay all taxes and assessments on said house and premises.

In witness whereof, &c.

Agreement for a Lease.

This agreement, made this   day of   , in the year eighteen hundred and eighty, between A. B. of   and C. D., of said city, merchant, *witnesseth*, That A. B. agrees, by indenture, to be executed on or before the   day of   next, to demise and let to the said C. D., a certain house and lot in said city, now or lately in the occupation of E. F., known as No.   , in   street, to hold to the said C. D., his executors, administrators, and assigns, from the   day of   , aforesaid, for and during the term of three years, at or under the clear yearly rent of   dollars, payable quarterly, clear of all taxes and deductions except the ground rent. In which lease there shall be contained covenants on the part of the said C. D., his executors, administrators and assigns, to pay the rent, (except in case the premises are destroyed by fire, the rent is to cease until they are rebuilt by the said A. B.,) and to pay all taxes and assessments, (except the ground rent;) to repair the premises, (except damages by fire;) not to carry on any offensive business on the same except by written permission of the said A. B.; to deliver the same up at the end of the term, in good repair, (except damages by fire, aforesaid;) with all other usual and reasonable covenants, and a proviso for the re-entry of the said C. D., his heirs and assigns, in case of the non-payment of the rent for the space of fifteen days after either of the said rent days, or the non-performance of any of the covenants. And there shall also be contained covenants on the part of the said A. B., his heirs and assigns, for quiet enjoyment; to renew said lease at the expiration of said term, for a further period of twenty-one years at the same rent, on the said C. D., his executors, administrators, or assigns, paying the said A. B., his executors, administrators, or assigns, the sum of five hundred dollars, as a premium for such renewal; and that in case of an accidental fire, at any time during the term, the said A. B. will forthwith proceed to put the premises in as good repair as before such fire, the rent in the meantime to cease. And the said C. D. hereby agrees to accept such lease on the terms aforesaid. And it is mutually agreed, that the cost of this agreement, and of making and recording said lease, and a counterpart thereof, shall be borne by the said parties equally.

As witness our hands and seals, the day and year first above written.

In presence of
J. S.

A. B. [L.S.]
C. D. [L.S.]

Landlord's Agreement of Lease.

This is to certify, that I have, this   day of   , 1881, let and rented unto Mr. C. D., my house and lot, known as No.   , in   street, in the city of   , with the appurtenances, and the sole and uninterrupted use and occupation thereof, for one year, to commence the   day of   next, at the yearly rent of   dollars, payable quarterly, on the usual quarter-days; rent to cease in case the premises are destroyed by fire.   A. B.

Tenant's Agreement.

This is to certify, that I have hired and taken from Mr. A. B., his house and lot, known as No.   , in   street, in the city of   , with the appurtenances, for the term of one year, to commence the first day of   next, at the yearly rent of   dollars, payable quarterly on the usual quarter-days. And I do hereby promise to make punctual payment of the rent in manner aforesaid, except in case the premises become untenantable from fire or any other cause, when the rent is to cease; and do further promise to quit and surrender the premises, at the expiration of the term, in as good state and condition as reasonable use and wear thereof will permit, damages by the elements excepted.

Given under my hand and seal, the   day of   , 1880.

In presence of   C. D. [L.S.]
    J. S.

Agreement for Part of a House.

Memorandum of an agreement entered into, the   day of   , 1881, by and between A. B., of   , and C. D., of, &c., whereby the said A. B. agrees to let, and the said C. D. agrees to take the rooms or apartments following, that is to say: an entire first floor, and one room in the attic story or garret, and a back kitchen and cellar opposite, with the use of the yard for drying linen, or beating carpets or clothes, being part of a house and premises in which the said A. B. now resides, situate and being in No.   , in   street, in the city of   , to have and to hold the said rooms and apartments, and the use of the said yard as aforesaid, for and during the term of half a year, to commence from the day of   , instant, at and for the yearly rent of   dollars, lawful money of Canada, payable monthly, by even and equal portions, the first payment to be made on the   day of   next ensuing the date thereof ; and it is further agreed that, at the expiration of the said term of half a year, the said C. D. may hold, occupy and enjoy the said rooms or apartments, and have the use of the said yard as aforesaid, from month to month, for so long a time as the said C. D. and A. B. may and shall agree, at the rent above specified ; and that each party be at liberty to quit possession on giving the other a month's notice in writing. And it is also further agreed, that when the said C. D. shall quit the premises, he shall leave them in as good condition and repair as they shall be in on his taking possession thereof, reasonable wear excepted.

Witness, &c., [*as in Agreement for a Lease.*]

LINE FENCES AND WATER COURSES. (ONTARIO.)

In a great agricultural country like the Province of Ontario, it was only natural that the matter of Line Fences and Water Courses should receive a large share of legislative attention. The Statute books, accordingly, of Upper Canada (as Ontario was called up to the rise of the New Dominion), contain various enactments regulating line or boundary fences, and the matter of drainage. Thirty-six years ago the law on these matters was amended and improved by 8 Vic., Chap. 20 ; and ultimately re-appeared in the Consolidated Statutes for Upper Canada (1859) in Chap. 57. The Legislature of Ontario has also devoted considerable attention to this subject in 37 Vic., Chap. 25, and 40 Vic., Chap. 29. In the Revised Statutes of Ontario, Chap. 198 is devoted to the single subject of Line Fences, and is amended by the short explanatory Act of 41 Vic.,

Chap. 10, to the effect that "occupied lands" shall only mean those parts of a lot, parcel or farm which are enclosed or fenced in, and in actual use and occupation. Chap. 199 of the Revised Statutes is devoted to the subject of Water Courses, but as it affects individual rights only. This Act was amended by 43 Vic., Chap. 30, and is now appended in its amended form. As it is highly desirable that the fullest and most accurate information, as regards the important matters of Line Fences and Water Courses, should be generally known to all those interested, we publish the applying Statutes in full. We may add that other local legislation makes the most ample provision for drainage, on a more extensive scale, by municipalities and companies.

REVISED STATUTES ONTARIO, CHAPTER 198.

An Act respecting Line Fences.

1. This Act may be cited as " *The Line Fences Act.*"

2. Owners of occupied adjoining lands shall make, keep up and repair a just proportion of the fence which marks the boundary between them, or if there is no fence, they shall so make, keep up and repair the same proportion, which is to mark such boundary ; and owners of unoccupied lands which adjoin occupied lands, shall, upon their being occupied, be liable to the duty of keeping up and repairing such proportion, and in that respect shall be in the same position as if their land had been occupied at the time of the original fencing, and shall be liable to the compulsory proceedings hereinafter mentioned.

3. In case of dispute between owners respecting such proportion, the following proceedings shall be adopted :

(*a*) Either owner may notify (Form 1) the other owner or the occupant of the land of the owner so to be notified, that he will, not less than one week from the service of such notice, cause three Fence-viewers of the locality to arbitrate in the premises.

(*b*) Such owners so notifying shall also notify (Form 2)

the Fence-viewers, not less than one week before their services are required.

(c) The notices in both cases shall be in writing, signed by the person notifying, and shall specify the time and place of meeting for the arbitration, and may be served by leaving the same at the place of abode of such owner or occupant, with some grown-up person residing thereat; or in case of such lands being untenanted, by leaving such notice with any agent of such owner.

(d) The owners notified may, within the week, object to any or all of the Fence-viewers notified, and in case of disagreement, the Judge hereinafter mentioned shall name the Fence-viewers who are to arbitrate.

4. An occupant, not the owner of land notified in the manner above mentioned, shall immediately notify the owner; and if he neglects so to do, shall be liable for all damage caused to the owner by such neglect.

5. The Fence-viewers shall examine the premises, and if required by either party, they shall hear evidence, and are authorized to examine the parties and their witnesses on oath, and any one of them may administer an oath or affirmation as in Courts of Law.

6. The Fence-viewers shall make an award (Form 3) in writing signed by any two of them, respecting the matters so in dispute; which award shall specify the locality, quantity, description and the lowest price of the fence it orders to be made, and the time within which the work shall be done, and shall state by which of the said parties the costs of the proceedings shall be paid, or whether either party shall pay some proportion of such costs.

(b) In making such award, the Fence-viewers shall regard the nature of the fences in use in the locality, the pecuniary circumstances of the persons between whom they arbitrate, and generally the suitableness of the fence ordered to the wants of each party.

(c) Where, from the formation of the ground, by reason of streams or other causes, it is found impossible to locate the fence upon the line between the parties, it shall be lawful for the Fence-viewers to locate the said fence either wholly or partially on the land of either of the said parties, where to them it seems to be most convenient; but such location shall not in any way affect the title to the land.

(*d*) If necessary, the Fence-viewers may employ a Provincial Land Surveyor, and have the locality described by metes and bounds.

7. The award shall be deposited in the office of the Clerk of the Council of the Municipality in which the lands are situate, and shall be an official document, and may be given in evidence in any legal proceeding by certified copy, as are other official documents; and notice of its being made shall be given to all parties interested.

8. The award may be enforced as follows:—The person desiring to enforce it shall serve upon the owner or occupant of the adjoining lands a notice in writing, requiring him to obey the award, and if the award is not obeyed within one month after service of such notice, the person so desiring to enforce it may do the work which the award directs, and may immediately recover its value and the costs from the owner by action in any Division Court having jurisdiction in the locality; but the Judge of such Division Court may, on application of either party, extend the time for making such fence to such time as he may think just.

9. The award shall constitute a lien and charge upon the lands respecting which it is made, when it is registered in the Registry Office of the County, or other Registration Division in which the lands are.

(*b*) Such registration may be in duplicate or by copy, proved by affidavit of a witness to the original, or otherwise, as in the case of any deed which is within the meaning of "*The Registry Act.*"

10. The Fence-viewers shall be entitled to receive two dollars each for every day's work under this Act. Provincial Land Surveyors and witnesses shall be entitled to the same compensation as if they were subpœnaed in any Division Court.

11. Any person dissatisfied with the award made may appeal therefrom to the Judge of the County Court of the

County in which the lands are situate, and the proceedings on such appeal shall be as follows:—

(a) The appellant shall serve upon the Fence-viewers, and all parties interested, a notice in writing of his intention to appeal within one week from the time he has been notified of the award; which notice may be served as other notices mentioned in this Act.

(b) The appellant shall also deliver a copy of such notice to the Clerk of the Division Court of the Division in which the land lies, and the Clerk shall immediately notify the Judge of such appeal, whereupon the Judge shall appoint a time for the hearing thereof, and, if he thinks fit, order such sum of money to be paid by the appellant to the said Clerk as will be a sufficient indemnity against costs of the appeal.

(c) The Judge shall order the time and place for the hearing of the appeal, and communicate the same to the Clerk, who shall notify the Fence-viewers and all parties interested, in the manner hereinbefore provided for the service of other notices under this Act.

(d) The Judge shall hear and determine the appeal, and set aside, alter, or affirm the award, correcting any error therein, and he may examine parties and witnesses on oath, and, if he so pleases, may inspect the premises; and may order payment of costs by either party, and fix the amount of such costs.

(e) His decision shall be final; and the award, as so altered or confirmed, shall be dealt with in all respects as it would have been if it had not been appealed from.

(f) The practice and proceedings on the appeal, including the fees payable for subpœnas and the conduct money of witnesses, shall be the same, as nearly as may be, as in the case of a suit in the Division Court.

12. Any agreement in writing (Form 4) between owners respecting such line fence may be filed or registered and enforced as if it was an award of Fence-viewers.

13. The owner of the whole or part of a division or line fence which forms part of the fence enclosing the occupied or improved land of another person, shall not take down or remove any part of such fence,

(a) Without giving at least six months previous notice of his intention to the owner or occupier of such adjacent enclosure ;

(b) Nor unless such last mentioned owner or occupier after demand made upon him in writing by the owner of such fence, refuses to pay therefor the sum, to be determined as provided in the sixth section of this Act ;

(c) Nor if such owner or occupier will pay to the owner of such fence or of any part thereof, such sum as the Fence-viewers may award to be paid therefor under the sixth section of this Act.

(*b*) The provisions of this Act relating to the mode of determining disputes between the owner of occupied adjoining lands ; the manner of enforcing awards and appeals therefrom ; and the schedules of forms attached hereto, and all other provisions of this Act, so far as applicable, shall apply to proceedings under this section.

14. If any tree is thrown down, by accident or otherwise, across a line or division fence, or in any way in and upon the property adjoining that upon which such tree stood, thereby causing damage to the crop upon such property or to such fence, it shall be the duty of the proprietor or occupant of the premises on which such tree theretofore stood, to remove the same forthwith, and also forthwith to repair the fence, and otherwise to make good any damage caused by the falling of such tree.

(*b*) On his neglect or refusal so to do for forty-eight hours after notice in writing to remove the same, the injured party may remove the same, or cause the same to be removed, in the most convenient and inexpensive manner, and may make good the fence so damaged, and may retain such tree to remunerate him for such removal, and may also recover any further amount of damages beyond the value of such tree from the party liable to pay it under this Act.

(*c*) For the purpose of such removal the owner of such tree may enter into and upon such adjoining premises for the removal of the same without being a trespasser, avoiding any unnecessary spoil or waste in so doing.

(*d*) All disputes arising between parties relative to this

section, and for the collection and recovery of all or any sums of money becoming due thereunder, shall be adjusted by three Fence-viewers of the Municipality, two of whom shall agree.

15. The forms in the Schedule hereto are to guide the parties, being varied according to circumstances.

SCHEDULE OF FORMS.

FORM 1.

(Section 3.)

NOTICE TO OPPOSITE PARTY.

Take notice, that Mr.   , Mr.   , and Mr.   , three fence-viewers of this locality, will attend on the   day of   , 18   , at the hour of   , to view and arbitrate upon the line fence in dispute between our properties, being Lots (*or* parts of Lots) *One* and *Two* in the Concession of the Township of   , in the County of   .

Dated this   day of   , 18 .

A. B.,
Owner of Lot 1.

To *C. D.*,
Owner of Lot 2.

FORM 2.

(Section 3.)

NOTICE TO FENCE-VIEWERS.

Take notice, that I require you to attend at   on the   day of   , A.D. 18 , at   o'clock A.M., to view and arbitrate on the line fence between my property and that of Mr.   , being Lots (*or* parts of Lots) Nos. *One* and *Two* in the   Concession of the Township of   , in the County of   .

Dated this   day of   , 18 .

A. B.
Owner of Lot 1.

FORM 3.

(Section 6.)

AWARD.

We, the fence-viewers of (*name of the locality*), having been nominated to view and arbitrate upon the line fence between

314   LINE FENCES AND WATER COURSES. (ONTARIO.)

by (*name and description of owner who notified*) and (*name and description of owner notified*), which fence is to be made and maintained between (*describe properties*), and having examined the premises and duly acted according to "*The Line Fences Act*," do award as follows: That part of the said line which commences at   and ends at   (*describe the points*) shall be fenced, and the fences maintained by the said   , and that part thereof which commences at   and ends at (*describe the points*) shall be fenced, and the fence maintained by the said   . The fence shall be of the following description (*state the kind of fence, height, material, &c.*), and shall cost at least   per rod. The work shall be commenced within   days, and completed within   days from this date, and the costs shall be paid by (*state by whom paid; if by both, in what proportion.*)

Dated this   day of   , A.B. 18 .

(*Signatures of fence-viewers.*)

FORM 4.

(*Section 12.*)

AGREEMENT.

We   and   , owners respectively of Lots (*or parts of Lots*) *One* and *Two* in the   Concession of the Township of   , in the County of.   , do agree that the line fence which divides our said properties shall be made and maintained by us as follows: *follow the same form as award.*)

Dated this   day of   , A.D. 18 .

(*Signatures of parties.*)

REVISED STATUTES OF ONTARIO CHAP. 199.

An Act respecting Ditching Water-courses.

1. This Act may be cited as "*The Ditches and Water Courses Act.*"

2. This Act shall not affect the Acts relating to Municipal Institutions or the Acts respecting Drainage, as this Act is intended to apply to individual, and not to public or local interests, rights, or liabilities.

3. In case of owners occupying adjoining lands which would be benefited by making a ditch or drain, or by deepening or widening a ditch or drain already made in a natural water-course, or by making, deepening or widening

a ditch or drain for the purpose of taking off surplus water from swamps or low miry land, in order to enable the owners or occupiers thereof to cultivate the same, such several owners shall open and make, deepen or widen a just and fair proportion of such ditch or drain, according to their several interests in the construction of the same; and such ditches or drains shall be kept and maintained so opened, deepened or widened, by the said owners respectively, and their successors in such ownership, in such proportions as they have been so opened, deepened or widened, unless in consequence of altered circumstances the Fence-viewers hereinafter named otherwise direct, which they are hereby empowered to do upon application of any party interested, in the same form and manner as is hereinafter prescribed in respect of the original opening, deepening or widening; and in case the Fence-viewers find no reason for such application, all costs thereby shall be borne by the applicant.

4. In case of dispute between owners respecting such proportion, the following proceedings shall be adopted :—

(*a*) Either owner may notify (Form 1) the other owner or the occupant of the land of the owner so to be notified, that he will, not less than one week from the service of such notice, cause three Fence-viewers of the locality to arbitrate in the premises.

(*b*) Such owner so notifying shall also notify (Form 2) the Fence-viewers not less than one week before their services are required.

(*c*) The notices in both cases shall be in writing, signed by the person notifying, and shall specify the time and place of meeting for the arbitration, and may be served by leaving the same at the place of abode of such owner or occupant, with some grown-up person residing thereat, or in case of a non-resident, by leaving such notice with any agent of such owner.

(*d*) The owner notified may, within the week, object to any or all of the Fence-viewers notified; and in case of disagreement the Judge hereinafter mentioned shall name the Fence-viewers who are to arbitrate.

5. An occupant not the owner of land notified in the manner above mentioned, shall immediately notify the own-

er; and if he neglects so to do, shall be liable for all damage caused to the owner by such neglect.

6. The Fence-viewers shall examine the premises, and if required by either party, they shall hear evidence, and are authorized to examine the parties and their witnesses on oath, and any one of them may administer an oath or affirmation as in Courts of Law.

7. The Fence-viewers shall make an award (Form 3) in writing, signed by any two of them, respecting the matters so in dispute, which award shall specify the locality, quality, and description and cost of the ditch or drain it orders to be made, and the time within which the work shall be done; and shall state by which of the said parties the costs of the proceedings shall be paid, or whether either party shall pay some proportion of such costs.

(b) In making such award the Fence-viewers shall regard the nature of the ditches or drains in use in the locality, and generally the suitableness of the ditch or drain ordered to the wants of the parties; and the Fence-viewers may, if they think necessary, employ a Provincial Land Surveyor for the purpose of taking levels, or of making a plan for the parties to follow in making the ditch or drain, or for other purposes.

(c) If the expense of the ditch or drain exceeds the expense as estimated by the Fence-viewers, the same Fence-viewers may be again notified in the same manner herein provided, and shall attend, and, if they see fit, make a supplementary award respecting such expenses which award shall have the same effect, and may be dealt with in all respects as if it were part of the first award.

4. If it appears to the Fence-viewers that the owner or occupier of any tract of land is not sufficiently interested in the opening up the ditch or water-course to make him liable to perform any part thereof, and at the same time that it is necessary for the other party that such ditch should be continued across such tract, they may award the same to be done at the expense of such other party; and after such award, the last mentioned party may open the ditch or water-course across the tract, at his own expense, without being a trespasser.

8. *(Repealed by 43 Vic., Chap. 30, as annexed hereto.)*

9. The award shall constitute a lien and charge upon the lands respecting which it is made when it is registered in the Registry Office of the County or other Registration Division in which the lands are.

(b) Such registration may be in duplicate or by copy, proved by affidavit of a witness to the original, or otherwise, as in the case of any instrument which is within the meaning of "*The Registry Act.*"

10. The award may be enforced as follows :—The person desiring to enforce it, provided the work is not done within the time specified by the award, may do the work which the award directs, and may immediately recover its value and the costs from the owner by action in any Division Court having jurisdiction in the locality : but the Judge of such Division Court may, on application of either party, extend the time for making such ditch to such time as he may think just.

11. The Fence-viewers shall be entitled to receive two dollars for every day's work under this Act. Provincial Land Surveyors and witnesses shall be entitled to the same compensation as if they were subpœnaed in any Division Court.

12. Any person dissatisfied with the award made may appeal therefrom to the Judge of the County Court of the County in which the lands are situate ; and the proceedings on such appeal shall be as follows :—

(a) The appellant shall serve upon the Fence-viewers and all parties interested, a notice in writing of his intention to appeal, within one week from the time he has been notified of the award, which notice shall be served as other notices mentioned in this Act.

(b) The appellant shall also deliver a copy of such notice to the Clerk of the Division Court of the Division in which the land or a portion thereof lies, and the Clerk shall immediately notify the Judge of such appeal, whereupon the Judge shall appoint a time for the hearing thereof, and, if he thinks fit, order such sum of money to be paid by the appellant to the said Clerk as will be a sufficient indemnity against costs of the appeal.

(*c*) The Judge shall order the time and place for the hearing of the appeal, and communicate the same to the Clerk, who shall notify the Fence-viewers and all parties interested, in the manner hereinbefore provided for the service of other notices under this Act.

(*d*) The Judge shall hear and determine the appeal, and set aside, alter, or affirm the award, correcting any error therein, and he may examine parties and witnesses on oath, and, if he so pleases, inspect the premises, and he may order payment of costs by either party, and fix the amount of such costs.

(*e*) His decision shall be final; and the award, as so altered or confirmed, shall be dealt with in all respects as it would have been if it had not been appealed from.

13. In case any Municipal Corporation would be benefited by the construction of such ditch or drain, such Corporation shall be in the same position as an individual owner under this Act.

14. In case any person during or after the construction of the ditches or drains herein provided for, desires to avail himself of such ditches or drains for the purpose of draining other lands than those contemplated by the original proceedings, he may avail himself of the provisions of this Act, as if he were or had been a party to such original proceedings; but no person shall make use of the ditches or drains constructed under the provisions of this Act unless under agreement or award pursuant to its provisions as to use of the land of others, as to enlargement of the original ditch or drain, so as to contain additional water therein, and as to the time for the completion of such enlargement.

15. Any agreement in writing (Form 4) between owners respecting such ditch, may be filed or registered, and enforced as if it was an award of the Fence-viewers.

16. The forms in the Schedule hereto are to guide the parties, being varied according to circumstances.

SCHEDULE OF FORMS.

FORM 1.

(Section 4.)

NOTICE TO OPPOSITE PARTY.

Take notice, that Mr.   , Mr.   and Mr.   three fence-viewers of this locality, will attend on the   day of   A.D. 18 , at the hour of   , to view our properties, being Lots (*or* parts of Lots) *One* and *Two* in the   Concession of the Township of   , in the County of   , and arbitrate respecting the ditch in dispute upon our said Lots.

Dated this   day of   , A.D. 18 .

                         A. B.,
                            Owner of Lot 1.

To *C. D.*,
    Owner of Lot 2. (*or as the case may be.*)

FORM 2.

(Section 4.)

NOTICE TO FENCE-VIEWERS.

Take notice, that I require you to attend to   on the   day of   , A.D. 18 , at   o'clock to view my property, and that of Mr.   being Lots (*or* parts of Lots) Nos. *One* and *Two* in the   Concession of the Township of   , in the County of   , and arbitrate on the ditch required on said Lots.

Dated this   day of   A.D. 18 .

                         A. B.,
                            Owner of Lot 1.

FORM 3.

(Section 7.)

AWARD.

We, the Fence-viewers of (*name of the locality*); having been nominated to view and arbitrate between (*name and description of owner who notified*) and (*name and description of owner notified*) upon a ditch required on the property of (*name of owner notified*), which ditch is to be made and maintained on said property; and having examined the premises and duly acted according to *The Act respecting Ditching Water-courses*, do award as follows: A ditch shall be made and maintained by the said   commencing at (*state point of commencement and then give course and point of ending*). The ditch shall be of the following description (*state kind of ditch, depth, width, &c.* ; *if a plan has been made by Provincial Land Sur-*

veyor, *describe course, kind of ditch, &c., by reference to plan*). The work shall be commenced within   days, and completed within   days from this date ; and the costs shall be paid (*state by whom to be paid, and if by both, in what proportion.*)

Dated this   day of   , A.D. 18 .
Witness :   (*Signatures of Fence-viewers.*)

FORM 4.

(*Section 15.*)

AGREEMENT.

We   and   owners respectively of Lots (*or parts of Lots*) *One* and *Two* in the   Concession of the Township of   , in the County of   , do agree that a ditch shall be made and maintained by us as follows (*follow same form as in award*).

Dated this   day of   , A.D. 18   ,
Witness :   /   (*Signatures of parties.*)

---

43 VIC. CHAPTER 30, (ONTARIO.)

Amending The Act respecting Ditching Water-courses.

1. Section three of Chapter one hundred and ninety-nine of the Revised Statutes is hereby amended by striking out the word "occupying," in the first line of said section and substituting therefor the word "of."

2. Sub-section three of section four of the said Act is hereby amended by striking out all the words after the word "resident" in the sixth line of the said sub-section and inserting the words "by mailing such notice to, or leaving the same with, any agent of such owner or by mailing such notice to the last known place of residence of such owner.

3. Sub-section three of section seven of the said Act is hereby amended by adding thereto the following proviso:

"Provided always that in the case of the death or removal from the municipality of any such fence-viewers or his or their ceasing to be fence-viewers, another or other fence-viewer or fence-viewers may be notified in the place of him or them so dying, removing out of the municipality or ceasing to be fence-viewers, but there shall be the same right of objecting to the substituted fence-viewers as is given by sub-section four of section four of this Act, and in case of such objection being made the judge shall name the fence-viewers who are to arbitrate."

4. The eighth section of the said Act is hereby repealed and the following substituted therefor:

8. The award and any plan made as above provided for, shall be deposited in the office of the clerk of the municipality in which the lands are situate, within ten days after the making thereof, and the award and plan shall be official documents, and may be given in evidence in any legal proceedings by certified copies, as are other official documents, and notice of their being made shall also be given by the clerk of such municipality to all parties interested, within three days after their deposit.

MARRIAGE AND RIGHTS OF MARRIED WOMEN.

In the Dominion of Canada the law of marriage is derived from three sources, namely, (1) the common and statute law of England up to the original founding, by Imperial enactments of its various Provinces; (2) the laws subsequently passed by the local legislatures of these Provinces; (3) and the French civil code of the Province of Quebec, to which Province that code is exclusively confined. In any Province where no legislation has taken place on the subject of marriage, its courts will be governed by the law of England, which provides that twenty one years shall be the age at which the duties of the married state may be voluntarily undertaken without the interference of parent or guardian. In the United States each separate state regulates for itself the nature of the marriage contract, and the age at which it may be legally consummated. In Ohio the legal age is 18 for males and 14 for females; in Massachusetts 17 for males and 14 for females; and in all the other states 14 for males and 12 for females. Idiots, lunatics, near relations and persons already married and not legally divorced, are incompetent to form a valid marriage in any part of the United States. There the basis of the marriage contract is the mutual voluntary consent of the parties, and subsequent cohabitation. In several of these states the ceremony of marriage is complete on the declaration of the parties, in the presence of one witness or more, that they take each other for man and wife respectively, or words to that effect, and subsequent cohabitation. No other ceremony is essential, and it is not necessary that marriage should be performed by any particular person. But even in these states marriage is usually performed by a clergyman or magistrate, and in New York and other States it must be performed by them to make it valid.

In England the marriage ceremony can only be performed by a clergyman of some legally recognized church. There the preliminary step is the publication of the banns by a clergyman for three successive Sundays, at the hour and place of Divine Service, or the purchase of a license. The degree of relationship in England within which marriage is prohibited may be found in the Book of Common Prayer; and the Imperial law as laid down there is also held to apply to this Dominion in the absence of any express legislation by its Parliament. In Ontario the law of marriage is very closely assimilated to the law in England.

With regard to Breach of Promise of Marriage, we may state that an engagement of marriage may be made in various ways. It may be made by a promise to marry in presence of one witness or more, or it may be made by the letters of either party, or it may be construed or inferred from a series of visits and particular attentions. If the parties are young when an engagement of marriage is made, and the period they had mutually agreed to wait for one another is not unreasonably long, the contract will be held good in law. If no specified time is agreed upon the law will infer that the contract must be performed within a reasonable time, and either party may call upon the other to fulfil his or her part of the agreement. In case of a refusal or neglect to fulfil it the demanding party may then treat the engagement as at an end, and bring an action for damages.

As it is highly desirable that the residents of Ontario should be as fully acquainted as possible with the marriage laws of their Province, we now give its applying Statutes in full.

REVISED STATUTES OF ONTARIO CHAP. 124.
An Act respecting the Solemnization of Marriages.

1. The ministers and clergymen of every church and religious denomination duly ordained or appointed according to the rights and ceremonies of the churches or denominations to which they respectively belong, and resident in Ontario, may, by virtue of such ordination or appointment, and according to the rites and usages of such churches or denominations respectively, solemnize the ceremony of marriage between any two persons not under a legal disqualification to contract such marriage.

2. No minister or clergyman shall celebrate the ceremony of marriage between any two persons, unless duly authorized so to do by license under the hand and seal of the Lieutenant-Governor, or his Deputy duly authorized in that behalf, or by a certificate under this Act, or unless the intention of the two persons to intermarry has been proclaimed once, openly, and in an audible voice, either in the church, chapel or meeting-house in which one of the parties has been in the habit of attending worship, or in some church, chapel, meeting-house, or place of public worship of the congregation or religious community with which the minister or clergyman who performs the ceremony is connected, in the local municipality, parish, circuit or pastoral charge, where one of the parties has, for the space of fifteen days immediately preceding, had his or her usual place of abode ; such proclamation to be on a Sunday, immediately before the service begins, or immediately after it ends, or at some intermediate part of the service.

3. A certificate in the form given in Schedule A or Schedule B to this Act, (according to the circumstances of the case) may at the option of the applicant, be substituted for a marriage license; and such certificate shall have the same legal effect as a license.

4. Such licenses or certificates shall be issued from the office of the Provincial Secretary, and shall be furnished to persons requiring the same by such persons as the Lieutenant-Governor in Council may name for that purpose.

5. Every license executed under the hand and seal of the Lieutenant-Governor, or his Deputy duly authorized in that behalf, and every certificate signed by the Provincial Secretary, or Assistant Provincial Secretary, for the purpose of solemnizing a marriage, shall be and remain valid, notwithstanding that the Lieutenant-Governor or Deputy, or Provincial Secretary, or Assistant Provincial Secretary has ceased to hold office before the time of the issue of the license or certificate.

6. If any person issues any license or certificate for the solemnization of marriage without being authorized by the Lieutenant-Governor in Council in that behalf, unless under the authority in the next section contained, he shall forfeit to Her Majesty the sum of one hundred dollars for every license or certificate so issued.

7. Any Issuer of marriage licenses or certificates may, with the approval, in writing, of the Mayor or Reeve of the City, Town, Township or incorporated Village wherein he resides, from time to time, when prevented from acting by illness or unavoidable accident, or where his temporary absence is contemplated, appoint, by writing under his hand, a Deputy to act for him.

(*b*) The said Deputy shall, while so acting at the residence or office or place of business of the said Issuer for whom the Deputy acts, possess the powers and privileges (as to administering necessary oaths and otherwise) of the Issuer appointing him.

(*c*) The Issuer shall, upon appointing a Deputy, forthwith transmit to the Provincial Secretary a notice of the appointment, and of the cause thereof, and of the name and official position of the person by whom the appointment has been approved, and the Lieutenant-Governor may at any time annul the appointment.

(d) In case it is necessary on account of illness, unavoidable accident, or contemplated temporary absence of any Issuer of marriage licenses, to appoint a Deputy, and there is no Mayor or Reeve to give the consent required by the provisions of sub-section one of this section, such Issuer of marriage licenses may, in the manner in other respects required by said sub-section, but without such consent, appoint such Deputy; and the licenses or certificates issued by such Deputy shall be deemed to authorize the solemnization of marriages at the same places as licenses or certificates issued by the principal for whom such Deputy acts; and no irregularity in the appointment of a Deputy Issuer shall affect the validity of a license or certificate by him issued.

8. Every Deputy so appointed shall sign each license and certificate issued by him, with the name of his principal as well as his own name, in the followidg manner—"*A. B., Issuer of Marriage Licenses, per C. D., Deputy Issuer,*" or to the like effect; but no irregularity in the issue of a license or certificate issued by an Issuer or Deputy Issuer to any person or persons obtaining the same, or acting thereon in good faith, shall invalidate a marriage solemnized in pursuance thereof.

9. Every Issuer of licenses or certificates aforesaid, or any other person having unissued licenses or certificates in his possession, power, custody or control, shall whenever required so to do, transmit to the Provincial Secretary every such license or certificate; and the property in all unissued licenses and certificates shall be and remain in Her Majesty.

10. All expenses incident to providing licenses and certificates, shall be paid by the Issuer of the licenses and certificates.

11. Before any license or certificate is granted by any Issuer or Deputy Issuer, one of the parties to the intended marriage shall personally make an affidavit which shall state

(a) In what County or District it is intended that the marriage shall be solemnized, and in what Town, Village or place in the County or District, and

(b) That he or she believes that there is no affinity, consanguinity, precontract, or other lawful cause, or legal impediment, to bar or hinder the solemnization of the marriage;

(c) That one of the parties has for a space of fifteen days immediately preceding the issue of the license or certificate had his or her usual place of abode within the County or judicial district, in which (for either municipal or judicial purposes) the local Municipality in which the marriage is to be solemnized lies ;

Or (if the County or District in which it is intended that the marriage shall be solemnized is not that in which either of the parties has, for a space of fifteen days immediately preceding the issue of the license or certificate, had his or her usual place of abode), that the reason of procuring the marriage to be solemnized in such place is not in order to evade due publicity or for any other improper purpose.

2. In case either of the parties, not being a widower or widow, is under the age of twenty-one years, the affidavit shall further state that the consent of the person whose consent to the marriage is required by law has been obtained thereto.

3. If there is no person having authority to give such consent, then, upon oath made to that effect by the party requiring the license or certificate, it shall be lawful to grant the license or certificate notwithstanding the want of any such consent.

4. The affidavit may be in the form set forth in Schedule C to this Act, and may be made before the Issuer of Licenses or his Deputy.

12. In case the person having authority to issue the license or certificate has personal knowledge that the facts are not as the eleventh section of this Act requires, he shall not issue the license or certificate; and if he has any reason to believe or suspect that the facts are not as aforesaid, he shall, before issuing the license or certificate, require further evidence to his satisfaction in addition to the said affidavit or deposition.

13. The father, if living, of any party under twenty-one years of age (not being widower or widow), or if the father is dead the guardian or guardians of the person of the party

so under age, lawfully appointed, or one of the guardians, if there are more than one; or in case there is no such guardian, then the mother of the minor, if the mother is unmarried, shall have authority to give consent to the marriage.

14. No fee shall be payable for any license or certificate, except the sum of two dollars, which the Issuer of the license or certificate shall be entitled to retain for his own use; but the Lieutenant-Governor in Council may from time to time reduce the sum so payable.

15. It shall not be a valid objection to the legality of a marriage that the same was not solemnized in a consecrated church or chapel, or within any particular hours.

16. Every clergyman or minister, who celebrates a marriage, shall, if required at the time of the marriage by either of the parties thereto, give a certificate of the marriage under his hand, specifying the names of the persons married, the time of the marriage, and the names of two or more persons who witnessed it, and specifying also whether the marriage was solemnized pursuant to license or certificate under this Act, or after publication of banns; and the clergyman or minister may demand twenty-five cents for the certificate given by him from the person requiring it.

17. Every clergyman or minister shall, immediately after he has solemnized a marriage, enter in a book, to be kept by him for the purpose, a true record of the marriage; which record shall specify all the particulars, given in Schedule B to *The Act respecting the Registration of Births, Marriages and Deaths.*

18. The Clerk of the Peace of every County shall, at the expense of the County, from time to time on demand, furnish all clergymen or ministers with the books to be kept; and such books shall have columns and headings printed on every page according to the form of said Schedule B; and the books shall be of such size and form as to admit of the necessary entries being conveniently made therein.

19. The book by whomsoever furnished shall be the property of the church or denomination to which the clergyman or minister, clerk or secretary belongs at the time of the first marriage which he records therein.

20. Every marriage duly solemnized between members of

the Religious Society of Friends, commonly called Quakers, according to the rights and usages thereof, shall be valid; and all the duties imposed by this Act, or by *The Act respecting the Registration of Births, Marriages and Deaths*, upon a minister and clergyman, shall, with regard to such marriage, be performed by the clerk or secretary of the Society, or of the meeting at which the marriage is solemnized.

21. No minister who performs any marriage ceremony after banns published, or after a license or a certificate under this Act issued, shall be subject to any action or liability for damages or otherwise by reason of there having been any legal impediment to the marriage, unless, at the time when he performed the ceremony, he was aware of the impediment.

SCHEDULE "A."
(Section 3.)

FORM OF CERTIFICATE BEFORE MARRIAGE WITHOUT BANNS, WHERE ONE OF THE PARTIES HAS RESIDED FOR FIFTEEN DAYS NEXT PRECEDING THE ISSUE OF THE CERTIFICATE IN THE COUNTY.

These are to certify that *A. B.*, of   and *C. D.*, of   being minded, as it is said, to enter into the contract of marriage, and being desirous of having the same duly solemnized, the said *A. B.* (or *C. D.*) has made oath, as required by law, that he (or she) believes that there is no affinity, consanguinity, precontract, or any other lawful cause or legal impediment to bar or hinder the solemnization of the said marriage, and that said *A. B.* or *C. D.* (*or both, as the case may be*), has (or have) had his (or her, or their) usual place of abode, for the space of fifteen days last past, within the City (County *or* District) of   namely, in the Township (Town *or* Village) of   in the said County (*or* District) of   and that the said *A. B.* and *C. D.* are of the full age of twenty-one years.

[*Or that A. B.* or *C. D.* is a widower or widow ; *or* is under the age of twenty-one years, and that the consent of *E. F.*, whose consent to said marriage is required by law, has been obtained ; *or* that the father of the said (*party under age*) is dead, no guardian of the person of said (*party*) has been appointed, and the mother of said (*party*) is dead (*or* married), and there is no person having authority to give consent to said marriage (*as the case may be*).]

And these are therefore to certify that the requirements of *The Act respecting the Solemnization of Marriages* have been complied with.

Given under my hand and seal at   this   day of   in the year of our Lord one thousand

eight hundred and   and in the   year
of Her Majesty's reign.
                              G. H.,
                   Issuer (or Deputy Issuer) of Licenses.

Issued from the office of the Provincial }
Secretary for Province of Ontario,   }
this   day of   18 .   }
       K. L.,
       Provincial Secretary.

SCHEDULE "B."
(Section 5.)

FORM OF CERTIFICATE FOR A MARRIAGE WITHOUT BANNS WHERE NEITHER OF THE PARTIES HAS RESIDED FOR FIFTEEN DAYS NEXT PRECEDING IN THE COUNTY.

These are to certify that *A. B.* of   and *C. D.* of
            being minded, as it is said, to enter into the contract of marriage, and being desirous of having the same duly solemnized, the said *A. B.* (*or C. D.*) has made oath that he (*or* she) believes that there is no affinity, consanguinity, precontract, or any other lawful cause or legal impediment to bar or hinder the solemnization of the said marriage, and having also otherwise made oath as required by law. These are therefore to certify that the requirements of *The Act respecting the Solemnization of Marriages* have been complied with.

Given under my hand and seal at   this
day of   in the year of our Lord one thousand
eight hundred and   and in the   year
of Her Majesty's reign.
                              G. H.,
                   Issuer (or Deputy Issuer) of Licenses.

Issued from the office of the Provincial   }
Secretary for the Province of Ontario,   }
this   day of   18 .   }
       K. L.,
       Provincial Secretary.

SCHEDULE "C."
(Section 11.)
FORM OF AFFIDAVIT.

I, *A. B.* (*or C. D.*) of   { Bachelor (*or* widower),
                                 { Spinster (*or* widow),
make oath and say as follows:

1. I, and *C. D.* of   { Spinster (*or* widow),
                                 { Bachelor (*or* widower),
            are desirous of entering into the contract of marriage, and of having our marriage duly solemnized at the Town (*or* Village, &c.) of   in the County (*or* District) of

2. According to the best of my knowledge and belief, there is no affinity, consanguinity, precontract, or any other lawful cause or legal impediment to bar or hinder the solemnization of the said marriage.

[3. I, *or* the said *C. D.* (*or both, as the case may be*) have (*or* has) had since the   day of   my (*or* his, *or* her, *or* our) usual place of abode within the Municipality of   in the said County (*or* District). (*Or if neither of the parties has, for the space of fifteen days immediately preceding the issue of the certificate or license, had his or her usual place of abode in the County or District in which it is intended that the marriage shall be solemnized;* The reason of procuring the marriage to be solemnized in   is not in order to evade due publicity, or for any other improper purpose.)]

4. I am of the age of   years, and the said *C. D.* is of the age of   years.

5. (*In case of one or both of the parties being under the age of twenty-one years*) I am a { widower / widow } *or* the said *C. D.* (*or A.B.* { is a } { widow / widower }

[*Or E. F.* of   is the person whose consent to said marriage is required by law, and the said *E. F.* consents to the said marriage]

[*Or* The father of the said (*party under age*) is dead, no guardian of the person of the said (*party under age*) has been appointed, and the mother of the said (*party under age*) is dead (*or* married), and there is no person having authority to give consent to said marriage (*as the case may be*)].

Sworn before me, at   } (Signed)   *A. B.*
in the   of   }   *or C. D.*
this   day of   18 .   }
          G. H.,
          (*Issuer of Licenses,* or
          Deputy Issuer of Licenses.)

Separate Rights of Property of Married Women.

Extracts from Chap. 125 Revised Statutes of Ontario.

4. The real estate of any woman married after the second day of March, one thousand eight hundred and seventy-two, whether owned by her at the time of her marriage, or acquired in any manner during her coverture, and the rents, issues and profits thereof respectively, shall, without prejudice and subject to the trusts of any settlement affecting the same, be held and enjoyed by her for her separate use, free from any estate therein of her husband during her lifetime, and from his debts and obligations, and from any

claim or estate by him, as tenant by the curtesy; and her receipts alone shall be a discharge for any rents, issues and profits of the same; but nothing herein contained shall prejudice the right of the husband as tenant by the curtesy in any real estate of the wife which she has not disposed of *inter vivos*, or by will.

5. Every woman who has married since the fourth day of May, one thousand eight hundred and fifty-nine, or who marries after the passing of this Act, without any marriage contract or settlement, shall and may, notwithstanding her coverture, have, hold and enjoy all her personal property, whether belonging to her before marriage or acquired by her by inheritance, bequest or gift, or as next of kin to an intestate, or in any other way after marriage, free from the debts and obligations of her husband, and free from his control or disposition, without her consent, in as full and ample a manner as if she continued sole and unmarried; but this clause shall not extend to any property received by a married woman from her husband during coverture.

6. Nothing herein contained shall be construed to protect the property of a married woman from seizure and sale on any execution against her husband for her torts; and in such case, execution shall first be levied on her separate property.

7. All the wages and personal earnings of a married woman, any acquisitions therefrom, and all proceeds or profits from any occupation or trade which she carries on separately from her husband, or derived from any literary, artistic or scientific skill, and all investments of such wages, earnings, moneys or property, shall, after the said second day of March, one thousand eight hundred and seventy-two, be free from the debts or dispositions of her husband, and shall be held and enjoyed by such married woman and disposed of without her husband's consent as fully as if she were a *feme sole*; and no order for protection shall hereafter be necessary in respect of any of such earnings or acquisitions; and the possession, whether actual or constructive of the husband, of any personal property of any married woman, shall not render the same liable for his debts.

8. Any married woman having a decree for alimony against her husband, or any married woman who lives apart

from her husband, having been obliged to leave him for cruelty or other cause which by law justifies her leaving him and renders him liable for her support, or any married woman whose husband is a lunatic with or without lucid intervals, or any married woman whose husband is undergoing sentence of imprisonment in the Provincial Penitentiary or in any gaol for a criminal offence, or any married woman whose husband, from habitual drunkenness, profligacy or other cause, neglects or refuses to provide for her support and that of his family, or any married woman whose husband has never been in this Province, or any married woman who is deserted or abandoned by her husband, may obtain an order of protection, entitling her, notwithstanding her coverture, to have and enjoy all the earnings of her minor children, and any acquisitions therefrom, free from the debts and obligations of her husband and from his control or dispositions, and without his consent, in as full and ample a manner as if she continued sole and unmarried.

9. The married woman may at any time apply, or the husband or any of the husband's creditors may at any time, on notice to the married woman, apply for the discharge of the order of protection; and if an order for such discharge is made, the same may be registered or filed like the original order.

10. Either order may issue in duplicate, and where the married woman resides in a City or Town in which there is a Police Magistrate, the order for protection or any order discharging the same shall be made by the Police Magistrate, and shall be registered in the Registry Office of the Registration Division in which the City or Town is situate.

15. Every married woman having separate property, whether real or personal, not settled by any ante-nuptial contract, shall be liable, upon any separate contract made or debt incurred by her before marriage, (such marriage being since the said fourth day of May, one thousand eight hundred and fifty-nine, or after this Act takes effect) to the extent and value of such separate property, in the same manner as if she were sole and unmarried.

17. A husband shall not, by reason of any marriage solemnized after the second day of March, one thousand eight hundred and seventy-two, be liable for the debts of his

wife contracted before marriage, but the wife shall be liable to be sued therefor, and any property belonging to her shall be liable to satisfy such debts, as if she had continued unmarried.

20. A married woman may maintain an action in her own name for the recovery of any wages, earnings, money and property, by this or any other Act declared to be her separate property, and shall have in her own name the same remedies, against all persons whomsoever for the protection and security of such wages, earnings, money, and property, and of any chattels or other her separate property for her own use, as if such wages, earnings, money, chattels and property belonged to her as an unmarried woman ; and any married woman may be sued or proceeded against separately from the husband in respect of any of her separate debts, engagements, contracts or torts, as if she were unmarried.

21. A married woman, in her own name, or that of a trustee for her, may insure for her sole benefit, or for the use or benefit of her children, her own life, or, with his consent, the life of her husband, for any definite period, or for the term of her or his natural life ; and the amount payable under said insurance shall be receivable for the sole and separate use of such married woman or her children, as the case may be, free from the claims of the representatives of her husband, or of any of his creditors.

22. Any married woman may become a stockholder or member of any bank, insurance company, or any other incorporated company or association, as fully and effectually as if she were a *feme sole*, and may vote by proxy or otherwise, and enjoy the like rights as other stockholders or members.

23. A married woman may make deposits of money in her own name in any savings or other bank, and withdraw the same by her own cheque ; and any receipt or acquittance of such depositor shall be a sufficient legal discharge to any such bank.

24. Nothing hereinbefore contained in reference to moneys deposited, or investments by any married woman, shall, as against creditors of the husband give validity to any deposit or investment of moneys of the husband made

in fraud of such creditors, and any money so deposited or invested may be followed as if this Act had not been passed.

25. The separate personal property of a married woman dying intestate shall be distributed in the same proportions between her husband and her children as the personal property of a husband dying intestate is to be distributed between his wife and children; and if there be no child or children living at the death of the wife so dying intestate, then such property shall pass or be distributed as if this Act had not been passed.

Respecting Dower.

Dower is the right possessed by every married woman at common law to the use, during her life-time, of one-third of her husband's real estate after his death. When a woman is entitled to dower she must join in every conveyance, mortgage, &c., of real estate by her husband, as otherwise her dower is not barred. Her right of dower must be conveyed personally, or by power of attorney to an agent under her hand and seal. A wife under twenty-one years of age is incapable of legally binding herself by any instrument. But the wife's right of dower operates against an estate only after all previous liens and incumbrances have been discharged. When divorced for adultery a wife forfeits all claim to dower.

Extracts from Chap. 126 Revised Statutes of Ontario.

WIDOWS TO BE ENTITLED TO DOWER IN CERTAIN CASES.

1. Where a husband dies beneficially entitled to any land for an interest which does not entitle his widow to dower out of the same at Law, and such interest, whether wholly equitable or partly legal and partly equitable, is an estate of inheritance in possession, or equal to an estate of inheritance in possession, (other than an estate in joint tenancy), then his widow shall be entitled in Equity to dower out of the same land.

2. Where a husband has been entitled to a right of entry or action in any land, and his widow would be entitled to dower out of the same if he had recovered possession thereof, she shall be entitled to dower out of the same although her husband did not recover possession thereof; but such dower shall be sued for or obtained within the period during which such right of entry or action might be enforced.

HOW DOWER MAY BE BARRED.

5. A married woman may bar her dower in any lands or hereditaments, by joining with her husband in a deed or conveyance thereof in which a release of dower is contained.

6. A married woman may also bar her dower by executing either alone, or jointly with other persons, a deed or conveyance to which her husband is not a party, containing a release of such dower; but no such deed or conveyance shall be effectual to bar her dower unless made in conformity with "*The Married Woman's Real Estate Act.*"

7. A power of attorney executed by a married woman authorizing the attorney to execute a deed barring or releasing her dower, shall be valid both at Law and in Equity, provided that the power of attorney is executed in conformity with said Act.

A Husband is bound to Maintain His Wife.

On the part of the husband the marriage contract of itself binds him to provide, in accordance with his condition and means of living, suitable necessaries for his wife, and if he fails to do this, and his wife contracts debts for those necessaries, he will be held legally liable for those debts. But he will not be held liable for debts contracted by her for what cannot be called necessaries; or for articles purchased not suitable to her condition in life; for a wife cannot recklessly plunge her husband into debt, and parties who supply her with goods or luxuries which cannot be called necessaries do so at their own risk. When a wife is in the habit of purchasing necessary articles for the use of herself and her family the husband becomes liable for debts so contracted, unless he notifies the merchant or shopkeeper not to supply her with any goods, and furnishes her with the required family necessaries himself. Should a husband desert his wife, or send her away from his home, or if they separate by mutual consent, without his having made any sufficient or suitable provision for her support, the law will hold him liable for her maintenance, and for the reasonable debts contracted by her for necessaries. But while the husband is willing to supply his wife with a home, and does his best to support her in accordance with his condition in life, and is not guilty of cruelty towards her, she is bound to live with him, and he cannot be held liable for her separate maintenance. When the wife deserts her husband without cause he is not bound to support her; but if she conducts herself with propriety during her absence, and offers to return to him he cannot refuse her permission to do so, although he may not be held legally liable for debts contracted during her absence. It is usual, however, when a wife deserts her husband for the latter to give public notice that such desertion has been made without reasonable cause, and that he will not be responsible for any debts contracted by her. If a wife's desertion or elopement is accompanied by adultery the husband is not bound to receive her back, and cannot be held liable for her support even should she offer to return to him. Persons supplying necessaries of life, such as food, clothing and lodging, to a married woman, living apart from her husband, are bound to make all due enquiries touching her actual position, and give her credit at their own risk. In humble life, where the husband earns his living by his daily toil, the law presumes that he shall use all reasonable exertions to support his wife and family, and where he is able to work for that support, and refuses to do so, he may be dealt with criminally as a vagrant, and imprisoned for any term up to six months at hard labor. Vide 32-33 Vic., Chap. 28 as amended by 37 Vic., Chap. 43.

MASTER AND SERVANT.

From a purely civil point of view, the law as regards the relation of Master and Servant lies within the jurisdiction of the various local legislatures of the Dominion. When we come to regard this relation from a penal point of view we find that it has been very materially altered by the Breaches of Contract Act of 1877, being 40 Vic., Chap. 35. This Act repeals all the criminal remedies of the master against the ordinary hired servant for non-fulfilment of agreement, and reduces the bargain between them to the level of a purely civil contract. Before the passage of this Act any servant who refused to perform his work, according to agreement, or left his employment without permission, or refused to obey the lawful commands of his master or agent, was liable, on conviction before a justice of the peace, to be fined or imprisoned. The Breaches of Contract Act entirely abolished this remedy, as regards the ordinary hired servant, in all the Provinces of the Dominion, and leaves the master without any remedy save the civil one for breach of contract. It makes however the following exceptions :—

2. Any person who wilfully and maliciously breaks any contract made by him, knowing or having reasonable cause to believe that the probable consequences of his so doing, either alone or in combination with others, will be to endanger human life, or to cause serious bodily injury, or to expose valuable property, whether real or personal, to destruction or serious injury ; and

(2.) Any person who, being under any contract made by him with any municipal corporation or authority, or with any company bound, agreeing or assuming to supply any city or any other place, or any part thereof, with gas or water, wilfully and maliciously breaks such contract, knowing or having reasonable cause to believe, that the probable consequences of his so doing, either alone or in combination with others, will be to deprive the inhabitants of that city or place, or part thereof, wholly, or to a great extent of their supply of gas or water ; and

(3.) Any person who, being under any contract made by him—

(*a*) With a railway company, bound, agreeing or assuming to carry Her Majesty's mails, or passengers or freight; or—

(*b*) With Her Majesty, or any one on behalf of Her Majesty, or of the Government, in connection with a Government railway on which Her Majesty's mails, or passengers or freight are carried,—

Wilfully and maliciously breaks such contract, knowing, or having reason to believe, that the probable consequences of his so doing, either alone or in combination with others, will be to delay or prevent the running of any locomotive engine, or tender, or freight or passenger train or car on the railway,—

Shall, on conviction thereof, be liable to be punished by fine not exceeding one hundred dollars, or by imprisonment for a term not exceeding three months, with or without hard labor.

3. Any municipal corporation or authority or any company, which, being bound, agreeing or assuming to supply any city, or any other place, or any part thereof, with gas or water, wilfully and maliciously breaks any contract made by such municipal corporation, authority, or company, knowing or having reason to believe that the probable consequences of its so doing will be to deprive the inhabitants of that city or place or part thereof, wholly or to a great extent, of their supply of gas and water ; and—

(2.) Any railway company which, being bound, agreeing or assuming to carry Her Majesty's mails or passengers or freight, wilfully and maliciously breaks any contract made by such railway company, knowing or having reason to believe that the probable consequences of its so doing will be to delay or prevent the running of any locomotive engine or tender or freight or passenger train or car on the railway, shall be liable to a penalty not exceeding one hundred dollars.

4. The word "maliciously," used in reference to any

offence against this Act, shall be construed in the same manner as it is required in the sixty-sixth section of the Act thirty-second and thirty-third Victoria, chapter twenty-two, intituled "*An Act respecting Malicious Injuries to Property,*" to be construed with reference to any offence committed against the last mentioned Act.

Under these circumstances Masters, for their own protection, should avoid paying servants in advance for services to be performed; and should always make payment of wages contingent on the due performance of the contract. If the Servant fails to fulfil his contract, according to its fair terms, and leaves his employment, a forfeiture of wages necessarily follows.

In order to constitute a contract of hiring and service, which creates the relation of master and servant, there must be a mutual agreement binding the master to employ and pay, and the servant to work, for some definite term. If the master simply agrees to pay as long as the servant continues to work, there is no contract made of hiring and service; but if the servant agrees to serve for a certain length of time, and the master, either expressly or by implication, promises to retain the servant for that time, the contract becomes binding on both, and constitutes one of hiring and service. A verbal or word of mouth agreement of hiring is only good for one year; and an agreement for a longer period must be in writing. In the absence of an express bargain between master and servant a hiring may be presumed from the fact of the performance of the service itself, unless in the case of near relations. Thus where one person serves another as a clerk, or servant of any sort, for a continued period, and that service is tacitly accepted, the law will presume a hiring, and the person so serving will be entitled to recover what will be considered as customary and reasonable wages. But if the service has been rendered to a parent, uncle, or other near relation, an express hiring must be proved in order to support a claim for wages. In the absence of such proof the law regards services rendered by one near relation to another, as acts of kindness, affection or charity, and not to be paid for unless under an express contract of hiring. When the employment of a servant is of a permanent nature and annual wages are to be paid the hiring is a yearly one, and can only be terminated by mutual consent before the end of the current year. In the same way a monthly hiring can only terminate with the end of the month, and a weekly hiring with the end of the week. After the contract of hiring and service has been entered into the master is bound to take the servant into his employment, and if he refuses or neglects to do so renders himself liable to an action for breach of contract. On the other hand the servant is bound to commence the service agreed on, and to serve his master faithfully and with due diligence ; but only as regards the duties he has undertaken to perform. If he refuses to perform these duties, or fails in the performance by incompetence or neglects, or does not obey the reasonable and lawful commands of his master, he becomes guilty of a breach of contract, and may be dismissed. If a household servant hired for a year, or for any shorter period, becomes disabled or falls sick, while doing his or her master's business, a wages' deduction cannot be made ; and if a servant is improperly dismissed, or prevented by the persecution or other improper conduct of his master to perform his duties, the Master can be compelled to compensate him for any injuries he may sustain.

Such is the general tenor of the relation of master and servant throughout the Dominion. Its special features will be learned from the acts of the several Local Legislatures.

Extracts from Revised Statutes of Ontario Chap. 133, being an Act respecting Master and Servant.

2. No voluntary contract of service or indentures entered

into by any parties shall be binding on them, or either of them, for a longer time than a term of nine years from the day of the date of such contract.

5. All agreements or bargains, verbal or written, between masters and journeymen, or skilled labourers, in any trade, calling or craft, or between masters and servants or labourers, for the performance of any duties or service of whatsoever nature, shall, whether the performance has been entered upon or not, be binding on each party for the due fulfilment thereof; but a verbal agreement shall not exceed the term of one year.

6. No tavern keeper or boarding-house keeper shall keep the wearing apparel of any servant or labourer in pledge for any expenses incurred to a greater amount than six dollars, and on payment or tender of such sum, or of any less sum due, such wearing apparel shall be immediately given up, whatever be the amount due by such servant or labourer; but this is not to apply to other property of the servant or labourer.

SUMMARY PROCEEDINGS BEFORE JUSTICES.

9. Any one or more of Her Majesty's Justices of the Peace may receive the complaints upon oath of parties complaining of any contravention of the preceding provisions of this Act, and may cause all parties concerned to appear before him or them, and shall hear and determine the complaint in a summary and expeditious manner.

10. Wherever the Justice takes the evidence of the complainant in support of his or her claim, the said Justice shall be bound to take the evidence of the defendant also, if tendered.

12. Any one or more of such Justices, upon oath of any such servant or labourer against his master or employer concerning any non-payment of wages, may summon such master or employer to appear before him or them at a reasonable time to be stated in the summons, and he or they or some other Justice or Justices shall, upon proof on oath of the personal service of such summons, examine into the matter of the complaint, whether the master or employer appears or not, and upon due proof of the cause of complaint, the Justice or Justices may discharge such servant or labourer from the service or employment of such master, and may

direct the payment to him of any wages found to be due, not exceeding the sum of forty dollars, and the said Justice or Justices shall make such order for payment of the said wages as to him or them seems just and reasonable, with costs, and in case of non-payment of the same, together with the costs, for the space of twenty-one days after such order has been made, such Justice or Justices shall issue his or their warrant of distress for the levying of such wages, together with the costs of conviction and of the distress.

Relating to Apprentices.

Chap. 135 of the Revised Statutes of Ontario, being an Act respecting Apprentices and Minors, provides that where a minor (that is, a person under twenty-one years of age) over the age of sixteen, who has no parent or legal guardian, or who does not reside with such parent or guardian, enters into an engagement, written or verbal, to perform any service or work, such minor shall be liable upon the same, and shall have the benefit thereof in the same manner as if of legal age.

A parent or other person, or any charitable society authorized by the Lieut.-Governor in Council, having the care or charge of a male minor not under the age of fourteen years may, with consent of the minor, put and bind him as an apprentice, by indenture, to any master-mechanic, farmer, or other person carrying on a trade or calling, until such minor attains twenty-one. A female minor, not under twelve years, may be bound until the age of eighteen.

When the father of an infant child abandons and leaves the child with the mother, the mother, with the approbation of two justices of the peace, may bind the child as an apprentice until the child attains twenty-one if a male, or eighteen if a female. The mother and the justices must sign the indenture. No child fourteen years old or upwards is to be so apprenticed without his or her consent.

The Mayor, or Police Magistrate of any city or town, and

in a county, the chairman of and at the General Sessions may apprentice orphan children, and children who have been deserted by their parents, or whose parents have been committed to gaol.

If the master of an apprentice dies, the apprentice by operation of law, and without any new writings, becomes transferred to the person (if any) who continues the master's business.

A master may transfer his apprentice, with his consent, to any person who is competent to receive or take an apprentice, and who carries on the same kind of business.

Every master must provide for his apprentice suitable board, lodging and clothing, or such money or other equivalent therefor as is mentioned in the indenture, and must also properly teach and instruct him, or cause him to be taught and instructed, in his trade or calling.

Every apprentice must faithfully serve his master, obey all his lawful commands, and not absent himself from his service, day or night, without consent.

A master convicted before any Justice, Mayor, or Police Magistrate, on the complaint of the apprentice, of any ill usage, cruelty or refusal of necessary provisions, is liable to a fine not exceeding twenty dollars and costs, and to imprisonment in default of payment of such fine and costs for a term not exceeding one month.

An apprentice convicted of refusal to obey lawful commands, or of waste or damage to property, or of any other improper conduct, may be imprisoned for a term not exceeding one month.

An apprentice absenting himself before the time of service expires, or who refuses to obey the lawful commands of his master, or neglects to perform his duty, may be compelled, on complaint to a justice of the peace, to make good the loss by longer service or pecuniary satisfaction ; and if he refuses or neglects to do so, may be committed to gaol for a term not exceeding three months; but the master must proceed to enforce such service or satisfaction within three years after the expiration of the term for which the apprentice contracted to serve.

Persons knowingly harboring or employing an absconding apprentice, are liable to pay the master the full value of the apprentice's labor.

The apprenticeship indentures may be cancelled if the apprentice becomes insane, or be convicted of felony, or be sentenced to the Provincial Penitentiary, or absconds. The master, must, within one month, give notice in writing to the other parties to the indenture of his intention to cancel the indentures, which notice must be served on the parties, or published in the Gazette, or in a local county or city newspaper.

Masters or apprentices may appeal to the General Sessions against any magistrate's decision.

Apprenticeship Indenture.

This Indenture, made the   day of   188 , Between W. J., of, &c., of the first part, H. J., his son, now the age of fifteen years, of the second part, and T. M., of, &c., printer, of the third part, Witnesseth, That the said W. J., with the consent of his said son H. J., (a minor now of the age of fifteen years or thereabout), testified by his being a party to and executing these presents, doth hereby put, place, bind and indent him, the said H. J., to the said T. M., to learn the art and trade of a printer, and with him, the said T. M., his executors, administrators and assigns, after the manner of an apprentice to dwell and serve from the day of the date hereof until the   day of   , 188   , being a period of   years, when the said minor will arrive at the age of twenty-one years.

And the said W. J. doth hereby, for himself, his heirs, executors and administrators, covenant, promise and agree to and with the said T. M., his executors, administrators and assigns, that during the said term of   years, the said H. J. shall well and faithfully serve the said T. M., his secrets keep, and lawful commands at all times obey, and shall give and devote to him his whole time and labor; that he shall not marry during the said term, nor use ardent spirits, nor practice gaming or any other unlawful sports, nor waste, injure or destroy the property of his master, but conduct himself in a sober, temperate, honest manner, and as a good and faithful apprentice ought to do, during all the time aforesaid.

And the said T. M., for himself, his heirs, executors and administrators, doth hereby covenant, promise and agree to and with the said W. J., his executors and administrators, that he, the said T. M., his executors and administrators, shall and will teach and instruct, or cause to be taught and instructed, the said H. J. in the art, trade and mystery of a Printer, and shall and will find and provide for the said apprentice sufficient meat, drink, apparel, washing and lodging during the said term; and at the expiration thereof shall and will give his said apprentice two suits of apparel (*any other special terms may be here inserted*); and the said T. M. further agrees to pay to the said W. J. father of the said H. J., the following sums of money, to wit: for the first year's service, twenty-five dollars; for the second year's service, seventy-five dollars; and for each and every subsequent year, until the completion of his term, one hundred dollars; which said payments are to be made on the first day of May in each year.

And for the true performance of all and singular the covenants and agreements hereinbefore contained, the said parties bind themselves each unto the other, jointly by these presents.

In witness whereof, the said parties to these presents have hereunto set their hands and seals, the day and year first above written.

Signed, sealed and delivered
in the presence of
    R. J.

    W. J. [L. S.]
    H. J [L. S.]
    T. M. [L. S.]

Indenture of Apprenticeship for a Girl to learn Housework, &c.

This Indenture, made the   day of   , 188 , Between M. F., of, &c., Widow, of the first part; S. F., her daughter, now of the age of fifteen years, of the second part; and R. H., of the same place, Farmer, of the third part, Witnesseth that the said S. F., by and with the consent of the said M. F. her mother, testified by her execution of these presents, hath bound and put herself, and by these presents doth bind and put herself, apprentice to the said R. H., with him to dwell and serve from the day of the date hereof until the full end of the term of six years next ensuing, fully to be completed and ended; during which term the said S. F., her said master, faithfully shall and will serve in all lawful business, according to her power and ability, and honestly and obediently in all things demean and behave herself towards her said master during the term aforesaid.

And the said R. H. shall and will teach and instruct, or cause to be taught and instructed, the said apprentice in sewing, knitting and house-wifery, the management of the dairy, and all matters connected with the calling of a farmer, properly to be taught to her the said apprentice, together with reading, writing and the other usual branches of a common school education; and shall and will during the said term find, provide and allow her sufficient meat, drink, clothing, lodging, washing, and all other necessaries; and at the expiration of the term aforesaid shall and will give unto the said apprentice two suits of apparel.

In Witness, &c., (*Conclude as in last form*).

Assignment of an Indenture of Apprenticeship.

Know all men by these presents, that I, the within named T. M., by and with the consent of H. J., my within named apprentice, and W. J., his father (*or as the case may be*), parties to the within Indenture, testified by their signing and sealing these presents, for divers good causes and consideration, have assigned and set over, and do hereby assign and set over, the within Indenture, and the said H. J., the apprentice within named, unto J. T., of, &c., Printer, his executors, administrators or assigns, for the residue of the within mentioned term, he and they performing all and singular the covenants therein contained on my part to kept and performed.

And I, the said H. J., do hereby covenant on my part, with the consent of my father, the said W. J., faithfully to serve the said J. T. as an apprentice for the residue of the term within mentioned, and to perform toward him all and singular the covenants within mentioned on my part to be kept and performed.

And I, the said J. T., for myself, my executors, administrators and assigns, do hereby covenant to perform all and singular the covenants within mentioned on the part of the said T. M. to be kept and performed toward the said apprentice.

Witness our hands and seals this   day of   , 188 .
Signed, sealed, &c.,   T. M. [L. S.]
    J. S.   H. J. [L. S.]
                           W. J. [L. S.]
                           J. T. [L. S.]

MORTGAGES.

The word Mortgage means a pledge, but in ordinary acceptation conveys the idea of the conveyance of an estate from one party to another, as security for money borrowed, with the right of redemption within a certain specified time on the repayment of the loan. In popular language, and speaking with reference to real estate, or landed property only, it may be called a pledge of land: whereby the *debtor or pledgor*, or, as he is commonly called, the *mortgagor*, conveys his land to the creditor or pledgee, or, as he is commonly called, the *mortgagee*, subject to a condition or proviso that, if the debt is discharged by a day named, the pledge shall be void, and the mortgagor shall be entitled to receive back and hold the lands, free from all claims created by the mortgage. By virtue of a mortgage, the right of property to the land mortgaged, passes to the creditor, subject to be divested by the payment of the debt at the appointed time. Assuming the mortgage to have been drawn in the usual form, with a proviso that on payment of the debt and interest, the mortgage should be void; upon payment, the property will revest in the mortgagor without any deed or instrument of re-conveyance. In practice, however, it is usual to take a discharge of mortgage, which operates as a re-conveyance. If the debt be not paid on the day named, the land, *at law*, becomes the absolute property of the mortgagee, and he may proceed to take possession of it: quietly, if he can; if not, by means of ejectment. A Court of Chancery, when such exists in any province, will, however, give the mortgagor liberty to redeem, at any time within *twenty years*, on payment of what is due for principal and interest. When the debt is paid *after* the appointed day, a re-conveyance or discharge of the mortgage is requisite in order to revest the property in the mortgagor.

A mortgagee may take a release of the equity of redemption from the mortgagor, or may purchase the same under a power of sale in his mortgage, without thereby merging his debt: that is to say, without thereby losing the right to hold the lands against any person having a claim on them *subsequent* to the mortgagee's, until his debt and interest be paid; and if such subsequent creditor should afterwards take proceedings in Chancery to foreclose his mortgage, he will only be allowed to do so, subject to the rights of the mortgagee who has so acquired the equity of redemption.

Mortgages should be executed in duplicate, and one part left in the registry or other office, where documents of this nature are placed on record, as in the case of a deed of land. A mortgagee has several remedies if his mortgage be not paid at maturity. He may bring an action at law upon the covenant to recover the amount of principal and interest due; or he may bring an action of ejectment, and take possession of the premises, in which case he will be entitled to hold the lands until the full amount of principal and interest has been discharged out of the rents and profits; or he may file a bill in equity to have the mortgage foreclosed, in which case he will acquire a title to the lands discharged of all equity of redemption; and the lands and premises will be sold under the direction of the Court, and the debt due paid out of the proceeds, if sufficient; and if insufficient, the mortgagor will be ordered to pay the deficiency. If the mortgage contains a power of sale, the lands may be sold without going into Court.

When a mortgage is paid off, a discharge should be signed and registered: it will then be marked as discharged in the books of the registry or other office. A discharge must be signed by the mortgagee, or his assignee, if the mortgage has been assigned; or by his executor or administrator, if he be dead. When a mortgage has been made in favor of a married woman, both husband and wife must sign the discharge. It is sufficient to sign in the presence of one witness; and the usual affidavit of execution must be made by him. Every Province in the Dominion has the right to legislate in the matter of mortgages, and in the absence of legislation the English practice will govern the courts. In Ontario a short form of mortgage has been created by statute, which is found to be a great improvement.

Mortgage of Lease.

This Indenture, made the   day of   , 188 , Between John Doe, of, &c., of the first part, and Richard Roe, of, &c., of the second part. Whereas, by an indenture of Lease, bearing date on or about the   day of   , 188   , and made between, &c., The said lessor therein named did demise and lease unto the said lessee therein named; his executors, administrators and assigns, All and singular that certain parcel or tract of land and premises situate, lying and being, &c., (*set out the lands,*) To hold the same, with their appurtenances, unto the said lessee, his executors, administrators and assigns, from the   day of   , 188   , for and during the term of
years from thence next ensuing, and fully to be completed and ended, at the yearly rent of $, and under and subject to the lessee's covenants and agreements in the said Indenture of Lease reserved and contained.

Now this Indenture witnesseth, that in consideration

of the sum of one thousand dollars of lawful money of Canada, now paid by the said party of the second part to the said party of the first part, (the receipt whereof is hereby acknowledged,) He, the said party of the first part, Doth hereby grant, bargain, sell, assign, transfer and set over unto the said party of the second part, his executors, administrators and assigns, All and singular the said parcel or tract of land, and all other the premises comprised in and demised by the said hereinbefore in part recited Indenture of Lease: Together with the said Indenture of Lease, and all benefit and advantage to be had or derived therefrom: To have and to hold the same, with the appurtenances thereunto belonging, unto the said party of the second part, his executors, administrators and assigns, from henceforth for and during all the residue of the said term granted by the said Indenture of Lease, and for all other the estate, term, right of renewal (if any), and other the interest of the said party of the first part therein. Subject to the payment of the rent, and the observance and performance of the lessee's covenants and agreements, in the said Indenture of Lease reserved and contained; and to the proviso for redemption hereinafter contained.

Provided always, that if the said party of the first part, his executors or administrators, do and shall well and truly pay, or cause to be paid, unto the said party of the second part, his executors, administrators or assigns, the full sum of $, with interest for the same, at   per cent per annum, on the days and times and in manner following, that is to say, (*here specify terms of payment*) without making any deduction, defalcation or abatement thereout, on any account whatsoever, then these presents, and every clause, covenant, matter and thing herein contained, shall cease, determine and be absolutely void to all intents and purposes whatsoever, as if the same had never been executed.

And the said party of the first part doth hereby, for himself, his heirs, executors and administrators, covenant, promise and agree to and with the said party of the second part, his executors, administrators and assigns, in manner following, that is to say:

That he, the said party of the first part, his executors and administrators, or some or one of them, shall and will well and truly pay, or cause to be paid, unto the said party of the second part, his executors, administrators or assigns, the said principal sum and interest in the above proviso mentioned, at the times and in manner hereinbefore appointed for payment thereof, without any deduction or abatement whatsoever, and according to the true intent and meaning of these presents.

And that the said hereinbefore in part recited Indenture of Lease is, at the time of the sealing and delivery of these presents, a good, valid, and subsisting lease in the law, and not surrendered, forfeited or become void or voidable ; and that the rent and covenants therein reserved and contained have been duly paid and performed by the said party of the first part, up to the day of the date thereof.

And that the said party of the first part now hath in himself good right, full power, and lawful and absolute authority to assign the said lands and premises in manner aforesaid, and according to the true intent and meaning of these presents.

And that in case of default in payment of the said principal money or interest, or any part thereof, contrary to the proviso and covenant aforesaid, it shall be lawful for the said party of the second part, his executors, administrators and assigns, to enter into and upon and hold and enjoy the said premises for the residue of the term grant by the said Indenture of Lease, and any renewal thereof (if any), for their own use and benefit, without the let, suit, hindrance, interruption, or denial of the said party of the first part, his executors, administrators and asigns, or any other persons whomsoever ; and that free and clear, and freely and clearly acquitted, exonerated and discharged, or otherwise, by and at the expense of the said party of the first part, his executors and administrators, well and effectually saved, defended and kept harmless of, from and against all former and other gifts, grants, bargains, sales, leases, and other incumbrances whatsoever.

And that the said party of the [first part, his executors, administrators and assigns, and all other persons claiming any interest in the said premises, shall and will, from time to time, and at all times hereafter, so long as the said principal sum or any part thereof shall remain due and owing on this security, at the request and costs of the said party of the second part, his executors, administrators or assigns, make, do and execute, or cause and procure to be made, done and executed, all such further assignments and assurances in the law of the said premises for more effectually assigning and assuring the said premises for the residue of the said term, and any renewal thereof (if any), subject to the proviso aforesaid, as by the said party of the second part, his executors, administrators or assigns, or his or their counsel in the law, shall be reasonably advised or required.

And that the said party of the first part, his executors, administrators or assigns, shall and will, from time to time, until default in payment of the said principal sum or the interest thereof, and until the said party of the second part shall enter into possession of the said premises as aforesaid, well and truly pay, or cause to be paid, the said yearly rent by the said Indenture of Lease reserved, and all taxes payable on the said premises, and perform and keep all the lessee's covenants and agreements in the said lease contained, and indemnify and save harmless the said party of the second part therefrom, and from all loss, costs, charges, damages, and expenses in respect thereof.

And also shall and will, from time to time, and at all times hereafter, so long as the said principal money and interest or any part thereof, shall remain due on this security, insure and keep insured the buildings erected or to be erected on the land hereby assigned, or any part thereof, against loss or damage by fire, in some Insurance Office, to be approved of by the party of the second part, in the full amount hereby secured, at the least, and, at the expense of the said party of the first part, immediately assign the Policy, and all benefit thereof to the said party of the second part, his executors, administrators and assigns, as additional security for the payment of the principal money and interest hereby secured; and that in default of such insurance it shall be lawful for the said party of the second part, his executors, administrators or assigns, to effect the same, and the premium or premiums paid therefor shall be a charge or lien on the said premises hereby assigned, which shall not be redeemed or redeemable until payment thereof, in addition to the said principal money and interest as aforesaid.

Provided, lastly that until default in payment of the said principal money and interest hereby secured, it shall be lawful for the said party of the first part, his executors, administrators or assigns, to hold, occupy, possess and enjoy the said lands and premises hereby assigned, with the appurtenances, without any molestation, interruption or disturbance of, from or by the said party of the second part, his executors, administrators or assigns, or any person or persons claiming or to claim by, from, through, under or in trust for him, them, or any of them.

In witness whereof the said parties to these presents have hereunto set their hands and seals, the day and year first above written.

Signed, sealed and delivered
in the presence of   JOHN DOE, [L. S.]
    JOHN SMITH.   RICHARD ROE, [L. S.]

Received on the date hereof, the sum of of $, being the full consideration above mentioned.

Witness,   JOHN DOE.
    JOHN SMITH.

Statutory Mortgage. (Ontario).

This Indenture, made (in duplicate) the   day of   A. D. 188   , in pursuance of the Act respecting Short Forms of Mortgages,   Between

WITNESSETH, that in consideration of   of lawful money of Canada, now paid by the said Mortgagee to the said Mortgagor (the receipt whereof is hereby acknowledged), the said Mortgagor   do grant and Mortgage unto the said Mortgagee   heirs and assigns for ever :

All and singular, th   certain parcel or tract of land and premises

Provided this Mortgage to be void on payment of
of lawful money of Canada, with interest   at
per cent per annum, as follows ;   and taxes and performance of statute labour.

The said Mortgagor   covenant   with the said Mortgagee that the Mortgagor   will pay the Mortgage money and interest, and observe the above proviso ;

That the Mortgagor   ha   a good title in fee simple to the said lands ; and that   he ha   the right to convey the said lands to the said Mortgagee   and that on default the

Mortgagee shall have quiet possession of the said lands, free from all incumbrances. And that the said Mortgagor will execute such further assurances of the said lands as may be requisite.

[TITLE DEEDS.]

And that the said Mortgagor ha   done no act to incumber the said lands; and that the said Mortgagor will insure the building on the said lands to the amount of not less than   currency; and the said Mortgagor   do release to the said Mortgagee all   claims upon the said lands, subject to the said proviso:

Provided that the said Mortgagee on default of payment for   month may   enter on and lease or sell the said lands:

Provided that the Mortgagee may distrain for arrears of interest; provided that in default of the payment of the interest hereby secured, the principal hereby secured shall become payable; provided that until default of payment the Mortgagor shall have quiet possession of the said lands.

In witness whereof, &c.

Signed, sealed, &c.

(Endorsation Receipt.)

Received on the day of the date of this Indenture, from the within named   the sum of   dollars, being the consideration in the said Indenture mentioned.

Witness,   A. B.
C. D.

Affidavit of Execution.

County of   } I,   of the   of
  To Wit :   }   in the County of   in
the Province of Ontario, and Dominion of Canada, make oath and say:

1st. That I was personally present and did see the within indenture,   duly signed, sealed, delivered and executed by the therein described   the parties thereto.

2nd. That the said Indenture   so signed, sealed, delivered and executed as aforesaid,   executed at the

3rd. That I know the said

4th. That I am a subscribing witness to the said within Indenture *(and duplicate if any.)*

Sworn before me at
in the county of
this   day of
A. D. 188

J. P., or A Commissioner, &c.

Mortgage with Dower. (Ontario).

This Indenture, made (in duplicate) the   day of
          A. D. 188   , in pursuance of the Act respecting Short Forms of Mortgages,
   Between   hereinafter called the Mortgagor of the first part ;   his wife of the second part ; and hereinafter called the Mortgagee, of the third part :
   Witnesseth, that in consideration of   of lawful money of Canada, now paid by the said Mortgagee   to the said Mortgagor (the receipt whereof is hereby acknowledged,) the said Mortgagor   do grant and Mortgage unto the said Mortgagee   heirs and assigns for ever :
   All and singular th   certain parcel   or tract   of land and premises situate, lying and being
   And the said   wife of the said mortgagor hereby bars her dower in the said lands.
   Provided this Mortgage to be void on payment of   of lawful money of Canada, with interest at   per cent per annum, as follows :   and taxes and performance of statute labour.
   The said Mortgagor covenant with the said Mortgagee that the Mortgagor will pay the Mortgage money and interest, and observe the above proviso.
   That the Mortgagor ha   a good title in fee simple to the said lands ; and that   he   ha the right to convey the said lands to the said Mortgagee   ; and that on default the said Mortgagee   shall have quiet possession of the said lands, free from all incumbrances.
   And that the said Mortgagor will execute such further assurances of the said lands as may be requisite.

   [TITLE DEEDS.]

   And that the said Mortgagor ha   done no act to encumber the said lands.
   And that the said Mortgagor   will insure the buildings

ed the said lands to the amount of not less than   dollars currency.

And the said Mortgagor   do   release to the said Mortgagee all claims upon the said lands, subject to the said proviso :

Provided that the said Mortgagee   in default of payment for   months, may, upon giving   notice in writing, enter upon and lease or sell the said lands ; provided that the Mortgagee   may distrain for arrears of interest ; provided that in default of the payment of the interest hereby secured the principal hereby secured shall become payable ; provided that until default of payment the Mortgagor   shall have quiet possession of the said lands.

In witness whereof, &c.

Signed, sealed, &c.

Received on the day of the date of this Indenture, &c.

(Affidavit of Execution.)

Mortgage to secure future advances. (Ontario).

This Indenture, made (in duplicate) the   day of   A. D. 188 , in pursuance of the Act respecting Short Forms of Mortgages :

Between   hereinafter called the Mortgagor, of the first part ;   his wife, of the second part ; and   hereinafter called the Mortgagee, of the third part ;

Whereas the Mortgagee has advanced to the said Mortgagor, value to the amount of   dollars, and it has been agreed for further advances, and the Mortgagor hath agreed to secure the Mortgagee (for the present debt of   and also for further debts to the said Mortgagee, whether the same be notes or book accounts owing by the Mortgagor) by the lands hereinafter mentioned :

Witnesseth, that in consideration of   of lawful money of Canada, now paid by the Mortgagee to the Mortgagor (the receipt whereof is hereby acknowledged) and also in consideration of further advances by the Mortgagee to the Mortgagor, the Mortgagor doth grant and Mortgage unto the said Mortgagee, his heirs and assigns forever, all and singular th   certain parcel   or tract   of land and premises, situate, lying and being in the

Provided this Mortgage to be void on payment of

dollars, of lawful money of Canada, with interest at   per cent, and all further advances by the Mortgagee to the Mortgagor as follows :   and taxes and performance of statute labour.

Provided that in default of the payment of the interest hereby secured, the principal hereby secured shall become payable.

The Mortgagor covenants with the Mortgagee, that the Mortgagor will pay the mortgage money and interest, and all further indebtedness of the Mortgagor to the Mortgagee, whether by note or account, and observe the above provisoes.

And that the Mortgagor has a good title in fee simple to the said lands.

And that he has the right to convey the said lands to the Mortgagee.

And that on default the Mortgagee shall have quiet possession of the said lands, free from all incumbrances.

The Mortgagor covenants with the Mortgagee that this Mortgage shall also form and be a security to the Mortgagee for future debts of the Mortgagor to the Mortgagee.

And that the Mortgagor will execute such further assurances of the said lands as may be requisite.

And that this Mortgage shall form a charge and claim against the aforesaid lands for all lawful indebtedness of the Mortgagor to the Mortgagee, whether due or to become due.

And that the Mortgagor doth release to the Mortgagee all his claims upon the said lands subject to the said proviso.

Provided that the Mortgagee on default of payment for one month may, without notice, enter upon and lease or sell the said lands.

Provided that the Mortgagee may distrain for arrears of interest.

And the said   the party of the second part, wife of the said party of the first part, hereby bars her dower in the said lands.

Provided that until default of payment the Mortgagor shall have quiet possession of the said lands.

And that this Mortgagee shall not be discharged until all lawful debts of the Mortgagor to the Mortgagee are fully paid and satisfied.

In witness, &c.

Signed, sealed, &c.

Received on the day of the date of this Indenture, &c.

(*Affidavit of Execution.*)

Discharge of Mortgage. (Ontario).

PROVINCE OF ONTARIO, }
                        DOMINION OF CANADA,
        To WIT :

To the Registrar of the do certify that ha satisfied all money due on or to grow due on a certain mortgage made by which mortgage bears date the day of A. D. 188 , and was registered in the registry office for the on the day of A. D. 188 at minutes past o'clock noon, in Liber - for as No. and that such mortgage has been assigned (*Here state whether mortgage assigned or not.*) And that I am the person entitled by law to receive the money ; And that such mortgage is therefore discharged.

Witness my hand this day of A. D. 188 .
Witness .

(*Affidavit of Execution.*)

ONTARIO : }   I,
County of   of the of
                   in the county of
         To WIT :   make oath and say :

1. That I was personally present and did see the within certificate of discharge of mortgage duly signed and executed by the part thereto.

2. That the said certificate of discharge of mortgage was executed at

3. That I know the said

4. That I am a subscribing witness to the said certificate of discharge of mortgage.

Sworn before me at
in the county of
this day of
A. D. 18

      J. P., or a Commissioner for taking affidavits, &c.

Discharge of part of Mortgaged Premises.
(Statutory.)

Province of Ontario, } Dominion of Canada.
'To Wit : }

To the Registrar of the   I   do certify that
        ha   satisfied the sum of   dollars, part of
the moneys mentioned in a certain mortgage made by
which mortgage bears date the   day of   A.
D. 188   and was registered in the registry office for the
        on the   day of   A. D. 188   , at
        minutes past   o'clock in the   noon, in
Liber   for   as No.   and that such mortgage   and that   the person entitled by law to
receive the money, and that such part of the lands as is
herein more particularly described, that is to say :
is therefore discharged.

Witness   hand this   day of   A. D. 188 .
Witness :
(*Same Affidavit of Execution as in discharge of Mortgage.*)

NATURALIZATION.

In constitutional countries, like the British Empire, where the institution of slavery has ceased to exist, their inhabitants may be said to be divided into three classes, which may be described as natives, denizens and aliens. A native of any country is one born therein ; a denizen is a naturalized citizen, but who has been born in some other country ; and an alien is one born in a foreign country, but who has not been naturalized. The proceeding, or process, of naturalization is the act by which an alien, or subject hitherto of a foreign state, is transformed into a denizen, or citizen, of his adopted country ; and becomes entitled to its protection and privileges as though he had been born there. In the Dominion of Canada any alien duly naturalized becomes entitled to all the rights and privileges of a natural-born subject of the British Crown, as regards every part of the Empire.

As it affects Canada the law of Naturalization is derived from two sources, namely, the act passed by the Dominion Parliament in 1868, being 31 Vic., Chap. 66, and the act of the Imperial Parliament, assented to by the Queen on the 12th May, 1870, being 33 Vic., Chap. 14. As it is highly requisite that the most precise information should be disseminated as regards Naturalization, we now, in order to effect that object, append the necessary parts of these Acts :—

Extracts from Dominion Statutes, 31 Vic., Chap. 66.

LOCALLY NATURALIZED SUBJECTS OF HER MAJESTY.

1. Each and every person who, being by birth an Alien, had, on or before the passing of this Act, become entitled to the privileges of British birth, within any part of Canada, by virtue of any general or special Act of Naturalization in force in such part of Canada, shall hereafter be entitled to all the privileges by this Act conferred on persons naturalized under this Act.

NATURALIZATION OF ALIENS.

2. Every Alien-born woman married to a natural-born British subject, or person naturalized under the authority of this Act or of any law either of the Province of Nova Scotia, or of the Province of New Brunswick, or of the late Province of Canada, or of the late Province of Upper Canada, or of the late Province of Lower Canada, shall be deemed to be herself naturalized, and shall have all the rights and privileges of a natural-born British subject.

3. Every such Alien (not being a woman married to a natural-born or naturalized British subject) now residing in, or who shall hereafter come to reside in any part of this Dominion, with intent to settle therein, and who after a continued residence therein for a period of three years or upwards, has taken the oaths or affirmations of residence and allegiance, and procured the same to be filed of record as hereinafter prescribed, so as to entitle him or her to a Certificate of

Naturalization as hereinafter provided, shall thenceforth enjoy and may transmit all the rights and capacities which a natural born subject of Her Majesty can enjoy or transmit.

4. Every such Alien (not being a woman married to a natural-born or naturalized British subject) in order to become entitled to the benefit of this Act, shall take and subscribe the following Oath of Residence, or being one of those persons who are allowed by the Laws of the Province in which he or she then is, to affirm in judicial cases, shall make affirmation to the same effect, that is to say:

Oath of Residence.

" I, A. B., do swear (*or, being one of the persons allowed
" by Law to affirm in judicial cases,* do affirm) that I have
" resided three years in this Dominion, with intent to settle
" therein, without having been during that time a stated
" resident in any foreign country. So help me God."

2. And every such Alien, in order to become entitled to the benefit of this Act, shall also take and subscribe the following Oath of Allegiance, (or being one of those persons who are allowed, by the Laws of the Province in which he or she then is, to affirm in judicial cases, shall make affirmation to the same effect,) that is to say:

Oath of Allegiance.

" I, A. B., do sincerely promise and swear (or, *being one
" of the persons allowed by Law to affirm in judicial cases,*
" do affirm) that I will be faithful and bear true allegiance
" to Her Majesty Queen Victoria, as lawful Sovereign of the
" United Kingdom of Great Britain and Ireland, and of the
" Dominion of Canada, dependent on and belonging to the
" said United Kingdom, and that I will defend Her to the
" utmost of my power against all traitorous conspiracies and
" attempts whatever which shall be made against Her Per-
" son, Crown and Dignity ; and that I will do my utmost
" endeavor to disclose and make known to Her Majesty,
" Her Heirs and Successors, all treasons and traitorous
" conspiracies and attempts which I shall know to be against
" Her or any of them ; and all this I do swear without any
" equivocation, mental evasion, or secret reservation. So
" help me God."

3. And every such oath or affirmation shall be taken and

subscribed by such Alien, and may be administered to him or her by any Judge of any Court of Record in that Province of Canada in which such Alien resides, or by any person authorized to administer oaths in any of the Courts hereinafter mentioned, or by any Commissioner to be appointed by the Governor for that purpose, or by any Justice of the Peace of the County or District within which such Alien resides; which said Judge, Commissioner, or Justice of the Peace, on being satisfied by evidence produced by such Alien, that he or she has been a resident of Canada, for a continuous period of three years or upwards, and is a person of good character, shall grant to such Alien a Certificate, setting forth that such Alien has taken and subscribed the said oath or affirmation, and that such Judge, Commissioner or Justice of the Peace, has reason to believe that such Alien has been so resident within Canada for a period of three years or upwards, that he or she is a person of good character, and that there exists to the knowledge of such Judge, Commissioner or Justice of the Peace, no reason why such Alien should not be granted all the rights and capacities of a Natural-born British Subject.

5. Such Certificate shall be presented to the Court of Quarter Sessions of the Peace, or the Recorder's Court of the County or City within the jurisdiction of which the Alien resides in Ontario, or to the Circuit Court in and for the Circuit within which he or she resides in Quebec, or to the Supreme Court if he or she resides in Nova Scotia, or to the Supreme Court of Judicature of New Brunswick, or County Court of the County in which he or she resides, if he or she resides in New Brunswick, in open Court, on the first day of some general sitting of such Court, and thereupon such Court shall cause the same to be openly read in Court; and if during such general sitting the facts mentioned in such Certificate are not controverted, or any other valid objection made to the Naturalization of such Alien, such Court, on the last day of such general sitting, shall direct that such Certificate be filed of record in the said Court, and thereupon such Alien shall be thereby admitted and confirmed in all the rights and privileges of British birth, to all intents whatever, as if he or she had been born within Canada.

6. Every such person shall be then entitled to receive a

Certificate of Naturalization under the seal of such Court, and the signature of the Clerk thereof, that he or she hath complied with the several requirements of this Act; which Certificate of Naturalization may be in the following form, or to to the like effect, that is to say :

Dominion of Canada,
 Province of
  Circuit, (*or* County *or* City) of
   to wit:
In the Court of

 Whereas A. B., of, &c. (*describing him or her as formerly of such a place, in such a Foreign Country, and now of such a place in Canada, and adding his or her addition*, hath complied with the several requirements of the *Act respecting Aliens and Naturalization*, and the certificate thereof has been read in open Court, and thereupon, by order of the said Court, duly filed of record in the same, pursuant to the said Act; These are therefore to certify to all whom it may concern, that under and by virtue of the said Act, the said A. B. hath obtained all the rights and capacities of a Natural-born British Subject, to have, hold, possess and enjoy the same upon, from, and after the   day of , (*the day of filing the Certificate of Residence*), in the year of our Lord, one thousand eight hundred and ; and this Certificate thereof is hereby granted to the said A. B., according to the form of the said law.

 Given under my Hand and the Seal of the said Court, this day of , in the year of our Lord, one thousand eight hundred and

   (*Signature,*) C. D.
       Clerk of the Peace,
(*or* Clerk of the Recorder's Court, *or* Clerk of the Circuit Court, *or* Clerk of the Supreme Court, *as the case may be.*)

 7. A copy of such Certificate of Naturalization may, at the option of the party, be registered in the Registry Office of any County or District or Registration Division within Canada, and a certified copy of such Registry shall be sufficient evidence of such Naturalization in all Courts and places whatsoever.

8. Any Alien entitled, at the time of the passing of this Act, to be naturalized under the provisions of any of the Acts mentioned in the twelfth and fourteenth sections of this Act, may take the oaths or affirmations of Residence and of Allegiance, and obtain Certificates as aforesaid, in the same manner as Aliens entitled to be naturalized under the provisions of the third section of this Act, and with the same effect, to all intents and purposes :

2. Notwithstanding anything in this Act, all Aliens now resident within the Province of Nova Scotia, and entitled to be naturalized by virtue of the thirty-fourth Chapter of the Revised Statutes of Nova Scotia, shall hereafter, on fulfilling the requirements of the said last mentioned Chapter, be entitled to all the privileges by this Act conferred on persons naturalized under this Act.

9. The Clerk of the Peace or Clerk of the Recorder's Court, or Clerk of the Circuit Court, or Clerk of the Supreme Court, shall, for reading and filing the Certificate of Residence, and preparing and issuing the Certificate of Naturalization under the Seal of the Court, be entitled to receive from such person the sum of twenty-five cents, and no more ; And the Registrar shall, for recording the said last mentioned Certificate, be entitled to receive from such person, the sum of fifty cents, and a further sum of twenty-five cents for every search and certified copy of the same, and no more.

14. The following Acts are hereby repealed, that is to say : The Act *respecting the Naturalization of Aliens*, forming the eighth chapter of the Consolidated Statutes of Canada, save and except the ninth section thereof, the thirty-fourth chapter of the Revised Statutes of Nova Scotia, third series, *Of the privileges and Naturalization of Aliens*, save and except the first, second and third sections thereof ; the Act of the Legislature of New Brunswick, passed in the twenty-fourth year of Her Majesty's reign, chapter fifty-four, intituled : *An Act relating to the Naturalization of Aliens;* and the Act of the same Legislature passed in the twenty-eighth year of Her Majesty's reign, chapter five, intituled : *An Act to amend the Act relating to the Naturalization of Aliens;* but nothing in this section contained shall impair or affect the naturalization of any person naturalized under the said Acts, or either of them, or any rights acquired by such

person, or by any other party, by virtue of such naturalization, all which shall remain valid, and be possessed and enjoyed by such person or party respectively.

Extracts from Imperial Statute, 33 Vic., Chap. 14.

EXPATRIATION.

6. Any British subject who has at any time before, or may at any time after the passing of this Act, when in any foreign State and not under any disability voluntarily become naturalized in such State, shall from and after the time of his so having become naturalized in such foreign State, be deemed to have ceased to be a British subject and be regarded as an alien : Provided,—

(a). That where any British subject has before the passing of this Act voluntarily become naturalized in a foreign State and yet is desirous of remaining a British subject, he may, at any time within two years after the passing of this Act, make a declaration that he is desirous of remaining a British subject, and upon such declaration, hereinafter referred to as a declaration of British nationality being made, and upon his taking the oath of allegiance, the declarant shall be deemed to be and to have been continually a British subject; with this qualification, that he shall not, when within the limits of the foreign State in which he has been naturalized, be deemed to be a British subject, unless he has ceased to be a subject of that State in pursuance of the laws thereof, or in pursuance of a treaty to that effect.

(b). A declaration of British nationality may be made, and the oath of allegiance be taken as follows; that is to say :—If the declarant be in the United Kingdom in the presence of a Justice of the Peace; it elsewhere in Her Majesty's dominions in the presence of any Judge of any Court of civil or criminal jurisdiction, of any Justice of the Peace, or of any other officer for the time being authorized by law, in the place in which the declarant is, to administer an oath for any judicial or other legal purpose. If out of Her Majesty's dominions, in the presence of any officer in the diplomatic or consular service of Her Majesty.

8. A natural-born British subject who has become an alien in pursuance of this Act, and is in this Act referred to as a

statutory alien, may, on performing the same conditions and adducing the same evidence as is required in the case of an alien applying for a certificate of nationality, apply to one of Her Majesty's Principal Secretaries of State for a certificate hereinafter referred to as a certificate of re-admission to British nationality, re-admitting him to the status of a British subject. The said Secretary of State shall have the same discretion, as to the giving or withholding of the certificate as in the case of a certificate of naturalization, and an oath of allegiance shall in like manner be required previously to the issuing of the certificate.

A statutory alien to whom a certificate of re-admission to British nationality has been granted shall, from the date of the certificate of re-admission, but not in respect of any previous transaction, resume his position as a British subject; with this qualification, that within the limits of the foreign State of which he became a subject he shall not be deemed to be a British subject unless he has ceased to be a subject of that foreign State according to the laws thereof, or in pursuance of a treaty to that effect. The jurisdiction by this Act conferred on the Secretary of State in the United Kingdom in respect of the grant of a certificate of re-admission to British nationality, in the case of any statutory alien being in any British possession may be exercised by the Governor of such possession; and residence in such possession shall, in the case of such person, be deemed equivalent to residence in the United Kingdom.

9. The oath in this Act referred to as the oath of allegiance shall be in the form following; that is to say:—

" I,   do swear that I will be faithful and bear true allegiance to Her Majesty Queen Victoria, her heirs and successors, according to law. So help me GOD."

PARTNERSHIP.

A partnership is an association of two or more persons, contributing, in equal or unequal proportions, money, labor, skill, care attendance or services in the prosecution of some trade or manufacture or the accomplishment of any other common object, upon the express, or implied understanding that the profit or loss, attending the transaction, is to be shared among the parties in certain proportions. The contract of partnership is founded wholly on the consent of parties, and may be created by their acts and deeds, and their common participation in the profit and loss of a trade or business, or of a particular speculation or adventure, as well as through the medium of an express contract. If parties are not to share the profit and loss, there can be no partnership as between themselves : whatever may be their apparent situation and position as regards the public. If one man joins another in the furtherance of a particular undertaking, and contributes work and labor, services and skill, towards the attainment of the common object, upon the understanding that the remuneration is to depend upon the realization of profits, so that, if the business is a losing business, he is to get nothing, he stands in the position of a partner in the undertaking, and not in that of a laborer or servant for hire. But a person who merely receives out of the profits the wages of labor, or a commission, as a hired servant or agent, such as a factor, foreman, clerk or manager, and who has no interest or property in the capital stock of the business, is not a partner in the concern, although his wages may be calculated according to a fluctuating standard, and may rise and fall with the accruing profits.

A partner in a private commercial partnership (not being a public joint-stock company with transferable shares) cannot introduce a stranger into the firm, as a partner, without the consent of all the members of the co-partnership.

Every person who stipulates with another for a share of the profits of the business, is a partner in the business as regards the public and third parties and liable as such, whatever may be the private stipulations and agreements between him and the parties who appear to the world as the managers and conductors of the business; because the profits form a portion of the fund on which the creditors have a right to rely for payment.

A *general* partnership is one formed for trade or business generally, without limitations. A *special* partnership is one in which the joint interest extends only to a particular concern, as, for example, in the erection of a hotel. A *limited* partnership is one in which one or more of the partners put in a certain amount of capital, which is liable for the contracts of the firm; but beyond that amount the party advancing is not liable.

A person who lends his name as a partner, or who suffers his name to continue in the firm after he has actually ceased to be a partner, is still responsible to third persons as a partner.

A partner may buy and sell partnership effects; make contracts in reference to the business of the firm: pay and receive money; draw and endorse and accept bills and notes; and all acts of such a nature, even though they be upon his own private account, will bind the other partners, if connected with matters apparently having reference to the business of the firm, and transacted with other parties, ignorant of the fact that such dealings are for the particular partner's private account. So also the representation, or misrepresentation, of any fact, made in any partnership transaction by one partner, or the commission of any fraud in such transaction, will bind the entire firm, even though the other partners may have no connection with, or knowledge of the same.

Dormant and secret partners, whose names do not appear to the world, may be made responsible for the engagement of a trading firm of which they are members.

Persons may become clothed with the legal liabilities and responsibilities of partners as regards the public and third parties, by holding themselves out to the world as partners, as well as by contracting the legal relationship of partners among themselves. If a man, therefore, allows himself to be published to the world as a member of a particular firm; if he permits his name to appear in the partnership name or to be used in the business; if he suffers it to be exhibited to the public over a shop-window; or to be written or printed in invoices or bills of parcels or prospectuses; or to be published in advertisements, as the name of a member of the firm, he is an ostensible partner and is chargeable as a partner, although he is not in point of fact a partner in the concern, and has no share or interest in the profits of the business. But if a man's name is used *without* his knowledge and consent, and he is represented by others to be a partner *without* his authority or permission, he cannot, of course, be made responsible as a partner, upon the strength of such false and fraudulent representation.

An in-coming partner, cannot be made responsible for the non-performance of contracts entered into by the firm *before* he became an actual or reputed member of it.

Dormant and secret partners may release themselves from all further liability by a simple relinquishment of their share in the profit and loss of the business; but, if they are not strictly *secret* as well as dormant partners, notice of the termination of their connection with the co-partnership must be given. A general notice is sufficient as to all but actual customers; these must have some kind of actual notice.

If no time has been limited for the dissolution of a general trading partnership, it is a partnership at will, and may be dissolved at any time at the pleasure of any one or more of the partners. If the partnership was established by deed, the renunciation and disclaimer of it by the party who withdraws from the firm ought to be made by deed. But if the partnership was contracted *without* deed, or, as it is technically called, by parole, it may be renounced in the same manner. If the partners have agreed that the partnership shall continue for a definite period, it cannot be dissolved before the expiration of the term limited, except on the mutual consent of all the parties, or by the outlawry, felony or death of any one or more of them, or by a decree of the Court of Equity. If a partnership for a definite term has been created by deed, duly executed under seal, (which is the proper mode of making all agreements of this nature,) the mutual agreement of the parties to dissolve it must be by deed also. The partnership is dissolved by the death or insolvency of one of the partners; or by an assigment by any partner of his share and interest in the business. A dissolution by one partner is a dissolution as to all.

An executor, administrator or personal representative continuing in the business after the death of a partner, is personally responsible as partner for all debts contracted.

Immediately after a dissolution, a notice of the same should be published in the public papers, for general information, and a special notice sent to every person who has had dealings with the firm. If these precautions be not taken, each partner will still continue liable for the acts of the others to all persons who have had no notice of the dissolution.

Since the formation of the Dominion of Canada, legislation as regards the matter of partnership, comes within the jurisdiction of the several provinces. Under the "Act respecting Limited Partnerships," Revised Statutes of Ontario, Chap. 122, limited partnerships for the transaction of any mercantile, mechanical, or manufacturing business within the Province of Ontario may be formed by two or more persons, upon certain terms and conditions; but the provisions of this act are not to be construed to authorize any partnership for the purpose of banking or insurance.

Such partnerships are to consist of one or more persons, called "general partners," and of one or more persons who contribute, in actual cash payments, a specific sum as capital to the common stock, and who are styled "special partners." General partners are jointly and severally responsible for all debts and engagements of the partnership, in the same manner as ordinary partners in any trade or business; but special partners are not liable for any debts beyond the amounts contributed by them to the capital. All business is to be transacted by the general partners alone, and they only are authorized to sign for and bind the partnership.

Persons desirous of forming a limited partnership must make and sign a certificate which is to contain : firstly, the name or firm under which the partnership is to be conducted ; secondly, the general nature of the business intended to be transacted : thirdly, the names of all the general and special partners interested therein ; distinguishing which are general and which are special partners, and their usual places of residence; fourthly, the amount of capital stock which each special partner has contributed; fifthly, the period at which the partnership is to commence, and the period at which it will terminate.

The certificate is to be in the form given in the act, and will be found therein, and must be signed by the several persons forming such partnership before a notary public, who will duly certify the same. The certificate so signed and certified must be filed in the office of the clerk of the County Court of the county in which the principal place of business of partnership is situate, and is to be recorded by him at full length in a book kept for the purpose and open to public inspection.

No partnership will be deemed to have been formed until such certificate has been made, certified, filed and recorded; and if any false statement be made in such certificate, all the persons interested in the partnership will be liable for all the engagements thereof as *general* partners.

If it is desired to renew or continue the partnership beyond the time originally fixed for its duration, a new certificate must be made, certified, filed and recorded in the manner required for its original formation; and every partnership otherwise renewed or continued will be deemed a general partnership.

If any alteration be made in the names of the partners, in the nature of the business, or in the capital or shares thereof, or in any other matter specified in the original certificate, it will be deemed a dissolution of the partnership; and every partnership in any manner carried on after any such alteration has been made will be deemed a general partnership, unless renewed as a special partnership in the way above mentioned.

The business of the partnership is to be conducted under a name or firm in which the names of the general partners, or some or one of them, only shall be used: and if the name of any special partner is used in such firm with his privity, he will be deemed a general partner.

No part of the sum which any special partner has contributed to the capital stock can be withdrawn by him, or paid or transferred to him in the shape of dividends, profits or otherwise, at any time during the continuance of the partnership; but any partner may annually receive lawful interest on the sum contributed by him, if the payment of such interest does not reduce the original amount of capital; and if, after the payment of such interest, any profits remain to be divided, he may also receive his portion of such profits. If, however, it should afterwards appear that by the payment of any interest or profits to any special partner the original capital has been reduced, the partner receiving such interest or profits shall be bound to restore the amount necessary to make good his share of the deficient capital with interest.

Special partners are at liberty, at all times, to examine into the state and progress of the partnership concerns, and may advise as to their management; but they must not transact any business on account of the partnership, nor be employed for that purpose as agents, attorneys or otherwise and if any special partner interferes in that manner, he will be deemed a general partner, and become liable as such.

General partners are liable to account to each other, and to the special partners, for their management of the concern, in the same manner as partners in any other trade or business.

A limited partnership may be dissolved before the expiration of the term specified in the original certificate, by filling a notice of dissolution in the office in which the original certificate was recorded, and publishing such notice once a week for three weeks in a newspaper published in the county or district where the partnership has its principal place of business, and for the same time in the *Ontario Gazette*.

The fee for filing or recording every certificate is fifty cents.

By the Revised Statutes of Ontario, Chap. 123, it is enacted that all persons, who, at the time of the passing of the act, or thereafter, should be associated in partnership for trading, manufacturing or mining purposes, shall cause to be delivered to the Registrar of the county, city or riding, or other registration division, in which they carry on business, a declaration in writing, signed by the members of the co-partnership: which declaration is to contain the names, surnames, additions and residences of each partner, and the style of the firm, and the period of the partnership; and also a statement that there are no other members. Under section 9 of this act a similar declaration must also be made by any person using any other name than his own, or adding the word *company* to his own name.

Such declaration must be filed within six months after the passing of the act, as to all partnerships in existence at that time; and within six months of formation, as to all others; and a similar declaration must be filed whenever any change is made in the names of the members, or the style of the firm, or place of residence.

The penalty for non-compliance with this act is one hundred dollars, to be sued for in a civil action; half of which goes to the informer, and half to the Crown.

For registering such declaration, the Registrar is entitled to 50 cents, if it does not contain more than 200 words, and 10 cents per folio of 100 words over 200.

Until a new declaration has been signed and filed, the members of the original partnership will remain liable.

DECLARATION OF (ORDINARY) CO-PARTNERSHIP.

Province of Ontario, }
  County of   }

      We   of   in   (*occu-pation*) and   of   in
(*occupation*), hereby certify

1. That we have carried on and intend to carry on trade and business as   at   in partnership, under the name and firm of   . (*Or*, I (*or we*) the undersigned, of   in   , hereby certify that I (*or we*) have carried on and intend to carry on trade and business as   at   in partnership with *C. D.* of   and *E. F.* of   (*as the case may be.*)

2. That the said partnership has subsisted since the   day of   one thousand eight hundred and

3. And that we, (or I (or we) and the said C. D. and E. F.) are and have been since the said day the only members of the said partnership.

Witness our hands at   this   day of   one thousand eight hundred and

---

DECLARATION OF DISSOLUTION OF PARTNERSHIP.

Province of Ontario, } I,
County of   } formerly a member of the firm carrying on business as
at   , in the County of   , under the style of   , do hereby certify that the said partnership was on the   day of   dissolved.

Witness my hand, at   , the   day of   , one thousand eight hundred and

---

Partnership Deed.

Articles of agreement, made the   day of   , 18   , Between A. B., of, &c., C. D., of, &c., E. F., of, &c., G. H., of, &c.

Whereas, the said parties hereto respectively are desirous of entering into a co-partnership in the business of   , at   , for the term and subject to the stipulations hereinafter expressed. Now, therefore, these presents witness that each of them, the said parties hereto respectively, for himself, his heirs, executors and administrators, hereby covenant with the others and other of them, their and his executors and administrators, in manner following, that is to say :

1st. That the said parties hereto respectively will henceforth be and continue partners together in the said business of   , for the full term of   years, to be computed from the   day of   , 18   , if the said partners shall so long live, subject to the provisions hereinafter contained for determining the said partnership.

2nd. That the said business shall be carried on under the style or firm of A. B. & Co.

3rd. That the said partners shall be entitled to the profits of the said business in the proportions following ; that is to say, (*here state the shares ;*) and that all losses in the said business shall be borne by them in the same proportions, unless the same shall be occasioned by the wilful neglect or default of either of the said partners, in which case the same shall be made good by the partner through whose neglect the same shall arise.

4th. That the said partners shall each be at liberty, from time to time during the said partnership, to draw out of the said business, weekly, any sum or sums, not exceeding for each the sum of $ per annum ; such sums to be duly charged to each of them respectively, and no greater amount to be drawn by either of the said partners, except by mutual consent.

5th. That all rents, taxes, salaries, wages and other out-goings and expenses incurred in respect of the said business shall be paid and borne out of the profits of the said business.

6th. That the said partners shall keep, or cause to be kept, proper and correct books of account of all the partnership moneys received and paid, and all business transacted on partnership account, and of all other matters of which accounts ought to be kept according to the usual and regular course of the said business ; which said books shall be open to the inspection of both partners, or their legal representatives ; and a general balance or statement of the said accounts, stock in trade, and business, and of accounts between the said partners, shall be made and taken on the   day of   , in each year of the said term, and oftener, if required.

7th. That the said partners will be true and just to each other in all matters of the said co-partnership, and will at all times during the continuance thereof diligently and faithfully employ themselves respectively in the conduct and concerns of the said business, and devote their whole time exclusively thereto, and will not transact or engage in any other business or trade whatsoever ; and will not either in the name of the said partnership, or individually in their own names, draw, accept or endorse any accommodation bill or bills, promissory note or notes, or become bail or surety for any person or persons, or knowingly or wilfully do, commit or permit any act, matter or thing, by which, or by means of which, the said partnership moneys or effects shall be seized, attached, or taken in execution for their own private debts or liabilities ; and in case either partner shall fail or make default in the performance of any of the agreements or articles of the said partnership in so far as the same is or are to be observed by him, then the other partner, or any one or more of them may give notice in writing to such partner offending in what respects he is deemed to be so in default; and in case such failure or default is not rectified by a time to be specided for that purpose, in such notice, the said partnership shall thereupon at once, or at any other time to be so specified as aforesaid, be dissolved and determined accordingly.

8th. That in case either of the said partners shall die before the expiration of the term of the said co-partnership, the said partnership shall thereupon cease, and the surviving partner or partners shall within six calender months after such decease, settle and adjust with the representative or representatives of such deceased partner, all accounts, matters and things relating to the said co-partnership.

In witness whereof, &c.

Dissolution of Partnership.

(By Indorsement.)

We, the undersigned, do hereby mutually agree that the partnership heretofore subsisting between us, as Wholesale Grocers, under the within articles of co-partnership, be, and the same is hereby dissolved, except for the purpose of the final liquidation and settlememt of the business thereof; and upon such settlement wholly to cease and determine.

In witness whereof, &c.

Notice thereof.

Notice is hereby given that the partnership heretofore subsisting between us, the undersigned, as Wholesale Grocers, has been this day dissolved by mutual consent. All debts owing to the said partnership are to be paid to A. B., at   , and all claims against the said partnership are to be presented to the said A. B., by whom the same will be settled.

Dated at   , this   day of   , A D. 18 .
Witness,   A. B.
Y. Z.   C. D.

Notice when business is to be continued.

Notice is hereby given that the partnership heretofore subsisting between us, the undersigned A. B., C. D., E. F. and G. H., as Wholesale Grocers, was this day dissolved by mutual consent, so far as regards the said A. B. All debts due to the said partnership are to be paid, and those due from the same discharged, at   , where the business will be continued by the said C. D., E. F. and G. H., under the firm of " *D. & Co.*"

Dated at   , this   day of   , A.D. 18 .

Witness,   A. B.
Y. Z.   C. D.

PATENTS OF INVENTION.

The Patent Laws of the Dominion of Canada are of the most liberal and progressive character, and are framed in a broad and comprehensive spirit, and with the special design to stimulate invention and to introduce new and useful improvements of every kind for the benefit of the public. Under the beneficial influence of these laws excellent results have already accrued to the Dominion, and its industrial resources have been very largely developed thereby. These benefits, as the country grows older, and more populous and prosperous, must be still more widely and generally diffused; and the property in patent rights of genuine merit and originality cannot fail to become very valuable. It must, however, be remembered, at the same time, that improvements and patents may neither be valuable nor legal. Parties therefore who take out patents should ascertain by proper researches in the Patent Office, at Ottawa, that they do not infringe the rights of other persons, and those who purchase any interest in patents should be equally or even still more cautious, and see that in every case they get good value for their money.

It would be well, therefore, before any person even makes application for a patent to have the Patent Office records properly searched, in order to ascertain if any similar invention is registered there. In this way much useless work in constructing models, preparing drawings and drafting documents, and needless anxiety as well, may be avoided. And if it should turn out that only a part of the invention had been patented, the applicant will then be in a position to alter or improve that part or to modify his claims so as not to infringe on the rights of the previous patentee. We may add that a personal appearance at the Patent Office in Ottawa is not at all necessary, and the applicant for a patent right can, as a rule, do his business much better by written correspondence. The officials at the Patent Office are always ready and willing to supply all requisite information, and to forward the applying Statutes, and the Rules, Regulations and Forms, of the Department, to every person who properly and courteously asks therefor. Correspondence with the Patent Department is carried by the mails free of postage, and should be addressed in all cases to the Commissioner of Patents. Under these circumstances every person who designs to apply for a patent should at once obtain from the Patent Office its rules, regulations and forms, and acquire for himself the necessary information otherwise by carefully reading up the applying statutes. If he does not feel competent to do this there is usually some lawyer or other person in his county town, who makes it a business to obtain patent rights, and to conduct correspondence with the Patent Office, whose assistance should be obtained. The

Acts of Parliament which govern the issue of Patent Rights are the Patent Act of 1872, being 35 Vic., Chap. 26, and the Amending Acts 36 Vic., Chap. 44, 37 Vic., Chap. 44, and 38 Vic., Chap. 14. Under Sec. 1 of the Patent Act, the Patent Office is constituted a branch of the Department of Agriculture, and the Minister of Agriculture, for the time being, shall be the Commissioner of Patents. Sec. 3 provides that the Commissioner may, from time to time, subject to the approval of the Governor in Council, make such rules and regulations as are necessary, under the Act, which shall have the force of law after publication in the *Canada Gazette*.

These explanations will enable any person desirous of obtaining a patent to take the proper steps to do so. We now append such extracts from the Patent Act of 1872 as may be generally useful to persons designing to apply for patents, as well as to the public generally :—

WHO MAY OBTAIN PATENTS.

6. Any person having invented any new and useful art, machine, manufacture, or composition of matter, or any new and useful improvement on any art, machine or manufacture, or composition of matter, not known or used by others before his invention thereof, and not being in public use, or on sale for more than one year previous to his application, in Canada, with the consent or allowance of the inventor thereof, may, on a petition to that effect presented to the Commissioner, and on compliance with the other requirements of this Act, obtain a patent granting to such person an exclusive property therein ; and the said patent shall be under the seal of the Patent Office and the signature of the Commissioner, or the signature of another member of the Privy Council, and shall be good and avail to the grantee, his executors, administrators or assigns for the period mentioned in such patent ; but no patent shall issue for an invention having an illicit object in view nor for any mere scientific principle or abstract theorem.

7. But an inventor shall not be entitled to a patent for his invention, if a patent therefor in any other country shall

have been in existence in such country more than twelve months prior to the application for such patent in Canada; and if during such twelve months any person shall have commenced to manufacture in Canada the article for which such patent is afterwards obtained, such person shall continue to have the right to manufacture and sell such article, notwithstanding such patent; and under any circumstances, where a foreign patent exists, the Canadian patent shall expire at the earliest date at which any foreign patent for the same invention expires.

8. The patent may be granted to any person to whom the inventor entitled under the sixth section to obtain a patent has assigned or bequeathed the right of obtaining the same, or in default of such assignment or bequest, to the executors or administrators or assigns of the deceased inventor.

9. Any person, who has invented any improvement on any patented invention, may obtain a patent for such improvement, but shall not thereby obtain the right of vending or using the original invention, nor shall the patent for the original invention confer the right of vending or using the patented improvement.

10. In cases of joint applications, the patent shall be granted in the names of all the applicants; and in such cases any assignment from one of the said applicants or patentees to the other or to any person, shall be registered in like manner as other assignments.

TARIFF OF FEES.

34. The following fees shall be payable to the Commissioner, before an application for any of the purposes hereinafter mentioned shall be entertained; that is to say:—

On petition for a patent for 5 years..........................$20 00
On petition for a patent for 10 years........................ 40 00
On petition for a patent for 15 years........................ 60 00
On petition for extension from 5 to 10 years................ 20 00
On petition for extension from 10 to 15 years.............. 20 00
On petition for extension from 5 to 15 years............... 40 00
On lodging a caveat... 5 00
On asking to register a judgment *pro tanto*................ 4 00
On asking to register an assignment......................... 2 00
On asking to attach a disclaimer to a patent................ 2 00
On asking for a copy of patent with specification........... 4 00
On petition to re-issue a patent after surrender, and on petition to extend a former patent to the Dominion for every

unexpired year of the duration of such patent, the fee shall be at the rate of.......... .. .. 4 00

On office copies of documents, not above mentioned, the following charges shall be made :

For every single or first folio of certified copy......... ......$0 50
For every subsequent hundred words (fractions from and under fifty being not counted, and over fifty being counted for one hundred)..,. 0 25

35. For every copy of drawings, the party applying shall pay such sum as the Commissioner considers a fair remuneration for time and labour expended thereon by any officer of the department, or person employed to perform such service.

36. The said fees shall be in full of all services performed under this Act, in any such case by the Commissioner or any person employed in the Patent Office.

37. All fees received under this Act shall be paid over to the Receiver-General, and form part of the Consolidated Revenue Fund of Canada, except such 'sums as may be paid for copies of drawings when made by persons not receiving salaries in the Patent Office.

38. No fee shall be made the subject of exemption in favor of any person; and no fee, once paid, shall be returned to the person who paid it, except,—

1. When the invention is not susceptible of being patented;
2. When the petition for a patent is withdrawn;

And in every such case the Commissioner may return one-half of the fee paid :

And in the case of withdrawal, a fresh application shall be necessary to revive the claim, as if no proceeding had taken place in the matter.

Extracts from General Rules of Patent Office.

1. A personal appearance of the applicant or his representative at the Patent Office is not required, unless specially called for by the Commissioner or Deputy Commissioner, the business being transacted in writing.

2. In all cases the applicant or depositor of any paper is responsible for the merits of his allegations and the validity of the instruments furnished by him or his agent.

3. Correspondence will be carried on with the applicant, or his agent, but only with one person.

4. All documents must be legibly and neatly written on foolscap paper (say 13 inches long and 8 wide), with an inner margin of one inch and a half wide.

5. All communications are to be addressed :—*"To the Commissioner of Patents, Ottawa."*

7. Models must be neat and substantial working ones, not to exceed eighteen inches on the longest side, unless otherwise allowed by special permission; models must be so constructed as to show exactly every part of the invention and its mode of working. In cases where samples of ingredients are required by law, they must be contained in glass bottles properly arranged; but dangerous or explosive substances are not to be sent. Both models and bottles must bear the name of the inventor, the title of the invention, and the date of the application; and must be furnished to the Patent Office free of charge and in good order.

8. All fees required to be paid by law must be transmitted with the application, in current, bankable funds, enclosed in registered letters. Post Office Orders are preferred. In no case should money be sent enclosed with models.

16. The Office cannot respond to enquiries as to the probability of an alleged invention being patented in advance of an application for a Patent; nor to enquiries founded on brief or imperfect descriptions, propounded with a view of ascertaining whether alleged improvements have been patented, and if so, by whom; nor can it act as an expounder of the Patent Law, nor as counsellor for individuals, except as to questions arising within the Office.

17. All business with this Office should be transacted in writing. The action of the Office will be based exclusively on the written record. No attention will be paid to any alleged verbal promise or understanding in relation to which there is any disagreement or doubt.

19. All cases connected with the intricate and multifarious proceedings arising from the working of the Patent Office, which are not specially defined and provided for in these Rules, will be decided in accordance with the merits of each case under the authority of the Commissioner; and such decision shall be communicated to the interested parties, through the Departmental correspondent of the Patent Office.

Notice.

I. Correspondence with the Department is carried through the Canadian Mail, free of postage.

II. Every paper forwarded to the office should be accompanied by a letter, and a separate letter should be written on every distinct subject.

III. In order to avoid unnecessary explanations and useless loss of time and labour, it is particularly recommended that reference be made to the law before writing on any subject to the Department; and it is also recommended, in every case, to have the papers and drawings prepared by competent persons, in the interest both of the applicant and of the public service.

VI. A copy of the rules with a particular section marked, sent to any person making an enquiry, is intended as a respectful answer by the Office.

POWER OF ATTORNEY.

What is technically termed a Power of Attorney, is a legal instrument in writing and under seal, whereby one person specially appoints another to perform some act or acts for him, or in his stead, with the same binding effect or force as though such were done by himself. The authority delegated to such attorney may be limited or extensive, general or particular, as the person appointing him shall consider expedient. Any man or woman may delegate, in this way, his or her authority to a substitute; and such substitute, or attorney, will be bound to act according to his powers or instructions in the instrument which appoints him. An attorney without permission from his principal cannot delegate his authority to a substitute; and where discretionary power is given he must perform the duty personally. The attorney must perform every act in the name of his principal, who may withdraw his power at discretion, unless such attorney should have a joint interest in the execution of the power, when his authorization cannot be revoked. When a power of attorney is revoked, the parties interested should be duly notified, and after such notification it will have full force and effect. When a power of attorney is to be used in any foreign country, it should be executed before a Justice of the Peace or Notary Public, and his signature certified to by the Consul of the country where it is to be used. When a power of attorney is given to sell real estate, it should be registered in the proper registry or other office where deeds are recorded. Under any circumstances the execution of a power of attorney should be witnessed, and usually it is better that there should be two witnesses in order to provide against the death of either of them.

General Power of Attorney.

Know all Men by these Presents : That I,   , of the   of   , in the county of   , and Province of   , have made, constituted and appointed, and by these presents do make, constitute and appoint,   , of   , my true and lawful attorney for me, and in my name, place and stead, to [*here insert the things which the atttorney is to do, specifying his authority in plain and direct language, so that it may not be misunderstood*], giving and granting unto my said attorney full power and authority to do and perform all and every act and thing whatsoever, requisite and necessary to be done, in and about the premises, as fully, to all intents and purposes, as I might or could do if personally present, with full power of substitution and revocation, hereby ratifying and confirming all that my said attorney or his substitute shall lawfully do or cause to be done by virtue hereof.

In witness whereof, I have hereunto set my hand and seal, this   day of   , one thousand eight hundred and

Signed, sealed and delivered } C. D.   A. B. [L.S.]
    in presence of   } E. F.

General Custom House Power.

Know all Men by these Presents: That I,   of the   of,   , in the county of   and Province of   , have made, constituted and appointed, and by these presents do make, constitute and appoint,   , of   , my true and lawful attorney, for me and in my name, to receive and enter, at the custom-house of the district of   , any goods, wares or merchandise imported by me, or which may hereafter arrive, consigned to me, to sign my name, to seal and deliver for me, and as my act and deed, any bond or bonds which may be required by the collector of the said district for securing the duties on any such goods, wares or merchandise. Also to sign my name to, seal and deliver for me, and as my act and deed, any bond or bonds requisite for obtaining the debenture on any goods, wares or merchandise when exported, and generally to transact all business at the said custom-house in which I am, or may hereafter be, interested or concerned, as fully as I could if personally present. And I hereby declare, that all bonds signed and executed by my said attorney shall be as obligatory on me as those signed by myself; and this power shall remain in full force until revoked by written notice given to said collector.

In witness whereof, &c. [*as in General Power of Attorney.*]

Power to sell and convey Real Estate.

Know all Men by these Presents: That I,   , of the   of   , in the county of   and Province of   , have made, constituted and appointed, and by these presents do make, constitute and appoint,   , of   , my true and lawful attorney, for me and in my name, place and stead, to enter into and take possession of all and singular, etc., [*here describe the land,*] and to grant, bargain and sell the same, or any part or parcel thereof, for such sum or price and on such terms as he shall think advisable, and for my benefit, and for me and in my name to make, execute and deliver good and sufficient deeds and conveyances for the same, with the usual covenants and warrantry; And until the sale thereof, my attorney is hereby authorized to lease the said real estate, on the most advantageous terms; and ask, demand, distrain for, collect, recover and receive all moneys or sums of money which shall become due and owing to me by means of such bargain and sale, or lease; giving and granting unto my said attorney full power and authority to do and perform all and every act and thing whatsoever, requisite and necessary to be done in and about the premises as fully, to all intents and purposes, as I might or could do if personally present ; with full power of substitution and revocation, hereby ratifying and confirming all that my said attorney or his substitute shall lawfully do or cause to be done by virtue thereof.

In witness whereof, &c., [*as in General power of Attorney.*]

Power of Attorney to transfer Stock.

Know all Men by these Presents : That I,   , of the   of   , in the county of   and Province of   , have made, ordained, nominated, constituted and appointed, and by these presents do make, ordain, nominate, constitute and appoint,   , of   , my true and lawful attorney, for me, and in my name, place and stead, to assign, transfer and make over to   , of   ,   shares of stock held by me in the   , upon which   per cent. is paid, hereby ratifying all and whatsoever my said attorney may lawfully do by virtue of these presents.

In witness whereof, &c., [*as in General Power of Attorney.*]

Proxy, or Power, to Vote at Election of Directors.

Know all Men by these Presents : That I,   , of the   of   , in the county of   and Province of   , do hereby constitute and appoint,   of   , my true and lawful attorney and agent, for me, and in my name, place and stead, to vote as my proxy at any election of directors of the   , according to the number of votes I should be entitled to give if there personally present.

In witness whereof, &c., [*as in General Power of Attorney.*]

Substitution to be Indorsed on the Power of Attorney.

Know all Men by these Presents : That I,   , of the   of   , in the county of   and Province of   , by virtue of the authority to me given by the within power of attorney, do substitute   , of the   of

, in the county of   and Province of   , as attorney in my stead, to do, perform and execute every act and thing which I might or could do by virtue of the within power of attorney, hereby ratifying and confirming all that the said substitute may do in the premises by virtue hereof and of the within power of attorney.*

In witness whereof, &c. [*as in General Power of Attorney.*]

*This power of substitution can only be used when the attorney has had the right of substitution expressly granted to him in his appointment by his principal.

Revocation of Power of Attorney.

Know all Men by these Presents : That I,   , of the   of   , in the county of   and Province of   , (*addition*), for divers good causes and considerations, me hereby especially moving, do by these presents revoke, countermand, annul and make void a certain power of attorney under my hand and seal bearing date the   day of   , A. D. 18 , to   , of the   of   , in the county of   and Province of   , (*addition*), given, delivered and executed, and all powers and authorities whatsoever therein expressed and delegated.

In witness whereof, &c. [*as in preceding forms.*]

PROTECTION OF GAME AND FISHING LAWS OF CANADA.

While legislation as to Game comes within the jurisdiction of the various Provinces of the Dominion, and must be sought for in their Statute books, the Dominion Parliament alone has the right to legislate on the matters of fishing and fisheries, both as regards our rivers and lakes and sea coasts. The Dominion Fisheries Act, being 31 Vic., Chap. 60, was extended to Manitoba by 37 Vic., Chap. 28, and amended by 38 Vic., Chap. 33. Under the 19th section of that Act the Governor General in Council has the right to make such regulations thereunder for the better management and regulation, as may be necessary or expedient, from time to time, of the sea-coast and inland fisheries, which regulations have the force of law after being published in the *Canada Gazette.* As orders in Council are now annually incorporated with the Dominion Statutes, and fully indexed, they can readily be referred to at any time. In order that our readers may have the fullest and most accurate information on the Game Law of Ontario, we now publish the applying Statute in full. We also give such extracts from the Fisheries Act, as may be necessary for the general public to become acquainted with.

43 VIC., CHAP. 31, (ONTARIO.)

An Act for the Protection of Game and Fur-bearing Animals.

1. The Act passed in the forty-first year of Her Majesty's reign, and chaptered eighteen, is hereby repealed.

2. None of the animals or birds hereinafter mentioned, shall be hunted, taken or killed within the periods hereinafter limited ; (1) deer, elk, moose, reindeer or caribou, between the fifteenth day of December and the first day of October ; (2) grouse, pheasants, prairie fowl or partridge, between the first day of January and the first day of September ; (3) wild turkeys or quail, between the first day of January and the first day of October ; (4) woodcock, between the first day of January and the first day of August ; (5) snipe, between the first day of January and the fifteenth day of August ; (6) water fowl, known as mallard, grey duck, black duck, wood or summer duck, between the first day of January and the fifteenth day of August ; (7) other ducks, swans or geese, between the first day of May and the fifteenth day of August ; (8) hares, between the first day of March and the first day of September.

3. No person shall have in his possession any of the said animals or birds, or any part or portion of any of such animals or birds during the periods in which they are so protected : Provided that they may be exposed for sale for

twenty days, and no longer, after such periods, and may be had in possession for the private use of the owner and his family at any time, but in all cases the proof of the time of killing, taking or purchasing shall be upon the person so in possession.

4. No eggs of any of the birds above mentioned shall be taken, destroyed, or had in possession by any person at any time.

5. None of the said animals or birds, except the animals mentioned in the seventh section of this Act, shall be trapped or taken, by means of traps, nets, snares, gins, baited lines, or other similar contrivances; nor shall such traps, nets, snares, gins, baited lines or contrivances be set for them, or any of them, at any time; and such traps, nets, snares, gins, baited lines or contrivances may be destroyed by any person without such person thereby incurring any liability therefor.

6. None of the contrivances for taking or killing the wild fowl, known as swans, geese or ducks, which are described or known as batteries, swivel guns, sunken punts or nightlights, shall be used at any time.

7. No beaver, muskrat, sable, martin, otter or fisher, shall be hunted, taken or killed or had in possession of any person between the first day of May and the first day of November; and no mink between the first day of April and the first day of November; nor shall any traps, snares, gins or other contrivances be set for them during such period; nor shall any muskrat-house be cut, broken or destroyed at any time; and any such traps, snares, gins or other contrivances so set may be destroyed by any person without such person thereby incurring any liability therefor: Provided that this section shall not apply to any person destroying any of the said animals in defence or preservation of his property.

8. Offences against this Act shall be punished upon summary conviction or information or complaint before a justice of the peace as follows: (1) in case of deer, elk, moose, reindeer or caribou, by a fine not exceeding fifty dollars, nor less than ten dollars, with costs, for each offence; (2) in case of birds or eggs, by a fine not exceeding twenty-five dollars, nor less than five dollars, with costs, for each bird or egg; (3) in case of fur-bearing

animals mentioned in the seventh section of this Act, by a fine not exceeding twenty-five dollars, nor less than five dollars, with costs, for each offence; (4) in the case of other breaches of this Act, by a fine not exceeding twenty-five dollars, nor less than five dollars, with costs.

9. The whole of such fine shall be paid to the prosecutor, unless the convicting justice has reason to believe that the prosecution is in collusion with and for the purpose of benefiting the accused, in which case the said justice may order the disposal of the fine as in ordinary cases.

10. In all cases confiscation of game shall follow conviction, and the game so confiscated shall be given to some charitable institution or purpose, at the discretion of the convicting justice.

11. In order to encourage persons who have heretofore imported or hereafter import different kinds of game with the desire to breed and preserve the same on their own lands, it is enacted that it shall not be lawful to hunt, shoot, kill or destroy any such game without the consent of the owner of the property wherever the same may be bred.

12. It shall not be lawful for any person to kill or take any animal protected by this Act by the use of poison or poisonous substances, nor to expose poison, poisoned bait or other poisoned substances in any place or locality where dogs or cattle may have access to the same.

13. No person shall at any time hunt, take, or kill any deer, elk, moose, reindeer, or caribou, for the purpose of exporting the same out of Ontario, and in all cases the onus of proving that any such deer, elk, moose, reindeer, or caribou, so hunted, taken or killed is not intended to be exported as aforesaid shall be upon the person hunting, killing, or taking the same;

(1) Offences against this section shall be punished by a fine not exceeding twenty-five dollars, nor less than five dollars for each animal.

14. No owner of any dog, trained or accustomed to hunt deer, shall permit any such dog to run at large (if such dog is accustomed or is likely to resort to the woods unaccompanied by such owner or any of his family or other person) during the period from the fifteenth day of November to the

first day of October, under a penalty, on conviction, of not more than twenty-five dollars, nor less than five dollars, for each offence. Any person harbouring or claiming to be the owner of any such dog, shall be deemed to be the owner thereof.

15. It shall be lawful for the council of any county, city, town, township or incorporated village, to appoint an officer who shall be known as the game inspector for such county, city, town, township or incorporated village, and who shall perform such duties in enforcing the provisions of this Act, and be paid such salary, as may be mutually agreed upon.

Extracts from Fisheries Act, being 31 Vic., Chap. 60.

FISHERY OFFICERS.

1. The Governor may appoint Fishery Officers, whose powers and duties shall be defined by this Act and Regulations made under it, and by instructions from the Department of Marine and Fisheries; and every Officer so appointed under oath of office and instructed to exercise magisterial powers, shall be *ex officio* a Justice of the Peace for all the purposes of this Act and the Regulations made under it, within the limits for which he is appointed to act as such Fishery Officer :

FISHERY LEASES AND LICENSES.

2. The Minister of Marine and Fisheries may, where the exclusive right of fishing does not already exist by law, issue or authorize to be issued fishery leases and licenses for fisheries and fishing wheresoever situated or carried on; but leases or licenses for any term exceeding nine years shall be issued only under authority of an Order of the Governor in Council.

(*d.*) Salmon fry, parr and smolt, shall not be at any time fished for, caught or killed, and no salmon or grilse of less weight than three pounds shall be caught or killed; but where caught by accident in nets lawfully used for other fish, they shall be liberated alive at the cost and risk of the owner of the fishery, on whom shall in every case devolve the proof of such actual liberation;

(e.) Meshes of nets used for capturing salmon, shall be at least five inches in extension, and nothing shall be done to practically diminish or nullify their size ;

(f.) The use of nets or other apparatus which capture salmon shall, except in the Provinces of Nova Scotia and New Brunswick, be confined to tidal waters, and any Fishery Officer may determine the length and place of each net or other apparatus used in any of the waters of the Dominion ; provided that nothing contained in this section shall prevent the use of nets for catching salmon in the lakes of the Province of Ontario, nor preclude the Minister from authorizing, by special fishery licenses or leases, the capture of salmon by nets in fresh water streams ;

10. No salmon shall be captured within two hundred yards of the mouth of any tributary creek or stream which salmon frequent to spawn ;

11. Except in the manner known as fly-surface-fishing with a rod and line, salmon shall not be fished for, caught or killed at any artificial pass or salmon leap, nor in any pool where salmon spawn ;

LAKE AND RIVER TROUT FISHERY.

8. It shall not be lawful to fish for, catch or kill any kind of trout (or "lunge") in any way whatever between the first day of October and the first day of January ; and no one shall at any time fish for, catch or kill trout by other means than angling by hand with hook and line, in any inland lake, river or stream, except in tidal waters ; Provided always, that as affecting the waters of the Province of Ontario, such prohibitions shall apply only to the kind known as "speckled trout."

WHITE-FISH AND SALMON TROUT FISHERY.

9. It shall not be lawful to fish for or catch white-fish in any manner between the nineteenth day of November and the first day of December, nor by means of any kind of seine, between the thirtieth day of May and first day of August, in the Province of Ontario, or thirty-first day of July and first day of December in the Province of Quebec, nor shall the fry of the same be at any time destroyed :

Extracts from Act to amend Fisheries Act, being 38 Vic., Chap. 33.

1. The first sub-section of the seventh section of the Act passed in the thirty-first year of Her Majesty's reign, and known as "*The Fisheries Act*," is hereby repealed; and the following shall be substituted in lieu thereof, that is to say:—

"7. Salmon shall not be fished for, caught, or killed, between the thirty-first day of July and the first day of May, in the Provinces of Ontario and Quebec, and in the River Restigouche; nor between the fifteenth day of August and the first day of March, in the Provinces of New Brunswick and Nova Scotia: Provided always, that it shall be lawful to fish for, catch, and kill salmon with a rod and line, in the manner known as fly-surface-fishing, between the thirtieth day of April and the thirty-first day of August, in the Provinces of Ontario and Quebec, and between the first day of February and the fifteenth day of September, in the Provinces of New Brunswick and Nova Scotia."

Order in Council 16th May, 1879.

By Order in Council of the 16th day of May, 1879, those parts of the General Fishery Regulations adopted by the Governor-General in Council on the 3rd day of April, 1875, fixing close seasons for bass, pickerel and maskinonge, were repealed, and the following Regulation adopted:—

"In the Provinces of Ontario and Quebec no person shall fish for, catch, kill, buy, sell or possess any bass, pickerel (doree) or maskinonge, between the 15th day of April and the 15th day of May in each year."

Vide Canada Gazette, Vol. 12, p. 1501.

Order in Council.

By Order in Council of the 16th of May, 1879, the following Fishing Regulation was made and adopted:—

"The close time for shad and gaspereaux shall extend from sunset on Friday evening to sunrise on Monday morning, in each week, during which time it shall be unlawful to fish for, catch or kill, any shad or gaspereaux in the Dominion of Canada.

Vide Canada Gazette, Vol. 12, p. 1501.

PROVINCE OF ONTARIO LAWS OF GENERAL INTEREST.

From Revised Statutes of Ontario.

CHAP. 24. *Free Grants and Homesteads' Act.* This Act provides that the Lieutenant Governor in Council, may make free grants to actual settlers of certain public lands in the districts of Algoma, Nipissing, and that lying between Georgian Bay and the Ottawa River. The person applying for a free grant of land must be at least eighteen years of age. He will have to perform certain settlement duties, and these fulfilled he will be entitled to his patent at the end of five years. If his settlement duties are not performed in that time he will forfeit his location. Land located under this Act is exempt from seizure before the issue of the patent and for fifteen years afterwards.

CHAP. 120. *The Mechanics' Lien Act.* This Act provides that, unless there is an express agreement to the contrary, every mechanic, machinist, builder, miner, labourer, contractor, or other person doing work upon or furnishing materials to be used in the construction, alteration or repair of any building or erection; or erecting, furnishing, or placing machinery of any kind in, upon or in connection with any building, erection, or mine, shall on notice of being so employed or furnishing have a lien or charge for the price of such work, machinery, or materials, upon such building, erection, or mine, and upon the lands occupied thereby, for the amount justly due to the person entitled to such lien. This lien shall be good for thirty days only if not registered, and suit cannot be brought after that period. If registered, in accordance with the provisions of the Act, the lien holds good for ninety days. To become fully acquainted with the proper mode of procedure the Act itself should be consulted.

CHAP. 113. *Mills and Mill-Dams.* Under this Act the owner or occupant of a mill is prohibited from taking more toll than a twelfth of the grain brought to him for grinding and bolting, under a penalty of forty dollars for each offence, recoverable by suit in the Division or other competent Court. Unless bags are marked, the miller is not obliged to make them good should they be lost. Where a river or stream is sufficiently deep to permit of logs being floated, mill owners must construct aprons or slides to their dams to allow the passage of timber, under a penalty of two dollars for each day in default, recoverable before a Justice of the Peace.

CHAP. 187. *Planting Trees along Highways.* The third section of this Act provides that in rural districts every shade tree, shrub and sapling, growing on either side of any public highway, shall be the property of the owner of the adjoining land, who has the privilege of planting trees along such highway, but not so as to become a nuisance, or to interfere with the travel thereon. Any person who ties any animal to such tree, shrub or sapling; or permits any animal in his charge to injure the same; or who removes them, or receives them knowing them to be so removed; shall upon conviction thereof before a Justice of the Peace, be liable to a fine of twenty-five dollars, or in default of payment to thirty days' imprisonment. Half the fine to go to complainant and the other half to municipality.

CHAP. 195. *An Act respecting Pounds.* This Act provides that the owner of land shall be responsible for damage by all animals in his charge, whether owned by himself or others. Pound-keeper to impound all animals or poultry running at large. Person impounding to give a statement in duplicate to the pound-keeper of his claim, which is not to exceed twenty dollars, within twenty-four hours, and an agreement to indemnify the owner of animals, &c., impounded, should the distress be illegal. The party impounding is also obliged to notify the owner of animals, &c., if known. Fence viewers to decide if boundary fences are lawful. Damages recoverable before a Justice of the Peace. (*Consult Act for further information.*)

CHAP. 159. *Protecting Cheese and Butter Manufacturers.* This Act provides that any person selling or supplying to any cheese or butter manufacturer, any skimmed, soured or watered milk, or who keeps back the strippings, shall be liable to a penalty of not less than one nor more than fifty dollars.

Any cheese or butter manufacturer who uses, or permits others to fraudulently use the cream or milk of his patrons, shall be liable to fifty dollars fine.

This Act makes penalties recoverable before two Justices of the Peace having no interest in the manufactory; or the aggrieved party may at option bring a civil action for damages in any competent court.

CHAP. 201. *For the Protection of Birds beneficial to Agriculture.* This Act does not apply to cage birds or poultry, or to the birds specified in the protection of Game Act. (43 Vic. Chap. 31.) It prohibits the shooting or selling any bird whatever, except eagles, falcons, hawks, owls, wild pigeons, king-fishers, jays, crows and ravens, which may be destroyed at will by any person. It also prohibits injuries to eggs of other birds, and provides that any person may arrest offenders, and take them before a Justice of the Peace, who can impose a penalty of not less than one dollar nor more than twenty, and imprison in default of payment.

CHAP. 189. *To Prevent the Profanation of the Lord's Day (Sunday.)* This Act provides that it shall not be lawful for any merchant, tradesman, artificer, mechanic, workman, labourer, or other person whatsoever, to sell or show forth, or expose or offer for sale, or to purchase anything, or do any business or work at his ordinary calling, other than conveying travellers or Her Majesty's mail by land or by water, selling drugs or medicines, or doing other work of necessity and charity. The Act also prohibits political meetings on the Sabbath, tippling at inns or taverns, to revel, or exhibit one's self in a state of intoxication, or to brawl or use profane language on any street or in the open air, or to create any riot or disturbance, to play at any game, or to shoot, hunt, or fish. On conviction, a Justice of the Peace may impose a fine on the offender of not less than one dollar nor more than forty dollars, and may imprison in default of payment for three months. A Justice may convict on his own view, that is when the offence is committed in his presence. (*See Act itself for further particulars.*) This Act does not extend to Indians.

CHAP. 36. *Registration of Births, Marriages and Deaths.* This Act makes each city, town, village or township a Registration Division; the Clerk of the same to be Division Registrar.

It provides that any clergyman or other person, authorized by law to baptize, marry, or perform the funeral service, in Ontario, shall keep a registry, showing the names of his congregation whom he has baptized, married or buried. The father or mother, or in case of death or sickness the persons acting in their place, must give notice to the Registrar of the birth of any child within thirty days. Clergymen must give notice of marriages performed by them, occupiers of tenements must give notice when deaths occur, and doctors must also give notice of deaths. Persons violating the provisions of this Act are liable to a penalty of twenty dollars, on conviction before one Justice of the Peace.

CHAP. 96. *Right of Property in Swarms of Bees.* This Act provides that bees living in a state of freedom shall be the property of the person finding them. The owner of a swarm leaving the hive shall have the right to follow them on the land of another person, unless the swarm settles in a hive already occupied. He must however notify beforehand the owner of the land on which his swarm settles, and compensate him for all damages. If the owner of a swarm declines to follow it, any other person may do so and keep the bees. If swarms are not followed they become the property of the person on whose land they settle. But unless he objects the first owner may secure the swarm.

CHAP. 76. *Returns of Convictions and Fines by Justices of the Peace.* This Act provides that every Justice of the Peace shall make a return (according to the form given) of all convictions made by him on or before the second Tuesday in the months of March, June, September and December, in each year, to the Clerk of the Peace, under a penalty of eighty dollars for default. When two or more justices join in a conviction they must make an immediate return. Parts of fines, or fines imposed in one quarter and collected in another, must also be returned. The making wilfully of any false, or partial, or incorrect return renders the Justice, or Justices, liable to the penalty. Actions to recover penalties must be brought within six months.

CHAP. 131. *Support of Illegitimate Children.* This Act provides that any person who furnishes food, clothing or lodging to an illegitimate child, still a minor, may recover the cost of the same from the father. If the mother (or the person to whom she has become accountable therefor) sues for the value of the necessaries so furnished, she must prove that the defendant is the father of her child by other evidence than her own. An action cannot be maintained against the reputed father in any case, unless the mother makes affidavit while pregnant or six months after its birth, that such person is the father of such child. The following form complies with the Act :—

Form of Affidavit of Affiliation under this Act.

ONTARIO,   ) I, Jane Roe, of the (*here in-*
County of   } *sert township, town, or other*
         To wit :) *place of residence,*) in the county of   , unmarried woman, make oath and say, that on the   18 , I gave birth to a female (*or male*) child, at   , in the county aforesaid, and that John Doe, of the   , in the county of   , is really the father of such female child.

Sworn before me at
in the county of
this   day of
A. D. 188
         J. P.
                              }   JANE ROE.

CHAP. 188. *To Prevent the Spreading of Canada Thistles.* This Act (as amended by 43 Vic., Chap. 29) provides that owners of land must cut down thistles before they go to seed where the land is not sown with grain. Overseers of highways must give notice to owners of land not later than the 25th of June to cut down thistles, and if they are not cut in accordance with said notice, may enter on the land and cut them down, and compel the owner to pay him for so doing by having the amount added to his or her taxes. Railway companies must keep thistles cut down, and road overseer must keep them cut down along the highways, and is to be paid by the municipality for so doing. Act provides for a penalty of ten dollars for knowingly selling seed mixed with thistle seed. Overseers of highways who neglect their duties under this Act are liable to a penalty of not less than ten nor more than twenty dollars. Penalties recoverable before a single Justice of the Peace.

CHAP. 193. *To Prevent Accidents by Threshing Machines.* This Act provides that all persons owning or running any threshing, wood-sawing, or other machine run by horse-power, shall have each of the knuckles, couplings, joints and jacks of such machine covered by wood, leather or metal, with tubes running through the same for oiling, so that the dress of a person cannot be caught by the same, under a penalty of not less than one nor more than twenty dollars. Prosecution to be commenced within thirty days after offence.

CHAP. 183. *Travelling on Public Highways and Bridges.* This Act provides that where vehicles meet on the public highway the driver of each shall turn to the right hand, and each give half the road. A person in a vehicle or on horseback overtaken by another travelling at greater speed, must turn to the right quietly and allow the other to pass. If the person so overtaken cannot turn out of the way he must stop and if necessary shall assist the other person to pass him without damage. Any person who is too drunk to ride or drive, or any person who races or drives furiously, or uses blasphemous or indecent language, or who has not at least two bells to his harness if travelling with a sleigh, or who drives faster than a walk over a bridge where a prohibitory notice has been put up, or removes such notice, shall be liable to certain penalties under this Act recoverable before any Justice of the Peace, who may commit to gaol in default of payment. No such fine or imprisonment to be any bar to the recovery of civil damages before any court of competent jurisdiction.

CHAP. 184. *Tolls on Turnpike Roads.* This Act exempts Volunteers in uniform, persons going to or returning from divine service on Sunday or legal holiday, or who own farms divided by toll roads, or when drawing manure from any city, town or incorporated village, from tolls.

CHAP. 29. 44 Vic. provides that notwithstanding anything contained in the Revised Statute respecting the Protection of Insectivorous and other Birds beneficial to Agriculture, chapter two hundred and one, any person may, during the fruit season, for the purpose of protecting his fruit from the attacks of such birds, shoot or destroy, on his own premises, the birds known as the Robin and Cherry Bird, without being liable to any penalty under the said Act.

PROVINCE OF NOVA SCOTIA LAWS OF GENERAL INTEREST.

Landlord and Tenant. Chap. 105, Revised Statutes of Nova Scotia (4th series), provides that when any house is let by the year three months' notice to quit, and when by the month, one month's notice, and when by the week, one weeks' notice, shall be given to or by the tenant in possession.

And in case of forcible entry or wrongful detainer when the possession is withheld from the party entitled thereto, for seven days' after notice, any two Justices of the Peace on complaint on oath being made, may by warrant cause the party in possession to be arrested and detained until he find security for his appearance at the next term of the Supreme Court or County Court.

The plaintiff shall file and serve his complaint, and the Defendant shall answer the same within fourteen days, and the case shall be tried in a summary way as a civil suit, and the Court may issue a writ of possession and award damages to the injured party.

By section 42 of the "County Court Act" (1880,) the landlord, when any tenant overholds, after the determination of his tenancy, may apply to the Judge of the County Court for the district, on affidavit of the facts, and obtain a summons to be served on the tenant or party in possession to show cause why a warrant should not issue to the Sheriff to put the party entitled into immediate possession ; and the costs of such proceedings shall be taxed by the Judge.

By section 7 Chap. 157 Revised Statutes (4th series,) the tenant's goods are not liable to be removed under execution until the rent, not to exceed one year's amount, is paid to the landlord. And by section 8 of the same Act, the landlord may seize goods fraudulently removed to avoid distress within twenty-one days after removal unless previously *bona fide* sold without notice of such fraudulent removal.

Rights of Married Women. Chap. 86 Revised Statutes (4th series,) provides that a wife deserted by her husband may obtain an order from the Supreme Court to protect her property and earnings, acquired after such desertion, from her husband and his creditors. Such order shall be entered with the Registrar of Deeds for the district, and the wife shall, during the continuance of such order, in regard to property and contracts, be in the like position as if she had obtained a decree of divorce. The husband or any creditor seizing property of the wife, after notice of such order, shall be liable, at the suit of the wife, to restore the same, and also a sum equal to the value of double the property so seized.

A husband may insure his life for the benefit of his wife, or wife and children; and the amount of such policy shall in no manner be liable for the debts of the husband.

Law of Inheritance. Chap. 82 Revised Statutes (4th series,) provides that undevised real estate shall descend to the children of the person leaving the same in equal shares, and in case of the decease of any of his children to such as shall legally represent them.

If the deceased shall leave no issue, one half of his real estate shall go to his father and the other half to his widow; and if there be no widow, the whole shall go to his father. If the deceased shall leave no issue, nor father, one half of his real estate shall go to his widow and the other half in equal shares to his mother and brothers and sisters, or their children by right of representation. And if there be no widow, the whole shall go to them; and in default of brothers and sisters his estate shall go to his next of kin in equal degree, but in no case shall representatives be admitted among collaterals after brother's and sister's children.

The degrees of kindred shall be computed after the manner of the Civil Law, and the kindred of the half blood shall inherit with those of the whole blood in the same degree.

If the intestate shall have no kindred, the whole shall go to his widow to her own use.

The interest of a party in lands held in trust for him, shall descend in the same manner as if he had died seized of such lands.

The widow shall be allowed all her own paraphernalia and the apparel of the minor children, and also such provisions and other articles necessary for the sustenance of herself and family for 'ninety days after the death of her husband. The remaining personal estate, after payment of debts, shall be distributed one-third to the widow, if any, and the residue among the persons who would be entitled to the real estate.

Any child born after the death of the father (there being no provision made in his will for such child) shall have the like interest in the real and personal estate of the father as if he had died intestate.

Any real or personal estate given by the intestate as an advancement to any child, shall be taken by such child as a portion of his share of the intestate's estate. (*The Act does not effect the title of a husband as tenant by the curtsey nor that of a wife as tenant in dower.*)

Wills of Real and Personal Property. Chap. 81 Revised Statutes (4th series) provides that no minor's will is valid but a married woman may make a will of real or personal estate, held in her own right, and may bequeath property so held by her, to her husband; and may, with her husband's consent in writing, make a will of her personal estate, not held to her own use. No will shall be valid unless in writting, signed at the foot or end by the testator, or by some other person in his presence, and by his direction, and such signature shall be made or acknowledged by the testator in the presence of two or more witnesses present at the same time; and such witnesses shall attest and shall subscribe the will in the presence of the testator, but no form of attestation is necessary.

Soldiers and sailors on service may dispose of personal estate as before the Act.

No will shall be invalid for incompetency of the witnesses; but all gifts or devises to a witness, or the wife or husband of a witness, shall be void, but the executor of the will is competent to be a witness to it.

No will shall be revoked otherwise than by another will, or by codicil duly executed, or by destroying the will with the intention to revoke it; but the marriage of a person after the making of a will will revoke the same, unless the same be re-executed after marriage.

Every will shall be construed with reference to the real and personal estate comprised in it, to speak and take effect as if executed immediately before the death of the testator, unless a contrary intention appear by the will.

A devise of real or personal estate without words of limitation shall be construed as a devise of all the testator's interest in the property devised, unless a contrary intention shall appear by the will itself,

A devise to testator's children who die before him shall not lapse if they have left issue living and all lapsed legacies shall be included in the residuary devise, unless a contrary intention shall appear.

Mechanic's Lien. The "Mechanic's Lien Act of 1879" provides that unless there be an express agreement in writing to the contrary, every contractor or sub-contractor shall have a lien or charge for the price of any work done or materials provided under a written agreement (which is to be filed with a statement of the claim according to a schedule given in the Act) upon the estate and interest of the person for whom such work is done, or materials furnished, in the building, erection, or mine, where such work is done or materials furnished, and in the lands usually enjoyed therewith, limited in amount to such sum as shall be justly due to the person entitled to such lien. Such lien shall attach upon the estate and interest, legal or equitable, of the person at whose request any such work is done or materials furnished. All persons furnishing materials under a written contract and who shall have obtained the consent of the owner or person against whom the lien is claimed, and who shall notify such owner or person within seven days after such material is furnished or work performed of an unpaid account, such lien holder shall be entitled to a charge therefor, *pro rata*, upon any amount payable by such owner or other person under said lien.

Within thirty days after the materials are furnished or the work performed, the party having the lien is required to file the written contract, and a statement of his claim, in the form prescribed by the Act, with the Registrar of Deeds for the county, and such lien shall expire within ninety days after registration, unless the lien holder take legal proceedings as provided by the Act to obtain a certificate of judgment from the Court, which, when registered, becomes a charge on the lands. (*The Act does not prevent creditors on any such contract from maintaining actions at common law, in like manner as if they had no such lien for the security of their debts.*)

Deeds, Bills of Sale, &c. There are no statutory forms of conveyances provided by any acts of the Legislature of Nova Scotia. Releases of mortgages, however, have to be by deed, and a certificate of discharge endorsed on a mortgage is not sufficient.

Deeds, and all other encumbrances affecting real estate have to be registered in the office of the Registrar of Deeds, where the lands lie, in order to guard against subsequent encumbrances or transfers. Certificates of judgment are also registered, and bind the real estate of the defendant from the date of the registry; and the judgment creditor after the expiration of one year may proceed to sell the lands of the judgment debtor under execution.

All deeds and instruments in writing require to be attested by at least one witness, and will be registered on the oath of any subscribing witness to the signatures of the parties.

Deeds may be proved out of the Province of Nova Scotia by the oath of a subscribing witness, or the acknowledgment of the parties under oath, such oath to be administered by a Judge of any court of record, by the Mayor of any city, by a Justice of the Peace, or by a Notary Public, residing respectively at or near the place where the deed is proved; and the attestation with the date to be certified under the seal of a court of record or of a city, or under the hand and seal of a Notary Public, and where a deed is proved in a foreign country the oath may be administered by and the attestation with the date certified under the hand and seal of any public Minister, Ambassador or Consul from the Court of Great Britain, or Vice-Consul, residing at or near the place where the deed is proved.

The registry of a deed executed by virtue of a power of attorney, shall not be valid unless the power of attorney, or a deed subsequently confirming the authority given thereby shall also be registered.

Bills of sale and chattel mortgages have also to be filed with the Registrar of Deeds for the county where the personal property or chattels are, otherwise the same may be taken under execution or otherwise disposed of.

Acts, deeds, &c., done in great Britain and Ireland and British Colonies, and authenticated legally there have the same effect as if sworn to in the Province of Nova Scotia.

Crown Land Grants. Chap. 11 Revised Statutes of Nova Scotia (4th series), provides that all Crown Lands fit for settlement are reserved for agricultural improvements, and are divided into lots of 100 acres, and any person may obtain a grant up to 300 acres upon making application therefor to the Commissioner of Crown Lands, which application shall be accompanied by an affidavit sworn before a Justice of the Peace, that the same is intended solely for cultivation and improvement. The price to be paid for the land is forty cents per acre. All necessary information respecting the lands can be obtained from the Deputy Surveyors of each county, the fees to be paid him are twenty cents for each search, and fifty cents for each plan. Immediate payment for the land must be made to the Provincial Secretary, and upon the grant being issued, the party shall be entitled to enter into possession, but not before. Any person or persons can obtain a grant for lumbering purposes, up to two thousand acres, paying the same price and under the same conditions as land for settlement.

Master's, Servant's and Apprentice's Act. Chap. 88 Revised Statutes (4th series), provides that children under the age of 14 years may be bound as apprentices or servants until that age, without their consent, by their father; and in case of his death or incompetency, by their mother or guardian, and if they have neither parents nor guardians, then they may bind themselves, with the approbation of two Justices of the Peace. Minors above the age of 14 years, may be bound in the same manner, provided their assent shall be expressed in the indenture and testified by their signing the same. Females may be bound to the age of 18 years, or the time of their marriage within that age, and males to the age of 21 years. The overseers of the poor may bind the children of any poor person or any other children whether under or above the age of 14 years, who have become chargeable to their district; females, to 18 years, or their marriage within that time, and males to 21 years, and provision shall be made in the contract for teaching such children to read, write and cypher, and such other instructions as the overseers may think fit.

All considerations of money paid by the master upon any contract of service or apprenticeship, shall be paid or secured to the sole use of the minor thereby bound. The parents, guardians or overseers shall enquire into the treatment of all children bound by them and protect them from all cruelty, neglect or breach of contract, on the part of their masters, and may make a complaint in writing to two Justices of the Peace, who, after investigating the cause, may order the minor to be discharged from his apprenticeship, and give costs against the master, and, if the complaint is not maintained, then against the complainant. And if any apprentice or servant, bound as aforesaid, unlawfully departs from the service of his master, or is guilty of gross misconduct, or refusal, or wilful neglect of his duty, any Justice of the Peace, on complaint on oath by the master, may issue his warrant and bring the servant or apprentice before him, and, if the charge prove to be true, may commit him to the common jail for any term not more than 20 days, unless sooner discharged by the master.

Nature and Jurisdiction of Small Debts Courts.—Magistrates' Courts. Chap. 91 Revised Statutes (4th series), provides that in actions for debt where the whole cause of action does not exceed $20, one Justice has jurisdiction, and where the cause of action is above $20 and under $80, two Justices have jurisdiction.

The suit is conducted in the same way and subject to the like defence as suits in the Supreme Court.

Particulars of the plaintiff's claim showing both debts and credits shall be annexed to the original summons, and a copy thereof with a copy of the summons shall be served on the defendant at least five days, where the amount is under $40; and at least ten days, when above $40, before the return day thereof.

The cause shall be tried between the hours of 10 A. M. and 6 P. M., of the return day of the writ, and may be continued by the Justice for sufficient cause till such further time not exceeding 30 days. If either party wishes, the cause may be tried by a jury of three. The defendant shall file his set off, if any, at least two days before the return day of the summons, and if it exceeds the plaintiff's amount, and is proved, he shall have judgment accordingly. If either party is not satisfied with the judgment he may appeal to the County Court. The party appealing must, within ten days. after judgment, enter into a bond with sufficient security in a penalty double the amount of the judgment, with a condition that he will prosecute the appeal and perform the judgment of the Court.

Stipendiary Magistrates within their jurisdiction have the same power as two Justices of the Peace.

County Court. "County Court Act, 1880" provides that the County Court has jurisdiction in actions *ex contractu* to the amount of $400, and *ex delicto* to $200. The practice is the same as in the Supreme Court, and the barristers of the Supreme Court practice in the County Court.

Limitations of Actions. Chap. 100 Revised Statutes (4th series), provides that actions for debt, or on simple contract, or for rent, or account, &c., must be brought within six years next after the cause of action accrued, and no promise or acknowledgement shall take the case out of the operation of the Act, unless in writing, and action by or against minors, married women or insane people must be brought within six years after the removal of the disability, and actions against persons out of the province may be brought within the same period after their return.

And any entry or distress or action to recover any land may be brought within twenty years after the time to make such entry or distress or bring such action first accrued, and persons under any disability shall have ten years after the removal of the disability, but such person shall only have forty years from the time when the right first accrued, although he may have remained under the disability the whole forty years.

Magistrate's Court.—Justices' Fees.

Each summons or capias, and copy thereof	$0 40
Affidavit for a capias and swearing	0 10
Subpœna	0 20
Tickets	0 10
Trial and judgment in all cases	0 20
Venire	0 20
Returning papers on appeal to County Court	0 20
Each execution	0 20
Affidavit of service of summons when required and swearing	0 10
Affidavit of appeal and swearing	0 10
Appeal Bond	0 50

(*When the defendant resides out of the county where the summons is issued, a deposit of 5c. per mile has to be made by the plaintiff with the Justice, to be paid to the defendant for his travelling fees, in the event of judgment being given for defendant.*

Constables' Fees.

Serving summons and making return...................	$0 20
Serving capias and making return.....................	0 20
Bail bond..	0 20
Summoning a jury....................................	0 20
Summoning each additional juror where there is not sufficient by-standers...............................	0 05
Serving subpœna, each witness.......................	0 10
Serving execution...................................	0 20
Poundage on execution on sale of goods...............	0 10
Poundage on execution where the amount is paid in money, for each four dollars................................	0 05
All travelling to be computed from residence of Justice to residence of defendant on summons, capias or execution; and from residence of officer to residence of witness, on subpœna, each mile when necessarily done.................	0 10
In cases of execution levied on the body, travelling to be computed from residence of officer to that of defendant, and thence to place of confinement, each mile.................	0 10

Where subpœnas are served by a constable, travel shall not be charged for serving each witness, but so much travel as may be necessarily and actually performed by the constable serving all the subpœnas.

WILLS AND INTESTACY.

The law with regard to Wills comes to us from two sources, if we except the Province of Quebec. One of these sources is the law of England, as it stood at the date of its introduction into Canada towards the close of the last century; the other source springs from the local Statutes of the various Provinces of the Dominion, all of which have jurisdiction as regards the descent of real and personal property. In ordinary acceptation the word Will means to determine by an act of choice, but in a legal point of view it refers to an instrument by which the owner of any real or personal property provides for the disposal of that property after his or her death. When a man makes a will he is termed a *testator*, while a woman who makes a will is termed a *testatrix*. When land, or real estate is given by a will, it is said to be *devised*, and the heir becomes the *devisee.* When personal or other chattel property is given it is said to be bequeathed. A person receiving a legacy under a will is termed the *legatee.* Any person of sound mind and understanding is competent to make a will. Where land is the subject of a will, the person making it must be of the full age of twenty-one years; but personal property may be bequeathed by males at the age of fourteen, and by females at the age of twelve, presuming that they have sufficient discretion to comprehend properly the nature of the act they are performing. The right to dispose of landed property in England, not entailed by the Crown Patent, was first permitted there by an Act of Parliament, passed in the reign of Henry VIII, called the Statute of Wills. Prior to the passage of that act personal or moveable property might, at common law, be bequeathed by will under certain limitations. For example, a man who died leaving a wife and children behind him could not deprive them by will of more than a third of his personal or moveable property. If he left a wife and no children he could only will one-half of his property; and if he had children and no wife they were also entitled at common law to half of his personal estate. At the present day no such limitation exists, and a man may, if sufficiently devoid of natural affection, give the whole of his property to strangers, and leave his own family or relations penniless. Under English law all wills require to be in writing, except the wills of soldiers when on service, and of seamen when at sea. A will of lands must not only be in writing but must also be signed by the maker in the presence of two witnesses, who must subscribe their names thereto in the presence of each other. As regards a will of personal property the same formalities are not required, although it is always desirable that they should be observed; and a simple memorandum in the hand-writing of the owner will be sufficient to control the disposition of his personal estate after death. A draft will prepared by a lawyer under instructions, although not executed, will have the same effect. But it should always be remembered that a will properly signed and witnessed, can be much more easily proved than any other, and so makes the disposal of personal property after death more secure. In every will bequeathing personal property, some person or persons should be appointed to carry it into practical effect, who should be of the full age of twenty-one, and who should legally qualify himself to execute it by complying with the law as to taking out letters of administration from the Surrogate or other similar Court of the Province. While the legatee of personal property can only get such property through the agent or executor, under the will, the devisee or heir, to whom land is given takes possession of it without the intervention of any third person. The moment a testator dies the executor or executrix is legally entitled to take possession of the whole of the personal property, and must first pay all the testator's lawful debts, and cannot legally pay a single legacy, or part with any of the property committed to his care, until that is done. If a married woman is possessed of property, real or personal, in her own right, she may dispose of the same by will to her children by such mode of division as she thinks fit; and failing children then to her husband or to whom she pleases. Such will must be in writing, and must be executed before two witnesses, neither of whom can be her husband. Should she die intestate her property is subject to the same distribution as that of her husband, presuming he should die without making a will.

The law does not supply any form for wills. But in drafting them great care should be taken that their language be plain and easily understood, and the wishes of the testator expressed in proper terms. A codicil is a supplement, or addition to a will, altering some of its provisions, or making new ones, and should be executed with the same formalities as the will itself. Wills are revoked by the marriage of the person making them or by subsequent wills.

In the Province of Ontario before an executor or executrix can act under a will, he or she must be clothed with the necessary lawful authority. This is done by proving the will in the Surrogate Court of the county where the testator had, at the time of his death, his fixed place of abode. If he had no fixed place of abode in the Province, or resided out of it, the will must be proved in the Surrogate Court of the county in which he had any personal or landed property. The first proceeding on the part of an executor is to take the will to the clerk of the Surrogate Court, who is usually the clerk of the County Court, at the county town. He will fill up the necessary affidavits and other documents, and have the will proved in due form. When a person dies intestate any of the next of kin may obtain letters of administration in the Surrogate Court, which will give the same authority as though he had been appointed executor under a will. In Ontario wills can be registered in the usual way at the County Registration Office.

Descent of Property of Persons dying intestate. (Ontario.)

In Ontario no law of primogeniture, or the preference of the eldest born, exists as regards the descent of real or personal property. Chap. 105 of its Revised Statutes makes full provisions for the descent of real and personal property transmissible to heirs. Descents before 1st July 1834 will still remain under the common law, after that date descents shall be traced from the purchaser. Sec. 13 of this Act provides that no brother or sister shall be considered to inherit immediately from his or her brother or sister, but that every descent from a brother or sister shall be traced through the parent. Sec. 15 provides that the male line shall be preferred to the female line. Sec. 22 provides that when any person dies intestate his fee simple estate, or leasehold estate if for the life of another person, shall pass—

1st. To his children and their descendants.
2nd. To his father.
3rd. To his mother.
4th. To his collateral relatives.

Sec. 23 provides that where there are several descendants equally related to the intestate the estate shall be divided in equal parts among them. Sec. 31 provides that in case of the failure of other heirs the descent shall be:—

1st. To the brothers and sisters of the father of the intestate in equal shares.

2nd. To the living brothers and sisters of the father of the intestate, and to the descendants of those who have died, in equal shares.

3rd. If all such brothers and sisters have died then to their descendants.

Descendants and relatives born after the death of intestate shall inherit equally with those living before death. Children who may have already received their full share or settlement of intestate's property cannot claim any further share. If they have not got their full share, they are entitled to the difference and no more. The value of any real or personal estate so absconded, unless the value has been acknowledged by an instrument in writing by the child, shall be estimated at its fair value when given. The maintaining or educating of a child, without a view to a portion or settlement in life, shall not be deemed an advancement under this Act.

Law of Ontario respecting Wills.

Extracts from Chap. 106, Revised Statutes of Ontario.

9. In the construction of the sections numbered ten to thirty-eight inclusive in this Act,

(*a.*) "Will" shall extend to a testament, and to a codicil, and to an appointment by will, or by writing in the nature of a will in exercise of a power, and also to a disposition by will and testament, or devise of the custody and tuition of any child, by virtue of the Act passed in the twelfth year of the reign of King Charles the Second, entititled "*An Act for taking away the Court of Wards, and liveries and tenures* in capite, *and by the knight's service and purveyance, and for settling a revenue upon His Majesty in lieu thereof*," and to any other testamentary disposition ;

(*b.*) "Real estate" shall extend to messuages, lands, rents and hereditaments, whether freehold or of any other tenure, and whether corporeal, incorporeal or personal, and to any undivided share thereof, and to any estate, right, or interest (other than a chattel interest) therein ;

(*c.*) "Personal estate" shall extend to leasehold estates and other chattels real, and also to moneys, shares of government and other funds, securities for money (not being real estates), debts, choses in action, rights, credits, goods, and all other property whatsoever which by law devolves upon the executor or administrator, and to any share or interest therein ;

(*d.*) "Person" and "Testator," shall include a married woman ;

(*e.*) "Mortgage" shall include any lien for unpaid purchase money, and any charge, incumbrance, or obligation of any nature whatever upon any lands or tenements of a testator or intestate.

10. Every person may devise, bequeath, or dispose of by will, executed in manner hereinafter mentioned, all real estate and personal estate which he may be entitled to, either at Law or in Equity, at the time of his death, and which, if not so devised, bequeathed, or disposed of, would devolve upon his heir at law, or upon his executor or administrator ; and the power hereby given shall extend to estates *pur autre vie*, whether there be or be not any special occupant thereof, and whether the same be a corporeal or incorporeal hereditament ; and also to all contingent, executory, or other future interests in any real or personal estate, whether the testator be or be not ascertained as the person or one of the persons in whom the same may respectively become vested, and

whether he be entitled thereto under the instrument by which the same were respectively created, or under any disposition thereof by deed or will, and also to all rights of entry for conditions broken and other rights of entry, and also to such of the same estates, interests and rights respectively, and other real and personal estate, as the testator may be entitled to at the time of his death, notwithstanding that he may become entitled to the same subsequently to the execution of his will.

11. No will made by any person under the age of twenty-one years shall be valid.

12. No will shall be valid unless it is in writing, and executed in manner hereinafter mentioned; that is to say, it shall be signed at the foot or end thereof by the testator, or by some other person in his presence, and by his direction; and such signature shall be made or acknowledged by the testator, in the presence of two or more witnesses present at the same time, and such witnesses shall attest and subscribe the will in the presence of the testator; but no form of attestation shall be necessary.

13. No appointment made by will, in exercise of any power, shall be valid, unless the same is executed in manner hereinbefore required; and every will executed in manner hereinbefore required shall, so far as respects the execution and attestation thereof, be a valid execution of a power of appointment by will, notwithstanding it has been expressly required that a will made in exercise of such power shall be executed with some additional or other form of execution or solemnity.

15. Every will executed in manner hereinbefore required shall be valid without any other publication thereof.

20. Every will shall be revoked by the marriage of the testator, except a will made in exercise of a power of appointment where the real or personal estate thereby appointed would not, in default of such appointment, pass to the testator's heir, executor or administrator, or the person entitled as the testator's next of kin under the Statute of Disributions.

22. No will or codicil, or any part thereof, shall be revoked otherwise than as aforesaid, or by another will or codicil executed in manner hereinbefore required, or by

some writing declaring an intention to revoke the same, and executed in the manner in which a will is hereinbefore required to be executed, or by the burning, tearing, or otherwise destroying the same, by the testator, or by some person in his presence and by his direction, with the intention of revoking the same.

23. No obliteration, interlineation or other alteration made in any will after the execution thereof, shall be valid or have any effect, except so far as the words or effect of the will before such alteration are not apparent, unless such alteration is executed in like manner as hereinbefore is required for the execution of the will; but the will, with such alteration as part thereof, shall be deemed to be duly executed, if the signature of the testator and the subscription of the witnessess are made in the margin or in some other part of the will opposite or near to such alteration, or at the foot or end of, or opposite to, a memorandum referring to such alteration, and written at the end or in some other part of the will.

24. No will or codicil, or any part thereof, which has been in any manner revoked, shall be revived otherwise than by the re-execution thereof, or by a codicil executed in manner hereinbefore required, and showing an intention to revive the same; and where any will or codicil which has been partly revoked, and afterwards wholly revoked, is revived, such revival shall not extend to so much thereof as was revoked before the revocation of the whole thereof, unless an intention to the contrary is shown.

25. No conveyance or other act made or done subsequently to the execution of a will, of or relating to any real or personal estate therein comprised, except an act by which such will is revoked as aforesaid, shall prevent the operation of the will with respect to such estate, or interest in such real or personal estate, as the testator had power to dispose of by will at the time of his death.

26. Every will shall be construed, with reference to the real and personal estate comprised in it, to speak and take effect as if it had been executed immediately before the death of the testator, unless a contrary intention appears by the will.

30. Where any real estate is devised to any person without any words of limitation, such devise shall be construed

to pass the fee simple, or other the whole estate or interest, which the testator had power to dispose of by will, in such real estate, unless a contrary intention appears by the will.

36. Where any person has died since the 31st day of December, 1865, or hereafter dies seised of or entitled to any estate or interest in any real estate, which, at the time of his death, was or is charged with the payment of any sum or sums of money by way of mortgage, and such person has not, by his will or deed or other document, signified any contrary or other intention, the heir or devise to whom such real estate descends or is devised shall not be entitled to have the mortgage debt discharged or satisfied out of the personal estate, or any other real estate of such person ; but the real estate so charged shall, as between the different persons claiming through or under the deceased person, be primarily liable to the payment of all mortgage debts with which the same is charged, every part thereof according to its value bearing a proportionate part of the mortgage debts charged on the whole thereof.

(b.) Nothing herein contained shall affect or diminish any right of the mortgagee on such real estate to obtain full payment or satisfaction of his mortgage debt, either out of the personal estate of the person so dying as aforesaid, or otherwise ; and nothing herein contained shall affect the rights of any person claiming under or by virtue of any will, deed, or document made before the first day of January, one thousand eight hundred and seventy-four.

37. In the construction of any will or deed or other document to which the next preceding section of this Act relates, a general direction that the debts or that all the debts of the testator shall be paid out of his personal estate shall not be deemed to be a declaration of an intention contrary to other than the rule in the said section contained, unless such contrary or other intention is further declared by words expressly or by necessary implication referring to all or some of the testator's debts or debt charged by way of mortgage on any part of his real estate.

A Short Form of Will.

This is the last will and testament of me, A. B., of, &c., made this   day of   , in the year of our Lord one thousand eight hundred and   , as follows :

I give, devise and bequeath all my messuages, lands, tenements and hereditaments, and all my household furniture, ready money, securities for money, money secured by life assurance, goods and chattels, and all other my real and personal estate and effects whatsoever and wheresoever, unto C. D., his heirs, executors, administrators and assigns, to and for his and their own absolute use and benefit, according to the nature and quality thereof respectively; Subject only to the payment of my just debts, funeral and testamentary expenses, and the charges of proving and registering this my will. And I appoint E. F., of   , executor of this my will; And hereby, revoking all other wills, I declare this only to be my last will and testament.

In witness whereof, I have hereunto set my hand and seal, the day and year above written.

A. B. [L. S.]

Signed, sealed, published and declared by the said A. B., the testator, as and for his last will and testament, in the presence of us, who at his request, and in the presence of each other, have hereunto subscribed our names, as witnesses to the due execution thereof.   R. S.
                                                                    X. Z.

General form of a Will to dispose of Real and Personal Estate, in Legacies.

I, T. T., of   , in the county of   , gentleman, being of sound and disposing mind and memory, do make and publish this my last will and testament, hereby revoking all former wills by me at any time heretofore made.

1st. I hereby constitute and appoint my wife, E. T., to be sole executrix of this my last will, directing my said executrix to pay all my just debts and funeral expenses, and the legacies hereinafter given, out of my estate.

2nd. After the payment of my said debts and funeral expenses, I give to each of my children the sum of   dollars, to be paid to each of them as soon after my decease, but within one year, as conveniently may be done.

3rd. And for the payment of the legacies aforesaid, I give and devise to my said executrix all the personal estate owned by me at my decease (except my household furniture and wearing apparel), and so much of my real estate as will be sufficient, in addition to the said personal estate herein given, to pay the said legacies.

4th. I give to my said executrix all my household furniture and wearing-apparel for her sole use.

5th. I devise to my said executrix all the rest and residue of my real estate, as long as she shall remain unmarried, and my widow, with remainder thereof, on her decease or marriage, to my said children and their heirs respectively, share and share alike.

In witness whereof, I have hereunto set my hand and seal, this   day of   , in the year of our Lord one thousand eight hundred and

T. T. [L. S.]

Signed, sealed, published and declared by the said T. T., as and for his last will and testament, in the presence of us, who in the presence of each other, and at his request, have subscribed our names as witnesses hereto.   Y. Z.
R. S.

Codicil to a Will.

This is a codicil to the last will and testament of me A. B., of, &c., bearing date the   day of   A. D., 18 , (*the date of the will.*)

I do hereby revoke the bequest of all my household furniture to my son John, and do give and bequeath the same to my daughter Jane, to and for her own absolute use and benefit forever.

I give and bequeath to my daughter Mary, in addition to the legacy bequeathed to her by my said will, the further sum of $400.

In all other respects I do confirm my said will.

In witness whereof, I have hereunto set my hand and seal, this   day of   , A. D. 18 .

A. B. [L. S.]

Signed, sealed, published and declared by the said A. B., the testator, as and for a codicil to his last will and testament, in the presence of us, who at his request, and in the presence of each other, have hereunto subscribed our names as witnesses to the due execution hereof.   R. S.
X. Z.

THE HISTORY OF CANADA.
From its First Discovery down to the present times.
BY J. M. McMULLEN, ESQ.

640 pages 8vo., beautifully printed on superfine paper. Price $2 in bevelled cloth, $3 in elegant half calf, or $4 in antique morocco, gilt edges, making a most elegant gift or prize book.

Published by McMullen & Co., Brockville, who will forward carriage prepaid by mail or otherwise, on receipt of above price.

THIS is the only complete History of Canada ever written, and brings its social and political record from its first discovery down to Dominion Day. The Author has had access to the most authentic sources of information, and has spared no pains to make his history a valuable book of reference to the public man, as well as a reliable and pleasant source of information to all those who desire to acquaint themselves with the annals of this Dominion. This work supplies the only full and complete history of the Province of Ontario, from its first settlement in 1784, in existence; while no event of any importance is omitted in the history of the Province of Quebec.

Extracts from Notices of the Press.

Mr. McMullen's work is a model of perspicuous writing and judious condensation of material.—Glasgow (Scotland) *Daily Herald.*

Mr. McMullen's work is evidently that of a truth-seeking and truth-loving historian. He is ardently patriotic, but his patriotism is that of a Canadian loyal to his sovereign and a lover of constitutional liberty.—Edinburgh (Scotland) *Evening Courant.*

Another interesting and useful volume, the first complete work of the kind—the first that has dealt with the whole of the period during which the Dominion has been the home of European settlers.—*London Saturday Review.*

By far the best English Canadian History.—*Montreal Gazette.*

We have no hesitation in recommending this history to our readers.—*Picton Gazette.*

Such a work must be welcomed by all classes of Canadian readers at the present time.—*Ottawa Daily Times.*

The author has treated public events, especially those of the last twenty years, in a singularly impartial way.—*Ottawa Daily Citizen.*

No English History of this country can in our opinion, compare with the work under notice. * * * * The Author possesses the happy art of presenting his facts, whatever may be the nature of the subject, in a style which cannot fail to captivate the reader.—*Quebec Daily Gazette.*

The composition is of a character to render the subject fascinating to the young as well as to the more advanced reader --*Montreal Daily Witness.*

www.ingramcontent.com/pod-product-compliance
Lightning Source LLC
Chambersburg PA
CBHW030551300426
44111CB00009B/941